ABOUT THE AUTHOR

Nick Redfern is the author of thirty books on UFOs, Bigfoot, conspiracies, and Hollywood scandals, including VIP's *Secret History: Conspiracies from Ancient Aliens to the New World Order*, *The Zombie Book: The Encyclopedia of the Living Dead* (with Brad Steiger), and *The Bigfoot Book: The Encyclopedia of Sasquatch, Yeti, and Cryptid Primates*. He has appeared on more than seventy TV shows, including: Fox News; the BBC's *Out of This World*; the SyFy Channel's *Proof Positive*; the Space Channel's *Fields of Fear*; the History Channel's *Monster Quest*, *America's Book of Secrets*, *Ancient Aliens*, and *UFO Hunters*; Science's *The Unexplained Files*; the National Geographic Channel's *Paranatural*; and MSNBC's *Countdown* with Keith Olbermann. Originally from the UK, Nick lives on the fringes of Dallas, Texas. He can be contacted at his blog, http://nickredfernfortean.blogspot.com.

ALSO FROM VISIBLE INK PRESS

Alien Mysteries, Conspiracies, and Cover-Ups
by Kevin D. Randle
ISBN: 978-1-57859-418-4

Angels A to Z, 2nd edition
by Evelyn Dorothy Oliver and James R Lewis
ISBN: 978-1-57859-212-8

Armageddon Now: The End of the World A to Z
by Jim Willis and Barbara Willis
ISBN: 978-1-57859-168-8

The Astrology Book: The Encyclopedia of Heavenly Influences, 2nd edition
by James R Lewis
ISBN: 978-1-57859-144-2

The Bigfoot Book: The Encyclopedia of Sasquatch, Yeti, and Cryptid Primates
by Nick Redfern
ISBN: 978-1-57859-561-7

Conspiracies and Secret Societies: The Complete Dossier, 2nd edition
by Brad Steiger and Sherry Hansen Steiger
ISBN: 978-1-57859-368-2

The Dream Encyclopedia, 2nd edition
by James R Lewis and Evelyn Dorothy Oliver
ISBN: 978-1-57859-216-6

The Encyclopedia of Religious Phenomena
by J. Gordon Melton
ISBN: 978-1-57859-209-8

The Fortune-Telling Book: The Encyclopedia of Divination and Soothsaying
by Raymond Buckland
ISBN: 978-1-57859-147-3

Hidden Realms, Lost Civilizations, and Beings from Other Worlds
by Jerome Clark
ISBN: 978-1-57859-175-6

Real Aliens, Space Beings, and Creatures from Other Worlds,
by Brad Steiger and Sherry Hansen Steiger
ISBN: 978-1-57859-333-0

Real Encounters, Different Dimensions, and Otherworldly Beings
by Brad Steiger with Sherry Hansen Steiger
ISBN: 978-1-57859-455-9

Real Ghosts, Restless Spirits, and Haunted Places, 2nd edition
by Brad Steiger
ISBN: 978-1-57859-401-6

Real Miracles, Divine Intervention, and Feats of Incredible Survival
by Brad Steiger and Sherry Hansen Steiger
ISBN: 978-1-57859-214-2

Real Monsters, Gruesome Critters, and Beasts from the Darkside
by Brad Steiger and Sherry Hansen Steiger
ISBN: 978-1-57859-220-3

Real Vampires, Night Stalkers, and Creatures from the Darkside
by Brad Steiger
ISBN: 978-1-57859-255-5

Real Zombies, the Living Dead, and Creatures of the Apocalypse
by Brad Steiger
ISBN: 978-1-57859-296-8

The Religion Book: Places, Prophets, Saints, and Seers
by Jim Willis
ISBN: 978-1-57859-151-0

The Spirit Book: The Encyclopedia of Clairvoyance, Channeling, and Spirit Communication
by Raymond Buckland
ISBN: 978-1-57859-172-5

Unexplained! Strange Sightings, Incredible Occurrences, and Puzzling Physical Phenomena, 3rd edition
by Jerome Clark
ISBN: 978-1-57859-344-6

The Vampire Book: The Encyclopedia of the Undead, 3rd edition
by J. Gordon Melton
ISBN: 978-1-57859-281-4

The Werewolf Book: The Encyclopedia of Shape-Shifting Beings, 2nd edition
by Brad Steiger
ISBN: 978-1-57859-367-5

The Witch Book: The Encyclopedia of Witchcraft, Wicca, and Neo-paganism
by Raymond Buckland
ISBN: 978-1-57859-114-5

"REAL NIGHTMARES" E-BOOKS BY BRAD STEIGER

Book 1: *True and Truly Scary Unexplained Phenomenon*

Book 2: *The Unexplained Phenomena and Tales of the Unknown*

Book 3: *Things That Go Bump in the Night*

Book 4: *Things That Prowl and Growl in the Night*

Book 5: *Fiends That Want Your Blood*

Book 6: *Unexpected Visitors and Unwanted Guests*

Book 7: *Dark and Deadly Demons*

Book 8: *Phantoms, Apparitions, and Ghosts*

PLEASE VISIT US AT VISIBLEINKPRESS.COM

THE MONSTER BOOK

CREATURES, BEASTS AND FIENDS OF NATURE

NICK REDFERN

VISIBLE
INK
PRESS

Detroit

THE MONSTER BOOK: CREATURES,
BEASTS, AND FIENDS OF NATURE

Visible Ink Press®
43311 Joy Rd., #414
Canton, MI 48187-2075

Visible Ink Press is a registered trademark of Visible Ink Press LLC.

Most Visible Ink Press books are available at special quantity discounts when purchased in bulk by corporations, organizations, or groups. Customized printings, special imprints, messages, and excerpts can be produced to meet your needs. For more information, contact Special Markets Director, Visible Ink Press, www.visibleink.com, or 734-667-3211.

Managing Editor: Kevin S. Hile
Art Director: Mary Claire Krzewinski
Typesetting: Marco DiVita
Proofreaders: Larry Baker and Janet L. Hile
Indexer: Shoshana Hurwitz

Cover images: Shutterstock

Library of Congress Cataloging-in-Publication Data

Names: Redfern, Nicholas, 1964- author.
Title: The monster book : creatures, beasts, and friends of nature / by Nick Redfern.
Description: 1st [edition]. | Detroit, MI : Visible Ink Press, 2016.
Identifiers: LCCN 2016021179| ISBN 9781578595754 (pbk. : alk. paper) | ISBN 9781578596294 (epub) | ISBN 9781578596287 (pdf)
Subjects: LCSH: Monsters.
Classification: LCC GR830 .R43 2016 | DDC 001.944--dc23
LC record available at https://lccn.loc.gov/2016021179

10 9 8 7 6 5 4 3 2 1

CONTENTS

UNEARTHLY CATS, DEADLY DOGS, WEREWOLVES

ΠΑΤΙΙRE GΟΠΕ ΜΑD

REPTILIAΠS, AMPHIBIAΠS, DIΠOSAURS, AΠD WORMS

Lake, River, and Ocean Menaces

CRYPTIC APES AND WILD MEN

NOT SO HUMAN

FLYING BEINGS

Vampires and Bloodsuckers

Monsters of Magic and Mind

UFO Creatures

ACKNOWLEDGMENTS

I would like to offer my sincere thanks to all of the following: my agent, Lisa Hagan, for her fine and much appreciated work; Roger Jänecke, Kevin Hile, and everyone else at Visible Ink Press for being a great company to work for.

PHOTO SOURCES

Alexandre Albore: p. 61.

Lux Amber: p. 275.

American Museum Journal: p. 267.

Angus (Wikicommons): p. 195.

David Barkasy and Loren Coleman: p. 192.

John Bauer: p. 367.

Tim Bertelink: p. 300.

Cryotank (Wikicommons): p. 69.

Gary Dee: p. 26.

Andreas Eriksson: p. 188.

J. Patrick Fischer: p. 90.

Alan Ford: p. 15.

Gelweo (http://www.gel-weo.com): p. 105.

Hamedog (Wikicommons): p. 171.

Dorothy Hardy: p. 13.

istolethetv (Wikicommons): p. 108.

Jared and Corin (Wikicommons): p. 128.

JNL (Wikicommons): p. 162.

Hansueli Krapf: p. 374.

Maciej Lewandowski: p. 270.

Library of Congress: p. 129.

Ltshears (Wikicommons): p. 143.

Jim Marrs: p. 253.

Mary Evans Picture Library: pp. 18, 34, 58, 59, 82, 96, 117, 120, 124, 134, 139, 146, 153, 242, 243, 265.

Ian Medcalf: p. 338.

Dr. Meierhofer (Wikicommons): p. 44.

Momotarou2012 (Wikicommons): p. 55.

Mostlymade (Wikicommons): p. 307.

Rolf Müller: p. 239.

Nam from D Block (Wikicommons): p. 294.

National Astronomy and Ionosphere Center: p. 331.

National Gallery of Art (Washington, D.C.): p. 348.
National Nuclear Security Administration: p. 272.
Alvin Padayachee: p. 38.
Mike Peel: p. 185.
pfly from Pugetopolis (Wikicommons): p. 121.
Geoff Pick: p. 10.
Pieter0024 (Wikicommons): p. 110.
Preus Museum: p. 369.
Arthur Rackham: p. 157.
Nick Redfern: p. 215.
Seo75 (Wikicommons): p. 244.
Shalom (Wikicommons): p. 333.
Anthony Shiels: p. 152.
Shutterstock: pp. 2, 9, 16, 19, 28, 37, 43, 47, 57, 63, 65, 72, 73, 76, 78, 88, 107, 113, 149, 156, 160, 173, 178, 192, 202, 210, 216, 226, 283, 289, 291, 303, 310, 311, 313, 321, 323, 325, 327, 335, 352, 358, 360, 372.
Sphilbrick (Wikicommons): p. 31.
Stanthejeep (Wikicommons): p. 230.
Angella Streluk: p. 259.
Subarite (Wikicommons): p. 207.
Testus (Wikicommons): p. 286.
University of Washington Freshwater and Marine Image Bank: p. 190.
Pieter VanderLinden: p. 79.
The Voice of Hassocks: p. 361.
Chris Whippet: p. 204.
Philip White: p. 315.
Wilson44691 (Wikicommons): p. 200.
Public domain: pp. 5, 11, 14, 24, 35, 39, 41, 53, 66, 68, 83, 98, 100, 103, 125, 167, 224, 235, 236, 254, 261, 297, 308, 346, 350, 357, 378.

INTRODUCTION

Monster. It's an emotive and ominous word that provokes a wide and varied body of responses, depending on the circumstances and the person. For little children, monsters are those terrifying things that, on bleak and stormy nights, lurk under the bed and in the shadowy recesses of the closet. They surface as their dark and warped moods take them, causing those same children to bury their heads under the sheets, praying the beasts do not take them away to their hidden lairs.

For cryptozoologists—those people who pursue such beasts as Bigfoot, the Chupacabra, and Mothman—monsters are all too real. They are things presently unknown to science, but that give every indication of being living, breathing entities. Their abodes are not the bedrooms of children, however. No: they dwell in huge lakes, dense forests, expansive jungles, deep caves and caverns, and on vast, icy mountain ranges.

For others who pursue terrifying beasts, the hideous things out there have supernatural—even occult—origins: we're talking about werewolves, the "Grinning Man," and deadly, phantom hounds, among many others.

As you will quickly come to appreciate, monsters are not merely the things of urban legends, hoaxes, and friend-of-a-friend tales. The shocking truth is that monsters—whether physical, supernatural, or even inter-dimensional—are all too chillingly real. And there are far more than a few of them, too.

Indeed, in the pages that follow you will quickly find yourself immersed in the worlds of giant flying monsters; winged humanoids; violent and hairy man-beasts; long-necked leviathans of lakes, rivers, and oceans; ferocious and deadly shape-shifters; and a multitude of other menacing, hideous, and dangerous things. They are creatures that scientists tell us don't exist, that zoologists assert cannot exist, and that historians assure us are nothing more than a mixture of ancient and modern folklore and mythology. I'm here to tell you they are wrong; each and every one of them. Monsters do exist. You're about to learn of no less than two hundred of them. Before you do so, however, ensure the doors and the windows are all locked. If it's a dark and stormy night, keep the lights on full. You never know what might be lurking outside, in the shadows, watching you as you read about them.

Unearthly Cats, Deadly Dogs, Werewolves

ALIEN BIG CATS

For decades, the British Isles have played host to a decidedly mysterious and marauding beast. It has become known as the "Alien Big Cat," or the ABC. Some cryptozoologists and monster hunters suggest the puzzle is an even older one, maybe even dating back centuries. Regardless of when, exactly, the controversy began, the fact is that pretty much every year, dozens upon dozens of reports surface of large cats roaming the wilder—and sometimes the not so wild—parts of Britain.

Very often, the cats are described as being huge, muscular and black in color. This has given rise to the term "black panther," which is actually incorrect, but frequently used by both the public and the press. It would be far more correct to suggest the creatures are probably leopards and jaguars displaying significant melanism—a condition in which there is an excess of a black pigment known as melanin.

As for how such creatures have come to be seen across pretty much the entirety of the British Isles, the theories are as many as they are varied. Some researchers hold that the animals have escaped from private zoos and enclosures and are now living and thriving very nicely in the nation's woods and forests. Others suggest that back in 1976, when the British Government significantly altered the rules and regulations governing the keeping of large, predatory animals, the owners of such cats—who couldn't afford to pay the new

Alien big cats are typically described as being black, very large, and very muscular.

fees—secretly released their pets into the wild. And today, so the theory goes, what people are seeing are the descendants of those large cats set free in the 1970s.

Other theories are far more controversial: one suggests the ABCs may have been with us since roughly 43 C.E., when invading Roman forces brought large cats to Britain in the form of mascots. Did some of those mascots escape and manage to survive and breed, largely undetected? Some say yes. Then there is the highly charged theory that Britain has in its midst an unidentified *indigenous* cat—one that science and zoology have yet to recognize or categorize.

Whatever the answer to the question of the origins of Britain's ABCs, the fact is that their presence is pretty much accepted by the general public and the media—although largely not by the government, which prefers to play down the matter whenever and wherever possible. But they are not literal monsters: they're simply regular animals, albeit seen in distinctly out of place environments, correct? Well … *maybe not.* They just might be monsters, after all.

Although many ABC researchers cringe and squirm when the matter is brought up, the fact is there are more than a few reports on record that place the ABCs in a category that is less flesh and blood-based and far more paranormally themed. There are cases of the ABCs vanishing—*literally*—before the eyes of astonished witnesses. People report large black cat encounters in old graveyards, within ancient stone circles, and even—on a few occasions—in association with UFO sightings. Whatever the truth of the matter, the ABCs of the U.K. aren't going away any time soon.

AUSTRALIAN MYSTERY BLACK CATS

Reports of large black cats proliferate in both the United States and the U.K. They have become known as "Alien Big Cats"—or ABCs—due to the fact that such creatures are seen in areas where they have no business being seen. After all, the U.K. is certainly not home to any known large cats.

And, ABCs in the United States are often spotted in areas where government officials maintain no such creatures roam. Far less well known is the equally curious saga of the ABCs of Australia.

A subject that, for years, typically only attracted the attention of cryptozoologists and monster hunters, it was thrust into the limelight in late 2008 when the Australian government decided to make its thoughts and data on the subject known publicly. It was September of that year when Nathan Rees, the Premier of New South Wales, Australia, declared openly and to the media that the stories of the ABCs roaming the land were not the stuff of hoaxes, misidentification, or fantasy. The creatures really existed—even if no one knew, exactly, what they were.

Notably, this statement was completely at odds with comments Rees made in August 2008, when he essentially stated that the subject had no merit whatsoever. What changed his opinion was a large dossier of ABC sightings in Australia—collected by elements of the Australian government—which was provided to him in early September and which made for impressive reading. It was because of Rees's words that Australian officials decided that rather than just *collect* such reports and file them away, they would finally embark on an *investigation* of those same reports. The program, which focused on the State of Victoria (a particular hotspot for alien big cat encounters), began in earnest in 2010, at the order of the Victorian National Party's Peter Ryan.

> The report ... concluded that no such creatures were prowling around, never mind slaughtering the nation's farm animals.

Two years later, specifically on September 18, 2012, the long awaited report was finally published. It was not the kind of thing that many people—and particularly farmers who claimed to have lost substantial numbers of animals to the ABCs—were anticipating and/or hoping for. The report—titled *Assessment of Evidence for the Presence in Victoria of a Wild Population of "Big Cats"*—concluded that no such creatures were prowling around, never mind slaughtering the nation's farm animals.

The Minister for Agriculture and Food Security, Peter Walsh, tried to assure the skeptical populace, as well as the doubtful media, that no Alien Big Cat had ever been "detected in a formal wildlife survey, shot by a hunter or farmer or killed by a vehicle and no skeletal remains have ever been found. Nor have 'big cats' been identified in wildlife studies involving the analysis of thousands of mammalian fecal samples."

So, what then *were* people seeing? According to Australian authorities, nothing stranger than overfed, regular cats that had turned feral. Many people who followed the story suggested and suspected that the government was playing the matter down, to avoid panicking the population by admitting that large and dangerous cats were on the loose. Despite extensive criticisms of the report, the Australian government was utterly unmoved: "On the basis of the report's conclusions, further work focusing on obtaining primary evidence to conclusively rule out the existence of 'big cats' is not warranted."

That is where matters still stand today—somewhat frustratingly. Ranchers and members of the Australian public continue to see Alien Big Cats, and on a disturbingly regular basis. And not just in Victoria, but all across Australia. Can so many people all be mistaken by nothing stranger than tubby feral cats? Australian authorities say, "Yes!" The eyewitnesses, however—and hardly surprisingly—hold very different views. Unless something unforeseen occurs out of the blue—such as the killing or capturing of an ABC in Australia—it's unlikely that situation will change.

BEAST OF BRAY ROAD

Since 1991, the Wisconsin town of Elkhorn has been the lair and hunting ground of a terrifying creature that is the closest thing one can imagine to a real-life werewolf. And, just maybe, that's exactly what it is. The monster has become known as the Beast of the Bray Road—on account of the fact that many of the initial sightings were made on that particular road. Without doubt, the expert on all things of a lycanthropic nature in Wisconsin is author and journalist Linda Godfrey, who has penned half a dozen books on werewolves, and who I interviewed about her research into this malignant beast. She told me:

"The story first came to my attention in about 1991 from a woman who had heard rumors going around here in Elkhorn, and particularly in the high school, that people had been seeing something like a werewolf, a wolf-like creature, or a wolf-man. They didn't really know what it was. But some were saying it was a werewolf. And the werewolf tag has just gotten used because I think that people really didn't know what else to call it.

"I started checking it out. I talked to the editor of *The Week* newspaper here, and which I used to work for. He said, 'Why don't you check around a little bit and see what you hear?' This was about the end of December. And being a weekly newspaper that I worked for, we weren't really hard news; we were much more feature oriented. So, I asked a friend who had a daughter in high school and she said, 'Oh yeah, that's what everybody's talking about.' So, I started my investigations and got one name from the woman who told me about it. She was also a part-time bus driver.

"In my first phone call to the bus driver, she told me that she had called the County Animal Control Officer. So, of course, when you're a reporter, anytime you have a chance to find anything official that's where you go. I went to see him and, sure enough, he had a folder in his file drawer that he had actually marked *Werewolf*, in a tongue-in-cheek way.

"People had been phoning in to him to say that they had seen something. They didn't know what it was. But from their descriptions, that's what he had put. So, of course, that made it a news story. When you have a public official, the County Animal Control Officer, who has a folder marked *Werewolf*, that's news. It was very unusual.

"It just took off from there and I kept finding more and more witnesses. At first they all wanted to stay private, and I remember talking about it with the editor and we thought we would run the story because it would be over in a couple of weeks. The story was picked up by Associated Press. Once it hit AP, everything broke loose, and people were just going crazy. All the Milwaukee TV stations came out and did stories, dug until they found the witnesses, and got them to change their minds and go on camera, which some of them later regretted. And which I kind of regret, because it really made them reluctant, and kind of hampered the investigation.

The otherwise peaceful berg of Elkhorn, Wisconsin, has been the hunting grounds of a werewolf since 1991.

"They were all mostly saying that they had seen something which was much larger than normal, sometimes on two legs and sometimes on four, with a wolfish head. Some described it as a German Shepherd-like head, pointed ears, very long, coarse, shaggy, and wild-looking fur. One thing they all mentioned was that it would turn and look at them and gaze fearlessly or leer at them, and it was at that point that they all got really frightened. Everybody who has seen it—with the exception of one—has been extremely scared because it's so out of the ordinary. It was something they couldn't identify and didn't appear to be afraid of them. It would just casually turn around and disappear into the brush. It was never just out in the open where it didn't have some sort of hiding place. There was always a cornfield or some brush or some woods. So, that was pretty much the start of it.

> I've had a woman write me who insists it's a wolf. And I think a lot of people subscribe to that theory....

"Once that got out, I started finding other people who called me and got in touch with me and I sort of became the unofficial clearinghouse. And we called it the Beast of Bray Road because I've always been reluctant to call it a werewolf. The original sightings were in an area known as the Beast of Bray Road, which is outside of Elkhorn.

"Everybody seems to have an opinion about this that they are eager to make known and defend. I personally don't think there are enough facts for anybody to come to a conclusion. I have a couple of dozen sightings, at least. A few of them are second-hand and they date back to 1936. And they aren't all around Bray Road. Quite a number are in the next county, Jefferson. I've had a woman write me who insists it's a wolf. And I think a lot of people subscribe to that theory; yes, it's definitely a wolf and can't be anything else. But that doesn't explain the large size.

"We've had all sorts of theories; mental patients escaping or some crazy guy running around. A hoaxer is another theory; that it's somebody running around in a werewolf suit. One or two could have been that, but I tend to have my doubts about that, because the incidents are isolated and not close together. One of the sightings was on Halloween, but that's also one of the people who got a really good look at it and they're sure it wasn't a human in a costume. Otherwise, most of them have been in really remote locations where, if you were going to hoax, the person would have to have been sitting out there in the cold just waiting for somebody to come along. So, if it's a hoaxer, my hat's off to them. But I tend not to think that's the case. I don't rule it out completely because once publicity gets out, things like that can happen.

"Two hunters quite a bit farther north saw what looked like two 'dog children' standing up in the woods. They were too scared to shoot when they saw them. They were not tall; they were juvenile-looking, standing upright, which is what scared them. But, otherwise, it's a single creature. Most of the sightings I receive aren't recent, and so people can't remember too well what the moon was like. But most of the sightings occur around the fall when the cornfields get big and there's really good hiding cover. So, that's anywhere from late August through November. And I've had some sightings from the spring. But there are other theories as well for what is going on.

"Occasionally I'll get letters from people who say they are lycanthropes themselves and their theory is that this is an immature, real werewolf and it cannot control its transformation, and that's why it allows itself to be seen occasionally. They are completely convinced of that. And there are people who believe it's a manifestation of satanic forces, that it's a part of a demonic thing. They point to various occult activities around here. There are also people who try to link it to UFOs. Then there's the theory it's just a dog. One woman, a medium, thought that it was a natural animal but didn't know what it was. And there are a lot of people out here that do wolf-hybridizations, and I've thought to myself you'd get something like that. But that doesn't explain the upright posture. Then there's the theory that it's a creature known as the Windigo or Wendigo, which is featured in Indian legends and is supposedly a supernatural creature that lives on human flesh. But none of the descriptions from the Windigo legends describe a creature with canine features.

//I've had people ask me, 'Are you sure this isn't Bigfoot?' Most of the sightings really don't sound like what people report as Bigfoot."

"There's another possibility: I think a lot of these people are seeing different things. And that when they heard somebody else talk about something, there's a tendency to say, 'Oh, that must be what I saw.' There's really no way to know. And there are differences in some of the sightings. I've had people ask me, 'Are you sure this isn't Bigfoot?' Most of the sightings really don't sound like what people report as Bigfoot. But a couple of them do. There's one man who saw it in the 1960s in a different area of the county, who insists positively that he saw a Bigfoot, but doesn't want anyone saying he saw a werewolf. And the terrain around here isn't really the typical sort of Bigfoot terrain of forests where people usually report these things. We do have woods and a big state forest, but it's a narrow band of forest. It's a lot of prairie and is not what you would think a Bigfoot would live in. But you never know. I've also had the baboon theory, which I find extremely unlikely.

Of her first book on the subject, *The Beast of Bray Road*, Godfrey said to me: "Part of the angle of the book is looking at this as a sociological phenomenon and how something that a number of people see turns into a legend. And it has become that, a little bit. Personally, I'm still happy to leave it an open mystery. I don't have a feeling that it has to be pinned down."

A quarter of a century after her investigations into the mystery of the Beast of Bray Road began, Linda Godfrey's research and writing continue and the sightings of the unearthly monster continue. Her published works now include *The Beast of Bray Road, Werewolves, Hunting the American Werewolf, The Michigan Dogman,* and *Real Wolfmen.* Collectively, they demonstrate something incredible: werewolves may not be creatures of fantasy, legend and mythology. They just might be all too real. And Bray Road may be just the place to see them.

CEMETERY WOLF-MAN

The United Kingdom is home to a wealth of strange and extraordinary animals, including Alien Big Cats, the Loch Ness Monster, and the Big Grey Man of Ben Macdhui. Then, there is the matter of the nation's werewolves. Reports of British wolf-men date back more than one millennia and contain the key and staple ingredients of so many werewolf reports, such as the matter of shape-shifting, a full moon, and even silver bullets. And while many reports of werewolves in the U.K. date from times long gone, that's most assuredly not always the case. Take, for example, the matter of a certain wave of werewolf sightings that occurred in central England in 2007. It was a wave that attracted the attention of not just the general public, but of the local and national media too.

//...It must have been about six to seven feet tall. I know it sounds absolutely mad, but I know what I saw."

It's intriguing to note that each and every encounter with the marauding man-wolf occurred in and around the very same place. It was a certain cemetery located in central England's expansive woods known as the Cannock Chase. The Commonwealth War Graves Commission notes:

"During the First World War there was a large military camp at Cannock Chase which became the base for the New Zealand Rifle Brigade. There was also a prisoner-of-war hospital with 1,000 beds, and both camp and hospital used the burial ground. Cannock Chase War Cemetery contains 97 Commonwealth burials of the First World War, most of them New Zealanders, and 286 German burials. There are also three burials of the Second World War. The 58 German burials in Plot 4 were all brought into the cemetery in 1963, as part of the German Government's policy to remove all graves situated in cemeteries or war graves plots not maintained by the Commonwealth War Graves Commission."

As for the monster of the graves, it became briefly infamous in April 2007, thanks to a story that appeared in the pages of the local *Stafford Post* newspaper. According to newspaper staff: "A rash of sightings of a 'werewolf' type creature prowling around the outskirts of Stafford have prompted a respected Midlands paranormal group to investigate. West Midlands Ghost Club says they have been contacted by a number of shocked residents who saw what they claimed to be a 'hairy wolf-type creature' walking on its hind legs around the German War Cemetery, just off Camp Road, in between Stafford and Cannock. Several of them claim the creature sprang up on its hind legs and ran into the nearby bushes when it was spotted."

Nick Duffy, of the West Midlands Ghost Club, is the person we have to thank for bringing the story to the attention of the newspaper, as it was the WMGC that was the recipient of the initial batch of reports. Duffy said: "The first person to contact us was a postman, who told us he had seen what he thought was a werewolf on the German War Cemetery site. He said he was over there on a motorbike and saw what he believed was a large dog. When he got closer, the creature got on his hind legs and ran away."

There was also a Cannock-based scout leader, who had an encounter with the creature, and right in the heart of the cemetery: "It just looked like a huge dog. But when I slammed the door of my car it reared up on its back legs and ran into the trees. It must have been about six to seven feet tall. I know it sounds absolutely mad, but I know what I saw."

It was the publicity given to these two cases, in particular, that prompted additional people to come forward with their sighting reports and theories as to what might have been afoot. Of a mysterious and disturbing series of missing animals in the area, one source told the *Stafford Post*: "It's a fact that there has been significant mining activity under Cannock Chase for centuries. And it's a fact there is a high rate of domestic pet disappearance in the area—especially dogs off the lead. Just ask anyone who walks their dog near the German War Cemetery."

It's intriguing to note that although the 2007 wave captured significant attention, and for a period of no less than three or four months, the area had been very briefly hit by a very similar wave in the previous year, 2006. For example, early on June

Over the centuries that the werewolf legend has developed, some common ingredients have come to include shape shifting and the importance of full moons and silver bullets.

28, 2006, numerous motorists driving to work on the M6 Motorway reported seeing a large, wolf-like animal racing across the six lanes of the Motorway, at the height of the rush hour. The Highways Agency looked into the matter quickly and in concerned fashion. They came up blank and baffled.

As I grew up in the area where the werewolf encounters occurred, the local press contacted me on several occasions for my views on the werewolf wave of both 2006 and 2007. When my comments were published—in both the *Stafford Post* and the *Chase Post* newspapers—it led several people to contact me with their own, hitherto unknown sightings.

They were all eerily similar. The location was the same: the old cemetery. The nature of the beast was the same, too: it had the ability to run on both two legs and four, and when standing on its hind legs it reached a height of around seven feet. And there was something else: all of the witnesses got a sudden feeling—but for reasons they couldn't fathom—that the beast was both supernatural and downright evil. In addition, the wave of publicity given to the 2007 encounters encouraged some people to come forward with reports that predated the then-current encounters. Certainly, the most fascinating account came from a man named Jim Broadhurst, who contacted me when my comments and observations on the beast were published in the *Chase Post* in 2007.

According to Broadhurst, on a bright, summer day in late June 2006 he and his wife were taking a leisurely and pleasant walk through the Cannock Chase woods when they saw, at what he estimated to have been a distance of around 150 feet, a very large wolf making its way through the trees. Broadhurst said that initial amazement and excitement were rapidly replaced by nothing less than cold-hearted fear. There was a very good reason for that: the animal suddenly reared up onto its hind limbs and stared intently in the direction of the petrified pair—making it abundantly clear it had seen them, and—as Broadhurst speculated—wanted to let them know it had seen them. As they watched, frozen to the spot, the "upright wolf," as Broadhurst described it, backed away further into the heart of the woods, and keeping its eyes firmly fixed on the pair until it was finally lost from sight. The Broadhursts, very understandably, wasted not a second in fleeing the area and heading for the safety of their car. They stayed silent on their encounter until 2007, when the similar events of that year prompted them to finally speak out publicly.

The path through Cannock Chase woods seems pleasant enough ... until one stumbles upon a large wolf where none should exist....

Thankfully, there were never any human casualties reported in this very unsettling affair, and the sightings of the cemetery werewolf finally faded away, as the summer of 2007 became the autumn, and as the days became shorter and the nights became longer. We may never know, for sure, what the creature was, from where it came, or to where it ultimately vanished. But for the people who live in the vicinity of the Cannock Chase German War Cemetery, it's likely to be a mayhem-filled few months that they will never, ever forget. After all, it's hardly every day that one finds a real-life werewolf in one's very own midst!

EIGI EINHAMIR OF NORWAY AND ICELAND

The Reverend Sabine Baring-Gould (1834–1924) was someone who had a deep fascination for stories of strange creatures, including werewolves, ghouls, and a menacing phenomenon known as the *eigi einhamir*. In Baring-Gould's own words:

"In Norway and Iceland certain men were said to be *eigi einhamir*, not of one skin, an idea which had its roots in paganism. The full form of this strange superstition was, that men could take upon them other bodies, and the natures of those beings whose bodies they assumed. The second adopted shape was called by the same name as the original shape, *hamr*, and the expression made use of to designate the transition from one body to another, was at *skipta hömum*, or *at hamaz*; whilst the expedition made in the second form, was the *hamför*. By this transfiguration extraordinary powers were acquired; the natural strength of the individual was doubled, or quadrupled; he acquired the strength of the beast in whose body he travelled, in addition to his own, and a man thus invigorated was called *hamrammr*."

But how, exactly, was transformation achieved? Baring-Gould researched this matter extensively and offered the following:

"The manner in which the change was effected, varied. At times, a dress of

Anglican priest and author Sabine Baring-Gould is often remembered for writing hymns such as "Onward, Christian Soldier." He was also fascinated by stories of werewolves, ghouls, and other beasts.

skin was cast over the body, and at once the transformation was complete; at others, the human body was deserted, and the soul entered the second form, leaving the first body in a cataleptic state, to all appearance dead. The second *hamr* was either borrowed or created for the purpose. There was yet a third manner of producing this effect—it was by incantation; but then the form of the individual remained unaltered, though the eyes of all beholders were charmed so that they could only perceive him under the selected form.

"Having assumed some bestial shape, the man who is *eigi einhammr* is only to be recognized by his eyes, which by no power can be changed. He then pursues his course, follows the instincts of the beast whose body he has taken, yet without quenching his own intelligence. He is able to do what the body of the animal can do, and do what he, as man, can do as well. He may fly or swim, if he is in the shape of bird or fish; if he has taken the form of a wolf, or if he goes on a *gandrei*, or wolf's-ride, he is full of the rage and malignity of the creatures whose powers and passions he has assumed."

FENRIR THE WEREWOLF

Dion Fortune was an occultist, mystic, and the author of a number of acclaimed works, and whose real name was Violet Mary Firth. Fortune, who died in 1946 at the age of fifty-five, was someone who was skilled at creating monsters in the mind and who then unleashed them into the world around her. Fortune made it very clear, however, that creating a mind-monster rarely has a positive outcome. It is something that each and every one of us should take careful heed of. Her story is as fascinating as it is disturbing:

"The artificial elemental is constructed by forming a clear-cut image in the imagination of the creature it is intended to create, ensouling it with something of the corresponding aspect of one's own being, and then invoking into it the appropriate natural force. This method can be used for good as well as evil, and 'guardian angels' are formed in this way. It is said that dying women, anxious concerning the welfare of their children, frequently form them unconsciously.

"I myself once had an exceedingly nasty experience in which I formulated a were-wolf accidentally. Unpleasant as the incident was, I think it may be just as well to give it publicity, for it shows what may happen when an insufficiently disciplined and purified nature is handling occult forces.

"I had received serious injury from someone who, at considerable cost to myself, I had disinterestedly helped, and I was sorely tempted to retaliate. Lying on my bed resting one afternoon, I was brooding over my resentment, and while so brooding, drifted towards the borders of sleep. There came to my mind the thought of casting off all restraints and going berserk. The ancient Nordic myths rose before me, and I thought of Fenrir, the Wolf-horror of the North. Immediately I felt a curious drawing-out sensation from my solar plexus, and there materialized beside me on the bed a large wolf. It was a well-materialized ecto-plasmic form. It was grey and colorless, and had weight. I could distinctly feel its back pressing against me as it lay beside me on the bed as a large dog might.

"I knew nothing about the art of making elementals at that time, but had accidentally stumbled upon the right method—the brooding highly charged with emotion, the invocation of the appropriate natural force, and the condition between sleeping and waking in which the etheric double readily extrudes."

In Norse mythology, Fenrir is a god wolf that, at the end times of Ragnarok, actually kills the god Odin.

GLOWING MONSTER OF THE CLIFFS

Throughout the summer and fall of 1997, the skies of South Devon, England, were filled with UFOs, bizarre aerial vehicles, and mystifying lights. Strange creatures—including large black cats resembling mountain lions, flying beasts that had the appearance of huge jellyfish, and ghostly black dogs with blazing, evil-filled eyes—provoked terror in those who encountered them.

Unidentified, robed, and hooded figures were seen prowling around local woods by moonlight, seemingly engaging in infernal, occult-driven rites and rituals. Animals were found dead, and hideously mutilated, under mysterious circumstances. And trying to make some sense of all this high strangeness of the very disturbing kind were two dedicated investigators of all things paranormal, Nigel Wright and Jon Downes. Wright is a well-known, long-time investigator of UFOs in England, while Downes is the director of the Devon-

Jon Downes is the director of the Centre for Fortean Zoology in Devon, England.

based Centre for Fortean Zoology—one of the few groups that investigates reports of such things as lake monsters, Bigfoot, and the Chupacabra on a full-time basis.

Such was the sheer scale of supernatural activity that descended on ancient Devon in that specific period, that Downes and Wright found themselves plunged into a dark and turbulent world, one that closely paralleled the menacing environment that threatened to swallow up John Keel, as he investigated the turbulent Point Pleasant, West Virginia, Mothman reports of 1965 to 1967. And in the same way that Keel had run-ins with the Men in Black, both Downes and Wright experienced something chillingly similar: hang-up phone calls in the middle of the night.

Any mention of "animal mutilations" invariably, and quite understandably too, provokes imagery of the notorious "cattle-mutilation" events that reached their peak in the southwest regions of the United States in the mid-to-late 1970s.

On the issue of whether or not the killing and mutilation of animals on a large scale was, and perhaps still is, the work of extraterrestrials, occult groups, government personnel engaged in biological warfare experimentation, scavengers, shadowy figures with concerns about exotic viruses entering the U.S. food chain, or a combination of all the above, the jury is very much still out. But less well known is that such events are not limited to the United States. One particular case stands out for truly memorable and macabre reasons, as will now become apparent. It all began on October 1, 1997, as Nigel Wright's journals reveal:

"Approximately three weeks ago two young men were swimming in Otter Cove [Lyme Bay, Exmouth, England]. As darkness drew in, they decided to make for the shore and change to go home. As they got changed, one of them looked out to sea. He saw what he described as a 'greenish' light under the surface. He called to the other young man and they both watched as this light 'rose' to the surface of the water. The next thing they knew there was a very bright light shining into their faces. They turned the scene and fled."

Meanwhile, on the top of the cliffs, equally strange things were afoot. The two young men raced for the car of a relative and breathlessly explained what had happened. Incredibly, she, too, had seen something highly unusual in precisely the same time frame on the road leading to Otter Cove: a strange animal that she likened to "an enormous cat." Whatever the origin of the beast, however, she was certain of one thing: it was, to quote her, "all lit up"— glowing almost.

On the following day, a dead whale was found washed upon the beach below the cliffs. This did not appear to have been merely a tragic accident, however. Rumors quickly circulated that the culprit was the monstrous, glowing, cat-like thing. On receiving reports that a whale had been found in precisely the area that anomalous lights and a strange creature were seen, Wright launched an investigation.

"The first thing that struck me as I looked on at this scene," recalls Wright, "was how perfect the carcass was. There was no decay or huge chunks torn from it. Then, as I wandered around it, I noticed that there was only one external wound: in the area of the genitals a round incision, the size of a large dinner plate, was cut right into the internal organs of the mammal. The sides of this incision were perfectly formed, as if some giant apple corer had been inserted and twisted around. From the wound hung some of the internal organs."

Wright continues: "I quizzed the official from English Heritage, who was responsible for the disposal of the carcass. He informed me that no natural predator or boat strike would have caused this wound. As I looked at this sight, the first thing that came into my mind was how this looked just like the cattle mutilation cases of recent times."

Wright was also able to determine that this was not the only time that unusual lights had been seen in the vicinity of Lyme Bay: "No precise date can be given for the evening when a fishing boat encountered a strange light over Lyme Bay," he wrote, "but, since this was told to me by the skipper of the vessel concerned, I can vouch for its authenticity. The vessel in question was five miles off Budleigh Salterton. The crew became aware of a bright, white-blue light which hovered some distance from the boat. At first they thought it was a helicopter but they heard no engine sounds, nor saw any navigation lights."

Wright was told by the captain of the vessel that the night had been "bright and clear" and that if the object had made any noise, it would certainly have been "audible for miles."

Glowing lights had been seen over Lyme Bay by the English Channel. They were bright, silent, and stationary.

"The light remained stationary for about one and a half hours. Judging by the mast of their vessel, which is twenty-eight feet high, the crew estimated that the light was not much higher than that," adds Wright. "It then very suddenly disappeared."

The mystery was never solved and the glowing cat-thing was never seen again.

HEXHAM HEADS

On December 10, 1904, a startling story appeared in the pages of the English newspaper, the *Hexham Courant*. Under the heading of "Wolf at Large in Allendale," it read:

"Local farmers from the village of Allendale, very near to Hexham, had reported the loss of their livestock, so serious that many sheep were being stabled at night to protect them. A shepherd found two of his flock slaughtered, one with its entrails hanging out, and all that remained of the other was its head and horns. Many of the sheep had been bitten about the neck and the legs—common with an attack made by a wolf."

The newspaper article continued:

"Hysteria soon set in. During the night, lanterns were kept burning to scare away the wolf, and women and children were ordered to keep to the busy roads and be home before dusk. The 'Hexham Wolf Committee' was soon set up to organize search parties and hunts to bring down the beast using specialized hunting dogs, the 'Haydon Hounds', but even they could not find the wolf. The Wolf Committee took the next step and hired Mr. W. Briddick, a trained tracker. But he was also unsuccessful, despite searching the woods."

On January 7, 1905, however, there was a major development: the *Hexham Courant* reported that the body of a wolf

The residents of Allendale near Hexham suspected a wolf in their midst, even though wolves had disappeared centuries before that. It seems some still survived.

had been found dead on a railway track at Cumwinton, Cumbria—which was approximately thirty miles from where the majority of the attacks had been occurring. However, it was the newspaper's firm opinion that this was not the same creature, but yet another one. In other words, the mystery beast of Hexham was still out there.

Indeed, according to some theorists, there was a whole pack of such animals wildly roaming the countryside of northern England by night. And although the searches for the animal, or animals, continued for some time, they were finally brought to a halt when the attacks abruptly stopped. Hexham's mysterious and wolfish visitor was gone.

In 1972, however, it may well have returned—albeit in a slightly different guise. And as evidence of this, we have to turn our attention to the bizarre story of the Hexham Heads. The strange saga all began in February 1972. An eleven-year-old boy, Colin Robson, and his younger brother, Leslie, were digging up weeds in their parents' back yard in the town of Hexham, when they unearthed two carved, stone heads, slightly smaller than a tennis ball and very heavy in weight.

The heads would move by themselves. Household objects were found inexplicably broken. And at one point the boys' sister found her bed showered with glass.

Crudely fashioned and weathered-looking, one resembled a skull-like masculine head crowned by a Celtic hairstyle; while the other was a slightly smaller female head that possessed what were said to be witch-like qualities, including the classic beaked nose. Shortly after the boys took the heads into their house, a number of peculiar incidents occurred in the family home. The heads would move by themselves. Household objects were found inexplicably broken. And at one point the boys' sister found her bed showered with glass. It was, however, the next-door neighbors who would go on to experience the most bizarre phenomena of all.

A few nights after the discovery of the heads, a mother living in the neighboring house, Ellen Dodd, was sitting up late with her daughter, who was suffering with a toothache, when both saw what they described as a hellish, "half-man, half-beast" enter the room. Naturally, both screamed for their lives and the woman's husband came running from another room to see what all the commotion was about. By this stage, however, the hairy creature had fled the room and could be heard "padding down the stairs as if on its hind legs." The front door was later found wide open and it was presumed that the creature had left the house in haste.

Soon after that incident, one Anne Ross—a doctor who had studied the Celtic culture and who was the author of several books on the subject, including *Pagan Celtic Britain* and *The Folklore of the Scottish Highlands*—took possession of the stone heads to study them herself. She already had in her possession a number of similar heads and, as a result, she was certain that the Hexham Heads were Celtic in origin, and probably nearly two thousand years old.

The doctor, who lived in the English city of Southampton and about 150 miles from Hexham, had heard nothing at that time of the strange goings-on encountered by the previous owners of the heads. Having put the two stone heads with the rest of her collection, however, Dr. Ross, too, encountered the mysterious werewolf-like creature a few nights later. She awoke from her sleep feeling cold and frightened and, upon looking up, found herself confronted by a horrific man-beast identical to that seen at Hexham.

Of the terrible creature, Dr. Ross said: "It was about six feet high, slightly stooping, and it was black, against the white door, and it was half animal and half man. The upper part, I would have said, was a wolf, and the lower part was human and, I would have again said, that it was covered with a kind of black, very dark fur. It went out and I just saw it clearly, and then it disappeared, and something made me run after it, a thing I wouldn't normally have done, but I felt compelled to run after it. I got out of bed and I ran, and I could hear it going down the stairs; then it disappeared toward the back of the house."

The fear-filled affair was not yet over, however: the man-monster manifested in the family home on several more occasions, usually on the staircase and making heavy, "padding" noises as it roamed around under cover of darkness. It wasn't just Dr. Ross who saw the beast: her daughter, Berenice, did too. It soon became clear to Dr. Ross that not only was her family being plagued by a monster, but the house itself appeared to be cloaked by an "evil presence."

Werewolves and wolfmen have been a part of British folklore for ages. In this fifteenth-century illustration, the beast is shown as a man with a wolf's head.

So, she did the only thing she could to rid the family of the turmoil: she got rid of the stone heads.

For a while they were actually on display at the British Museum, later falling into the hands of a man named Don Robins, the author of a book titled *Circles of Silence*, on the subject of ancient, sacred sites. Robins, apparently concerned by the air of negativity that descended upon him when he came into possession of the heads, passed them onto a dowser by the name of Frank Hyde. He decided to try and lessen the malevolent powers of the stones by coating them in a mesh made of copper, which he believed would prevent any supernatural phenomena from being released.

Hyde, however, had no wish to hold onto the heads for too long and, as a result, they made their way around more than a few researchers of ancient anomalies. It's most revealing that no one kept them for long. Today, the location, and ownership, of the Hexham Heads is a mystery.

LYCANTHROPES

For those who believe in the existence of literal werewolves, the image of the hairy shape-shifting beast that is part-human and part-wolf, and that embarks on a marauding killing spree at the sight of a full moon, is no joke. But if such creatures really exist, are they true werewolves of the type that have been so successfully portrayed onscreen time and again by Hollywood movie moguls? Or could at least some of them be deranged souls, afflicted by a variety of mental illnesses and delusions? The answer might very well be "yes" to the second question.

Clinical lycanthropy is a rare psychiatric condition that is typified by a delusion that the afflicted person has the ability to morph into the form of a wild animal—and very often that of a berserk, killer wolf. Of course, this does not fully explain why so many such people believe they are changing into a specific animal—such as a wolf—rather than just experiencing random changes in, say, their arms or legs. But, nevertheless, it is without doubt a significant part of the puzzle. And there is another aspect to this affair that may go some way towards explaining the inner-workings of the mind of the clinical lycanthrope.

Linda Godfrey, a leading authority on werewolves in the United States, and the author of *Hunting the American Werewolf*, *The Beast of Bray Road*, and *The Michigan Dogman*, states: "One other medical explanation that turns up frequently in relation to lycanthropy is the ergot equation. A fungus that affects rye, ergot is now widely

Some mentally ill people believe that they can transform themselves into animals, usually vicious wolves.

regarded as a possible cause of the bestial madness. According to this theory, it was not demonic influence but the ingestion of *Claviceps purpurea* (which contains a compound similar to LSD), which led to the demented behavior."

And then there are just the plain deranged and evil characters who have been lumped in with lycanthropy. Beyond any shadow of doubt at all, one of the most notorious serial killers of all time was Peter Stumpp (sometimes referred to as Peter Stuube, see below), a German farmer who became infamously known as the Werewolf of Bedburg. Born in the village of Epprath, Cologne, Stumpp was a wealthy, respected, and influential farmer in the local community. But he was also hiding a dark and diabolical secret—one that surfaced graphically and sensationally in 1589, when he was brought to trial for the crimes of murder and cannibalism.

> **//According to this theory, it was not demonic influence but the ingestion of *Claviceps purpurea* (which contains a compound similar to LSD), which led to the demented behavior."**

Having been subjected to the torture of the rack, Stumpp confessed to countless horrific acts, including feasting on the flesh of sheep, lambs and goats, and even that of men, women, and children, too. Indeed, Stumpp further revealed that he had killed and devoured no fewer than fourteen children, two pregnant women and their fetuses, and even his own son's brain. Stumpp, however, had an extraordinary excuse to explain his actions. He maintained that since the age of twelve, he had engaged in black magic, and on one occasion had succeeded in summoning the Devil, who provided him with a "magical belt" that gave him the ability to morph into "the likeness of a greedy, devouring wolf, strong and mighty, with eyes great and large, which in the night sparkled like fire, a mouth great and wide, with most sharp and cruel teeth, a huge body, and mighty paws."

The court, needless to say, was not impressed, and Stumpp was put to death in brutal fashion: flesh was torn from his body, his arms and legs were broken, and, finally, he was beheaded. The Werewolf of Bedburg was no more. Stumpp was not alone, however.

MAN-DOG MONSTER

If, like me, you're a fan of the writings of Linda Godfrey—and particularly her werewolf-themed book, *The Michigan Dogman*, then what I'm about to share with you now is likely to be of deep interest. It's an old newspaper story—dating back more than a century—that is eerily reminiscent of some of

Linda's findings. And, it demonstrates that when we dig into the past, we can sometimes find fascinating tales that have a direct bearing on the present.

The story in question was published in the pages of several newspapers, including the *Pittsburgh Press* on May 3, 1905, and the Rake, Iowa, *Register* on June 15, 1905. The *Register's* article has the eye-catching title of "Dog with a Human Face." Its sub-title: "Strange Monstrosity Seen By Many Persons in Colorado Hills—Attempt Capture in Vain." According to the newspaper staff, an unidentified creature had then recently been seen "roaming the hills" of Buena Vista, Colorado, and specifically in the vicinity of Wildhorse—a station on the Colorado Midland Railway.

The *Register* reporter continued that "a prominent ranchwoman" driving across the Arkansas River had the shock of her life when something terrible loomed into view. As she crossed one particular bridge, the woman was shocked to see a "monstrosity" standing in the road. It was terrifying enough to cause her horse to panic, "almost throwing her from the rig." Interestingly, the *Register* said that the river was "where the animal has its lair."

As for the creature's physical description, it went like this: "It was about the size and build of a full-grown greyhound and of a drab color, its glistening sides being covered with black spots as large as silver dollars." Its eyes were set close together and its pointed ears stood tall. But, then came the most remarkable part of the story: the long-tailed animal "had an almost human face, and a bristling red moustache ornamented the proper place upon its physiognomy."

The story continued that the animal uttered a "piteous cry" and slunk away through the surrounding brush, turning back to look at the woman as it reached the top of a nearby hill. That's not all, though. There was something far more incredible to come. As it stood atop the hill the beast "punctured the rarefied atmosphere with sounds that reverberated among the crags" and rose up onto its hind legs.

As she crossed one particular bridge, the woman was shocked to see a "monstrosity" standing in the road.

Not surprisingly, the sight of this menacing, screaming, bipedal dog-thing "compelled a pace on the part of the usually staid horse that was a revelation to the driver."

So, what was it that the woman saw? The references to a long tail and black spots, and its size and build being similar to that of a greyhound, give rise to the possibility of a large cat of some sort. The human-like face, however—if not a fabrication or a genuine mistake—is far more difficult to explain. As is the ability of the creature to apparently walk on both four legs and two. And yet, this latter issue is something that turns up time and time again in many of the accounts that Linda Godfrey has uncovered.

Plus, the fact that the location of the encounter was a bridge is notable. Bridges often play key roles in creature cases of a definitively supernatural kind. Take, for example, Mothman's association to Point Pleasant, West Virginia's ill-fated Silver Bridge, which collapsed into the Ohio River, in December 1967. Then there is the spectral, hairy humanoid known as the Man-Monkey, which haunts Bridge 39 on England's Shropshire Union Canal. And, as one more example of many, there is the Goat-Man of Denton, Texas's Old Alton Bridge.

Everything about this case practically screams "high strangeness!" An early Dogman report? Maybe that's exactly what it is.

MILITARY WEREWOLF

In 2007, I penned an article for my *There's Something in the Woods* blog. The article was titled "Do Werewolves Roam the Woods of England?" It was an article that focused on a strange wave of sightings of hairy, upright bipedal creatures that looked like hair-covered humans and which were seen in the heart of England's Cannock Chase woods. But there was one big difference: the heads of the terrible beasts closely resembled those of wolves. No wonder, then, that word very quickly got out that a pack of deadly werewolves was on the loose in the area. Such is the strength with which the old traditions and folklore still prevail in the U.K.; even the local newspaper, the *Chase Post*, gave the reports significant coverage. And they did so in serious, rather than fun-poking, tones. That the vast majority of the encounters occurred in the vicinity of an old cemetery only served to increase the anxiety that quickly spread throughout the local villages and hamlets.

//I was in a secure weapons storage area when I encountered it. It seemed shocked and surprised to been caught off guard and I froze in total fright."

When my article appeared online, it quickly provoked numerous comments. One of those comments came from a former member of the U.S. military who, in 1970, was stationed at a certain British Royal Air Force facility in the U.K. Using the name of "Wes," he related the following:

"I encountered a werewolf (lack of better description) in England in 1970, I was 20 yrs. old when I was stationed at RAF Alconbury. I was in a secure weapons storage area when I encountered it. It seemed shocked and surprised to been caught off guard and I froze in total fright. I was armed with a .38 and never once considered using it. There was no aggression on its part. I could not comprehend what I was seeing.

"It is not human. It has a flat snout and large eyes. Its height is approx. 5 ft. and weight approx. 200 lbs. It is very muscular and thin. It wore no clothing and was only moderately hairy. It ran away on its hind legs and scurried over a chain link fence and ran deep into the dense wooded area adjacent to the base.

"I was extremely frightened but the fear developed into a total commitment of trying to contact it again. I was obsessed with it. I was able to see it again a few weeks later at a distance in the wooded area. I watched it for about 30 seconds slowly moving throughout the woods and I will never forget my good fortune to encounter it ... and to know this 'creature' truly does lives among us."

As incredible as it may sound, and taking into consideration the bizarre events of 2007 in the mysterious woods of the Cannock Chase, Wes is undeniably correct in his stance that such infernal monsters are "among us." It's a chilling thought that werewolves are not merely the product of horror writers, Hollywood, and ancient folklore and mythology. It would be wise to remember that if, late one night, you find yourself walking through dense and ancient woodland, or taking a short-cut through a creepy, old graveyard, and particularly so on a night when the moon shines brightly and full, pray you don't hear a loud, animalistic howl.

It's a chilling thought that werewolves are not merely the product of horror writers, Hollywood, and ancient folklore and mythology.

MORPHING BLACK BEAST

In the summer of 2007, a falconer named Martin Whitley, of the English county of Devon, obtained a number of photographs of a very curious, black-colored, dog-like animal on the wilds of Dartmoor—where Sir Arthur Conan Doyle set his classic Sherlock Holmes novel, *The Hound of the Baskervilles*. As Whitley noted, it was June 9 when the strange affair went down. In his own words:

"I was flying a hawk on Dartmoor with some American clients when one of them pointed out this creature. It was walking along a path about 200 yards away from us. It was black and gray and comparable in size to a miniature pony. It had very thick shoulders, a long, thick tail with a blunt end, and small round ears. Its movement appeared feline; then 'bear-like' sprang to mind. There was a party climbing on the Tor opposite, making a racket, but this it ignored completely."

This is a 1901 illustration from Sir Arthur Conan Doyle's *The Hound of the Baskervilles,* which was set in Devon County, England, where a falconer observed a dog beast a century later.

Merrily Harpur, a noted authority on mystery animals in the U.K., offered her thoughts on the handful of photos of the creature that one of the Americans with Whitley took:

"Martin's American clients took a series of photos. They show the Dartmoor landscape, the school party on the Tor, and in the middle distance an animal which seems to change shape in each frame, from cat, to bear, to pony, to boar, to various breeds of dog. Indeed, members of the BCIB [the Big Cats in Britain research group] invoked nearly the whole of Crufts [the British version of the Westminster Kennel Club show] in attempting to give the creature a 'rational' explanation, while the proximity of Hound Tor suggested to some a possible kinship to Devon's spectral Wisht Hounds."

Martin Whitley may not have known what the beast was, but he was certain it was not just a dog. On this matter he expanded: "I have worked with dogs all my life and it was definitely not canine. I have also seen a collie-sized black cat in the area, about ten years ago, and it was not that—this was a lot bigger."

Jon Downes, of the monster-hunting Centre for Fortean Zoology, took a more skeptical approach and suspected that the animal was indeed a large dog, and that the seeming ability of the creature to shape-shift resulted from nothing stranger than the technical limitations of the camera that was used to capture the shots. The dog angle was also championed by the U.K.'s *Daily Mail* newspaper. Its staff spoke with a local woman, Lucinda Reid, who believed that what had been photographed was actually her pet Newfoundland dog, Troy! Certainly, Troy, like all Newfoundland's, was a formidable and sizable animal. As evidence, he weighed in at just under 170 pounds.

Reid told the *Daily Mail:* "I was in stitches when I read that someone thought Troy was the Beast of Dartmoor. I spotted it was him right away—you can tell by the shape and the way he is walking. We go up to that spot on Dartmoor all the time. It is only ten minutes away from our home and Troy loves to run about there. A lot of people don't have a clue what he is, because he's so big. Troy frightens the life out of everyone because of his size and he doesn't look like a dog from a distance. He sometimes disappears off round the rocks on his own, and that's when he must have been photographed. But Troy is certainly nothing to be afraid of; he's a big softie. So, if anyone else sees him on the more, there's no need to panic."

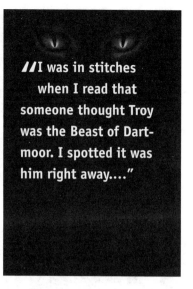

//I was in stitches when I read that someone thought Troy was the Beast of Dartmoor. I spotted it was him right away...."

Not everyone was quite so sure that Troy was the cause of the sensational story. Aside from the fact that the animal in the photos does appear to change shape, there is the matter of the location where the picture was taken. It's extremely close to a place known locally as Bowerman's Nose. It's a granite outcrop on the north slopes of Hayne down and only about a mile from a place called—wait for it—Hound Tor. And there is a very weird legend attached to the tor and how it got its name.

According to ancient, local folklore, roughly one thousand years ago there lived on the wilds of Dartmoor a man named Bowerman. He was a skilled hunter and someone who knew the old, mysterious landscape very well. On one particular day, while out hare hunting, his pack of hunting dogs stumbled upon something else: a secret coven of witches, hidden deep within a series of previously unknown caves on the moorland. Bowerman's dogs raced around the caves in chaotic fashion, knocking over a huge cauldron that was a significant part of an ancient ritual the witches were about to perform. Bowerman managed to take control of his dogs and fled the area. The witches, however, were determined to have their cold, deadly revenge.

One of the crone-like coven shape-shifted into a hare and coldly lured Bowerman and his dogs into marshy ground that quickly swallowed up one and all. The witches were not done with Bowerman and his pack, however. They hauled their dead bodies out of the marsh and turned them to stone. So the old legend goes, a line of rocks at the peak of Hound Tor is comprised of the dogs-turned-to-stone, while an outcrop called Bowerman's nose is all that remains of the dogs' master. And still the story continues.

The very same area of landscape is the home of what are known as the Wisht Hounds—briefly referred to above by Merrily Harpur. Like the monster-dog in Sir Arthur Conan Doyle's *The Hound of Baskervilles* (which was actually based, in part, on the old legends), the Wisht Hounds were huge, black, deadly dogs of a paranormal kind that sported blazing red eyes. They preyed upon the bodies and souls of the unfortunate people who dared to intrude upon their territory. On top of that, not at all far away is Buckfastleigh, which, in the seventeenth century, was the home of Squire Richard Cabell—the inspiration for evil Sir Hugo Baskerville in Conan Doyle's much-loved novel. Local lore tells of how, on the night Cabell died, a vicious pack of savage, black hounds was seen racing across the moonlit moor.

Wistman's Woods in Dartmoor, the home of the bloodthirsty Wisht Hounds.

Taking into consideration the sheer number of strange and centuries-old stories of supernatural hounds in the very same area where Martin Whitley's friends photographed, well, *something*, it's no wonder that the idea it was Troy the Newfoundland is met with much skepticism by monster hunters. While the matter was never resolved to the satisfaction of everyone, it did provide Troy with brief, nationwide fame!

ORANGE, TEXAS, SHAPE-SHIFTER

Solomon was someone I interviewed back in 2003—when he was in his mid-80s—about a startling encounter he had with a shape-shifting creature no fewer than seven decades earlier, when he was just a young teenager. The location was a dense area of woodland in Orange, Texas. It was a normal Sunday morning when Solomon and several friends were exploring the woods and having a good time. After a couple of hours of scouting around, they found a place to sit and heartily tucked into the lunches they had brought with them.

All was good until one of the group experienced that eerie sensation we all get from time to time: namely, that of being watched. And watched very closely. Then, the rest of the group experienced it too. Almost in unison they looked across the small stream that was before them, only to see nothing less than a large, wolf-like head peering directly at them, and from within the dense foliage.

When the creature realized it had been seen, however, it suddenly broke through the undergrowth and paced along the water's edge in a disturbing, prowling fashion. All four boys wondered if they were being sized up for lunch. As the beast made its presence fully known, the friends were shocked to see that although it resembled a wolf, the monster-thing was around ten feet in length and had a huge, muscular body—far beyond that of any normal wolf. On several occasions the monster stopped and stared at the boys, growling at them in a dark and deep, low and guttural fashion. Not surprisingly, the friends were too frightened to move. Then, suddenly, something very strange happened.

It was suddenly surrounded by an eerie, green fog, at which point the monster changed its stance: its hind legs noticeably morphed....

The massive wolf-creature suddenly sat down and "started to shake," as Solomon worded it. Even more amazing, it was suddenly surrounded by an eerie, green fog, at which point the monster changed its stance: its hind legs noticeably morphed, to the point where it was able to rear up onto those same hind legs and loom over the now near-hysterical boys at a height of around ten feet. As for its front limbs, they took on distinctly human-looking form, albeit covered in thick hair. For a few moments the man-beast snapped and snarled at the group, still from the other side of the stream, after which it suddenly turned and vanished into the woods—never to be seen again.

It was the one and only paranormal experience in Solomon's life—and he was very happy to keep it that way, too.

PHANTOM BLACK DOG

In his absolutely definitive book *Explore Phantom Black Dogs*, the author and researcher Bob Trubshaw wrote the following: "The folklore of phantom black dogs is known throughout the British Isles. From the Black Shuck of East Anglia to the Mauthe Dhoog of the Isle of Man there are tales of huge spectral hounds 'darker than the night sky' with eyes 'glowing red as burning coals.'" While a number of intriguing theories exist to explain the presence and nature of such spectral-like beasts, certainly the most ominous of all is that they represent some form of precursor to—or instigator of—doom, tragedy, and death.

One of the most infamous of all black dog encounters in the British Isles occurred at St. Mary's Church, Bungay, Suffolk, England, on Sunday, August 4, 1577, when an immense and veritable spectral hound from Hell materialized within the church during a powerful thunderstorm and mercilessly tore into the terrified congregation with its huge fangs and razor-sharp claws. In fact, so powerful was the storm that it reportedly killed two men in the belfry as the church tower received an immense lightning bolt that tore through it and shook the building to its ancient foundations.

According to an old, local verse: "All down the church in midst of fire, the hellish monster flew. And, passing onward to the quire, he many people slew." Then, just as suddenly as it had appeared, the beast bounded out of St. Mary's and was reported shortly thereafter at Blythburgh Church, about twelve miles away, where it allegedly killed and mauled even more people with its immense and bone-crushing jaws—and where, it is said, the scorch marks of the beast's claws can still be seen to this day, infamously imprinted upon the ancient door of the church.

Even more intriguing is the fact that Bungay's legend of a satanic black hound parallels that of yet another local legend: that of Black Shuck, a giant, spectral dog that haunts the Norfolk and Suffolk coasts. Such is the popularity of the Bungay legend that it has resulted in an image of the beast being incorporated into the town's coat of arms—and the Black Dogs is the name of the Bungay Town Football Club.

The stark, disturbing and memorable image that the infamous devil dog, or the phantom hound, as described above undoubtedly conjures up is that of a definitively sinister beast that stealthily prowls the towns and villages of ancient England by nothing more than silvery moonlight or to the accompanying background of a vio-

St. Mary's Church in Bungay, Suffolk, is the site of a famous 1577 sight of a beastly black dog.

lent, crashing thunderstorm. It is, however, a little known fact outside of dedicated students of the phenomenon that sightings of such creatures have also taken place in modern times: in both the twentieth and twenty-first centuries, even, as is evidenced by the following reports from my files.

First, there is the story of the Bradley family of the city of Leeds who had the very deep misfortune to encounter one of the now-familiar hounds of Hell in early 2009: at no less a site than the English city of Lichfield's famous and historic cathedral, which has the distinction of being the only English cathedral to be adorned with three spires.

According to the Bradleys, while walking around the outside of the cathedral one pleasant Sunday morning, they were startled by the sight of a large black dog racing along at high speed and adjacent to the side of the cathedral. The jaw-dropping fact that the dog was practically the size of a donkey ensured their attention was caught and held. But that attention was rapidly replaced by overwhelming fear, when the dog allegedly "charged the wall" of the cathedral and summarily vanished right into the brickwork as it did so! Perhaps understandably, the Bradleys chose not to report their mysterious encounter to cathedral officials or to the police.

The jaw-dropping fact that the dog was practically the size of a donkey ensured their attention was caught and held.

And then we have the account of Marjorie Sanders. Although Sanders's account can be considered a new one in the sense that it only reached my eyes and ears in August 2009, during which time I was on a week-long return trip to England, it actually occurred back in the closing stages of the Second World War, when the witness was a girl of ten or eleven. At the time, Sanders was living in a small village not too far from England's Tamworth Castle—which overlooks the River Tame, and which has stood there since it was built by the Normans in the eleventh century, although an earlier Anglo-Saxon castle is known to have existed on the same site, and which was constructed by the forces of Ethelfreda, the Mercian queen and the eldest daughter of King Alfred the Great of Wessex.

According to Sanders, "probably in about early 1945," her grandfather had "seen a hell-hound parading around the outside of the castle that scared him half to death when it vanished in front of him." For reasons that Sanders cannot now remember or comprehend, her grandfather always thereafter memorably referred to the animal in question as "the furnace dog." Whether or not this is an indication that the spectral dog had the seemingly ubiquitous fiery red eyes that so many witnesses have reported remains unfortunately unknown; but, it would not at all surprise me if that was one day shown to be the case.

Then we have the brief, but highly thought-provoking, account of Gerald Clarke, a Glasgow baker whose father claimed to have briefly seen a large, black-colored, phantom hound with bright, electric-blue-colored eyes on the grounds of a military base in central England—called Royal Air Force Stafford—in the late 1950s, and while on patrol late one winter's evening. As was the case with so many other witnesses to such disturbing entities, the elder Clarke quietly confided in his son that the creature "just vanished: first it was there and then it wasn't."

In view of all the above, one can only say: "Beware of the Dog!"

SHAPE-SHIFTING BLACK DOGS

Up until the end of season four of *The Walking Dead*, we were familiar with seeing our straggling bunch of heroes hunkered down in a fortified Georgia prison, doing battle with both the dead and their arch-villain, the one-eyed Governor. But the resurrected dead, people feeding on people, and prisons also have a place in the real world. Our story, however, revolves around monsters, rather than virally created zombies of the undead variety.

In the latter part of the sixteenth century, London, England's Newgate Prison was the site of a horrific series of deaths that would have made even the average walker proud in the extreme—if such creatures possess significant numbers of brains to be proud. Due to a pronounced lack of regular food, on more than a few occasions the prisoners targeted the weakest members of the pack and turned them into food. It was very much a case of having to eat the living to avoid becoming one of the dead. We are, then, talking about cannibals in the cell block.

> *Once again the mysterious dog manifested before the farmer, but this time, incredibly, it was supposedly heard to speak, in rumbling tones....*

One of those savagely killed and partially eaten by the prisoners was an unnamed man who did exactly what the bitten and the equally semi-devoured of the prison of *The Walking Dead* did on so many occasions: he rose again. Not, however, as a voracious devotee of raw, human flesh, but as a ghastly and ghostly black dog with a pair of blazing red eyes.

The actions of this undead man-hound were not at all unlike those of its television-based equivalents. The creature violently slaughtered all of those who had taken its human life by savagely biting down on their necks with its immense and powerful jaws. Death swiftly followed for

Ruins of Newgate Prison, where, it is said, underfed prisoners killed and ate some of their fellow inmates back in the sixteenth century.

the guilty parties. Reanimation, however, did not. When the deed was done, the man—in spectral dog form—vanished, never, ever to be seen again.

Then, there is the very similar, and very weird, tale of a pair of brothers: William and David Sutor. The dark saga all began late one night in December 1728, when William, a Scottish farmer, was hard at work in his fields and heard an unearthly shriek that was accompanied by a brief glimpse of a large, dark-colored dog, far bigger than any normal hound, and one possessed of a pair of glowing red eyes—just like the beast from Newgate Prison.

On several more occasions in both 1729 and 1730, the dog returned, always seemingly intent on plaguing the Sutor family. It was, however, in late November of 1730 that the affair ultimately reached its paranormal pinnacle. Once again the mysterious dog manifested before the farmer, but this time, incredibly, it was supposedly heard to speak, in rumbling tones, and directed William to make his way to a specific, nearby piece of ground within thirty minutes.

He did as he was told, and there waiting for him was the spectral hound of Hell. A terrified William pleaded to know what was going on. The hideous hound answered that he was none other than David Sutor—William's brother—and that he had killed a man at that very spot some thirty-five years earlier.

As David had directed his own savage dog to kill the man, David had himself—as punishment—been returned to our plane of existence in the form of a gigantic hound. The dogman instructed William to seek out the buried bones of the murder victim, and then place them within consecrated ground, which William duly did, in the confines of the old Blair Churchyard.

The ghostly black dog—the spirit of David Sutor in animal form—vanished. Like the beast of Newgate Prison, when its work was done, it never made a reappearance.

STUUBE, PETER

Back in 1590, George Bores wrote a fascinating, but horrific, report on one of the most notorious cases of lycanthropy on record. It told the story of a deranged and homicidal man named Peter Stuube, who went on murderous killing sprees, while—so he claimed—in the form of a terrifying werewolf. Bores began....

"In the towns of Cperadt and Bedbur near Collin in high Germany, there was continually brought up and nourished one Stubbe Peeter [note: there are several variations of spelling in the records], who from his youth was greatly inclined to evil and the practicing of wicked arts even from twelve years of age till twenty, and so forwards till his dying day, insomuch that surfeiting in the damnable desire of magic, necromancy, and sorcery, acquainting himself with many infernal spirits and fiends, insomuch that forgetting the God that made him, and that Savior that shed his blood man's redemption: In the end, careless of salvation gave both soul and body to the Devil forever, for small carnal pleasure in this life, that he might be famous and spoken of on earth, though he lost heaven thereby."

Bores continues that the Devil himself had pledged to provide Stuube "whatsoever his heart desired during his mortal life: whereupon this vile wretch neither desired riches nor promotion, nor was his fancy satisfied with any external or outward pleasure, but having a tyrannous heart and a most cruel bloody mind, requested that at his pleasure he might work his malice on men, women, and children, in the shape of some beast, whereby he might live without dread or danger of life, and unknown to be the executor of any bloody enterprise which he meant to commit."

The Devil, added Bores, perceived Stuube as being someone who was "a fit instrument to perform mischief as a wicked fiend pleased with the desire of wrong and destruction." The horned one gave Stuube a girdle which, upon being placed around his waist, mutated him into "the likeness of a greedy, devouring wolf, strong and mighty, with eyes great and large, which in the night sparkled like unto brands of fire, a mouth great and wide, with most sharp and cruel teeth, a huge body and mighty paws. And no sooner should he put off the same girdle, but presently he should appear in his former shape, according to the proportion of a man, as if he had never been changed."

> The horned one gave Stuube a girdle which, upon being placed around his waist, mutated him into "the likeness of a greedy, devouring wolf...."

It was then, having been given—by the Devil, no less—the ability to transform himself from man to monster and back again, Stuube went on to commit his gruesome acts. Or, as Bores worded it, Stuube "proceeded to the execution of sundry most heinous and vile murders; for if any person displeased him, he would incontinent thirst for revenge, and no sooner should they or any of theirs walk abroad in the fields or about the city, but in the shape of a wolf he would presently encounter them, and never rest till he had plucked out their throats and tear their joints asunder. And after he had gotten a taste hereof, he took such pleasure and delight in shedding of blood, that he would night and day walk the fields and work extreme cruelties."

Bores went into much detail regarding how, exactly, Stuube would go about his deadly, infernal business: "And sundry times he would go through the streets of Collin, Bedbur, and Cperadt, in comely habit, and very civilly, as one well known to all the inhabitants thereabout, and oftentimes was he saluted of those whose friends and children he had butchered, though nothing suspected for the same. In these places, I say, he would walk up and down, and if he could spy either maid, wife, or child that his eyes liked or his heart lusted after, he would wait their issuing out of the city or town. If he could by any means get them alone, he would in the fields ravish them, and after in his wolfish likeness cruelly murder them."

Stuube, in werewolf form, had more than just murder in mind, when it came to the women of the area:

"Yea, often it came to pass that as he walked abroad in the fields, if he chanced to spy a company of maidens playing together or else a milking their kine, in his wolfish shape he would incontinent run among them, and while the rest escaped by flight, he would be sure to lay hold of one, and after his filthy lust fulfilled, he would murder her presently. Beside, if he had liked or known any of them, look who he had a mind unto, her he would pursue, whether she were before or behind, and take her from the rest, for such was his swiftness of

A 1517 illustration from a German book depicts how people of the time really believed werewolves existed to menace the innocent.

foot while he continued a wolf that he would outrun the swiftest greyhound in that country; and so much he had practiced this wickedness that the whole province was feared by the cruelty of this bloody and devouring wolf."

Bores then spelled out the sickening history of Stuube's mad and murderous actions: "Thus continuing his devilish and damnable deeds within the compass of a few years, he had murdered thirteen young children, and two goodly young women big with child, tearing the children out of their wombs, in most bloody and savage sort, and after ate their hearts panting hot and raw, which he accounted dainty morsels and best agreeing to his appetite."

Eventually, and thankfully, however, Peter Stuube's abominable reign was brought to a close, as Bores revealed:

"Thus being apprehended, he was shortly after put to the rack in the town of Bedbur, but fearing the torture, he voluntarily confessed his whole life, and made known the villainies which he had committed for the space of 25 years; also he confessed how by sorcery he procured of the Devil a girdle, which being put on, he forthwith became a wolf, which girdle at his apprehension he confessed he cast it off in a certain valley and there left it, which, when the magistrates heard, they sent to the valley for it, but at their coming found nothing at all, for it may be supposed that it was gone to the Devil from whence it came, so that it was not to be found. For the Devil having brought the wretch to all the shame he could, left him to endure the torments which his deeds deserved."

Having spilled his guts as a result of "fearing the torture," Stuube had far more to say, as Bores duly noted in his extensive study of Stuube and his rampaging:

"After he had some space been imprisoned, the magistrates found out through due examination of the matter, that his daughter Stubbe Beell and his gossip Katherine Trompin were both accessory to diverse murders committed, who for the same as also for their lewd life otherwise committed, was arraigned, and with Stubbe Peeter condemned, and their several judgments pronounced the 28 of October 1589, in this manner, that is to say: Stubbe Peeter as principal malefactor, was judged first to have his body laid on a wheel, and with red hot burning pincers in ten several places to have the flesh pulled off from the bones, after that, his legs and arms to be broken with a wooden ax or hatchet, afterward to have his head struck from his body, then to have his carcass burned to ashes. Also his daughter and his gossip were judged to be burned quick to ashes, the same time and day with the carcass of the aforesaid Stubbe Peeter. And on the 31st of the same month, they suffered

The execution of Peter Stubbe was carried out on a "breaking wheel," and his violent demise (all three men on the wheels are Stubbe in different phases of the torture) for being a werewolf (depicted at top, left). His mistress and daughter (in the background at right) were burned.

death accordingly in the town of Bedbur in the presence of many peers and princes of Germany."

Peter Stuube's reign of lycanthropic terror was finally over.

Equally as horrific as the actions of Stumpp were those of an unnamed man who, in the final years of the sixteenth century, became known as the Werewolf of Chalons. A Parisian tailor who killed, dismembered, and ate the flesh of numerous children he had lured into his shop, the man was brought to trial for his crimes on December 14, 1598. Notably, during the trial, it was claimed that on occasion the man also roamed nearby woods in the form of a huge, predatory wolf, where he further sought innocent souls to slaughter and consume. As was the case with Stumpp, the Werewolf of Chalons was sentenced to death and was burned at the stake.

As I have noted in previous entries in the pages of this book, some reports of werewolves do appear to involve monstrous creatures of unknown origin. But, as the above clearly shows, sometimes the exact opposite is true. And sometimes, regrettably, one of the worst monsters is one of us, the human race.

SUPERNATURAL HOUNDS OF SOUTH AMERICA

Few people who have read Sir Arthur Conan Doyle's classic Sherlock Holmes novel *The Hound of the Baskervilles* can forget those immortal words uttered by Dr. James Mortimer to the world's most famous fictional detective: "Mr. Holmes, they were the footprints of a gigantic hound!"

It may come as a surprise to some people to learn that Conan Doyle's novel was actually based upon real legends of giant, devilish hounds that were said to haunt Britain's villages and countryside, bringing doom, tragedy, and death in their spectral and demonic wake. Yes, Britain has a long, rich, and varied history of encounters with what have generally become known as "Phantom Black Dogs."

Usually much larger than normal dogs, they are said to possess a pair of large, glowing eyes (very often red); they frequent graveyards, old roadways, crossroads, and bridges; and are almost unanimously associated with the realm of the dead. In some cases, the beasts appear to be demonstrably evil; while in other reports evidence is exhibited of a helpful—perhaps even concerned—nature. But whatever these critters are, they are not your average flesh and blood animal. Not at all. They might just be your worst nightmare.

While the image of the Phantom Black Dog is most associated with the British Isles and mainland Europe, the beast has been seen in many other locations, too—including throughout Latin America. The leading researcher in this field is Simon Burchell, the author of *Phantom Black Dogs in Latin America*. Running at thirty-eight pages, Burchell's work is obviously very much a booklet rather than a full-length book. But that doesn't detract from the most important thing of all: its pages are packed with case after case, each offering the reader little-known and seldom-seen information on the definitive Latin American cousin to Britain's more famous counterpart.

Notably, Burchell's publication details the truly startling wealth of similarities between those creatures seen centuries ago in England, and those reported throughout Latin America in the last 100 years.

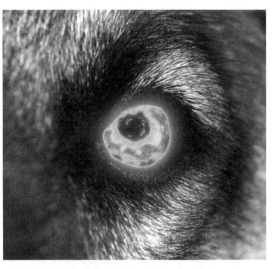

The supernatural dogs of South America possess glowing eyes, according to those who have reported seeing them.

Namely, the diabolical, glowing eyes; the association that the phantom hound has with life after death; how seeing the beast may be a precursor to doom and tragedy; its occasional helpful and guiding qualities; the fact that the animal is usually witnessed in the vicinity of bridges, crossroads, and cemeteries; its ability to shape-shift and change in size; and not forgetting the most important thing, of course: its perceived paranormal origins.

Burchell also reveals how the legends of the phantom black dog of some Latin American nations—such as Guatemala—have been exploited by those with draconian and outdated morals. For example, there are widespread tales of people who enjoy having a drink or several, incurring the dire wrath of the phantom black dog—which, as Burchell says, "was certainly popularized by the Catholic Church which used this legend and others as moralizing tales."

Winged hounds—whose appearance and activities smack strongly of the modern day Chupacabras of Puerto Rico—are discussed, as are copious amounts of data that make a link with tales of a truly dark and satanic nature. Burchell also reveals intriguing data suggesting that at least some tales of the black dog might be based upon cultural memories and stories of very real, large and ferocious hounds brought to the New World by the Conquistadors centuries ago—"savage and ferocious dogs to kill and tear apart the Indians."

That said, however, it is clear that the overwhelming majority of reports of the phantom black dog in Latin America parallel those of Britain to a truly striking, eerie, and extraordinary degree—in the sense that they appear to be something other than flesh-and-blood entities. As Burchell states:

"Although the Black Dog may appear at first glance to be a British or north European phenomenon, it exists in essentially the same form across the entire length and breadth of the Americas. Much has been written upon the presumed Germanic, Celtic or Indio-European origin of the legend but such an origin would not explain how a highland Maya girl can meet a shape-shifting Black Dog at a Guatemalan crossroads. It appears that the Black Dog, much like the poltergeist, is a global phenomenon."

TEXAS CHUPACABRA

Over the course of the last few years, I have found myself doing more and more radio, newspaper, magazine, and TV interviews on the phenomenon of the so-called "Texas Chupacabras"—those admittedly very strange-looking, hairless beasts that have predominantly been reported within woods and fields in and around the Austin and San Antonio areas, but that are now being seen with increasing frequency in the vicinity of the city of Dallas, very near to where I live.

One of the questions that keeps on surfacing during those same interviews is how, and under what particular circumstances, did these mysterious beasts manage to migrate from the island of Puerto Rico—where the Chupacabra reports began to surface in the mid-1990s—to the heart of the Lone Star State? Well, the answer to that question is very simple: they didn't.

While Puerto Rico's most infamous monster may very well share its name with that which haunts the woods, ranches, and wilds of Texas, that's pretty much where the connection ends. Notably, when I have mentioned this to certain media outlets, there's nothing but outright disappointment in response. So, let's take a look at what is really afoot, and how the creatures of Texas have become entwined with those of Puerto Rico.

I have been on a number of expeditions to Puerto Rico in search of the island's bloodsucking beasts, and there's no doubt in my mind that they exist. I have interviewed numerous ranchers, veterinarians, civil-defense employees, and members of the

This illustration by Alvin Padayachee depicts a chupacabra as a hairless, doglike monster.

public who have either seen the creatures, or who have been witness to their bloodsucking activities.

In most cases, the Chupacabras of Puerto Rico are described as bipedal creatures with large eyes, vicious claws and teeth, hairless monkey-like bodies, a row of spikes running down the backs of their heads and necks—punk-rock Mohawk-style—and even, occasionally, sporting membranous bat-like wings.

As for their mode of attack, most of the interviewees stated that the Chupacabras kill their prey by a bite to the neck and then proceed to drink the blood.

Turning to Texas, however, we see something very different at work. In each and every case on record, the Texas Chupacabras are most certainly not described as being bipedal in nature. Rather, they walk on four legs. There are no wings, no huge eyes, and certainly not any spikes running down their heads.

But that doesn't mean that high strangeness is not afoot. It most certainly is. In those cases where we have been fortunate to secure the body of a Texas Chupacabra—either after it has been shot or hit by a vehicle—DNA analysis has proven with 100 percent certainty that these creatures have canine origins. Yes, they look weird, but they are from the dog family, of that there is no doubt.

The story doesn't end there, however. Canine they are, but normal they're most certainly not. The lack of hair has led many commentators to suggest that the animals are afflicted by mange—which may be true. However, not only are we now seeing pups with the adult creatures, but young and old all seem to be adapting quite well to living without hair. There's none of the usual intense itching and scratching—to the point of bleeding—that is typical in animals affected by mange, and the lack of hair doesn't appear to have any bearing on their ability to roam quite happily and com-

In contrast to the Chupacabras in Texas, those described in Puerto Rico are very different: bipedal, large-eyed alien-like creatures with spikes down their backs.

fortably in the pulverizing summer heat of Texas. And as someone who shaves his head to the bone daily, I can say with certainty that the Texan sun can certainly do some damage to the skin without adequate protection!

In addition, in some cases the front legs of the animals appear to be much shorter than one would consider normal—which gives them a weird hopping, kangaroo-type gait. Others have elongated upper jaws, many have cataracts, and they act in a highly aggressive nature around people—which is quite unlike normal, wild canines which will usually steer clear of humans.

And then there is their mode of attack—which a number of ranchers have said involves bites to the neck of farm animals and a sizable amount of blood drained from the bodies. And, it is this latter point—and, arguably, this latter point alone—that has led many people to believe that the Puerto Rican Chupacabras and the Texan Chupacabras are one and the same. But they're not. The term Chupacabra is a great marketing tool. It provokes intrigue and terror and is a journalist's dream come true. And the whole thing has now gone viral within the media, on the Net, and in monster hunting circles.

So, in other words, we have two distinctly different phenomena in evidence: one is borne out of sightings of, and encounters with, truly unknown beasts on the island of Puerto Rico, and the other is focused upon weird-looking, Texas canines that may have some extraordinary changes going on at a genetic level, too. Beyond that, however, all we can say for certain about the real Chupacabra is that just like Las Vegas, what happens in Puerto Rico continues to stay in Puerto Rico.

WERECATS

Throughout history, folklore, and mythology, one can find accounts of shape-shifting creatures, with the most famous example surely being the werewolf. The deadly monster of the full moon is far from being alone, however. In Africa, there are legends of werehyenas. Wererats have been reported in Oregon. Cynanthropy is a condition in which a person believes he or she can shape-shift into the form of a dog. And then there are werecats.

Tales of werecats exist in numerous locations: South America, Asia, Africa, and Europe. Sometimes the werecats are nothing less than transformed humans. Leopards, lions, tigers, and jaguars are typically the werecat forms into which a human shape-shifter mutates. Others are regular cats, altered by dark magic into something hostile and terrible. All of which brings us back to the werecats of Britain.

The earliest case I have on file dates from 1953, specifically the month of August. The location: Abbots Bromley, a village in the English county of Staffordshire, the origin of which dates back to at least 942 C.E. The witness was a now-deceased man, Brian Kennerly. In 2002, Kennerly's family told me of how he often spoke of the occasion when, as he walked through Abbots Bromley on what was a warm, summer' night, he was confronted by a large black cat—one that he described as the typical "black panther."

Not surprisingly, Kennerly was frozen in his tracks. His amazement turned to outright fear when the beast suddenly rose up onto its back limbs, giving it a height of around five and a half feet. The creature reportedly issued a low growl and flicked its dangling front paws in Kennerly's direction. Notably, Kennerly's daughter told me her father said that as the ABC rose up, "its back legs changed shape, probably to support it when it was standing upright." A few seconds later, the creature dropped back to the ground and bounded out of sight.

This 1763 illustration depicts a weretiger, a half-human beast originating from Asia.

A similar report, this one from the centuries-old village of Blakeney—in the English county of Norfolk—occurred in 1967. In this case, the witness, who was driving to Blakeney on a cold, winter's night, caught a brief glimpse of a creature standing at the side of the road that was eerily similar to the one seen by Brian Kennerly fourteen years previously. In this case, the woman said: "It stood like a person, but stooped, but had a cat's head. Even the pointed ears."

The final two cases in my files are separated by seven years—1981 and 1988—but the location was the same: the German War Cemetery located within the heavily wooded Cannock Chase, Staffordshire. The Chase has long been a hotbed for weirdness: Bigfoot-type creatures, werewolves, huge serpents, ghosts, UFOs, and much more of a supernatural nature have been reported in the depths of the Chase.

As for the two reports of werecat-type creatures seen at the cemetery, one was a daytime event involving a beast that was black in color, taller than

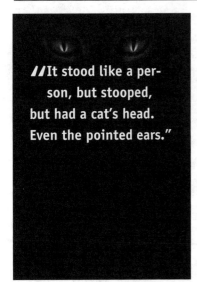

//It stood like a person, but stooped, but had a cat's head. Even the pointed ears."

the average man, and seen leaning on one of the gravestones. That is, until it realized it was being watched and it dropped to all fours and raced off into the trees. The second case concerned a van driver crossing the Chase late at night and who was forced to bring his vehicle to a halt—very near the cemetery—as a result of the presence in the road of a huge black cat. It was a cat that stared intently at the shocked driver, until it "sort of jumped onto its back legs." According to the man, Don Allen, the creature remained in view for no more than about twenty seconds, after which it headed towards the cemetery, making a curious "hopping and bouncing" movement as it did so.

Are infernal werecats really roaming the British Isles? Granted, the number of reports is small. And yet, the witnesses—and, in the case of Brian Kennerly, his family—are adamant that what they encountered were large, black, upright cats that displayed vaguely human characteristics. Perhaps the old myths and legends are not just folklore after all. Just maybe, the monstrous werecat really *does* roam the old landscapes of the British Isles.

WEREWOLF OF KLEIN-KRAMS

In 1879, Karl Bartsch wrote that in the vicinity of Klein-Krams, near Ludwigslust, Germany, there existed in earlier centuries huge woods that "were so rich with game that the dukes often came to this region to hold their great hunts. During these hunts they almost always saw a wolf who—even though he came within shooting distance—could never be killed by a huntsman. Indeed, they even had to watch as he took a piece of game before their very eyes and—something that was most remarkable to them—ran with it into the village."

Bartsch continued that, on one particular occasion, a hussar from Ludwigslust was making his way through the village to meet with a man named Feeg. When the unnamed hussar arrived at the home of the man in question, he got far more than he bargained, as Bartsch recorded:

"When he entered the house a flock of children stormed out of the house with a loud cry and hurried out into the yard. When he asked them about their wild behavior, they told him that except for a small boy, no one from the Feeg family was at home, and that he—as was his custom when no one was at home—had transformed himself into a werewolf, and that they were running away from him, because otherwise he would bite them."

Soon afterwards, Bartsch continued, the much-feared wolf-boy appeared, but by now he was back in his human form. The hussar demanded that the child tell him what manner of devilry was afoot in the village. Although the boy was initially reluctant to say anything at all, he finally relented. In Bartsch's words: "The child told him that his grandmother had a strap, and that if he put it on he would instantly become a wolf. The hussar kindly asked the boy to make an appearance as a werewolf. At first the boy refused, but finally he agreed to do it, if the strange man would first climb into the loft, so that he would be safe from him. The hussar agreed to this, and to be sure pulled up the ladder with which he had climbed into the loft."

By Bartsch's account, the incredible transformation from boy to monster happened quickly:

"As soon as this had happened the boy ran into the main room, and soon came out again as a young wolf and chased away all those who were standing in the entryway. After the wolf had run back into the main room and come back out as a boy, the hussar climbed down and had the Feeg child show him the magic belt, but he could not discover anything unusual about it."

In no time at all, the astonished and concerned hussar went to a forester in the vicinity of Klein-Krams and told him what he had experienced in the Feeg house. On listening to the tale, the forester, "who had always been present at the great hunts near Klein-Krams, immediately thought about the werewolf who could not be wounded. He now thought that he would be able to kill the werewolf."

At the very next hunt the forester told his friends, as he carefully inserted a silver bullet into the barrel of his rifle: "Today the werewolf will not escape from me!" His concerned friends looked on in silence.

According to Bartsch: "The hunt soon began, and it did not take long before the wolf showed himself once again. Many of the huntsmen shot at him, but he remained unwounded. Finally he approached the forester, who brought him to the ground. Everyone could see that the wolf was wounded, but soon he jumped up again and ran into

The boy was reluctant at first to show himself as a wolf, but he eventually agreed to do so by using the magical belt.

the village. The huntsmen followed him, but the werewolf outran them and disappeared into the Feeg farmyard."

There was, however, an unforeseen ending to this strange saga of shapeshifting in Germany of centuries past. The werewolf killed by the forester was not the young Feeg boy, after all. Bartsch revealed the twist in the story: "In their search, the huntsmen came into the house, where they found the wolf in the grandmother's bed. They recognized it from the tail that was sticking out from under the covers. The werewolf was no one other than Feeg's grandmother. In her pain she had forgotten to take off the strap, and thus she herself revealed the secret."

WEREWOLVES AND THE BROTHERS GRIMM

Jacob and Wilhelm Grimm, far better known as the Brothers Grimm, were born in Hanau, Germany—Jacob in 1875 and Wilhelm in the following year. They are renowned for their popularization of folklore, myths, and legends, and for promoting the likes of Rapunzel, Cinderella, Hansel and Gretel, and Rumpelstiltskin. They also had an interesting tale to tell of werewolves. In 1816, they wrote:

"A soldier related the following story, which is said to have happened to his grandfather. The latter, the grandfather, had gone into the forest to cut wood with a kinsman and a third man. People suspected that there was something not quite right about this third man, although no one could say exactly what it was. The three finished their work and were tired, whereupon the third man suggested that they sleep a little. And that is what they did. They all laid down on the ground, but the grandfather only pretended to sleep, keeping his eyes open a crack. The third man looked around to see if the others were asleep, and when he believed this to be so, he took off his belt (or, as others tell the story, put on a belt) and turned into a wolf.

The Grimm Brothers (immortalized here in a statue in Hanau, Germany), wrote about werewolves in some of their stories.

"However, such a werewolf does not look exactly like a natural wolf, but somewhat different.

"Then he ran to a nearby meadow where a young foal was grazing, attacked it, and ate it, including skin and hair. Afterward he returned, put his belt back on (or took it off), and laid down, as before, in human form.

"A little later they all got up together and made their way toward home. Just as they reached the town gate, the third man complained that he had a stomachache. The grandfather secretly whispered in his ear: 'That I can well believe, for someone who has a horse, complete with skin and hair, in his belly.'

"The third man replied: 'If you had said that to me in the forest, you would not be saying it to me now.'

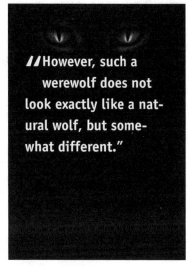

// However, such a werewolf does not look exactly like a natural wolf, but somewhat different."

"A woman had taken on the form of a werewolf and had attacked the herd of a shepherd, whom she hated, causing great damage. However, the shepherd wounded the wolf in the hip with an ax blow, and it crawled into the brush. The shepherd followed, thinking that he could finish it off, but there he found a woman using a piece of cloth torn from her dress to stop the blood gushing from a wound.

"At Lüttich in the year 1610 two sorcerers were executed because they had turned themselves into werewolves and had killed many children. With them they had a boy of twelve years whom the devil turned into a raven whenever they were tearing apart and eating their prey."

WOLF-MAN

In 1898, F. Asmus and O. Knoop wrote that by using what was called a wolf strap, it was possible for just about anyone to transform his- or herself into a werewolf. If, however, someone were to call the werewolf by their human name, they would transform back into human form. As for what, exactly, a wolf strap was, the pair noted that it was "a gift from the devil." They continued:

"A person who possessed such a strap could not get rid of it, however much he wanted to. Anyone who accepted a wolf strap also had entered into brotherhood with the devil, surrendering body and soul to him. If real wolves were feared in earlier times, werewolves were feared all the more. A real wolf could be shot dead or lured into a so-called wolf pit, where it would perish from

> **//** A person who possessed such a strap could not get rid of it, however much he wanted to. Anyone who accepted a wolf strap also had entered into brotherhood with the devil...."

hunger. However, a werewolf could not be brought down with a rifle bullet, nor would it ever fall into a wolf pit."

Asmus and Knoop put this question to their readers: "What is the use of running around as a werewolf?" It was, indeed, a good question. The pair answered it, themselves:

"This was not done for no good reason. When the pantries and meat containers were empty, one would only have to fasten on the wolf strap, run off as a wolf, seek out a fat sheep that was wandering off toward the edge of the woods, creep towards it, seize it, and drag it into the woods. In the evening one could bring it home without anyone noticing. Or the werewolf would know when a peasant was going through the woods with a lot of money. He would ambush him, rob him, then run off across the field with the booty."

In earlier times, the pair expanded, and after the horses had been unhitched from a wagon or a plow, "they would be driven out to a community pasture where they would be watched until morning by two herdsmen. Even colts were put out for the night. People took turns watching after them." There was a very good reason for that: the fear the horses would become the victims of the deadly werewolves in their very midst.

WOLF STONE BEAST-WOMAN

In a century long past and in a valley in the Fichtel Mountains, Bavaria, Germany, said Alexander Schöppner, a shepherd was tending his flock in a green meadow in 1874. Several times, it happened that after driving his herd home he discovered that one of the animals was missing. On each and every occasion, the search for the animals ended in complete failure. They were, said Schöppner, "lost and they remained lost."

On one occasion, however, the shepherd spied a huge wolf-like animal stealthily exiting the woods and attacking, and quickly killing, a small lamb. The shepherd gave chase but was not quite quick enough. The wolf-thing was near-instantaneously gone, as was the unfortunate lamb. Schöppner noted that the shepherd was not going to give up quite that easily, however, and he formulated a plan:

"The next time he took an expert marksman with him. The wolf approached, but the marksman's bullets bounced off him. Then it occurred to the hunter to load his weapon with the dried pith from an elder bush. The next day he got off a shot, and the robber ran howling into the woods. The next morning the shepherd met an old neighbor woman with whom he was not on the best of terms. Noticing that she was limping, he asked her: 'Neighbor, what is wrong with your leg? It does not want to go along with you.'"

The old woman, eying the shepherd with suspicion, replied: "What business is it of yours?" She didn't wait for an answer and quickly went on her way. The shepherd, said Schöppner, took careful note of her reply. Chiefly because the old woman "had long been suspected of practicing evil magic. People claimed to have seen her on the Heuberg in Swabia, the Köterberg, and also on the Hui near Halberstadt. He reported her. She was arrested, interrogated, and flogged with rod of alder wood, with which others suspected of magic, but who had denied the charges, had been punished. She was then locked up in chains. But suddenly the woman disappeared from the prison, and no one knew where she had gone."

That was not the end of the story, however. Sometime later, Schöppner recorded, the shepherd encountered the wolf again, yet again on the fringes of the forestland and late at night. On this occasion it was not the shepherd's animals that the beast had come for. No. It was the shepherd himself that the monster had in its deadly, predatory sights. A violent battle between the two erupted, during which the shepherd "gathered all of his strength together against the teeth and claws of the ferocious beast."

Despite the shepherd's determination to slay the beast, it quickly became clear that he was overwhelmed when it came to the matter of sheer, brute force and strength. The shepherd would have died had it not been for a hunter who quickly happened upon the scene and who "fired a shot at the wolf, and then struck it down with his knife. The instant that blood began to flow from the wolf's side, the old woman from the village appeared in the field before them, writhing and twisting terribly. They finished killing her and buried her twenty feet beneath the earth."

Schöppner concluded his account as follows: "At the place where they buried the woman they erected a large stone cross, which they named the 'Wolf Stone' in memory of these events. It was never peaceful and orderly in the vicinity of the stone."

The conflict between man and wolf goes back centuries. Bad enough to have to defend one's flock of sheep from wolves, but worse still if it is not really a wolf....

World War II Monster Hound

From a woman who—as a young girl—had a traumatic encounter with an infernal, supernatural hound at the height of World War II, we have the following:

"At the time, because of the war, my mother and I usually stayed with an elderly gentleman, who had kindly taken us in as 'refugees' from London. We only went back to the capital when the bombing ceased. The cottage where we lived is still in existence, in Bredon, Worcestershire. My encounter took place one late afternoon in summer, when I had been sent to bed, but was far from sleepy.

"I was sitting at the end of the big brass bedstead, playing with the ornamental knobs, and looking out of the window, when I was aware of a scratching noise, and an enormous black dog had walked from the direction of the fireplace to my left. It passed round the end of the bed, towards the door. As the dog passed between me and the window, it swung its head round to stare at me—it had very large eyes, which glowed from inside as if lit up, and as it looked at me I was quite terrified, and very much aware of the creature's breath, which was warm and as strong as a gust of wind.

"The animal must have been very tall, as I was sitting on the old-fashioned bedstead, which was quite high, and our eyes were level. Funnily enough, by the time it reached the door, it had vanished. I assure you that I was wide awake at the time, and sat on for quite some long while wondering about what I had seen, and to be truthful, too scared to get into our bed, under the clothes and go to sleep. I clearly remember my mother and our host, sitting in the garden in the late sun, talking and hearing the ringing of the bell on the weekly fried-fish van from Birmingham, as it went through the village! I am sure I was not dreaming, and have never forgotten the experience, remembering to the last detail how I felt, what the dog looked like."

Wulver

In her 1932 book, *Shetland Traditional Lore*, the noted folklorist Jessie Margaret Edmondston Saxby wrote: "The Wulver was a creature like a man with a wolf's head. He had short brown hair all over him. His home was a cave dug out of the side of a steep knowe, half-way up a hill. He didn't molest folk if folk didn't molest him. He was fond of fishing, and had a small rock in the deep water which is known to this day as the 'Wulver's Stane.' There he would sit fishing sillaks and piltaks for hour after hour. He was reported to have frequently left a few fish on the window-sill of some poor body."

Unlike the traditional werewolf, the Wulver was not a shape-shifter. Its semi-human, semi-wolf appearance was natural and unchanging. One of the most fascinating, and certainly disturbing, accounts of a Wulver came from Elliott O'Donnell. Shortly after the start of the twentieth century, O'Donnell interviewed a man named Andrew Warren, who had a startling story to tell. O'Donnell carefully recorded every word that Warren had to say. The priceless account reads:

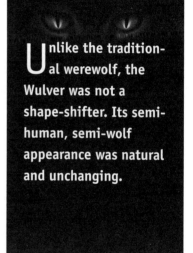

Unlike the traditional werewolf, the Wulver was not a shape-shifter. Its semi-human, semi-wolf appearance was natural and unchanging.

"I was about fifteen years of age at the time, and had for several years been residing with my grandfather, who was an elder in the Kirk [Church] of Scotland. He was much interested in geology, and literally filled the house with fossils from the pits and caves round where we dwelt. One morning he came home in a great state of excitement, and made me go with him to look at some ancient remains he had found at the bottom of a dried-up tarn [lake].

"'Look!' he cried, bending down and pointing at them, 'here is a human skeleton with a wolf's head. What do you make of it?' I told him I did not know, but supposed it must be some kind of monstrosity. 'It's a werwolf [sic]!" he rejoined, 'that's what it is. A werwolf! This island was once overrun with satyrs and werwolves! Help me carry it to the house.'

"I did as he bid me, and we placed it on the table in the back kitchen. That evening I was left alone in the house, my grandfather and the other members of the household having gone to the kirk. For some time I amused myself reading, and then, fancying I heard a noise in the back premises, I went into the kitchen. There was no one about, and becoming convinced that it could only have been a rat that had disturbed me, I sat on the table alongside the alleged remains of the werewolf, and waited to see if the noises would recommence.

"I was thus waiting in a listless sort of way, my back bent, my elbows on my knees, looking at the floor and thinking of nothing in particular, when there came a loud rat, tat, tat of knuckles on the window-pane. I immediately turned in the direction of the noise and encountered, to my alarm, a dark face looking in at me. At first dim and indistinct, it became more and more complete, until it developed into a very perfectly defined head of a wolf terminating in the neck of a human being.

"Though greatly shocked, my first act was to look in every direction for a possible reflection—but in vain. There was no light either without or within, other than that from the setting sun—nothing that could in any way have produced an illusion. I looked at the face and marked each feature intently. It was unmistakably a wolf's face, the jaws slightly distended; the lips wreathed in a savage snarl; the teeth sharp and white; the eyes light green; the ears pointed. The expression of the face was diabolically malignant, and as it gazed straight at me my horror was as intense as my wonder. This it seemed to notice, for a look of savage exultation crept into its eyes, and it raised one hand—a slender hand, like that of a woman, though with prodigiously long and curved finger-nails—menacingly, as if about to dash in the window-pane.

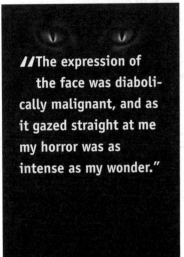

//The expression of the face was diabolically malignant, and as it gazed straight at me my horror was as intense as my wonder."

"Remembering what my grandfather had told me about evil spirits, I crossed myself; but as this had no effect, and I really feared the thing would get at me, I ran out of the kitchen and shut and locked the door, remaining in the hall till the family returned. My grandfather was much upset when I told him what had happened, and attributed my failure to make the spirit depart to my want of faith. Had he been there, he assured me, he would soon have got rid of it; but he nevertheless made me help him remove the bones from the kitchen, and we reinterred them in the very spot where we had found them, and where, for aught I know to the contrary, they still lie."

Dr. Karl Shuker, who has made a careful study of this particular case, says: "Quite aside from its highly sensational storyline, it is rather difficult to take seriously any account featuring someone (Warren's grandfather) who seriously believed that the Hebrides were '…once overrun with satyrs and werewolves'! By comparison, and despite his youthful age, Warren's own assumption that the skeleton was that of a deformed human would seem eminently more sensible—at least until the remainder of his account is read. Notwithstanding Warren's claim that his account was factual, however, the arrival of what was presumably another of the deceased wolf-headed entity's kind, seeking the return of the skeleton to its original resting place, draws upon a common theme in traditional folklore and legend."

Nature Gone Mad

BEAR-MONSTER

Neil Arnold, a noted authority on monsters, shared the following, which tells a story of very curious proportions: "For several decades Clapham Woods in West Sussex, [England,] has been the subject of many a dark whisper and wicked rumor. Tales of ghosts, murders and black magic often emerge from the ancient woods.

"My favorite and certainly, creepiest story pertaining to Sussex, and there are many, concerns a sighting of a truly dreadful creature. This manifestation even made the *Littlehampton Gazette*, in 1975, around the autumn. Even national radio and the popular, topical BBC program *Nationwide*, featured the story. At the time the area was caught up in a flap of high strangeness. Newscrews, journalists, UFO investigators, and paranormal enthusiasts flocked to the area, but rarely after dark.

"Two dogs had gone missing in the area, and when researchers stumbled across a footprint measuring eight-inches long and almost four-inches wide, but showing four-claw mark indentations (and a fifth claw mark towards the rear of the main pad), it was clear that something bizarre was going on. Twelve inches in front of the print, was another, almost identical print. The investigators were equipped with a Geiger counter, as well as other paraphernalia. Suddenly, the needle of the counter began to act oddly when the counter was swept over the prints, and then, from the darkness a grey pillar of mist

> **//It was once rumored that a bear cult operated clandestinely in the thickets....**

appeared. With the main A27 road in ear shot, the researchers decided it best to head for home, but then the monster appeared. The hazy shaft of mist before them took on the form of a great bear-like creature. The apparition then faded within ten seconds.

"From then on Clapham Woods would become known for its paranormal activity. It was once rumored that a bear cult operated clandestinely in the thickets, and maybe they'd raised some kind of tulpa-like energy forever to haunt the shadows of the 'birdless grove.'

"Strange symbols, time lapses, animal sacrifice, phantom hounds, secret societies and several obscure cults: Clapham Woods is certainly one of those special places. Blue Bell Hill in Kent, and Cannock Chase in Staffordshire seem to offer similar bouts of high strangeness, whether in the form of strange animal sightings or peculiar activity and folklore. Whether by strange coincidence, the grounds of Verdley Castle, situated also in West Sussex, are supposedly haunted by a giant bear. It is alleged to have been the last bear in England."

BLACK FOREST BEASTS

Robert R. Lyman Sr. (1870–1963) was someone who spent decades carefully collecting and chronicling reports of odd events, curious tales, and spooky legends, all from the Black Forest of north-central Pennsylvania. It was an area that Lyman had a particular fondness for. While many of the accounts were of the ghostly and supernatural variety, others were of a distinctly beastly kind. And they were varied and weird in the extreme.

Lyman said that "old timers" and "yarn spinners" in Potter County told him of the so-called "Sidehill Mootie." A bizarre beast, it had one leg shorter than the other! Lyman explained that, according to his sources, "It was built for the county's steep hills and could travel only in one direction around the hill. If alarmed, so that it turned around, it tumbled down the hill and could easily be captured alive." It was, he added, "very ferocious."

Lyman also recorded that local Native Americans told of "the most dreaded of strange, forest animals." It was a creature with the very odd name of the "Hide-Behind." Lyman explained: "No one ever saw one of the creatures because they always hid behind a tree. But everyone knew that they often followed travelers through the woods."

He expanded further on the nature of this near-unique critter of the woods: "If a person was afraid of them and kept looking back, the hide-behind would torment him into a panic. It took a brave man to be the last in line with a group walking through the woods. Old woodsmen said the only way to overcome the fear of the hide-behinds was to ignore them."

The Black Forest was also reportedly the home of a terrifying serpent, the "Hoop Snake." Once again, Lyman had intriguing data to impart on the nature of this deadly thing, which moved across the ground by placing its tail in its mouth and rolling along like a wheel! He elaborated: "As it came close it snapped its tail loose and struck its prey with a poison stinger. Escape was possible by jumping into a tree. The snake would strike the tree with its stinger and, unable to pull it out of the wood, the snake could easily be killed. The stung tree usually died."

Other unique creatures of the forest included the Fulleramo Bird, which flew in a very odd fashion: backwards, no less! Recognizing the humor in this, Lyman said: "It never saw where it was going and often hit people in the face! It could make a weird whistle through its tail."

Far less humorous was the "Sharp-Tailed Hodag." According to Lyman, "It was equipped with massive jaws and stout dorsal spines. It was very fond of

This undated photograph supposedly captures an image of a hodag in action. Of course, it's pretty obviously not a real hodag.

yman explained that, according to his sources, "It was built for the county's steep hills and could travel only in one direction around the hill...."

live dogs which it sopped in mud before devouring. It could be tamed and taught to cut grain with its scythe-shaped tail."

Of course, Lyman was no fool, or uncritical commentator. In that sense, he recognized that these Black Forest tales had an air of the mythological and the folkloric about them. He didn't, however, rule out the possibility that the accounts may have had some basis in reality. He closed his study of the bizarre beasts of the Black Forest with the following words:

"During the long, winter evenings story-tellers would yarn away for hours about all these, and more, impossible creatures. Mothers would tell these tales to wide-eyed children to make them fear the forest, so they would not wander away and get lost. They grew up half believing that the strange animals were an ever present hazard. Today, these weird creatures have all passed away, and so have the talented story-tellers who kept their memory alive. Except for a few recorded accounts, we would never know the entertainment provided by the folklore tales of our ancestors."

Giant Beaver

John Warms, who has extensively studied reports of monstrous beasts in Manitoba, Canada, has uncovered tales of giant, marauding beavers in not just Manitoba but also in areas stretching from Alaska to Florida. The term "giant" is not an exaggeration, as we're talking about beavers the size of people and even larger! As incredible as it may sound, such beasts really did once exist. Warms says:

"Today we know from recovered bones that the giant beaver is in a separate classification from the one we know so well as *Castor canadensis*. It has been named *Castoroides ohioensis* after the state where its remains were first documented."

Warms also notes that he has a number of reports on file of "bear-sized beavers," as well as sightings of huge beaver lodges, ones that come close to the size of an average house. It's hardly surprising that their lodges would be so huge. After all, not much else would be suitable for creatures that reached heights of seven feet and weights of in excess of 250 pounds. Although the

Giant beavers actually once roamed the earth in what is now North America. This is a fossilized skeleton of one such animal, the *Castoroides ohioensis*.

giant beaver is believed to have become extinct around 10,000 years ago—the same timeframe in which the Mammoth and the Mastodon became no more.

It's important to note that reports like those obtained by Warms are nothing new. One can find reports of huge, violent beavers that cover both the United States and Canada and which date back centuries. As a perfect example, in 1808, Alexander Henry the Younger was exploring the Red River in Manitoba, when he encountered a Native man near the forks of the Red and Assiniboine Rivers—today, the site of the city of Winnipeg. Henry's journal for that time contains a notable entry that confirms the giant beaver story having been told to him by his Native friend:

"A Salteaux, who I found here tented with the Courtes Oreilles, came to me this evening in a very ceremonious manner, and after having lighted and smoked his pipe informed me of his having been up a small river, a few days ago, upon a hunting excursion, when one evening while upon the water in his Canoe, watching the Beaver to shoot them, he was suddenly surprised by the appearance of a very large animal in the water. At first he took it for a Moose Deer, and was preparing to fire at it accordingly. But on its approach towards him he perceived it to be one of the Kitche Amicks or Large Beavers. He dare not fire but allowed it to pass on quite near his canoe without molesting it. I had already heard many stories concerning this large Beaver among the Saulteaux, but I cannot put any faith in them. Fear, I presume, magnifies an ordinary size Beaver into one of those monsters, or probably a Moose Deer or a Bear in the dark may be taken for one of them as they are seen only at night, and I am told they are very scarce."

While Henry's words clearly demonstrate his skepticism, they are important in the sense that they confirm that accounts of giant beavers existed centuries ago. As for John Warms's extensive research, it suggests that the giant beaver is still with us, albeit in deep stealth.

GIANT SPIDERS

For vast numbers of the human population spiders provoke a sense of creepiness and dread. And for people with arachnophobia, outright terror. And that's often as a result of an encounter with a small spider. Imagine, then, encountering a spider the size of a dog! You think it couldn't happen? It's time to think again. For decades, accounts have surfaced of giant-sized spiders, ones that easily rival anything conjured up by the world of Hollywood.

The largest known spider is the South American bird-eating spider, which goes by the name of *Theraphosa blondi*. One particular specimen, a twelve-year-old named Rosi, has an impressive leg-span of just under twelve inches, making her the largest, living spider on record—ever. That does not mean nothing larger than Rosi exists. It simply means we haven't formally classified it or them. But, more than a few people claim to have seen such things.

In 2001, English cryptozoologist Dr. Karl Shuker heard a fascinating story from explorer Bill Gibbons, who spent a great deal of time investigating reports of the Congo's most famous monster, the long-necked Mokele M'Bembe. The story dates back to 1938 and the experiences of a pair of explorers, Reginald and Margurite Lloyd. While negotiating a jungle pathway in the heart of the Belgian Congo, they saw something very strange step out in front of them. Their first thoughts were: was it a small crouching person, or a similarly crouched monkey? To their eternal horror, it quickly became clear it was neither. What it actually was, was a gigantic spider, one that had legs that spanned four feet! Reginald Lloyd, realizing the enormity of the situation—never mind the enormity of the creature—quickly reached for his camera. Unfortunately, the beast raced across the track and vanished into the undergrowth before he could capture what would, most assuredly, have been a priceless picture. The pair had no doubt about what they had encountered, however: a truly giant, eight-limbed monstrosity.

The amazing account of the Lloyds does not stand alone: the local Baka pygmy people have longstanding stories of these goliath spiders, which are said to be far rarer today than they once were; although, reportedly, one of their tribespeople saw such a terrifying thing in 2003. As for the lairs of the beasts, the Baka maintain they create something akin to huts, which are fashioned out of leaves and vegetation. They are also skilled weavers of massive,

It doesn't take a huge spider to scare many people. Arachnophobia is that creepy, eerie, terrifying feeling many get just seeing a tiny, eight-legged creature crawling toward them.

thick webs, which they build to ensnare their prey, which can include anything up to about the size of a small antelope.

Moving on to the United States, there is the 1948 report of William Slaydon, his wife, and grandchildren—which eerily echoes the report coming out of the Congo a decade earlier. The location was Leesville, Louisiana, and the family was walking to a nearby church for an evening of worship and prayer when their journey was suddenly interrupted—and in horrific fashion. As the Slaydons strolled along the road, to their horror, a giant spider— described as being "the size of a washtub"—surfaced out of a nearby ditch and raced across the road. Never again did the family walk that particular stretch of Louisiana road.

Now, it's time for a trip to Papua New Guinea. From there, we have a story told by Debbie and Peter Hynes—noted Australian cryptozoologists— and which came from the father of one of Debbie's friends. He was a man who had a bone-chilling encounter with a massive spider while serving in Papua New Guinea with the Australian military, during the Second World War. As the Hyneses note:

"One day he had to take himself off into the scrub in answer to a call of nature. While thus engaged he noticed he was crouched down next to a very large cobweb—not the classic 'fishing-net' sort but the fine, snow-white cottony stuff that spread all over the ground and tree trunk etc. His eye followed

In this c. 1890s illustration from *The Strand* a spider attacks a man in the jungle (part of a short fiction story). People have long had nightmares about large spiders, and fiction writers take advantage of that fear.

it one way and then the other—seems it was very extensive, like 10 to 15 ft. either way. Then he noticed the spider itself, only a foot or so away from his face. It was a real horror—the body, i.e. thorax + abdomen, he described as the 'size of a small dog or puppy,' it was colored jet black, the legs were thick and hairy but not as long as the classic 'dinner plate tarantula' type spider that owes its size to the spread of its legs. This thing had more body bulk than spread. Needless to say he backed out of there *very* slowly and carefully."

Dr. Karl Shuker says of this particularly creepy phenomenon:

"This is not the only report of a giant mystery spider encountered in Papua New Guinea during World War II. During an interview with cryptozoologist Rob Morphy of AmericanMonsters.com on the U.S. radio show 'Coast to Coast AM' a couple of years ago, a telephone caller named Craig recounted how his grandfather, while serving in Papua New Guinea during WW2, encountered a monstrous spider in a web that scared him so much he hacked it to death with his machete. According to Craig's grandfather, the spider measured an immense 3 ft. from tip to tip, and, unexpectedly, was not hairy like many big spiders are. Instead, it was shiny, and was emerald green in color. This nightmarish arachnid was encountered near Port Moresby, the capital of Papua New Guinea."

GIGANTIC INSECTS

Is it possible that the southwest region of the United States is home to giant-sized insects that feed upon us, the human race? Such a thing sounds not just unlikely and incredible, but just like the kind of scenario presented in the classic 1954 sci-fi movie *Them!* It's a movie in which massive, radioactive ants terrorize and slaughter the people of a small New Mexico town and threaten to do likewise to not just the rest of the country, but to the entire planet, too. Which brings us to an important question: might truth be stranger than fiction? Yes, just possibly.

Danielle B. is a woman who, for a number of years, lived in the New Mexican town of Aztec—which, just like the far more famous New Mexican town of Roswell, has a crashed UFO legend attached to it. It's a legend that dates back to March 1948, when, reportedly, a near-intact flying saucer and its crew of diminutive dead pilots were found. But, according to Danielle, she encountered something far stranger at Aztec than deceased extraterrestrial dwarfs and a wrecked flying saucer.

It was on one particular day in May 2004 that Danielle decided to spend a few hours hanging out in Aztec's Hart Canyon—which, curiously enough, is *exactly* where the alleged UFO is said to have fallen to earth, back in the 1940s. It was also where Danielle had an encounter with something far worse than aliens. On what was a warm and sunny day, Danielle found a place to sit, where she could read a book and have her snacks and drinks at hand. It was a perfect way to spend a day off work. Or, for a while it was, at least.

Gigantic ants menace humans in the 1954 sci-fi horror movie *Them!*

All was normal for a couple of hours. That is, until Danielle noticed a small, black helicopter approaching her in the distance. Far more correctly, she *assumed* that it was a helicopter. Certainly, at a distance that's what it appeared to be. But it was no normal helicopter: there was no "thud-thud" sound that one associates with the fast-moving blades of a helicopter. And, on top of that, it appeared to be carrying below it a small calf, held tightly in place by thick ropes! Most definitely not the kind of thing you see every day. When the helicopter got close to Hart Canyon, however, Danielle could see that the helicopter was actually nothing of the sort. It was a large, obscene-looking insect of around four meters in length. The presumed rotor-blades of the helicopter were actually the fast-beating wings of the monster-creature. As for those ropes, they were nothing less than powerful-looking black limbs.

> **D**anielle could see that the helicopter was actually nothing of the sort. It was a large, obscene-looking insect of around four meters in length.

Danielle could only stare—in a mixture of awe, fascination, fear, and horror—as the huge creature flew overhead, dropped the poor calf on a nearby peak, and then swooped to the ground with frightening speed, pounced on the animal, and viciously tore into it. In less than half an hour the giant insect was done with its feasting and took to the skies. Danielle had been too shocked to flee the area at the time, the result of which was that the terrible event was forever embedded in her memory, even though she clearly wished this was not the case. Suspecting—probably correctly—that if she told local law enforcement officials of what she saw, she would likely be booked for wasting police time, Danielle finally made her shaky way home. She stayed silent on the matter until she confided in me, roughly three years later.

Even I have to admit that Danielle's story stretches credibility to the max—despite the fact that she came across as nothing less than absolutely credible, down-to-earth, and normal. And while many might be inclined to dismiss such a bizarre account, I don't. Not because, in *X-Files*-style, "I want to believe," but because of something very different. It may come as a surprise to a lot of people to learn that, in the distant past, huge insects—not unlike the one described by Danielle—really did exist.

For example, in the Jurassic Period there existed in what today is the United States a dragonfly called *Meganeura monyi*. This was no regular dragonfly, however. It had a wingspan in excess of *three feet*. As another example, in 2001 Ohio State University geologists discovered the fossilized remains of a centipede in an old mine. It was a centipede *five feet long*. Then there were the ancient remains of a sea scorpion unearthed from a German quarry in 2007; an arthropod, the sea scorpion is of the same group as insects and spiders. There

A fossil of a *Meganeura monyi,* a species of huge dragonfly that lived during the Jurassic Period. They could have wingspans over 25 inches (65 centimeters) wide.

was something very notable about this particular sea scorpion, however: it was slightly more than *eight feet* in length.

Of course, none of these oversized things were alive at the time of their discovery. Indeed, they lived, walked, and flew millions of years ago. But, is it feasible that in certain parts of the United States—and amid a great deal of stealth and, perhaps, underground caves and caverns—certain similar things exist, today? Most people might say "no." But try asking Danielle and you will get a very different response. To this very day she has no doubt that these things are all too real. At the time of this writing, she is working on her own book; it's a book that ties in the predations of these hideous things with the so-called "cattle mutilation" phenomenon, which has plagued and puzzled ranchers, police officers, and even the FBI for decades. And particularly so in the southwest. In Danielle's scenario, the cattle-mutilators are not satanic cults, aliens, or covert military units conducting biological warfare operations. No. The mutilators are giant creatures from eras long gone that are feeding on the nation's cattle herds late at night.

Perhaps, one day, Danielle's story will finally be vindicated. If such a thing does happen, let's hope it's not because the huge insects have decided to turn their predatory attentions towards us, the human race. The possibility that *Them!* may one day become reality—rather than the stuff of sci-fi—is as chilling as it is disturbing.

INDIAN DEVIL

In 1899, a decidedly curious creature was encountered in Alaska by a man named Alfred L. Dominy and a colleague named Weyhrich. It was a terrifying, shape-shifting nightmare that became known as the Indian Devil. Dominy, a resident of Los Angeles, California, told his story to the press, which was all too keen to publish his saga of the sinister kind. It went like this:

"In the spring of 1899 myself and partner were going up the Francis River when we came across an animal which apparently had been drowned and left by high water on a gravel bar. It was about the size and shape of a small bear, would weigh about 300 pounds, snow white, hair about the same length and thickness as a bear's, short stub tail, heavy neck, head, teeth and ears like a wolf, legs short, not over a foot in length, and feet and claws like a large dog or wolf. Mr. Weyhrich and I examined it thoroughly, but were unable to determine what it was. I am satisfied there are still living specimens of the same animal further to the north.

"The following winter while hunting near the lower end of McPherson Lake I came upon queer fresh track which crossed the trail where I had been not an hour previous. The snow was pretty deep, and owing to the animal's short legs it was dragging its body through the snow. Satisfying myself it was the same kind of animal I had found dead farther south, and being on a good pair of snow shoes, and this animal plowing through the snow, I thought it an easy task to overtake and capture the snow plow, as I called it.

> They declared it was an Indian devil, said it had no heart and could not be killed by shooting: had the power of changing into the form of any other animal it chose.

"I found it could plow snow and then beat me. After following it the entire length of Lake McPherson, about seven miles, and two or three miles up a small stream that flows into the north end of McPherson, darkness overtook me and I had to camp for the long night. I saw tracks afterwards but never gave chase again."

The strangest, and most monstrous, part of the story was still yet to come, as Dominy noted:

"When I saw Indians the following spring near Deace Post, I described the animal to them, but could get no satisfaction out of them. They declared it was an Indian devil, said it had no heart and could not be killed by shooting: had the power of changing into the form of any other animal it chose. They told wonderful tales of its ferocity, and endurance. The Indians are very superstitious about it and seldom if ever visit this particular locality. It is carnivorous and not hibernating, as I saw signs of it during the entire winter, while the bear were taking their long sleep under the snow. What was it?"

What, indeed!

KINIK (KOKOGIAK)

❞ Nathaniel Neakok, the mighty hunter of polar bears, has quit scoffing at reports about the great Kinik being seen in this northernmost region of North America," reported the Idaho Falls, Idaho *Post-Register*, on May 15, 1958. The story continued:

"A Kinik is the name Eskimos give to a bear they say is too big to come out of the water. Its size varies with the individual story. But all agree he is a monster of great size and strength and appetite. Several weeks ago, Neakok laughed so loudly when told Raymond Lalayauk had reported seeing a 30-foot bear that his hearty guffaws echoed and re-echoed across the great, frozen polar wastes. But Neakok isn't laughing anymore. He has seen a Kinik with his very own eyes.

"This Kinik, Neakok says, was grayish white and only its head was visible as it swam through the water. It was so large he did not attempt to shoot it. Neakok said its head alone must have been five or more feet long—and almost as wide. This was not the first time a monster was reported by respected men of the village. Floyd Ahvakana and Roxy Ekownna, elders in the Presbyterian Church and men of undoubted veracity, tell of seeing a tremendous sea monster in 1932 while hunting with a third Eskimo, now deceased. All three thought it was a Kokogiak [another Eskimo word for Kinik] or 10-legged bear which occupies a prominent role in Eskimo legend.

"Until now there have been many scoffers in the village, especially about Kokogiak. And that white men have been known to make reference to the 'coming tourist season' or 'another abominable snowman.' But since the respected Neakok

Kiniks are bears that are so large that they stay in the water all the time, presumably so that buoyancy of the water will allow them to move their huge bulk.

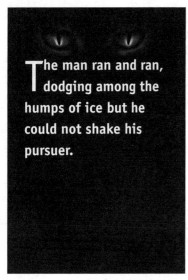

The man ran and ran, dodging among the humps of ice but he could not shake his pursuer.

added his testimony, the scoffers are strangely quiet. Even fearful. You don't even hear much about how the Arctic's strange mists distort distances or size, creating weird optical illusions. But you do hear told and retold stories about Kokogiak, the 10-legged bear of Eskimo legend.

"The stories could go something like this:

"Once upon a time there was a lazy Eskimo. He was the laziest man in the village. One evening after he had heard the village hunters tell of their experiences, the lazy one went out on the ice. He came to a large hole where some seal lungs were floating, showing that a large bear had eaten seal, leaving only the lungs. The man watched and waited by this hole and, sure enough, a monstrous bear came up. As he started out onto the ice, the man rammed his spear in first one eye and then the other, blinding the bear.

"However, the bear came right on out of the water and following this scent gave chase after the fleeing hunter. The man ran and ran, dodging among the humps of ice but he could not shake his pursuer. Finally, he saw ahead two towering walls of ice, with only a narrow corridor between.

"Through this pass he ran but the bear, following close upon his heels, was too big and he stuck fast, unable to back out. The hunter ran around and succeeded in killing the giant, 10-legged bear.

"Many Eskimos—possibly even some white men—still believe there are Kokogiak out there somewhere in the Arctic vastness. And, says wide-eyed Nathaniel Neakok, a 30-foot polar bear too big to shoot."

LONDON'S BEAR-MONSTER

Elliot O'Donnell, a renowned collector and investigator of ghost stories, told a fascinating story of a strange, ghostly, bear-like monster seen in none other than London, England's Tower of London. O'Donnell said:

"Edmund Lenthal Swifte, appointed in 1814 Keeper of the Crown Jewels in the Tower of London, refers in an article in *Notes and Queries*, 1860, to various unaccountable phenomena happening in the Tower during his residence there. He says that one night in the Jewel Office, one of the sentries was alarmed by a figure like a huge bear issuing from underneath the Jewel Room door.

"He thrust at it with his bayonet, which, going right through it, stuck in the doorway, whereupon he dropped in a fit, and was carried senseless to the guard-room. When on the morrow Mr. Swifte saw the soldier in the guard-room, his fellow-sentinel was also there, and the latter testified to having seen his comrade, before the alarm, quiet and active, and in full possession of his faculties. He was now, so Mr. Swifte added, changed almost beyond recognition, and died the following day.

"Mr. George Offer, in referring to this incident, alludes to queer noises having been heard at the time the figure appeared. Presuming that the sentinel was not the victim of an hallucination, the question arises as to the kind of spirit that he saw. The bear, judging by cases that have been told me, is by no means an uncommon occult phenomenon. The difficulty is how to classify it, since, upon no question appertaining to the psychic, can one dogmatize. To quote from a clever poem that appeared

Back in 1860, a huge, bearlike figure was spotted in London's Tower of London.

in the January number of the *Occult Review*, to pretend one knows anything definite about the immaterial world is all 'swank.'

"At the most we—Parsons, Priests, Theosophists, Christian Scientists, Psychical Research Professors—at the most can only speculate. Nothing—nothing whatsoever, beyond the bare fact that there are phenomena, unaccountable by physical laws, has as yet been discovered. All the time and energy and space that have been devoted by scientists to the investigation of spiritualism and to making tests in automatic writing are, in my opinion—and, I believe, I speak for the man in the street——hopelessly futile.

"No one, who has ever really experienced spontaneous ghostly manifestations, could for one moment believe in the genuineness of the phenomena produced at séances. They have never deceived me, and I am of the opinion spirits cannot be convoked to order, either through a so-called medium falling into a so-called trance, through table-turning, automatic writing, or anything else. If a spirit comes, it will come either voluntarily, or in obedience to some Unknown Power—and certainly neither to satisfy the curiosity of a crowd of sensation-loving men and women, nor to be analyzed by some cold, calculating, presumptuous Professor of Physics whose proper sphere is the laboratory.

"But to proceed. The phenomenon of the big bear, provided again it was really objective, may have been the phantasm of some prehistoric creature whose bones lie interred beneath the Tower; for we know the Valley of the Thames was infested with giant reptiles and quadrupeds of all kinds (I incline to this theory); or it may have been a Vice-Elemental, or—the phantasm of a human being who lived a purely animal life, and whose spirit would naturally take the form most closely resembling it."

MAN-EATING PLANTS

The idea that there could be monstrous, man-eating beasts of an unknown nature, lurking in the wilder parts of our planet, is not at all implausible. But, what about man-eating plants and trees? As incredible as it may sound, there is no shortage of reports of flesh-eating flora. In 1878, a German explorer named Carl Liche traveled to the island of Madagascar, where he witnessed nothing less than a human sacrifice to a tree! The horrific details were laid out in a letter penned by Liche himself and sent to the *South Australian Register* in 1881. According to Liche, the unfortunate victim was a woman of the Mkodo tribe, who was tied to the terrible tree, seemingly as a gift to it. Liche said:

"The slender delicate palpi, with the fury of starved serpents, quivered a moment over her head, then as if instinct with demoniac intelligence fastened upon her in sudden coils round and round her neck and arms; then while her awful screams and yet more awful laughter rose wildly to be instantly strangled down again into a gurgling moan, the tendrils one after another, like great green serpents, with brutal energy and infernal rapidity, rose, retracted themselves, and wrapped her about in fold after fold, ever tightening with cruel swiftness and savage tenacity of anacondas fastening upon their prey."

Researcher Brent Swancer says of the flesh-devouring tree that it "was described as being around 8 feet in height, and having an appearance reminiscent of a pineapple, with eight long, pointed leaves that hung down from its top to the ground. The trunk

An 1887 illustration of the man-eating tree described by Carl Liche.

of the tree was topped with a sort of receptacle that contained a thick liquid said to have soporific qualities that drugged potential prey and was believed to be highly addictive. Surrounding this receptacle were long, hairy tendrils with six white palpi resembling tentacles. The tree possessed white, transparent leaves that reminded Liche of the quivering mouthparts of an insect."

Moving on, the *American Weekly*, on January 4, 1925, included in its pages an article titled "Escaped from the Embrace of the Man-Eating Tree." It described an encounter in the Philippines, in which a man—referred to only as Bryant from Mississippi—and his native guide came across a truly unusual tree, around thirty-five feet in height and roughly ninety feet in diameter. Rather ominously, the tree stunk of rotting flesh, and a human skull could be seen at its base. It was the curious dimensions—which gave it something of a bulbous shape—that first caught the attention of the man; it wasn't long at all before something else grabbed his attention—as in literally. As the man stood and stared at the tree, he realized to his horror that it was reaching out to him. The *American Weekly* said of what happened next:

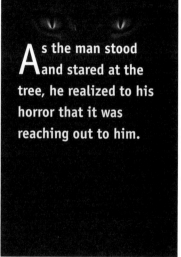

As the man stood and stared at the tree, he realized to his horror that it was reaching out to him.

"The whole thing had changed shape and was horribly alive and alert. The dull, heavy leaves had sprung from their compact formation and were coming at him from all directions, advancing on the ends of long vine-like stems which stretched across like the necks of innumerable geese and, now that the old man had stopped his screaming, the air was full of hissing sounds. The leaves did not move straight at their target, but with a graceful, side-to-side sway, like a cobra about to strike. From the far side, the distant leaves were peeping and swaying on their journey around the trunk and even the tree top was bending down to join in the attack. The bending of the trunk was spasmodic and accompanied by sharp cracks.

"The effect of this advancing and swaying mass of green objects was hypnotic, like the charm movements of a snake. Bryant could not move, though the nearest leaf was within an inch of his face. He could see that it was armed with sharp spines on which a liquid was forming. He saw the heavy leaf curve like a green-mittened hand, and as it brushed his eyebrows in passing he got the smell of it—the same animal smell that hung in the surrounding air. Another instant and the thing would have had his eyes in its sticky, prickly grasp, but either his weakness or the brown man's strength threw them both on their backs. The charm was broken. They crawled out of the circle of death and lay panting in the grass while the malignant plant, cracking and hissing, yearned and stretched and thrashed to get at them."

Despite the incredible nature of the story, it's important to note that it was written for the *American Weekly* by a very credible source: a botanist and

Botanist Willard Nelson Clute, a professor and founder of the American Fern Society, wrote about the dangerous plant in the Philippines.

naturalist named Willard Nelson Clute, who was the author of numerous books, including *The Useful Plants of the World* and *A Dictionary of American Plant Names.* Who knows? Perhaps the deadly, people-eating plant of the Philippines still exists, still luring the unwary into its deadly embrace.

Finally, there is the 1881 account of Philip Robinson, who, in *Under the Punkah,* wrote of his uncle's near-death experience with a plant hungry for human flesh somewhere along the Nile River:

"This awful plant, that rears its splendid death-shade in the central solitude of a Nubian fern forest, sickens by its unwholesome humors all vegetation from its immediate vicinity, and feeds upon the wild beasts that, in the terror of the chase, or the heat of noon, seek the thick shelter of … the birds that, flitting across the open space, come within the charmed circle of its power, or innocently refresh themselves from the cups of its great waxen flowers; upon even man himself when, an infrequent prey, the savage seeks its asylum in the storm, or turns from the harsh foot-wounding sword-grass of the glade, to pluck the wondrous fruit that hang plumb down among the wondrous foliage. And such fruit!

"Glorious golden ovals, great honey drops, swelling by their own weight into pear-shaped translucencies. The foliage glistens with a strange dew, that all day long drips on to the ground below, nurturing a rank growth of grasses, which shoot up in places so high that their spikes of fierce blood-fed green show far up among the deep-tinted foliage of the terrible tree, and, like a jealous body-guard, keep concealed the fearful secret of the charnel-house within, and draw round the black roots of the murderous plant a decent screen of living green."

MONTAUK MONSTER

Joe Nickell is a senior research fellow of the Committee for Skeptical Inquiry (CSI) and "Investigative Files" Columnist for *Skeptical Inquirer.* A former stage magician, private investigator, and teacher, he is the author of numerous books, including *Inquest on the Shroud of Turin* (1998), *Pen, Ink and Evidence* (2003), *Unsolved History* (2005), and *Adventures in Paranormal Investigation* (2007).

He writes: "In July 2008, the carcass of a creature soon dubbed the 'Montauk Monster' allegedly washed ashore near Montauk, Long Island, New York. It sparked much speculation and controversy, with some suggesting it was a shell-less sea turtle, a dog or other canid, a sheep, or a rodent—or even a latex fake or possible mutation experiment from the nearby Plum Island Animal Disease Center."

The strange saga of the admittedly very weird beast was one that caught the attention of not just national, but international, media. This was hardly surprising,

Prominent paranormal researcher and critic Joe Nickell wrote about the Montauk Monster.

since the animal appeared to have a beak-like face, large claws, and a dog-like body. While the controversy rolled on for a long time—and provoked deep rumors about what "the government" was doing, an answer to the riddle finally came, as Dr. Darren Naish noted:

"Is the carcass that of a dog? Dogs have an inflated frontal region that gives them a pronounced bony brow or forehead, and in contrast the Montauk monster's head seems smoothly convex. As many people have now noticed, there is a much better match: Raccoon *Procyon lotor*. It was the digits of the hands that gave this away for me: the Montauk carcass has very strange, elongated, almost human-like fingers with short claws. Given that we're clearly dealing with a North American carnivoran, raccoon is the obvious choice: raccoons are well known for having particularly dextrous fingers that lack the sort of interdigital webbing normally present in carnivorans. The match for a raccoon is perfect once we compare the dentition and proportions. The Montauk animal has lost its upper canines and incisors (you can even see the empty sockets), and if you're surprised by the length of the Montauk animal's limbs, note that—like a lot of mammals we ordinarily assume to be relatively short-legged—raccoons are actually surprisingly leggy (claims that the limb proportions of the Montauk carcass are unlike those of raccoons are not correct)."

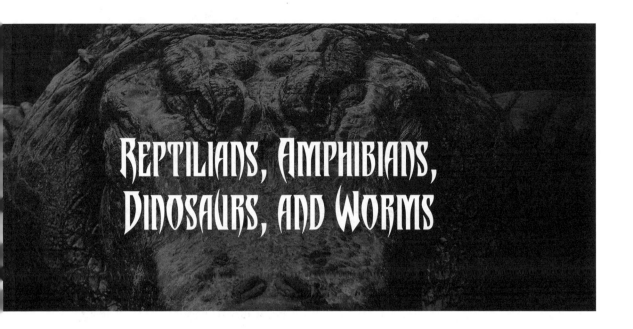

REPTILIANS, AMPHIBIANS, DINOSAURS, AND WORMS

ALLIGATORS IN THE SEWERS

Perhaps the most terrifying of all monsters are those that we *know* exist. And, when they are right under our feet—as in literally—they become even more fear-inducing. Take, for example, the alligators of New York. We're talking about those immense, bone-crunching beasts that lurk deep within the winding sewers and subways beneath the Big Apple. Most people assume that the stories of New York's people-eating alligators are nothing more than the stuff of myth and urban legend. The reality is they could not be further from the truth.

Proof that alligators have been on the loose in the city for decades was provided way back in February 1935 by none other than the *New York Times*. The story was spelled out in an article titled "Alligator Found in Uptown Sewer: Youths Shoveling Snow See the Animal Churning in Icy Water." As the newspaper noted, the gang of boys, led by Salvatore Condoluci, actually managed to capture the approximately seven-foot-long animal and beat and stabbed it to death, after it was seen lurking in the sewers on 123rd Street, close to the Harlem River.

For more than three decades, Teddy May was the Commissioner of Sewers in New York. He has gone on record as stating that he heard tales of alligators roaming the sewers of the city as far back as the 1930s—the same timeframe in which the *New York Times* reported on the violent encounter at

Are there man-eating crocodilians in New York City's sewer system? The rumors persist....

123rd Street. May conceded that he took little interest in the reports, since he felt it was all a case of folklore and legend, and certainly not reality.

As the reports grew in number, however, May decided that enough was enough and it was time for him to take a look for himself at what—possibly—was going on way below New York. To May's amazement and terror, after descending into that darkened, mysterious, subterranean realm, he stumbled upon a number of significantly sized alligators swimming in the sewer waters. The stories, he instantly realized, were not just stories, after all. Not surprisingly, May beat a hasty retreat.

Then there is the story of Mark Cherry, a man who maintains that one night in 1966, he was the solitary passenger standing on the platform at 149th Street Grand Concourse, when he was forcefully grabbed by a pair of police officers who told him there had been a flooding in one of the tunnels and he had to leave immediately. The somewhat heavy-handed approach of the officers puzzled Cherry—that is, until he caught sight of something as he was being practically frog-marched away from the platform.

According to Cherry, what he saw was a group of subway employees hauling the body of a large, albino alligator out of one of the tunnels, along with a body bag of the type in which a human body would be placed. Significantly, said Cherry, the body bag was clearly not empty. The implication was that the unfortunate soul inside had been attacked and killed by the alligator—which, in turn, had been killed by the police. Realizing that Cherry now knew what really happened, the officers sternly warned him not to speak of what he had seen—which Cherry did not, until 2004. It is a good indication of the fear that was drilled into Cherry back in 1966 that he was still concerned, nearly forty years later, that someone in authority might pay him a visit and silence him again—but this time permanently. Fortunately, nothing so conspiratorial ever occurred. Indeed, taking any kind of retaliatory action against Cherry would only have validated his story.

While sightings and claims of alligators in the sewers of New York are nowhere near as prevalent as they were decades ago, the controversy still provokes intrigue and fascination. And, just maybe, if we are to believe Mark Cherry, more than a few New Yorkers may have become the victims—and the dinners—of huge, vicious alligators.

AVEBURY WORM

Malcolm Lees enlisted in the British Royal Air Force in the early 1950s and retired in the late 1960s. In 1962 he received a posting to an RAF station in the county of Wiltshire, which he declined to name, and worked in the prestigious and secretive world of intelligence gathering. Most of the work, Lees explained, was routine and even mundane and he laughed heartily at the idea, spouted by many, that intelligence work was a glamorous one full of James Bond-style escapades. Nevertheless, Lees said, there was one aspect of his career that really was stranger than fiction. Early one September morning in 1962, a call came into the base from someone who had seen a UFO hovering in the vicinity of the ancient standing-stones in the historic English village of Avebury, Wiltshire.

UFO reports reached the base from time to time, said Lees. They were always handled by the RAF's Provost and Security Services. For the most part they were mind-numbingly mundane and related to little more than sightings of unidentified lights in the sky that could, in reality, have been anything or nothing. Invariably, he said, the reports were a week, or even more, old by the time they were received. And so, they were simply filed and passed up the chain of command—that was then at Government Buildings, Acton, and which relocated to Rudloe Manor in 1977. But this particular case was a little different, said Lees.

The witness was a middle-aged lady who had lived in Avebury all of her adult life and who was fascinated by archaeological history. A "spinster" (as the files describe her), she would often stroll among the Stonehenge-like formations at night, marveling at their creation and musing upon their history. It was on the night in question that she had been out walking at around 10:30 P.M. when she was both startled and amazed to see a small ball of light, perhaps two feet in diameter, gliding slowly through the stones. Transfixed and rooted to the

Dating back to about 2600 B.C.E., the Avebury stones in Wiltshire, England, are almost as well known as Stonehenge. They have also been the place where UFO sightings have occurred.

The creature, she said, was about five feet long, perhaps eight or nine inches thick, and its skin was milk-white.

spot, she watched as it closed in on her at a height of about twelve feet. The ball then stopped fifteen feet or so from her, and small amounts of what looked like liquid metal slowly and silently dripped from it to the ground. Then, in an instant, the ball exploded in a bright, white flash.

For a moment she was blinded by its intensity and instinctively fell to her knees. When her eyes cleared, however, she was faced with a horrific sight. The ball of light had gone, but on the ground in front of her was what she could only describe as a monstrous, writhing worm.

The creature, she said, was about five feet long, perhaps eight or nine inches thick, and its skin was milk-white. As she slowly rose to her feet, the creature's head turned suddenly in her direction and two bulging eyes opened. When it began to move unsteadily towards her in a caterpillar-like fashion, she emitted a hysterical scream and fled the scene. Rushing back home, she slammed the door shut and frantically called the airbase, after having been directed to it by the less-than-impressed local police.

The Provost and Security Services were used to dealing with UFO reports, said Lees, and a friend of his in the P&SS was dispatched early the next day to interview the woman—amid much hilarity on the part of his colleagues, all of whom thought that the story was someone's idea of a joke. On returning, however, Lees's friend and colleague had a very serious and grim look on his face, and informed him guardedly that whatever had taken place, it was definitely no hoax.

The woman, he said, had practically barricaded herself in her home, was almost incoherent with fear, and only agreed to return to the scene after lengthy coaxing. Lees's colleague said that he found no evidence of the UFO. The worm, or whatever it was, was clearly long gone. On the ground near the standing stone, however, was a three-foot long trail of a slime-like substance, not unlike that left by a snail. Lees's colleague quickly improvised and, after racing back to the woman's house, scooped some of the material onto a spoon and into a drinking glass.

After assuring the woman that her case would be taken very seriously, and requesting that she discuss the events with no one, he headed back to the base, the slimy substance in hand. A report was duly prepared and dispatched up the chain of command—along with the unidentified slime. For more than a week, said Lees, plainclothes military personnel wandered casually among the stones, seeking out evidence of anything unusual. Nothing else was ever found, however.

Lees said that he was fascinated by this incident because it was one of the few UFO-related cases he heard about that was taken very seriously at an official level and that had some form of material evidence in support of it. He did not know the outcome of the investigation but he never forgot about it.

BASILISK

Anomalies researcher and writer Mike Dash says: "Few creatures have struck more terror into more hearts for longer than the basilisk, a monster feared for centuries throughout Europe and North Africa. Like many ancient marvels, it was a bizarre hybrid: a crested snake that hatched from an egg laid by a rooster and incubated by a toad."

Tales of the Basilisk really came to the fore in 79 C.E., in the pages of Pliny the Elder's *Natural History*. He said of the beast:

"It is produced in the province of Cyrene, being not more than twelve fingers in length. It has a white spot on the head, strongly resembling a sort of a diadem. When it hisses, all the other serpents fly from it: and it does not advance its body, like the others, by a succession of folds, but moves along upright and erect upon the middle. It destroys all shrubs, not only by its contact, but those even that it has breathed upon; it burns up all the grass, too, and breaks the stones, so tremendous is its noxious influence. It was formerly a general belief that if a man on horseback killed one of these animals with a spear, the poison would run up the weapon and kill, not only the rider, but the horse, as well. To this dreadful monster the effluvium of the weasel is fatal, a thing that has been tried with success, for kings have often desired to see its body when killed; so true is it that it has pleased Nature that there should be nothing without its antidote. The animal is thrown into the hole of the basilisk, which is easily known from the soil around it being infected. The weasel destroys the basilisk by its odor, but dies itself in this struggle of nature against its own self."

None other than Leonardo da Vinci told a very similar story. He said that the monster "…is found in the province of Cyrenaica and is not more than 12 fingers long. It has on its head a white spot after the fashion of a diadem. It scares all serpents with its whistling. It resembles a snake, but does not move by wriggling but from the center forwards to the right. It is said that one of these, being killed with a spear by one who was on horse-back, and its venom flowing on the spear, not only the man but the horse also died. It spoils the wheat and not only that which it touches, but where it breathes the grass dries and the stones are split."

Without doubt the most notable account of the Basilisk comes from the Polish city of Warsaw and dates from 1587. In a Smithsonian.com 2012 article

A basilisk is an odd creature that is part rooster and part reptile. Feared since medieval times, it supposedly had poisonous breath and a lethal stare.

by Mike Dash, Midori Snyder says of this case that it revolved around "a terrifying encounter and eventual capture of a Basilisk hiding in the cellar of a house who is suspected of bringing the plague." So the old story went:

"The 5-year-old daughter of a knifesmith named Machaeropaeus had disappeared in a mysterious way, together with another little girl. The wife of Machaeropaeus went looking for them, along with the nursemaid. When the nursemaid looked into the underground cellar of a house that had fallen into ruins 30 years earlier, she observed the children lying motionless down there, without responding to the shouting of the two women. When the maid was too hoarse to shout anymore, she courageously went down the stairs to find out what had happened to the children. Before the eyes of her mistress, she sank to the floor beside them, and did not move. The wife of Machaeropaeus wisely did not follow her into the cellar, but ran back to spread the word about this strange and mysterious business. The rumor spread like wildfire throughout Warsaw. Many people thought the air felt unusually thick to breathe and suspected that a basilisk was hiding in the cellar."

CHATHAM ISLAND SAURIAN

F. W. Kemp was an officer with the Provisional Archives who, with his wife, had an extraordinary encounter in the early 1930s. It was an encounter with something that can only be classified as a monster. Indeed, Kemp's words make that abundantly clear. So impressed was he by the encounter, Kemp prepared the following statement for interested parties:

"On August 10, 1932, I was with my wife and son on Chatham Island in the Strait of Juan de Fuca. My wife called my attention to a mysterious something coming through the channel between Strong Tide Island and Chatham Island. Imagine my astonishment on observing a huge creature with head out of the water traveling about four miles per hour against the tide. Even at that speed a considerable wash was thrown on the rocks, which gave me the impression that it was more reptile than serpent to make so much displacement.

"The channel at this point is about 500 yard wide. Swimming to the steep rocks of the Island opposite, the creature shot its head out of water on the rock, and moving its head from side to side, appeared to [be] taking its bearings. Then fold after fold its body came to surface. Towards the tail it appeared serrated with something moving flail-like at the extreme end. The movements were like those of a crocodile. Around the head appeared a sort of mane, which drifted round the body like kelp.

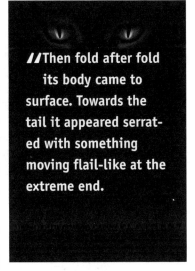

//Then fold after fold its body came to surface. Towards the tail it appeared serrated with something moving flail-like at the extreme end.

"The Thing's presence seemed to change the whole landscape, which make it difficult to describe my experiences. It did not seem to belong to the present scheme of things, but rather to the Long Ago when the world was young. The position it held on the rock was momentary. My wife and sixteen-year-old son ran to a point of land to get a clearer view. I think the sounds they made disturbed the animal. The sea being very calm, it seemed to slip back into deep water; there was a great commotion under the surface and it disappeared like a flash.

"In my opinion, its speed must be terrific and it senses of smell, sight and hearing developed to a very high degree. It would be terribly hard to photograph, as its movements are different from anything I have ever seen or heard of. I should say its length to be not less than eighty feet. There were some logs on Strong Tide Island which gave me a good idea as to the size of monster as it passed them. I took a measurement of one the next day which was over sixty feet in length, and the creature overlapped it to a large extent at each end. I put a newspaper on the spot where it rested its head and took an observation from our previous point of vantage. The animal was very much larger than the double sheet of newspaper. The body must have been at least five feet thick, and was of a bluish-green color which shone in the sun like aluminum. I could not determine the shape of the head, but it was much thicker than the body."

CHINESE DRAGON

In 1916, explorer Irwin J. O'Malley told a fascinating story of his discovery of the fossilized remains of a massive animal. That the creature was never formally identified has led to rumors that what O'Malley came upon were the remains of nothing less than an example of a legendary Chinese dragon! His story goes like this:

"During the latter part of a holiday trip to the Yangtze Gorges undertaken by my wife and self in November, 1915, we met Mr. M. Hewlett, British Consul at Ichang, and his wife, and in their company spent a day in the Ichang Gorge, landing at various points to climb the cliffs and explore some of the numerous caves. While exploring a large cave on the right of the bank of the river, and about one mile above the Customs Station at Ping Shon Pa, we discovered the fossils about to be described. The cave is reputed by the Chinese to extend some twenty miles to a point near Ichang.

"It is reported that a party from *H.M.S. Snipe* spent three days in the cave some years ago and that they failed to reach the end. Evidence that the party penetrated beyond the point where the discovery was made exists in the name of their ship painted on the cave walls at a point considerably further in.

"The Chinese name of the cave is Shen K'an Tzu, which means 'The Holy Shrine,' and one of the characters forming the word K'an is the Chinese character for 'dragon.' A large rock is seen at the entrance, and some eight to ten yards behind this there is a peculiar piece of curved rock bearing some

Chinese dragons are an integral part of the culture and are seen frequently in everything from pottery to architecture to paintings and even parades.

slight resemblance to a portion of a dragon's body; the resemblance is possibly suggestive enough to impress the Chinese mind, but altogether fails to impress the foreigner.

"After proceeding some hundreds of yards inside the cave we found ourselves walking on a peculiar ridge in order to avoid the surrounding pool of water. The ridge curved backward and forward across the width of the cave like the curves of a large serpent, the suggestion being so strong we lowered our lamps in order to examine the ridge more closely. To our astonishment and delight, we found that we were in very truth walking along a perfect fossil of some huge reptile. Further inspection revealed the presence of six or eight of these enormous monsters. Having taken a few small specimens of loose portions of scale for examination in a better light, we left, to return the following morning for the purpose of measurement.

"On our return the following morning we selected one of the largest fossils lying for a great part of its length isolated from the others, the coils of the remainder being rather entangled. The isolated portion measured seventy feet, so that is absolutely certain that the length is at least seventy feet, and as far as

One witness compared the head of a Chinese dragon to that of the skull of a Mosasaurus (above).

we could ascertain, this same specimen extended for another sixty or seventy feet. However, I admit that error is possible here, owing to the interlacing coils of the reptiles. The depth of the body seen in the foreground is two feet. The head is partially buried in the cave wall and appears to be a large, flat head similar to that of *Mosasaurus comperi*.

"About twelve or fourteen feet from the head two legs are seen partially uncovered, and again to more about fifty feet from the head. The fact that several persons have penetrated this cave in former years beyond the point where the discovery was made seems to indicate the fossils have been but recently uncovered; by a heavy discharge of water through the cave. It seems probable that these reptiles were trapped by some volcanic disturbance and starved to death; the size of the bodies compared to their length would indicate this.

"A point of peculiar interest is the resemblance to the Chinese dragon of these fossils. I believe that it has therefore been supposed that the Chinese borrowed their idea of the dragons from Western mythology. The discovery has created a great stir among the local Chinese and foreigners, who are daily flocking to view the fossils. I am attempting to interest the Chinese authorities in Peking and also the Chinese Monuments Society in order that the specimens may be preserved from damage."

Richard Freeman has suggested that what O'Malley examined were the fossilized remains of a huge Chinese sauropod named Mamenchisaurus. On the other hand, O'Malley's reference to the remains having a "resemblance to the Chinese dragon" has given rise to the possibility that, just possibly, in the distant past, fire-breathing dragons really did exist.

CIA's Super-Snake

While there are numerous reports of people encountering massive snakes in the jungles of our world, certainly the strangest case on record is one that involves none other than the Central Intelligence Agency—the CIA. The story is an intrigue-filled one, which is part James Bond and part Indiana Jones. And it all began—and violently ended, too—in 1956.

CIA personnel based out of the American Embassy in Bolivia were used to dealing with unpredictable and strange events. But, even by their standards, the events that went down in August 1956 were off the scale. In the early days of the month, CIA staff received reports of a gigantic snake on the loose in a nearby, rarely explored cave that was buried deeply within the mountainous jungle environment. And when I say gigantic, we're talking about somewhere between thirty and fifty feet long.

Worse still, a spate of mysterious disappearances of people from a nearby tribe had just about everyone on edge. The tribespeople were sure that the culprit was the deadly beast, and there were even rumors that the monster possessed supernatural powers. Time came when something had to be done and a call was put into the CIA by local Bolivian authorities, asking for help. While hunting for a giant snake was hardly the kind of thing that CIA agents typically got involved in (to say the least!), they agreed to give it a go.

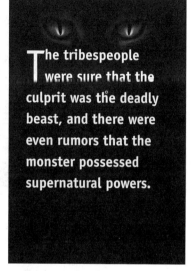

The tribespeople were sure that the culprit was the deadly beast, and there were even rumors that the monster possessed supernatural powers.

A six-person team was put together by a man we only know as "Lee," who led the group deep into the jungle. They were prepared to take on the man-eater, but as circumstances would demonstrate, it turned out to be a very close call. The supersized snake was not about to go down without a fight. As Lee's team climbed the heavily wooded hill and arrived at the small entrance to the cave where the snake made its lair, one and all stayed as silent as possible and began to prepare for a potentially deadly confrontation with the massive beast.

Each and every man had several tear gas canisters, and they were all equipped with .45s. We are, after all, talking about secret agents! They had something else with them too: a large canvas sack with zippers at both ends that had been created by CIA employees and which, it was hoped, the snake could be enticed into and then shot and killed before it could do any harm. It sounded like a most unlikely situation and something guaranteed to fail.

Nevertheless, each and every man strategically positioned himself at varying points around twenty feet from the cave entrance. It was then up to Lee to creep up to the shadowy opening. His first action was to encase the entrance with that large sack and, via a small space, hurl one of the canisters into the heart of the cave. He did so and then quickly retreated. It was a very wise move.

In less than a minute as the tear gas did its thing, the huge snake came charging out of the cave. The rumors of such a monster living in the cave were suddenly, and chaotically, rumors no more. Even the agents in question were shocked by the sight of the coiling thing before them: it was around forty feet in length and had a body thicker than an oil drum. As for its fang-filled head, it was around the size of a horse's head. To their utter consternation, in seconds it tore its way out of the sack, ripping it to shreds in the process. And then it began to move slowly forwards. One and all backed away another thirty or forty feet, as the huge creature stared malevolently at them—no doubt

Stories of monstrously large snakes in the jungles of South America go back literally centuries. This 1820 illustration shows a snake attacking a horse!

trying to decide which one to attack and devour first. Lee quickly realized it was a case of now or never and he fired a salvo of bullets into the snake's head. By all accounts it took more than several bullets to bring the violent beast down.

Of course, it must be said that this entire story has somewhat of an unlikely feeling to it; a sense of urban myth or of a friend-of-a-friend tale. There is, however, good evidence to suggest that the event occurred exactly as described above. All of this brings us to a man named David Atlee Phillips. A significant figure in the CIA in the 1950s, he was someone who spent a great deal of time in Mexico, Cuba, and Chile. Phillips crossed paths with Lee at a cocktail party in La Paz, Bolivia, in 1958. As the pair swapped stories of the espionage kind, the matter of the giant snake surfaced. Phillips admitted to Lee that he was dubious of the whole story. Nonplussed, Lee agreed to show him the snake's skin, which Lee had preserved in the Embassy's basement! Even when he was finally able to see the evidence, however, Phillips still doubted the story behind how the huge skin was obtained. He suspected Lee had gotten it from a collector and had created the story of a violent confrontation with the monster to impress a girlfriend or several. It turns out that was not the case.

Phillips apparently developed quite an obsession with the snake saga and brought it up, some months later, with one Darwin Mervill Bell, a man who had ties to both the CIA and the Agency for International Aid in Bolivia. Over drinks, Phillips tackled Bell on the matter of the snake legend—since Lee was a friend to both Phillips and Bell. Phillips said, as he discussed the story of how the snake was killed: "To this day, Lee claims they made a canvas sack with zippers at both ends. Now, did you ever hear anything about that?"

For a few moments, Bell was silent, seemingly musing on Phillips's question. Then, he answered: "Mr. Phillips, I certainly have heard about that. I was the tail zipper man."

Finally, Phillips was convinced.

As for what the snake actually was, there's a distinct possibility it may have been a surviving relic of a massive snake that lived in what is now

Colombia, but tens of millions of years ago. Its name was Titanoboa, and it has a lineage that connects it to both the boa constrictor and the anaconda of today. It could grow to lengths of fifty feet and weighed in at around a hefty ton. Certainly not a monster one would want to cross paths with. Did secret agents of the CIA, back in the 1950s, take out of circulation the very last of the Titanoboas? Possibly, yes!

CRESTED SNAKE-CREATURE

According to numerous accounts, there existed in the Caribbean of the nineteenth century a curious, crested, snake-like monster that instilled fear in all who encountered it. One such account came from an impeccable source: a Victorian naturalist named Philip Henry Gosse. He revealed how, during the course of his research, he uncovered details of the story. It all occurred when he spent time roaming the area, between 1845 and 1846. From a respected medical man, said Gosse, came a fascinating story. In Gosse's words:

"He had seen, in 1829, a serpent about four feet in length, but of unwonted thickness, dull ochre in color with well-defined dark spots, having on its head a sort of pyramidal helmet, somewhat lobed at the summit, of a pale red hue. The animal, however, was dead, and decomposition was already setting in. He informed me that the Negroes of the district were well acquainted with it; and that they represented it as making a noise, not unlike the crowing of a cock, and being addicted to preying on poultry."

Gosse had a friend named Richard Hill, who had also heard of this odd beast, from a Spanish acquaintance on Hispaniola. Those in the know said that it dwelled in the eastern regions of the island, in what is now the Dominican Republic. Gosse said of Hill:

"My friend's Spanish informant had seen the serpent with mandibles like a bird, with a cock's nest, with scarlet lobes or wattles; and he described its habits—perhaps

Philip Henry Gosse was an English naturalist especially noted for his knowledge of marine biology, but he was only nineteen when he came across the serpent in the Caribbean.

from common fame rather than personal observation—as a frequenter of hen-roosts, into which it would thrust its head, and deceive the young chickens by its imitative physiognomy, and its attempts to crow."

A further account reached Gosse from a Jamaican man, Jasper Cargill. Gosse recorded of his meetings with Cargill that "…when visiting Skibo, in St. George, an estate of his father's, in descending the mountain-road, his attention was drawn to a snake of dark hue, that erected itself from some fragments of limestone rock that lay about. It was about four feet long and unusually thick bodied. His surprise was greatly increased on perceiving that it was crested, and that from the far side of its cheeks depended some red colored flaps, like gills or wattles. After gazing at him intently for some time, with its head well erect, it drew itself in, and disappeared among the fragmentary rocks."

Rather notably, Cargill's son managed to shoot and kill just such a beast a few years later. Back to Gosse, who noted of this development:

"Some youngsters of the town came running to tell me of a curious snake, unlike any snake they had ever seen before, which young Cargill had shot, when out for a day's sport in the woodlands of a neighbor. They described it as a serpent in all respects, but with a very curious shaped head, with wattles on each side of its jaws. After taking it in hand and looking at it, they placed it in a hollow tree, intending to return for it when they should be coming home, but they had strolled from the place so far that it was inconvenient to retrace their steps when wearied with rambling."

When the lads returned the following day, however, the snake-thing was gone, presumably taken by a hungry scavenger. The stories were far from over, however. Gosse also recorded the experience of a man named Ulick Ramsay, who "…had seen in the hand of the barrack-master at the barracks of a Spanish town, a curious snake, which he, too, had shot among the rocks of a little line of eminences near the railway, about two miles out, called Craigal-lechie. It was a serpent with a curious shaped head, and projections on each side, which he likened to the fins of an eel, but said were close up to the jaws."

Today, the true identity of the crested snake that apparently had the ability to mimic the cries of chickens, remains the downright enigma it was back then.

FORTY-FOOT SNAKE

In 1868, a Frenchman named Raud made a truly extraordinary statement regarding a monstrous, near-dragon-like snake seen in the California countryside, earlier in that very same year, and which was estimated to have an overall length of around forty feet. Despite the controversial nature of the story, it was supported by his friend and colleague, F. C. Buylick—both of whom were cutting wood and burning charcoal when the immense creature loomed into view. Raud, who broke off from the wood-cutting to pursue nothing more threatening than a hare, said the following of the beast, which appeared to dwell deep in the woods, swamps, and fields of the area:

// Coiled up not more than twenty feet from where I stood was an immense serpent— the most hideously frightful monster that ever confronted mortal man."

"I had proceeded twenty-five yards, perhaps, when I emerged into an open space not to exceed thirty feet in diameter. As I entered it the hare dragged itself into the brush on the opposite side, and I quickened my steps in pursuit. Almost at the same instant I was startled by a loud, shrill, prolonged hiss, a sound that closely resembled the escape of steam from the cylinder of a locomotive when starting a heavy train. I stopped as suddenly as if my progress had been arrested by a rifle bullet, and looking toward the upper end of the plat my eyes encountered an object the recollection of which even now makes me shiver with horror.

"Coiled up not more than twenty feet from where I stood was an immense serpent—the most hideously frightful monster that ever confronted mortal man. It was a moment before my dazed senses could comprehend the dreadful peril that threatened me. As the truth of my terrible situation dawned upon me, my first impulse was to fly; but not a limb or muscle moved in obedience to the effort of my will. I was as incapable of motion as if I had been hewn in marble: I essayed to cry for help but the effort at articulation died away in a gurgling sound upon my lips.

"The serpent lay in three great coils, its head, and some ten feet of its body projecting above, swaying to and fro in undulatory [sic] sinuous, wavy convulsions, like the tentacles of an octopus in the swift current of an ebbing tide. The monster stared at me with its great, hateful, lidless eyes, ever and anon darting its head menacingly in my direction, thrusting out its forked tongue, and emitting hisses so vehemently that I felt its baleful breath upon my cheek. Arching its neck the serpent would dilate its immense jaws until its head would measure at least eighteen inches across, then dart toward me, distending its mouth and exhibiting its great hooked fangs that looked like the talons of a vulture.

"As I stood in momentary expectation of feeling the tusks and being crushed in the constricting fold of the scaly monster, my situation was appalling beyond description—beyond the conception of the most vivid imagination. The blood ran down my back cold as Greenland ice and congealed in my veins. Every pulse in my body seemed to stand still and my heart ceased to beat. Even respiration was slow and painful. There was a choking, suffocating sensation in my throat, and my lips became dry and parched. There was a ringing in my ears, dark spots floated before my eyes, and I should have fainted but for the horrifying reflection that if I gave way to such weakness my doom was inevitable. A cold clammy perspiration oozed from every pore, and so intense was my agony of fear that I suffered the tortures of the damned augmented a thousand fold. While all my physical capacities were prostrated and paralyzed, every mental faculty seemed preternaturally sharpened. It appeared as if the terrible tension of my nerve and bodily incapacity immeasurably increased my range of vision, and rendered my perceptive faculties critically acute.

"Not the slightest movement of the serpent escaped me, and every detail of its appearance—size, color, shape and position—is, alas! Only too strongly photographed upon my recollection. As I stated before, the serpent lay in three immense coils, the triple thicknesses of its body standing as high as my shoulders. The monster was fully twenty inches in diameter in the largest place. Its head was comparatively large. Its tremendous jaws that at times dilated to twice their natural size, having enormous hooked fangs that fitted in between each other when the mouth was shut. The neck was slender and tapering. The belly of the serpent was a dirty whitish color, deeply furrowed with transverse corrugations. With the exception of about ten feet of the neck and contiguous parts which were nearly black, the body of the snake was brown, beautifully mottled with orange-colored spots on the back. How long I confronted this terrible shape I do not know. Probably only a few moments; but to me it seemed ages.

> **//Its tremendous jaws that at times dilated to twice their natural size, having enormous hooked fangs that fitted in between each other when the mouth was shut."**

"At length the serpent began slowly to uncoil, but whether for the purpose of attacking me or retreating I could not fathom. You can have but a faint conception of my relief and joy when I discovered that it was the latter. Lowering its crest and giving vent to a venomous hiss, the monster went slowly crashing, through the chaparral, its head being plainly visible above the jungle. For a moment I could scarcely realize that I was no longer threatened by a death too horrible to contemplate.

"There was a tingling sensation through my body from the top of my head to the soles of my feet as the blood again commenced circulating in my veins. I attempted to step forward, but so benumbed were my limbs that I fell heavily to the earth. Recovering, I staggered through the chaparral into the open country. As I emerged from the thicket I saw my partner a short distance up the ridge and motioned him to approach. When he did so he was greatly alarmed at my haggard appearance, and excitedly inquired the cause. In reply I pointed to the serpent, then some 100 yards distant—a sight that threw him into the utmost consternation. We watched the monster until it disappeared from view in the rocky recesses of a cliff that overhangs the river. We were enabled to measure the length of the serpent very exactly by its passing parallel with two trees, its head being even with one while its tail reached the other. Mr Buylick has since ascertained that the trees are forty feet apart."

GIANT BOA

The Hagenbecks were a family of collectors of all manner of animals who supplied the world's zoos with a wide variety of exotic animals for more than a century. It's hardly surprising, therefore, that they came across a number of extraordinary tales—and extraordinary animals, too. Indeed, one of the Hagenbecks' explorers was the very first person to encounter a pygmy hippopotamus, on February 28, 1913. In addition, explorer Lorenz Hagenbeck had a particular interest in snakes, but not snakes of the average variety. It was super-sized snakes that fascinated him, to the point where he made it his business to collect just about as many credible reports as possible. A fascinating story came to Hagenbeck from a pair of Roman Catholic priests, Father Victor Heinz and Father Protesius Frickel. Father Heinz's story was particularly notable, since it revolved around the sighting of a truly colossal monster. Heinz prepared a statement that told the entire, shocking story:

"During the great floods of 1922 on May 22—at about three o'clock to be exact—I was being taken home by canoe on the Amazon from Obidos; suddenly I noticed something surprising in midstream. I distinctly recognized a giant water snake at a distance of some thirty yards. To distinguish it from the sucuriju, the natives who accompanied me named the reptile, because of its enormous size, sucuriju gigante (giant boa).

"Coiled up in two rings the monster drifted quietly and gently downstream. My quaking crew had stopped paddling. Thunderstruck, we all stared at the frightful beast. I reckoned that its body was as thick as an oil drum and that its visible length was some eighty feet. When we were far enough away and my boatmen dared to speak again they said the monster would have crushed us like a box of matches if it had not previously consumed several large capybaras."

Such was the extraordinary nature of the encounter, Father Heinz was hooked on finding all he could on the immense beast and its ilk. He learned

Even "normal" boas are impressive animals in size, as this trained animal handler demonstrates.

that yet another huge boa had been shot and killed, one day previously, as it tried to devour a capybara—the world's largest rodent which can reach the size of a dog. It wasn't long before Father Heinz had a second sighting of a massive snake:

"My second encounter with a giant water snake took place on 29 October 1929. To escape the great heat I had decided to go down river at about 7:00 P.M. in the direction of Alemquer. At about midnight, we found ourselves above the mouth of the Piaba when my crew, seized with a sudden fear, began to row hard towards the shore. 'What is it?' I cried, sitting up. 'There is a big animal,' they muttered very excited. At the same moment I heard the water move, as if a steamboat had passed. I immediately noticed several meters above the surface of the water two bluish-green lights like the navigation lights on the bridge of a riverboat, and shouted: 'No, look, it's the steamer! Row to the side so that it doesn't upset us.'"

It was no steamer:

"Petrified, we all watched the monster approach; it avoided us and re-crossed the river in less than a minute a crossing that would have taken us ten to fifteen minutes as long. On the safety of dry land we took courage and shouted to attract the attention of the snake. At this very moment a human figure began to wave an oil-lamp on the other shore, thinking, no doubt, that someone was in danger. Almost at once the snake rose on the surface and we were able to appreciate clearly the difference between the light of the lamp and the phosphorescent light of the monster's eyes. Later, in my return, the inhabitants of this place assured me that above the mouth of the Piaba there dwelt a sucuriju gigante."

// Almost at once the snake rose on the surface and we were able to appreciate clearly the difference between the light of the lamp and the phosphorescent light of the monster's eyes."

And, finally, there is the following account of Reymondo Zima, a Portuguese merchant, who Father Heinz had the good fortune to interview. Zima told the priest:

"On 6th July 1930 I was going up the Jamunda in company with my wife and the boy who looks after my motor-boat. Night was falling when we saw a light on the river bank. In the belief it was the house I was looking for I steered towards the light and switched on my searchlight. But then we noticed that the light was charging towards us at an incredible speed. A huge wave lifted the bow of the boat and almost made it capsize. My wife screamed in terror. At the same moment we made out the shape of a giant snake rising out of the water and performing a St. Vitus's dance around the boat. After which the monster crossed this tributary of the Amazon about half a kilometer wide at fabulous speed, leaving a huge wake, larger than any of the steamboats make at full speed. The waves hit our 13-meter boat with such force that at every moment we were in danger of capsizing. I opened my motor flat out and made for dry land. Owing to the understandable excitement at the time it was not possible for me to reckon the monster's length. I presume that as a result of a wound the animal lost one eye, since I saw only one light. I think the giant snake must have mistaken our searchlight for the eye of one of his fellow snakes."

It was, to be sure, a lucky escape.

GIANT SALAMANDER

Reports of lake monsters abound across the planet. Amongst the most famous ones are Scotland's Loch Ness Monster, Ogopogo of Lake Okanagan, and Champ of Lake Champlain. The big question is: if the creatures are real, then what, exactly, are they? Monster hunters suggest they may be relic populations of plesiosaurs, marine reptiles that are believed to have become extinct tens of millions of years ago. Other theorists suggest the creatures might be immense eels. Then there is the giant salamander scenario.

Salamanders are amphibians that are noted for their long tails, blunt heads, and short limbs and which—in the case of the Chinese giant salamander—can reach lengths of six feet. But, is it possible that some salamanders could grow much larger, even to the extent of fifteen to twenty-five feet? Incredible? Yes. Implausible? Maybe not. Steve Plambeck is a noted authority on the giant salamander theory when it comes to the matter of the Loch Ness Monster. He says:

"Nessie is a bottom dwelling, water breathing animal that spends very little time on the surface or in mid-water, although just enough to be spotted visually or by sonar on very rare occasions. Its forays up from the depths are most likely made along the sides of the Loch, to feed on the fish which are predominantly found along the sides, in shallower water above the underwater cliffs that precipitously drop off into the 750-foot [229-meter] abyss. Such

The Chinese giant salamander can reach lengths of nearly six feet (1.8 meters).

behavior is only consistent with a fish, or aquatic amphibian, which can extract all of its needed oxygen directly from the water.

"Yet as seldom as it happens, and for reasons known only to the animal itself, Nessie also *leaves the water* for apparently brief stretches, as observed most famously in the Spicer and Grant sightings of 1933 and 1934 respectively. It may be said that this is nothing new: it's a centuries old tradition among the Highlanders that the *kelpie* or water horse of Loch Ness comes ashore. That's a key behavioral trait to take into account if we are distinguishing fish from amphibians."

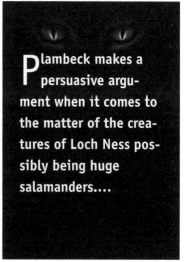

In that sense, Plambeck makes a persuasive argument when it comes to the matter of the creatures of Loch Ness possibly being huge salamanders, or, at the very least, another kind of large, unknown amphibian. It's a theory also noted by researcher "Erika." She says of such a scenario:

Plambeck makes a persuasive argument when it comes to the matter of the creatures of Loch Ness possibly being huge salamanders....

"This might seem ridiculous at first, but in China there is a species of giant salamander that can grow up to six feet long. Certainly this is an animal which is long enough, and odd enough, that if it surfaced in a lake, onlookers could be forgiven for mistaking it for a monster.

"There are other similarities which make this a plausible theory. The Chinese giant salamander lives in very cold fresh water, which describes Loch Ness handily. They are found in the rocky streams and mountain lakes of remote northern China, where they are as elusive as they are endangered.

"Best of all (for this purpose), the Chinese giant salamander is a very sluggish animal. It rarely surfaces, and spends most of its time lying at the bottom, waiting for prey to swim past. It strikes quickly and then retreats. This is not an active animal, and it's entirely possible they could live in a lake as big as Loch Ness without ever being seen at the surface."

Loch Ness Monster authority Roland Watson has also waded into this controversy: "Before long neck stories began to dominate peoples' thinking, some held to the view that Nessie was some form of outsized amphibian and in particular the salamander. I am a bit partial to a fish-like amphibian or amphibian-like fish theory myself, so we are in agreement to some degree there. An amphibian has its issues just like any other Nessie theory but I am sure it can hold its own in the Nessie pantheon."

Watson has also commented on the theories of Steve Plambeck: "One major block to a salamander interpretation is the traditional long neck of the creature. Salamanders do not have long necks. Steve however suggests that the long tail of the salamander can account for this apparent problem. I can see merit in that idea and have no problem believing that a long tail can be mistaken for a long neck by eyewitnesses."

Seekers of unknown animals might be disappointed by the possibility that some of our most famous lake monsters are merely salamanders and nothing else. But, when actually confronted, at close quarters, by such a creature—and one of twenty to twenty-five feet in length—very few would probably quibble with the notion that such a thing should be classed as a monster!

HORSHAM HORROR

Printed in 1614 by John Trundle of London is a pamphlet with the extraordinarily long title of *True and Wonderful, A DISCOURSE Relating A STRANGE AND MONSTROUS SERPENT OR DRAGON Lately Discovered and yet living to the great Annoyance and divers Slaughters both Men and Cattell, by his strong and violent Poyson. In Sussex, two Miles from Horsam, in a Woode called St. Leonards Forrest, and thirtie Miles from London, this present Month of August, 1614.*

It tells the strange, seventeenth-century story of a terrible monster that instilled fear into the people of the English town of Horsham and reads as follows, in quaint, old English style:

"In Sussex, there is a pretty market-town called Horsham, near unto it a forest, called St. Leonards forest, and there, in a vast and unfrequented place, heathy, vaulty, full of unwholesome shades, and overgrown hollows, where this serpent is thought to be bred; but, wheresoever bred, certain and too true it is that there it yet lives.

"Within three or four miles compass are its usual haunts, oftentimes at a place called Faygate, and it hath been seen within half a mile of Horsham, a wonder, no doubt, most terrible and noisome to the inhabitants thereabouts. There is always in his track or path left a glutinous and slimy matter (as by a small similitude we may perceive in a snail's) which is very corrupt and offensive to the scent, insomuch that they perceive the air to be putrified withal, which must needs be very dangerous.

"For though the corruption of it cannot strike the outward part of a man, unless heated into his blood, yet by receiving it in at any of our breathing organs (the mouth or

> **T**here is always in his track or path left a glutinous and slimy matter (as by a small similitude we may perceive in a snail's) which is very corrupt and offensive to the scent....

nose) it is by authority of all authors, writing in that kind, mortal and deadly, as one thus saith: *Noxia serpentum est admixto sanguine pestis.*

"The serpent, or dragon, as some call it, is reputed to be nine feet, or rather more, in length, and shaped almost in the form of an axletree of a cart, a quantity of thickness in the midst, and somewhat smaller at both ends. The former part, which he shoots forth as a neck, is supposed to be an ell long, with a white ring, as it were, of scales about it.

"The scales along his back seem to be blackish, and so much as is discovered under his belly appeareth to be red; for I speak of no nearer description than of a reasonable occular distance.

"For coming too near it hath already been too dearly paid for, as you shall hear hereafter. It is likewise discovered to have large feet, but the eye may be there deceived; for some suppose that serpents have no feet, but glide upon certain ribs and scales, which both defend them from the upper part of their throat unto the lower part of their belly, and also cause them to move much the faster.

"For so this doth, and rids way, as we call it as fast as a man can run. He is of countenance very proud, and, at the sight or hearing of men or cattle, will raise his neck upright, and seem to listen and look about, with arrogancy. There are likewise on either side of him discovered two great bunches so big as a large foot-ball, and, as some think, will in time grow to wings; but God, I hope, will defend the poor people in the neighbourhood, that he shall be destroyed before he grow so fledged.

"He will cast his venom about four rod from him, as by woeful experience it was proved on the bodies of a man and woman coming that way, who afterwards were found dead, being poisoned and very much swelled, but not preyed upon.

"Likewise a man going to chase it and, as he imagined, to destroy it, with two mastiff dogs, as yet not knowing the great danger of it, his dogs were both killed, and he himself glad to return with haste to preserve his own life. Yet this is to be noted, that the dogs were not preyed upon, but slain and left whole; for his food is thought to be, for the most part, in a cony-warren, (rabbit warren) which he much frequents, and it is found much scanted and impaired in the increase it had wont to afford.

"These persons, whose names are hereunder printed, have seen this serpent, beside divers others, as the carrier of Horsham, who lieth at the White Horse, in South wark, and who can certify the truth of all that has been here related."

JOHN STEELE.
CHRISTOPHER HOLDER.
And a Widow Woman dwelling near Faygate.

IRISH "CROCODILE"

The idea that crocodiles might be living in Ireland stretches credulity not just to its limit, but way beyond it, too! Nevertheless, creatures that at least superficially resemble crocodiles have been seen and reported across the land and for centuries—and particularly in Ireland's lakes and loughs. A particularly fascinating account of just such a monster was chronicled by Roderick O'Flaherty (Ruaidhrí Ó Flaithbheartaigh) in his 1684 book, *A Description of West or H-Iar Connaught*. The location was the waters of Lough Mask. O'Flaherty said:

"There is one rarity more, which we may term the Irish crocodile, whereof one, as yet living, about ten years ago (1674) had said experience. The man was passing the shore just by the waterside, and spyed [sic] far off the head of a beast swimming, which he took to be an otter, and took no more notice of it; but the beast it seems lifted up its head; to discern whereabouts the man was; then diving swam under the water till he struck ground; whereupon he run out of the water suddenly and took the man by the elbow whereby the man stooped down, and the beast fastened his teeth in its pate, and dragged him into the water."

What had begun for the man as a sighting of an unusual animal, was now nothing less than a fight for life and limb. O'Flaherty continued with his extraordinary account:

> **"… water suddenly and took the man by the elbow whereby the man stooped down, and the beast fastened his teeth in its pate, and dragged him into the water."**

"Where the man took hold of a stone by chance in his way, and calling to mind he had a knife in his jacket, took it out and gave a thrust of it to the beast, which thereupon got away from him into the lake. The water about him was all bloody, whether from the beast's blood, or his own, or from both he knows not. It was the pitch of an ordinary greyhound, of a black slimey [sic] skin, without hair as he imagines."

O'Flaherty then made an intriguing statement on the nature of the beast and its history—to the extent that its history was known:

"Old men acquainted with the lake do tell there is such a beast in it, and that a stout fellow with a wolf dog along with him met the like there once; which after a long struggling went away in spite of the man and his dog, and was a long time after found rotten in a rocky cave of the lake when the waters decreased. The like they say is seen in other lakes in Ireland, they call it Dovarchu, i.e. water-dog, or anchu which is the same."

Peter Costello, a noted authority on Irish lake monsters, has studied this case carefully and makes a number of thought-provoking comments. Just before we get to Costello, it's important that we first have an awareness of a footnote that appears in an 1866 edition of O'Flaherty's book, which was published by the Dublin, Ireland-based Archaeological Society. The editor of this particular edition said in the footnote:

"In these western parts, this animal is generally called Each Usage, which means a water-horse, and he is described as having a black shining skin and switch tail without hair. The story related by our author is yet told in the neighborhood of Lough Mask."

On this issue, Peter Costello says:

"There seems to be some confusion here. The word 'Dovarchu' does sometimes mean an otter in Irish. But Hardiman seems to be mixing up two creatures which are carefully distinguished in the folk tradition. In 1843 the author of *Wild Sports of the West* observed that in Connaught 'animals of extra-ordinary [sic] formation, and strange virtues, are supposed to inhabit lakes and rivers. Among these the sea-horse and the master-otter are pre-eminent. By a singular anomaly, the first is said to be found in certain island lochs, and his appearance is imagined to be fatal to the unfortunate person who encounters it.'"

Costello adds to this: "O'Flaherty's Irish crocodile is presumably the master-otter, while the sea-horse is the uisge of Gaelic stories.... It has often been suggested that some reports of lake monsters could be sightings of large otters," adding that suggestions have been made to the effect of "the Loch Ness animal might be a long-necked otter-like animal."

LAMBTON WORM

The River Wear is a sixty-mile-long body of water that dominates much of northern England and which, in medieval times, was said to have been the lair of a marauding, giant worm-like monster—one that provoked unrelenting terror across the land, devouring animals and people, and causing mayhem wherever it crawled and slithered. That is, until its reign of fear was brought to a fatal halt when a brave hero decided that the creature had to die. One person who dug deeply into the strange but engaging saga of the Lambton Worm

CHURCHMAN'S CIGARETTES

THE LAMBTON WORM

The legend of the Lambton Worm is such a part of English folklore that there was even once a cigarette package illustrated with the beast.

was Joseph Jacobs, a noted Australian folk-lorist who, in the 1800s, focused much of his research and writings on the matter of strange creatures, fabulous beasts, and marauding monsters reported throughout the British Isles. And, it's to Jacobs who we now turn, and his personal, nineteenth-century account of this legendary monster of the deep:

"A wild young fellow was the heir of Lambton, the fine estate and hail by the side of the swift-flowing Wear. Not a Mass would he hear in Brugeford Chapel of a Sunday, but a-fishing he would go. And if he did not haul in anything, his curses could be heard by the folk as they went by to Brugeford.

"Well, one Sunday morning he was fishing as usual, and not a salmon had risen to him, his basket was bare of roach or dace. And the worse his luck, the worse grew his language, till the passers-by were horrified at his words as they went to listen to the Mass-priest.

"At last young Lambton felt a mighty tug at his line. 'At last,' quoth he, 'a bite worth having!' and he pulled and he pulled, till what should appear above the water but a head like an elf's, with nine holes on each side of its mouth. But still he pulled till he had got the thing to land, when it turned out to be a Worm of hideous shape. If he had cursed before, his curses were enough to raise the hair on your head.

"'What ails thee, my son?' said a voice by his side, 'and what hast thou caught, that thou shouldst stain the Lord's Day with such foul language?'

"Looking round, young Lambton saw a strange old man standing by him.

"'Why, truly,' he said, 'I think I have caught the devil himself. Look you and see if you know him.'

"But the stranger shook his head, and said, 'It bodes no good to thee or thine to bring such a monster to shore. Yet cast him not back into the Wear;

thou has caught him, and thou must keep him,' and with that away he turned, and was seen no more.

"The young heir of Lambton took up the gruesome thing, and taking it off his hook, cast it into a well close by, and ever since that day that well has gone by the name of the Worm Well.

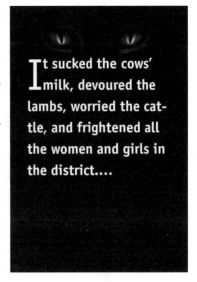

It sucked the cows' milk, devoured the lambs, worried the cattle, and frightened all the women and girls in the district....

"For some time nothing more was seen or heard of the Worm, till one day it had outgrown the size of the well, and came forth full-grown. So it came forth from the well and betook itself to the Wear. And all day long it would lie coiled round a rock in the middle of the stream, while at night it came forth from the river and harried the countryside. It sucked the cows' milk, devoured the lambs, worried the cattle, and frightened all the women and girls in the district, and then it would retire for the rest of the night to the hill, still called the Worm Hill, on the north side of the Wear, about a mile and a half from Lambton Hall.

"This terrible visitation brought young Lambton, of Lambton Hall, to his senses. He took upon himself the vows of the Cross, and departed for the Holy Land, in the hope that the scourge he had brought upon his district would disappear. But the grisly Worm took no heed, except that it crossed the river and came right up to Lambton Hall itself where the old lord lived on all alone, his only son having gone to the Holy Land. What to do? The Worm was coming closer and closer to the Hall; women were shrieking, men were gathering weapons, dogs were barking and horses neighing with terror. At last the steward called out to the dairymaids, 'Bring all your milk hither,' and when they did so, and had brought all the milk that the nine kye of the byre had yielded, he poured it all into the long stone trough in front of the Hall.

"The Worm drew nearer and nearer, till at last it came up to the trough. But when it sniffed the milk, it turned aside to the trough and swallowed all the milk up, and then slowly turned round and crossed the River Wear, and coiled its bulk three times round the Worm Hill for the night.

"Henceforth the Worm would cross the river every day, and woe betide the Hall if the trough contained the milk of less than nine kye. The Worm would hiss, and would rave, and lash its tail round the trees of the park, and in its fury it would uproot the stoutest oaks and the loftiest firs. So it went on for seven years. Many tried to destroy the Worm, but all had failed, and many a knight had lost his life in fighting with the monster, which slowly crushed the life out of all that came near it.

"At last the Childe of Lambton came home to his father's Hall, after seven long years spent in meditation and repentance on holy soil. Sad and desolate he found his folk: the lands untilled, the farms deserted, half the trees of the park uprooted, for none would stay to tend the nine kye that the monster needed for his food each day.

"The Childe sought his father, and begged his forgiveness for the curse he had brought on the Hall.

"'Thy sin is pardoned,' said his father; 'but go thou to the Wise Woman of Brugeford, and find if aught can free us from this monster.'

"To the Wise Woman went the Childe, and asked her advice.

"''Tis thy fault, O Childe, for which we suffer,' she said; 'be it thine to release us.'

"'I would give my life,' said the Childe.

"'Mayhap thou wilt do so,' said she. 'But hear me, and mark me well. Thou, and thou alone, canst kill the Worm. But, to this end, go thou to the smithy and have thy armour studded with spear-heads. Then go to the Worm's Rock in the Wear, and station thyself there. Then, when the Worm comes to the Rock at dawn of day, try thy prowess on him, and God gi'e thee a good deliverance.'

"'This I will do,' said Childe Lambton.

"'But one thing more,' said the Wise Woman, going back to her cell. 'If thou slay the Worm, swear that thou wilt put to death the first thing that meets thee as thou crossest again the threshold of Lambton Hall. Do this, and all will be well with thee and thine. Fulfil not thy vow, and none of the Lambtons, for generations three times three, shall die in his bed. Swear, and fail not.'

"The Childe swore as the Wise Woman bid, and went his way to the smithy. There he had his armour studded with spear-heads all over. Then he passed his vigils in Brugeford Chapel, and at dawn of day took his post on the Worm's Rock in the River Wear.

"As dawn broke, the Worm uncoiled its snaky twine from around the hill, and came to its rock in the river. When it perceived the Childe waiting for it, it lashed the waters in its fury and wound its coils

An 1890 illustration of the Lambton Worm from the book *English Fairy and Other Folk Tales* by Edwin Sidney Hartland.

round the Childe, and then attempted to crush him to death. But the more it pressed, the deeper dug the spear-heads into its sides. Still it pressed and pressed, till all the water around was crimsoned with its blood. Then the Worm unwound itself, and left the Childe free to use his sword. He raised it, brought it down, and cut the Worm in two. One half fell into the river, and was carried swiftly away. Once more the head and the remainder of the body encircled the Childe, but with less force, and the spear-heads did their work. At last the Worm uncoiled itself, snorted its last foam of blood and fire, and rolled dying into the river, and was never seen more."

LINDORM

Scandinavian history and folklore are filled with tales of all manner of monsters, rampaging beasts, and deadly creatures of a fantastic nature. Very few, however, were as feared as the lethal lindorm. It was a huge, wriggling, snake-like animal that, like today's lake monsters such as Nessie, Champ, and Ogopogo, chose to live in deep, massive lakes. There was one big difference between the lindorms and other, similar monsters, however. The lindorm never stopped growing. This, rather ironically, was its very own downfall: as it grew bigger and bigger, it got heavier and heavier, something that eventually ensured it could no longer support its own weight and it would sink to the lake bed, unable to ever again move its massive bulk, and where it would eventually die.

as it grew bigger • • • and bigger, it got heavier and heavier, something which eventually ensured it could no longer support its own weight and it would sink to the lake bed....

There are stories in Scandinavian legend of lindorms having a particular hatred of Christian churches and chapels, which they would reportedly coil around and crush into rubble with their powerful, flexible bodies. Perhaps this was a result of the fact that the dragon was a beast revered in pagan times, but far less so when Christianity was brought to Europe. There are also tales of huge bulls reared to fight lindorms—and to the death, no less. Fortunately for the bulls, they were well trained and very often successfully killed the snake-like monstrosities with their powerful horns.

While the lindorm is, today, a creature relegated to the world of myth, Scandinavia can boast of being home to a multitude of lake monsters and sea serpents. With that in mind, perhaps the lindorm is still with us, but just under another name.

LINTON WORM

Our world has no shortage of modern day monsters, as we have seen time and again in the pages of this book. The world of the past had no shortage, either, as the strange saga of what became known as the Linton Worm makes very clear. A tale that dates back to the 1100s, it tells of a horrific, man-eating, giant, worm-like beast that terrified the good folk of Linton, Roxburghshire, which is located on the Southern Uplands of Scotland. Interestingly, and as will soon become apparent, the monster has parallels with a number of Scottish lake monsters, and particularly so Nessie of Loch Ness and Morag of Loch Morar.

According to the old tales, the Linton Worm was somewhere between ten and twelve feet in length, which, if true, effectively rules out any known

An illustration of *The Worme of Lintoni* tale by artist James Torrance (1859–1916).

British animal—wild or domestic—as being the culprit. Rather oddly, so the old legend went, the huge worm had two homes. In part, it lived in the heart of Linton Loch—a small, boggy area and the ideal place for a monster to hide. Its other, dark abode was Linton Hill, which even today is referred to as Worm's Den, such is the enduring nature of the legend. That the beast apparently had the ability to leave the water and slither across the landscape of Scotland brings to mind the small number of reports of both the aforementioned Morag and Nessie being seen on land.

By all accounts, the worm was a creature to be avoided at all costs: cows, sheep, pigs, vegetables, and even people, were all food for the monster. Quite naturally, the people of Linton were thrown into a collective state of fear when the slithering thing decided to target their little village. People became petrified to leave their homes, lest they became the victims of the marauding beast. Doors and windows remained locked. Farmers stayed home. That is, until a man named John de Somerville came upon the scene.

When told of the nature of the monster that had brought terror to Linton, de Somerville—known as the "Laird of Lariston"—had a local blacksmith create for him a razor-sharp spear, which he, de Somerville, intended to use to slay the mighty beast. Fortunately, he did exactly that, by setting the spear aflame and plunging it into the throat of the monster, after seeking it out at Worm's Den. The beast fought back, its wormy form writhing and turning and twisting violently atop the hill, but it was to no avail. Exhausted, and on the verge of death, the beast retreated to its labyrinthine lair within Linton Hill. It was neither seen nor heard of again.

The Linton folk never forgot the valiant act of John de Somerville, and a sculpture commemorating de Somerville's brave act was created in Linton Church, as William Henderson noted in his 1879 book, *Notes on the folk-lore of the northern counties of England and the borders*. He said:

"The sculptured effigy of the monster, which may still be seen with the champion who slew it, at the south-western extremity of Linton church, differs from both accounts. A stone, evidently of great antiquity, is there built into the wall. It is covered with sculpture in low relief, and bears figures which, though defaced by time, can yet be made out pretty clearly. A knight on horseback, clad in a tunic or hauberk, with a round helmet, urges his horse against two large animals, the foreparts of which only are visible, and plunges his lance into the throat of one. Behind him is the outline of another creature, apparently of a lamb. The heads of the monsters are strong and powerful, but more like those of quadrupeds than of serpents. It is perplexing also to see two of them, but not the less does popular tradition connect the representation with the Linton Worm."

Today, both church and effigy still remain intact—and still provoking wonder, and perhaps even a little fear, in those who visit the little village of Linton.

LOVELAND FROG

Loveland is a city in southwest Ohio that has a population of around 12,000, and which was settled back in 1795. It's a small, picturesque town, filled with mountains of history and old buildings. Then there are Loveland's resident frog-people. Yes, you did read that right. The controversy all began in the summer of 1955—specifically in the month of July. It was around 4:00 one morning, and all was black and shadowy. Robert Hunnicutt, a volunteer with the local Civil Defense unit, was driving on a road on the fringes of Loveland when he spotted something amazing and terrifying in equal measures: a group—of three or four, Hunnicutt wasn't sure—of small, humanoid creatures standing under a bridge. Incredibly, they were described as around three feet tall, walking on two legs and with "lopsided chests, wide, lipless, froglike mouths, and wrinkles rather than hair."

A shocked Hunnicutt stopped and stared at the beasts for a few minutes, after which one of the frog-things pointed a device—a weapon, or something else, Hunnicutt never knew—into the air, which gave off electric-blue flashes. Hunnicutt, at that point, wasted no time in getting out of the area as soon as possible. His destination: the headquarters of the Loveland Police, where he spoke to the Chief of Police, John Fritz. Evidently, the strange story was taken seriously, as Fritz had one of his armed deputies keep a vigil at the bridge, to try and ascertain what Hunnicutt had seen.

Incredibly, they were described as around three feet tall, walking on two legs and with "lopsided chests, wide, lipless, froglike mouths, and wrinkles rather than hair."

Interestingly, Leonard Stringfield, a noted UFO researcher in Ohio at the time, looked into the affair. He uncovered something intriguing: "Despite my special affiliations with the Ground Observer Corps and the Air Defense Command, I was unable to get any details of official action from the Loveland Civil Defense Authority, from Frank Whitecotton, Coordinator for the Hamilton County GOC, or from the Loveland Chief of Police, John Fritz. However, I was able to learn from a member of the Loveland School Board that the incident had been investigated by the FBI."

The odd encounter was big news for a while, but ultimately faded into obscurity. That is, until 1972, when a new report surfaced and which, for the city's oldtimers, instantly brought back memories of Robert Hunnicutt's face-to-face stand-off with a group of monsters all those years earlier.

Mirroring the Hunnicutt affair, it was when the area was in darkness that the sighting of Ray Shockey took place. What is particularly notable is the fact that Shockey was a Loveland police officer, on patrol at the time in the vicinity of the Little Miami River. As he drove past the river, Shockey spied what, at first, he believed was a dog, sitting at the side of the road. Given that it was a freezing, wintry, icy night, Shockey slowed down to see if the dog was okay. It quickly became apparent that the "dog" was something else entirely.

As Shockey's cruiser closed in, the four-foot-tall animal leapt up onto its hind limbs, and stared directly at Shockey—which allowed the officer to see its strange, frog-like appearance. For a few minutes the frog-man and the officer stared at each other, after which the creature leapt over the guard rail and vanished into the heart of the shadowy river. Shockey raced back to headquarters and quickly prepared a report on his astonishing sighting, such was his conviction he had seen something truly out of this world. In the wake of the Shockey sighting, other accounts surfaced, all of a "frog-" or "lizard-like" nature.

Whatever the true nature of the frog-people of Loveland, Ohio, their origins remain, today, the mystery they were all those years ago, when the lives of two terrified men were forever changed.

MARCO POLO'S MONSTER

One of the most fascinating of all monster-themed stories comes from the renowned explorer Marco Polo (1254–1324), who told of animals that eerily sound like dragons in the province of Carajan, which falls under the region of Yunnan, in southern China. Polo's description of the beasts is as intriguing as it is bizarre and puzzling. In his own, legendary words:

"In this province are found snakes and great serpents of such vast size as to strike fear into those who see them, and so hideous that the very account of them must excite the wonder of those to hear it. I will tell you how long and big they are.

"You may be assured that some of them are ten paces in length; some are more and some less. And in bulk they are equal to a great cask, for the bigger ones are about ten palms in girth. They have two forelegs near the head, but for foot nothing but a claw like the claw of a hawk or that of a lion. The head is very big, and the eyes are bigger than a great loaf of bread. The mouth is large enough to swallow a man whole, and is garnished with great [pointed] teeth. And in short they are so fierce-looking and so hideously ugly, that every man and beast must stand in fear and trembling of them. There are also smaller ones, such as of eight paces long, and of five, and of one pace only.

The famous explorer Marco Polo traveled extensively throughout Asia in the Middle Ages. Among the things he saw were large snakes that had forelegs.

"The way in which they are caught is this. You must know that by day they live underground because of the great heat, and in the night they go out to feed, and devour every animal they can catch. They go also to drink at the rivers and lakes and springs. And their weight is so great that when they travel in search of food or drink, as they do by night, the tail makes a great furrow in the soil as if a full ton of liquor had been dragged along.

"Now the huntsmen who go after them take them by certain gyn which they set in the track over which the serpent has past, knowing that the beast will come back the same way. They plant a stake deep in the ground and fix on the head of this a sharp blade of steel made like a razor or a lance-point, and then they cover the whole with sand so that the serpent cannot see it. Indeed the huntsman plants several such stakes and blades on the track. On coming to the spot the beast strikes against the iron blade with such force that it enters his breast and rives him up to the navel, so that he dies on the spot and the crows on seeing the brute dead begin to caw, and then the huntsmen know that the serpent is dead and come in search of him.

"This then is the way these beasts are taken. Those who take them proceed to extract the gall from the inside, and this sells at a great price; for you must know it furnishes the material for a most precious medicine. Thus if a person is bitten by a mad dog, and they give him but a small pennyweight of this medicine to drink, he is cured in a moment. Again if a woman is hard in labor they give her just such another dose and she is delivered at once. Yet again if one has any disease like the itch, or it may be worse, and applies a small quantity of this gall he shall speedily be cured. So you see why it sells at such a high price.

"They also sell the flesh of this serpent, for it is excellent eating, and the people are very fond of it. And when these serpents are very hungry, sometimes they will seek out the lairs of lions or bears or other large wild beasts, and devour their cubs, without the sire and dam being able to prevent it. Indeed if they catch the big ones themselves they devour them too; they can make no resistance."

It's worth mentioning that noted cryptozoologist Richard Freeman is of the opinion that Marco Polo may have been describing nothing stranger than crocodiles. Perhaps that is indeed the case; although we can never be one hundred percent sure that he wasn't speaking of something that, today, is no longer with us, but which once earned the title of a real-life monster.

MEGALANIA PRISCA

Is it feasible that the subtropical rainforests of Australia (no, contrary to popular belief, the continent is *not* one largely of a desert nature and nothing

An artist's rendering of what the *Megalania prisca* may have looked like.

else) are home to gigantic, man-eating lizards of twenty to thirty feet in length? Could such *Jurassic Park*-like beasts really remain hidden, undetected, and free to rampage around in unstoppable fashion? The Australian government's wildlife department scoffs at such scenarios. Witnesses, however, strongly suggest otherwise. As for the creature itself, it's not something created out of the minds of the fantasy-driven and the deluded. Thousands of years ago, Australia really was home to such immense beasts. The big question is: do they still live, despite the fact that they have been declared completely and utterly extinct—in the long-gone past?

The creature in question went by the name of *Megalania prisca*, a huge, vicious, monitor lizard that roamed Australia at least as late as 40,000 years ago. It got its name thanks to one Richard Owen, a paleontologist of the 1800s—a man who has gone down in history as coining the term Dinosauria, or, in English, "terrible reptile." As for *Megalania prisca*, it very appropriately translates to "ancient giant butcher."

Many might consider it utterly absurd to believe that packs of thirty-foot monster-lizards could exist in stealth, in the wilds of modern-day Australia, and not be found. But, let's take a look at what we know of this undeniably controversial saga. For decades, reports have surfaced out of Australia of such creatures—to the extent that Australian monster hunter Rex Gilroy has been able to put together an extensive dossier of such accounts. One, in particular, is well worth noting.

Gilroy, during the course of his investigations into claims that *Megalania prisca* still lives, had the good fortune to meet with a soldier named Steve, who told Gilroy a fascinating and terrifying story. It was in October 1968 that Steve, serving in the Australian military at the time, was taking part in an exercise in Queensland—specifically on what was termed the Normandy Range. One part of the exercise required Steve's unit to negotiate a particularly treacherous and dense, swampy area.

As the team did so, they came upon something highly disturbing: the viciously ripped-to-pieces body of a cow. Not only that, from the surrounding ground, Steve and his comrades could see that something had dragged the cow for a considerable time, before savagely eating huge chunks out of the poor animal. More significant, lizard-like prints were found in the muddy ground— all of which were close to two feet in length—as was an area of flattened ground, which suggested to the group that the unknown beast had a long, heavy tail that dragged behind it. No one needed to be told twice: the soldiers got the hell out of the swamp as quickly as possible.

As amazing as Steve's story was, and still is, it may very well have been nothing less than a close and highly hazardous encounter with a marauding monster that science and zoology assure us became extinct tens of thousands of years ago—but which, against all the odds, might still be with us. Remember that, if you ever choose to take a trek through the subtropical terrain of Australia.

MINNESOTA GIANT FROG

The state of Minnesota is known as "the land of 10,000 lakes." And with very good reason, too: it's positively teeming with lakes. The actual figure is a highly impressive 11,842. Which brings us to a certain event that occurred in 2013 at Lake Itasca, which is located in northcentral Minnesota. As you may guess, we are talking about a lake monster. But, we're not talking about something akin to Ogopogo or Nessie. And we're not talking about a huge, expansive body of water, either. Lake Itasca is actually less than two square miles (5.18 square kilometers) in area and has a depth of thirty-five feet (10.67 meters). But for such a small lake, it is home to a big mystery and to a big monster, too. Unlike the aforementioned Nessie and Ogopogo, however, to the best of my knowledge, the creature of Lake Itasca has only been seen and reported on once.

Don is a keen outdoorsman who lives in Minnesota's Clearwater County (which is also the home of Lake Itasca) and someone who had an extraordinary encounter at the lake in March 2013. Yes, it was with a leviathan of the deep. But, no, it was not of the famous, long-necked, humpbacked variety so often reported at Loch Ness. Don's experience involved nothing less than a huge, monstrous frog. We're talking about a frog of around four feet in length.

According to Don, it was as he strolled along the lake shore with his German Shepherd, Ben, that he saw a sudden disturbance in the water, at a distance of around fifty feet. Puzzled, he continued walking, and kept his dog on a tight leash just in case. It was probably a very wise move. As Don closed in, he was both

Lake Itasca, like many lakes in Minnesota, is a popular place for recreation and tourism.

shocked and horrified to see a huge frog crawl out of the water and, for a couple of seconds, peer intently and eerily in his direction. Don, somewhat concerned for his and Ben's safety, stood frozen to the spot for a few moments, as did Ben. Don quickly thought about taking a picture with his iPhone, at which point the monstrous mutant flopped back into the water, with a powerful splash, and was gone. Such was Don's amazement, he raced home, got a bunch of provisions, food, and bottled water and spent the entire day and night staking out that specific area of the lake. Unfortunately, the beast did not return.

While the idea of a four-foot-long frog might seem like something out of a 1950s-era sci-fi movie, there is something genuinely intriguing about Don's story. As fellow monster hunter Ken Gerhard said to me:

"If you remember, back in 1995, there were an incredibly large number of deformed frogs that were found in a pond in southwest Minnesota. It made big, national news. It was kind of looked at as a sign of the times: there was so much pollution that man's impact on the environment was causing these really bizarre frog mutations, where they would have extra limbs, missing limbs, weird eyes, and things like that. So, it has occurred to me over the past couple of years that, perhaps, we're looking at something very similar here in Texas. It is likely that one or more combinations of chemicals, biological, and physical factors are responsible for causing the malformations."

I most certainly *did* remember the Minnesota mutations. Such was the concern surrounding a series of bizarre genetic and physical changes in the frog population, none other than the U.S. government's Department of the Interi-

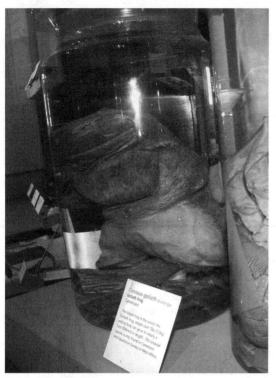

As far as biologists know, the goliath frog is the largest existing species (a specimen in the Harvard Museum of Natural History is shown here). They can grow to over seven pounds (3.25 kilograms).

or, U.S. Geological Survey, undertook careful and concerned studies. Its staff noted at its website: "Malformed frogs first became the topic of national news in August 1995 when students at a middle school in southern Minnesota discovered one-half of all the frogs they caught in a nearby pond were malformed. Since then, malformed frogs have been reported throughout Minnesota and elsewhere in the United States and Canada."

As the USGS said, the mutations were downright weird: "Malformations included missing limbs, missing digits, extra limbs, partial limbs, skin webbing, malformed jaws, and missing or extra eyes."

On the matter of how, exactly, the mutations might have occurred, the USGS had a few ideas. All of them were controversial and disturbing:

"Pesticides are known to cause malformation or death of frogs when present in sufficient concentrations. Studies in Canada show a relation between the percentage of malformed frogs and pesticide use. Methoprene, an insecticide widely used to control mosquitoes, also has been suspected as having caused malformations. Endocrine disruptors also are being studied to determine if they are responsible for some of the frog malformations in Minnesota. Endocrine disruptors are natural and human-made chemicals that interfere with or mimic natural hormones that control development, growth, and behavior of organisms. The number of endocrine disruptors is unknown; only during the last decade has screening of chemicals begun to evaluate endocrine disrupting activity."

The conclusion of the USGS:

"It is likely that one or more combinations of chemicals, biological, and physical factors are responsible for causing the malformations in Minnesota frogs. Chemical combinations may be mixtures of natural and human-made organic chemicals, each of which is harmless on its own but toxic when combined. The number of possible combinations of chemicals, biological, and physical factors is enormous, which may explain why finding the causes for frog malformations has been a difficult task."

So, what we have here is official confirmation that frogs—in Minnesota, no less, where Don's encounter occurred—have been subjected to certain "factors" that have provoked bizarre and extraordinary mutations, such as extra eyes and limbs. In view of that, it may not be out of the question that gigantism may be the latest development in the strange saga of Minnesota's mutated frogs.

And, it should be noted that there is a precedent for accounts of huge and monstrous frogs, as Dr. Karl Shuker notes: "On 31 December 1945, an article penned by Harvard University herpetologist Arthur Loveridge was published in the zoological journal *Copeia*, concerning an attack some months earlier upon an askari (native policeman) at Tapili, Niangara, in what was then the Belgian Congo (later renamed Zaire, and now called the Democratic Republic of Congo). Loveridge's source of information concerning this incident was a Mr. C. Caseleyr, then Administrator of the Niangara Territory. The askari had come to Caseleyr to inform him that while walking by a pool earlier that evening, he had been bitten on one of his legs by what proved to be a very large frog—he'd lunged out at his attacker with a large club that he was carrying and had killed it outright. And as conclusive proof of his statement, the askari had brought with him the frog's body to show it to Caseleyr."

> //The number of possible combinations of chemicals, biological, and physical factors is enormous, which may explain why finding the causes for frog malformations has been a difficult task."

MONGOLIAN DEATH WORM

Known and feared by those who call the Gobi Desert their home, the Mongolian Death Worm is a beast that has become legendary in monster hunting circles. That, at least, is its westernized title. For the people of Mongolia, it's *Allergorhai horhai*, which translates into English as "intestine worm." Its distasteful and monstrous moniker is derived from eyewitnesses to the creature, who say that in physical appearance it resembles the stomach of a cow and is blood red in color. The Mongolian Death Worm can grow to a length of five feet, is as thick as a man's arm, and is best avoided at all costs. Indeed, it didn't get its memorable name without reason. In addition, it predominantly lives underground.

The creature has two ways in which it brings down its prey—which often includes people. It has the ability to spit, over distances of up to around twelve feet, an acid-like venom that can burn through clothing, skin, muscle, and right down to the bone, which causes the skin of the victim to turn a sickly, jaundice-like yellow. The coiling terror can also emit a powerful and fatal electric shock that—in a fashion not unlike an electric eel—kills or stuns its prey, thus allowing it to move in and partake of a good meal.

It was not until the mid-1920s that word of this hideous thing reached the west; prior to that time it was a case of what happens in the Gobi Desert stays in the Gobi Desert. The news that Mongolia was home to one of the most terrifying of all monsters came from one Professor Roy Chapman Andrews, who was not only the author of the 1926 book *On the Trail of Ancient Man*, but he was also the inspiration for one of Hollywood's most famous characters of the gung-ho kind, Indiana Jones. It was while seeking evidence of the presence of ancient man in Mongolia that Andrews heard some very weird tales about a certain deadly beast that lived below the sands.

In his book, Andrews said: "This is probably an entirely mythical animal, but it may have some little basis in fact, for every northern Mongol firmly believes in it and gives essentially the same description. It is said to be about two feet long, the body shaped like a sausage, and to have no head or legs; it is so poisonous that even to touch it means instant death. It is reported to live in the most arid, sandy regions of the western Gobi. What reptile could have furnished the basis for the description is a mystery!"

The next data of significance surfaced in 1967, when a Czech adventurer and explorer named Jaroslav Mareö learned of the monster's legendary and

An artist's interpretation of what the Mongolian Death Worm might look like.

lethal reputation. One source told Mareö: "My brother, living in Oboto Cha-jun aimak, knew of a man who encountered an *Allergorhai horhai*, one herds-man told me. His name was Atlan. Once he returned with a friend from a neighboring camp. They were riding their horses, and it was just after noon, one day in July. The sun was shining.

"Suddenly, Atlan's horse fell down. The rider stood up and went to the horse, but suddenly cried out and fell again. Atlan was five meters behind, and saw a big, fat worm slowly crawling away. Atlan stood in horror and then ran to his friend. But he was dead and so too was his horse."

A great deal more was learned about the Mongolian Death Worm in the summer of 1990. That's when a cryptozoologist named Ivan Mackerle trav-eled to one particular part of Mongolia: an area of desert southwest of Dalandzadgad. One of the U.K.'s most respected cryptozoologists, Richard Freeman, says of one particularly intriguing account that Mackerle uncovered:

"The expedition's interpreter, Sugi, told them of a dramatic incident from his childhood. A party of geologists had been visiting Sugi's home region. One of them was poking into the sand with an iron rod when he suddenly col-lapsed as it poleaxed. His colleagues rushed to his aid only to find him dead. As they examined the ground into which he had shoved, they saw the sand begin to churn violently. Out of the dune came a huge bloated death-worm."

Reports of the Mongolian Death Worm continue to surface periodical-ly, suggesting that one should be very careful when crossing the Gobi Desert, lest one has some warped desire to end up as the meal of a monster.

ROCK MONSTER

What was surely one of the strangest stories to ever grace the pages of a newspaper was that which appeared in the pages of the *Illustrated London News* on February 9, 1856. It is such a strange story that the only way to do it justice is to present it for you, today, as it appeared midway through the nine-teenth century:

"A discovery of great scientific importance has been made at Culmout (France). Some men employed in cutting a tunnel to unite the St. Dizier and Nancy Railways, has just thrown down an enormous block of stone by means of gunpowder, and were in the act of breaking it to pieces, when from a cavity in it they suddenly saw emerge a living being of monstrous form."

There then followed a detailed and amazing description of the beast:

"This creature, which belongs to the class of animals hitherto considered to be extinct, has a very long neck, and a mouth filled with sharp teeth. It

// This creature ... has a very long neck, and a mouth filled with sharp teeth. It stands on four legs, which are united together by two membranes...."

stands on four legs, which are united together by two membranes, doubtless intended to support the animal in the air, and are armed with four claws terminated by long and crooked talons. Its general form resembles that of a bat, differing only in its size, which is that of a large goose. Its membranous wings, when spread out, measure from tip to tip three meters twenty-two centimeters. Its color is a vivid black; its skin is naked; thick and oily; its intestines only contain a colorless liquid like clear water."

The unnamed journalist then proceeded to reveal what happened after the monster emerged from its confinement in the rock:

"On reaching the light the monster gave some signs of life, by shaking its wings, but soon expired, uttering a hoarse cry. This strange creature, to which may be given the name of a living fossil, has been brought to Grey, where a naturalist well versed in the study of paleontology, immediately recognized it as belonging to the genus Pterodactylanas."

While the story is as intriguing as it is both amazing and unlikely, nothing else ever surfaced on this curious affair. The *Illustrated London News* was not a publication known for planting spurious stories in its pages. So, true or not, the staff appear to have published it in good faith. Admittedly, however, the idea that such an animal could have survived, encased in rock, for who knows how long sounds unlikely.

There is another possibility: recall that the workmen were blasting one particular area of tunnel. Perhaps the great explosion did not—as the workmen thought—release the beast, after all. Maybe it was hiding in the same portion of the tunnel, doing its utmost to avoid the men. Then, when the blasting occurred it was their assumption that it was encased in the great stone, rather than—hypothetically—actually being in its near-vicinity, elsewhere in the tunnel. Granted, it's just a theory, but it does at least go some way to explaining the downright oddness of the tale.

ROPEN

Is it possible that, against all the odds, the presumed long-extinct pterosaurs of the Jurassic era are still with us? Did they survive extinction in some of the more remote and jungle-based environments? The questions are without doubt inflammatory. The answer to both questions, however, may well be an incredible "Yes!" While reports have surfaced all around the world—and for literally millennia—of large, unidentified winged creatures, there's no doubt that the most credible and enduring cases come from east of Papua New Guinea, specifically the islands of Rambutyo and Umboi. Locally, the beast is known as the Ropen. Its name translates to "Demon Flyer," a most apt title indeed.

Unlike the enormous pterodactyls of yesteryear, today's Ropen appears to be a scaled-down equivalent of its ancient ancestor. Its wingspan is often described as being in the region of four to six feet, which is not large for a pterosaur, since they were immense creatures. That does not stop today's equivalents from being formidable predators, however. By all accounts the Ropen has a mouth filled with vicious-looking fangs, a tail that is reptilian in appearance, and is a beast that can fly at fantastic speeds. Horrifically, it is said to deliberately target funeral processions on the island—due to the fact that its incredible sense of smell attracts it to the odor of decaying, putrid, human flesh. Ropens have also been reported attacking the boats of fishermen at sea, as a means to try and steal their catches of tasty fish.

Funerals and fishing-boat activity aside, the Ropen is largely a nocturnal animal, preferring to lurk in its mountainous cave lair during the day and hunt when the sun has set and darkness is upon the land. This is when the

Unlike a pterodactyl, the Ropen has a long, reptilian tail and teeth.

monster is at its most dangerous and deadly. The people of Rambutyo say that sightings, today, are far fewer in number than they were in decades past. That they may be on an evolutionary decline is not impossible. Nevertheless, reports still continue to surface.

One of the most diligent pursuers of the Ropen is Jonathan Whitcomb, the author of a full-length book on the subject, *Searching for Ropens: Living Pterosaurs in Papua New Guinea*. Whitcomb has taken the welcome, proactive approach of traveling to the area and speaking with the witnesses directly. That includes Gideon Koro, his brother, Wesley, and a friend of theirs, Mesa. In 1994, they were hiking in the vicinity of Lake Pung—which is known for its volcanic activity—when they saw a huge Ropen, one with a wingspan of around twenty feet, which is far more in accordance with the size of the pterosaurs of tens of millions of years ago. Its tail was long and it had a row of curious, prominent ridges running down the length of its back.

> **//The wings were the most definite leathery feature, they were shaped in a triangular arch, similar to a very elongated shark fin."**

Moving onto mainland Papua New Guinea, such reports surface from there too: unlike the beasts of both Umboi and Rambutyo, the Ropens of Papua New Guinea are almost always of the size reported by the Koro brothers. One of those fortunate enough to see such an immense beast was an American G.I. named Duane Hodgkinson. In 1944, as the Second World War still raged, Hodgkinson was stationed near Finschhafen, Papua New Guinea, when he saw something amazing and daunting. He said that, along with a friend in the military, "…we had the opportunity to witness a pterodactyl take off from the ground, and then circle back overhead, giving us a perfect view, which clearly showed the long beak and appendage protruding from the back of its head. It was a big one! I have a *Piper* aeroplane, which has a wing-spread of twenty-six feet, and it appeared to be about that size. The frequency of its wing flaps was estimated to be about one or two seconds. With each flap we could hear a loud swish, swish and the plants and brush immediately beneath its take off were deflected by the down rush of air."

Papua New Guinea: a real-life *Jurassic Park*? Just maybe, that's *exactly* what it is.

It's worth noting that Papua New Guinea is not at all far from Australia. In light of this, we might consider relevant and related the story of a married couple from Perth, Australia, who, in December 1997, had an encounter with something that sounded like one of the Papua New Guinea monsters, but on the Perth coastline. The wife, Penny, said:

"Within a minute or so it had reached our position and was about 250 or 300 feet above us and slightly inland. The area was moderately well lit and I saw that it seemed to be a light reddish-tan color. It did not appear to be covered with feathers but had a leathery texture. Soon after it passed us it flew over a more brightly lit area which highlighted even more the leathery appearance also bringing more detail to view. The wings were the most definite leathery feature, they were shaped in a triangular arch, similar to a very elongated shark fin. The body also still appeared leathery, though textured as though possibly covered with fine hair or small scales, the distance preventing any finer observation than that it was slightly different texture than the wings. The shape of the body was a streamlined torpedo shape, slightly broadest at the chest and tapering slightly back to the hip, then tapering more quickly after the hips to a moderately thin tail which was slightly longer than the body."

Incredibly, the wingspan of the flying monster was in the region of *thirty feet.*

SUPER-SIZED SNAKE OF SPRING VALLEY

A sixty-foot-long, deadly snake roaming around California? It sounds incredible, and yet that is precisely the story that came out of Spring Valley, California, in the summer of 1868. The story was told in the pages of the *Calaveras Chronicle* newspaper, whose staff said:

"On the 12th of August, 1868, the serpent was first seen in the vicinity of Zane's ranch, near Spring Valley. Several persons—reputable people—saw the monster on two or three occasions, but always at a considerable distance—never nearer than a quarter of a mile. The reptile created the most intense excitement in the neighborhood, and at one time the getting up of a party to hunt it down was strongly agitated.

"What were then thought to be the most extravagant stories regarding the size of the serpent were told, but recent events prove that the truth was not exaggerated. The snake was seen in an open field in broad daylight, and described as 'being from forty to sixty feet long, and as large around as a barrel.' The mark of the monster in the dust where it crossed the road bore witness to its immense proportions. There was a difference of opinion regarding its method of locomotion, some maintaining that it progressed by drawing itself into immense folds, after the manner of a caterpillar, while others were equally certain that its motion was similar to others of the ophidian family.

"The serpent disappeared for several months, and was seen by Mr. W. P. Peek, of this place, while coming up the hill from the Gwin mine. Mr. Peek was driving a two horse team and had got about half way up the steep hill that

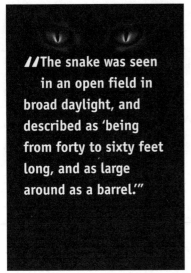

//The snake was seen in an open field in broad daylight, and described as 'being from forty to sixty feet long, and as large around as a barrel.'"

has to be ascended in leaving the mine, when he heard what he supposed to be the loud 'screeching' noise sometimes made by a wagon brake. Certain that a team was coming down the grade, and being in a favorable place for passing, he turned out of the road.

"After waiting until out of patience, and no team appearing, he drove on. He had gone but a short distance when a movement in the dense chaparral that lined the road, attracted his attention, and, advancing in the direction, he was horrified by the sight of a portion of the body of an immense serpent. At the same time his horse became unmanageable, and while Mr. Peek's utmost endeavors were put forth to prevent the escape of the frightened team, the monarch moved slowly off into the brush, making the hissing sound he had mistaken for the brake of an approaching wagon.

"About a year subsequently the serpent was seen by a couple of boys in the vicinity of Mosquito, the youths being so badly frightened that they could scarcely reach home and tell the story. Such is briefly the story of the Calaveras serpent up to Saturday of last week, when the experiences had with it at once settled all doubts as to its reality, and fix the fact beyond question that one of the largest boas of which we have knowledge has its residence in this county."

THETIS LAKE MAN-REPTILE

Nineteen seventy-two was the year in which the people of Thetis Lake, British Columbia, Canada, found themselves thrust into a saga of monstrous proportions—as in literally monstrous proportions. On August 19, two young men, Robin Flewellyn and Gordon Pile, encountered a scaly, humanoid monster that looked like the deadly, fictional beast of the 1954 Universal movie *Creature from the Black Lagoon*. Rather oddly for something that seemed reptilian in nature, the monster was silver in color. And, the pair didn't just encounter the thing: they were chased by it, too. Fortunately, despite its attempts to clearly try and injure or kill them, the friends managed to avoid its deadly clutches and headed for the nearest police station. Such was the state of fear into which Flewellyn and Pile had been plunged, that the police considered their story to be a true one.

It was a story bolstered by the fact that four days later the monster was seen again—and also at Thetis Lake, except that this time the thing was roaming around the opposite side of the lake. The witnesses were Michael Gold and Russell Van Nice, who confirmed the silver color of the creature, the scaly skin, and that it appeared to have a spike—or spikes—protruding from the top of its head.

Flewellyn and Pile said the monster looked like the one from the 1954 movie *Creature from the Black Lagoon.*

One day later, the story was big news: it was covered in the pages of the *Victoria Times*, along with a graphic drawing of the monster of Thetis Lake. Interest and concern were growing. Perhaps in an effort to try and lay the matter to rest, and to ensure that concern didn't erupt into full-blown hysteria, the police maintained—and maintained very quickly—that they had solved the affair. What the witnesses had seen, the police assured the media and the local population, was nothing stranger than an escaped pet tegu lizard. Cryptozoologist Dr. Karl Shuker made an important comment on this most unlikely scenario:

"Native to South America, tegus can grow up to four feet long, but are not bipedal or humanoid in shape, do not have crests, are not silver in color, have typical five-toed, lizard-like feet as opposed to three-toed flippers, do not have a fish-like mouth, but do have a very long, noticeable tail (unlike the Thetis Lake monster)."

Shuker adds: "Not surprisingly, given the considerable morphological discrepancies noted above, investigators of this case do not share the police's enthusiasm for accepting a tegu as the Thetis Lake monster's identity."

Lake, River, and Ocean Menaces

ATTACKING THE *PAULINE*

On January 18, 1875, the *Pauline* was sailing twenty miles off Cape Rogue, on the northeastern side of Brazil, when, at around 11:00 A.M., something remarkable occurred, as George Drevar, the master of the *Pauline*, made abundantly clear, in a carefully prepared report. It's a fascinating, historical document that deserves to be presented in its entirety:

"The weather fine and clear, the wind and sea moderate. Observed some black spots on the water, and a whitish pillar, about thirty-five feet high, above them [sic]. At the first glance I took all to be breakers, as the sea was splashing up fountain-like about them, and the pillar, a pinnacle rock bleached with the sun; but the pillar fell with a splash, and a similar one rose. They rose and fell alternately in quick succession, and good glasses showed me it was a monster sea-serpent coiled twice round a large sperm whale.

"The head and tail parts, each about thirty feet long, were acting as levers, twisting itself and victim around with great velocity. They sank out of sight about every two minutes, coming to the surface still revolving, and the struggles of the whale and two other whales that were near, frantic with excitement, made the sea in this vicinity like a boiling cauldron; and a loud and confused noise was distinctly heard.

"This strange occurrence lasted some fifteen minutes, and finished with the tail portion of the whale being elevated straight in the air, then waving

The crew of the *Pauline* witnessed a sea serpent attacking a whale (illustration based on a sketch by the ship's chaplain).

backwards and forwards, and … [lashing] the water furiously in the last death-struggle, when the whole body disappeared from our view, going down head-foremost towards the bottom, where, no doubt, it was gorged at the serpent's leisure; and that monster of monsters may have been many months in a state of coma, digesting the huge mouthful.

"Then two of the largest sperm whales that I have ever seen moved slowly thence towards the vessel, their bodies more than usually elevated out of the water, and not spouting or making the least noise, but seeming quite paralyzed with fear; indeed, a cold shiver went through my own frame on beholding the last agonizing struggle of the poor whale that had seemed as helpless in the coils of the vicious monster as a small bird in the talons of a hawk. Allowing for two coils round the whale, I think the serpent was about one hundred and sixty or one hundred and seventy feet long, and seven or eight in girth. It was in colour much like a conger eel, and the head, from the mouth being always open, appeared the largest part of the body. I think Cape San Roque is a landmark for whales leaving the south for the North Atlantic.

"I wrote thus far, little thinking I would ever see the serpent again; but at 7 A.M., July 13th, in the same latitude, and some eighty miles east of San Roque, I was astonished to see the same or a similar monster. It was throwing its head and about forty feet of its body in a horizontal position out of the water as it passed onwards by the stern of our vessel. I began musing why we were so much favored with such a strange visitor, and concluded that the band of white paint, two feet wide above the copper, might have looked like a fellow-serpent to it, and, no doubt, attracted its attention.

"While thus thinking, I was startled by the cry of 'There it is again,' and a short distance to leeward, elevated some sixty feet in the air, was the great leviathan, grimly looking towards the vessel. As I was not sure it was only our free board it was viewing, we had all our axes ready, and were fully determined, should the brute embrace the *Pauline*, to chop away for its backbone with all our might, and the wretch might have found for once in its life that it had caught a Tartar. This statement is strictly true, and the occurrence was witnessed by my officers, half the crew, and myself; and we are ready, at any time, to testify on oath that it is so, and that we are not in the least mistaken. A vessel, about three years ago, was dragged over by some sea-monster in the Indian Ocean."

BIG WALLY

On November 5, 1885, the *Wallowa Chieftain* newspaper ran an article on its resident monster, which has been given the distinctly non-monstrous name of "Big Wally." It is said to dwell in Wallowa Lake, Oregon, an approximately fifty-one-square-mile body of water with a depth of around 300 feet (91.4 meters). The article states:

"A prospector, who refuses to give his name to the public, was coming down from the south end of the lake on last Friday evening in a skiff shortly after dusk, when about midway of the lake he saw an animal about fifty yards [45.7 meters] to the right of the boat, rear its head and neck up out of the water ten or twelve feet, but on setting him it immediately dived. He ceased rowing and gazed around in astonishment, for the strange apparition which he had just seen, when it raised about the same distance to the left, this lime [sic] giving a low bellow something like that of a cow. It also brought its body to the surface, which the prospector avers was one hundred feet in length. The monster glided along in sight for several hundred yards. It was too dark to see the animal distinctly, but it seemed to have a large, flat head, something like that of a hippopotamus, and its neck, which was about ten feet in length, was as large around as a man's body.

"Now this story may have been coined in the imagination of the narrator, but he was very earnest in his recital. However, it is a known fact that there is a tradition among the Indians that the lake has a big sea cow in it, which on one occasion, many years ago, came up one evening and swallowed a young warrior and his dusky bride as they were gliding over the surface of the lake in a canoe. And to this day an Indian of the tribes who formerly frequented its shores cannot be induced to go upon its waters. The lake has been sounded to the depth of 270 feet [82.3 meters], and it is a bare probability that some monster does inhabit its unexplored depths."

It's unlikely that this was a hoax—on, or by, the newspaper—as other reports have since surfaced. In 1978, a couple with the

Wallowa Lake, with the town of Joseph in the distance, is seen from the top of Mt. Howard.

last name of Bryant saw Big Wally on not just one occasion but two! On the first occasion, they saw three hump-like protrusions break the surface of the lake, albeit briefly. Some months later, the Bryant watched an approximately twenty-foot-long, snake-like animal circle a certain portion of the lake for several minutes. Three years later, Bert Repplinger and Joe Babic were amazed by the brief sight of a three-foot-long head and neck that broke the surface of Lake Wallowa. While the number of sightings of Big Wally is scarcely anywhere near the likes of some of its far more famous cousins, the fact that occasional reports continue to surface is a fairly good indication that the lake is home to something unusual. Exactly what it may be, however, remains unknown.

BLOOP

It's rare that a story of a monster crosses paths with the world of conspiracy. But, that's exactly what happened when it came to the matter of a mysterious creature—or, rather, an alleged mysterious creature—said to have surfaced in the 1990s. It quickly became the subject of U.S. Navy interest. To fully understand the controversy, it's necessary to go back in time to the 1960s, when the Cold War was still in full force. It was in that decade that the Navy established a top secret program known as SOSUS. It stood for Sound Surveillance System. Essentially, it was a vast network of underwater microphones that spanned much of the planet and were designed to monitor for Russian submarines—and particularly so those that were equipped with atomic weapons. Today, the Cold War is over. The world, however, is still a dangerous place. Maybe even more so than back in the old days when we had only one enemy to worry about: the Soviets. As a result, the SOSUS detectors still exist, picking up on sound waves in what is termed the Deep Sound Channel.

It's not just Russian (and, today, Chinese) subs that the U.S. military has recorded on its SOSUS equipment. Ships, earth tremors, and even whales have been detected by the highly sophisticated technology. Its technology that has been significantly improved upon since the old days and which is now overseen by the National Oceanic and Atmospheric Administration (NOAA), which is a section of the government's Department of Commerce. All of which brings us to a certain, deeply puzzling, event that occurred in 1997. That was the year in which NOAA recorded a very weird, and very large, "something" in the waters of the South Pacific Ocean, west of South America's most southern tip.

Whatever "it" was, it certainly caught the attention of NOAA and the military, who nicknamed the anomaly "Bloop." Whatever Bloop was, he, she, or it was of a certain amplitude to be picked up on tracking equipment more than 5,000 kilometers from where its movements were recorded. More intriguing, within both NOAA and the Navy there were those who suspected the signature was suggestive of Bloop being a massive, unknown animal, such as a squid of unparalleled proportions. One might even be justified in saying something akin to H. P. Lovecraft's Cthulhu or the legendary Kraken.

Needless to say, the controversy surrounding Bloop attracted a great deal of interest. One of those who took a great deal of interest in the matter was a man named Phil Lobel. He was a marine biologist based at Boston University. Although Lobel was admittedly doubtful of the hypothesis that Bloop was a huge squid, he did not dismiss the possibility of it being something living. In fact, Lobel suggested it probably was some form of animal.

When the media latched onto the story, NOAA admitted that this was far from being the first occasion upon which such anomalies—which may well have been giant, unknown animals—had been detected in the world's oceans. Each and every one of them had been given specific names, including Whistle, Upsweep, Train, and Slowdown. As for NOAA's stance on the matter of Bloop today, the prevailing theory within the agency is that Bloop was nothing weirder than a large iceberg that was beginning to collapse, and which provoked the sounds that were recorded and provoked so much debate. True or not, the legend of Bloop lives on, still giving hope to some that Cthulhu is something more than just fiction.

BUNYIP

A creature believed by many to have supernatural—and perhaps even hellish—origins, the Bunyip is a monster that lurks within the creeks and swamps of Australia, and which has been known to the Aboriginal people for centuries, maybe even longer. As for its appearance, in 1845 the *Geelong Advertiser* told its readers:

"The Bunyip, then, is represented as uniting the characteristics of a bird and of an alligator. It has a head resembling an emu, with a long bill, at the extremity of which is a transverse projection on each side, with serrated edges like the bone of the stingray. Its body and legs partake of the nature of the alligator. The hind legs are remarkably thick and strong, and the fore legs are much longer, but still of great strength. The extremities are furnished with long claws, but the blacks say its usual method of killing its prey is by hugging it to death. When in the water it swims like a frog, and when on shore it walks on its hind legs with its head erect, in which position it measures twelve or thirteen feet in height."

One of the most fascinating reports of an encounter with a Bunyip came from a man who has taken on near-legendary status in Australia. His name was William Buckley. Born in Cheshire, England, in 1780, Buckley was an unforgettable and imposing figure, who stood at around six feet eight inches and had a head of wild, long, black hair. He enlisted in the King's Foot Regiment and fought against the army of none other than Napoleon Bonaparte. In what was certainly a miscarriage of justice, Buckley was found guilty of theft and given a sentence of fourteen years. Buckley was shipped off to Australia to serve his time in jail, but not for long. In December 1803, Buckley managed to escape and, as a result, spent an incredible thirty years living with the Wathaurung Aborigines and, in doing so, took two wives. In July 1835, Buckley finally came out of hiding and was soon thereafter pardoned for the crime that never was.

The nineteenth-century heroic figure William Buckley was a legend in Australia. Among his many adventures was an encounter with a bunyip.

Then in 1852, a man named John Morgan wrote a celebrated and highly entertaining book on Buckley. The very appropriate title was *Life and Adventures of William Buckley*. One of the highlights of the book was Buckley's claim to Morgan that while living in the wilds of Australia, he encountered a bunyip. Buckley told his chronicler:

"We next went about forty miles, I should think, to a place they call Kironamaat; there is near to it a lake about ten miles in circumference. It took us several days to accomplish this march, as we hunted all the way; we halted near a well of fresh water, the lake being brackish, and there was a great plain near us. We here made nets with strips of bark, and caught with them great quantities of shrimps. We lived very sumptuously and in peace for many months at this place, and then went to the borders of another lake, called Moodewarri: the water of which was perfectly fresh, abounding in large eels, which we caught in great abundance.

"In this lake, as well as in most of the others inland, and in the deep water rivers, is a very extraordinary amphibious animal, which the natives call Bunyip, of which I could never see any part, except the back, which appeared to be covered with feathers of a dusky grey color. It seemed to be about the size of a full grown calf, and sometimes larger; the creatures only appear when the weather is very calm, and the water smooth. I could never learn from any of the natives that they had seen either the head or tail, so that I could not form a correct idea of their size; or what they were like."

Buckley continued: "Here, the Bunyip—the extraordinary animals I have already mentioned—were often seen by the natives, who had a great dread of them, believing them to have some supernatural power over human beings, so as to occasion death, sickness, disease, and such like misfortunes. They have also a superstitious notion that the great abundance of eels in some of the lagoons where animals resort, are ordered for the Bunyip's provision; and they therefore seldom remain long in such neighborhoods after having seen the creature.

"When alone, I several times attempted to spear a Bunyip; but, had the natives seen me do so, it would have caused great displeasure. And again, if I had succeeded in killing or even wounding one, my own life would probably have paid forfeit—they considering the animal, as I have already said, something supernatural."

The Australian office of the Centre for Fortean Zoology notes the following, on this very unusual animal:

"Naturalist George French Angas collected a description of a bunyip as a 'water spirit' from the Moorundi people of the Murray River before 1847, stating it was 'much dreaded by them.... It inhabits the Murray; but ... they have some difficulty describing it. Its most usual form ... is said to be that of an enormous starfish.' Robert Brough Smyth's *Aborigines of Victoria* of 1878 devoted ten pages to the bunyip, but concluded 'in truth little is known among the blacks respecting its form, covering or habits; they appear to have been in such dread of it as to have been unable to take note of its characteristics.'"

The Centre for Fortean Zoology notes that although the Australian Aborigines believed the Bunyip was a monster of

An 1890 illustration of what a Bunyip supposedly looks like.

supernatural proportions (and still believe that to be the case), there may be a more down-to-earth explanation: "In many 19th-century newspaper accounts the bunyip was variously attributed a dog-like face, dark fur, a horse-like tail, flippers, and walrus-like tusks or horns or a duck-like bill. Many modern-day researchers now believe the descriptions may have referred to seals or walruses, or even a cultural memory of megafauna such as the diprotodon."

Whatever the truth of the Bunyip, the legend and lore that surrounds it is, today, as robust as it always has been.

CADDY

A Nessie-like creature, Caddy—an abbreviation of *Cadborosaurus willsi*—has struck a deep chord with the people of Cadboro Bay, British Columbia, Canada. It's a chord with a long history. For the skeptics, sightings of the Caddies can be explained away as whales, sharks, sea-lions, and serpent-like oarfish. Not everyone, however, is quite so sure that the monsters of Cadboro Bay can be dismissed quite so easily. Take, for example, the 1933 encounter of two duck hunters, Cyril Andrews and Norman Georgeson. They were in the bay's Gowlland Head. What began as a duck hunt rapidly changed into something very different, as Andrews noted, when he went public with the story shortly afterwards:

"I succeeded in shooting a golden-eye duck, but as I had only broken its wing, it began swimming to a kelp bed about fifty yards from shore. Seeing I could not get the wounded bird I sent Norman home for a small punt, five feet long. Returning, he was paddling across the bay towards me as I walked over a little rise to see if he was coming. As I looked across the water I heard a disturbance some distance out. From where I was standing I could plainly see the whole body of a sea monster just moving a foot underneath the surface.

"Thinking I might alarm Norman I did not draw his attention to what I saw, so he came along and picked me up at the point from which we had shot the bird. From there we paddled to the wounded bird in the kelp bed. I was sitting in front of the punt ready to pick the bird up, when about ten feet away from it, out of the sea rose two coils. They reached a height of at least six feet above me, gradually sinking under the water again, when a head appeared. The head was that of a horse, without ears or nostrils, but its eyes were in front of its head, which was flat just like a horse.

"I attracted Georgeson's attention to it and he saw one coil and the head well clear of the water. Then the whole thing, except the head, which remained out of the water, sank. I was still only ten feet away from it, with the duck right beside the thing, when to my horror it gulped the bird down its throat. It then looked at me, its mouth wide open, and I could plainly see its teeth and tongue, which were those of a fish. I would swear to the head being three feet long and two feet wide. When it closed its mouth, all the loose skin folded in neatly at the corners while its breathing came in short, sharp pants, like a dog after a run. At that point a number of seagulls swooped down at the creature, which snapped at them when they came too close. Shortly after this it sank beneath the surface."

It's important to note there were other witnesses, too. Georgeson and Andrews wasted no time in contacting the local Justice of the Peace, G. F. Parkyn, who prepared a detailed affidavit for the pair. In addition, the monster soon returned and was actually seen by an astonished Parkyn himself, along with eleven others. Yet again, it was fiercely and furiously snapping at the local seagulls.

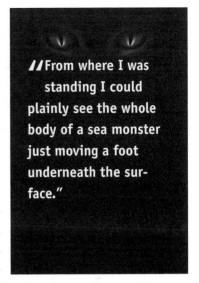

// From where I was standing I could plainly see the whole body of a sea monster just moving a foot underneath the surface."

CHAMP

Located on the U.S.–Canadian border, and covering parts of Vermont, Quebec, and New York, Lake Champlain has long been the reputed domain of a huge serpent known as Champ. Indeed, reports extend back more than 150 years. Certainly, one of the most fascinating developments in the story of Champ occurred in 1881. That was the year in which a huge skeleton was unearthed by one H. H. Burge. Of this sensational discovery, the May 27, 1881, issue of the *Middlebury Register* reported:

"The proprietors of the Champlain Granite Works, located near Barn Rock on Lake Champlain claim to have uncovered a petrified sea serpent of mammoth proportions, being about 8 inches in diameter and nearly fifty feet long. The surface of the stone bears evidence of the outer skin of a large serpent while the inner surface shows the entrails. The proprietors are intending soon to begin excavations along the place where it lies embedded in the dirt and granite, to ascertain its size."

Additional data surfaced on June 8 of the following year, 1882, in the *Elizabeth Town Post & Gazette*:

"The report of finding a monster in the limestone deposit of the 'North Shore' I heard many times and considered it a story originating with someone anxious to be the author of a sensation. Last summer, a party, part of whom were scientific gentlemen by education and profession called at the cottage and almost demanded admission to the apartments of the monster. The Superintendent was busy at the time superintending his many laborers engaged in the quarry, and told the gentlemen he could not leave his business and go down to the house, and furthermore, he was not prepared to exhibit what he had found, as there was so little of it, but at some time in the future he would be glad to show to all his serpent. I had heard the above from one of the party, and made my mind up to say nothing of the serpent when I went there. Just about to bid the good folks good-day, the Superintendent said: 'I am not in show business, as many have thought, neither am I showing snakes, but I have something to show you.'

"On the carpet in an upper room lay six or seven feet in length, pieces of an enormous petrified snake. Some portions were six inches long and some fifteen or more. The pieces were placed together and fitted so nicely that was no room for doubt of their having been broken apart. The largest end was

Champ has become such a popular legend in Vermont that a minor league baseball team called the Vermont Lake Monsters adopted it as the official mascot.

eight or nine inches in diameter, and only three or four feet from the terminal of the entrails, and two or three feet beyond. The entrails were petrified, but much darker and quite open or porous and containing many bright and glistening crystals. The vertebra was visible at each broken end, and the flesh part showed traces of what had at one time been veins.

"The skin was readily distinguished from the flesh as would have been had the monster been cut in two whilst living. After an examination of each piece, and comparing the gradual enlargement of the cavity, thickness of flesh and skin on the belly, and the gradual thickening towards the back, left no room in my mind to entertain the thought that it was an accident or freak of nature with molten rock. During this hour of examination at the south side of the window with bright sunlight, the Superintendent had sat quietly and had said nothing but answer a very few questions. I said I did not want to be inquisitive, but would like to know in what kind of rock he was found and his general position. He said he was not in the rock but was merely attached to the limestone, and his position was as if he had placed himself for rest or sleep, and he had traced his body by actual measurement over sixty feet, and his weight to several tons when all removed. The portions the Superintendent has removed he has secured alone, but will be obliged to have help in getting the remainder or leave the monster to rest in his slumber of death. When the proper time comes the scientific men of different localities will be called upon to make an examination and publish to the world their verdict."

Famous circus owner P. T. Barnum is said to have bought and displayed a specimen of the lake creature, but it later disappeared without a trace.

Cryptozoologist Richard Freeman, who has taken a deep, personal interest in this particularly intriguing saga, says: "The remains are next mentioned in *The Burlington Free Press* of November 4th 1886 and, apparently, were on show at a bank-sponsored exhibition held in Vergennes, Vermont. They were subsequently purchased by the famous showman P. T. Barnum (1810–1891) for his museum. From then on the specimen seems to have vanished. Searches of Barnum's records have so far been fruitless. Barnum's collections were twice ravaged by fire but both of these incidents were before he bought the remains."

Freeman asks the questions: "What was the skeleton? Some kind of fossil?"

He answers the question himself: "The strata around Lake Champlain is too young for dinosaurs or their contemporary marine reptiles. Archaeocetes are also much too old for the strata. The only fossil whales that have been uncovered in the area are modern species such as the beluga (*Delphinapterus leucas*). The presence of skin and soft organs is unusual. These are only preserved under exceptional circumstances. This raises the possibility that it was a sub-fossil or in other words fairly recent in origin."

DRAGONS OF THE DEEP

Afascinating and harrowing encounter with a monster of the oceans occurred on May 30, 1903, and involved highly credible individuals. They were Captain W. H. Bartlett, Second Officer Joseph Ostens Grey, and the rest of the crew of the cargo steamer *Tresco*. Captain Bartlett and his crew had sailed from Philadelphia just forty-eight hours earlier. All was well and completely normal—for a while, at least. When they reached a point around ninety miles off of Cape Hatteras, however, the crew noticed that the water appeared decidedly disturbed and inexplicably oily. High strangeness was afoot.

Suddenly, and rather incredibly, a group of around three to four dozen sharks were seen racing through the waters, almost as if something terrifying and deadly was in hot pursuit. It turns out that was exactly what was going on. And, it must be said, there are very few things that frighten sharks! Shortly afterwards, and at a distance, the crew saw what they first took to be a boat, possibly one that had capsized and with the bottom of the hull protruding out of the water. A boat it was not. That much was in evidence when a huge head and neck surfaced from the water, revealing that what the crew had encountered was a huge animal of a distinctly unknown and massive kind. An understanding of the sheer size of the leviathan can be gained from the description of the neck. It was, said Captain Bartlett, "as thick as a cathedral pillar."

> An understanding of the sheer size of the leviathan can be gained from the description of the neck. It was, said Captain Bartlett, "as thick as a cathedral pillar."

As the crew tentatively closed in, they were astonished to see that the monster most closely resembled a classic dragon of ancient Chinese lore and mythology! What was perceived to be nothing stranger than a legend just might have been something else entirely. It was described as being in excess of 100 feet in length, had a width of around eight feet, and had a pair of wing-like protuberances, one on each side of its long body. The entire body was scaly and green in color—further amplifying the dragon-like associations. The most detailed and amazing description came from Second Officer Grey, who had the good presence of mind to quickly write the details down as soon as the encounter was over. He committed the following to paper:

"There was something unspeakably loathsome about the head, which was five feet long from nose to upper extremity. Such a head I never saw on any denizen of the sea. Underneath the jaw seemed to be a sort of pouch, or drooping skin. The nose, like a snout upturned, was somewhat recurved. I can remember seeing no nostrils or blow-holes. The lower jaw was prognathous, and the lower lip was half projecting, half pendulous. Presently I noticed something dripping from the ugly lower jaw. Watching I saw it was saliva, of a dirty drab color. While it displayed no teeth, it did possess very long and formidable molars, like a walrus's tusks. Its eyes were of a reddish color. They were elongated vertically. They carried in their dull depths a somber baleful glow, as if within them was concentrated all the fierce menacing spirit that raged in the huge bulk behind."

Clearly aware it was being watched, the dragon made a menacing warning in the direction of the crew: it violently thrashed its tail in the water for a few moments, which shook the boat in a precarious fashion. Fortunately, and evidently, when the monster was done and satisfied that it had made its point, it sank beneath the waves, never to be seen again by the crew of the *Tresco*.

GALVESTON SEA SERPENT

It's not often that one sees a story of a giant monster splashed across the front page of the *New York Times*! That, however, is exactly what happened on July 1, 1908. The article was headlined: "200-FOOT SEA SERPENT. Seen at 3 Bells in Gulf of Mexico—Enormous Rattles on Its Tail." *Times* staff said:

"What is confidently believed to be a sea serpent has been sighted and narrowly inspected by the officers crew, and fifteen passengers of the steamship *Livingstone* of the Texas-Mexican Line. All of the witnesses made a sworn affidavit to this effect before United States Consular Agent Charles W. Rickland at Frontera, Mexico.

"The statement is signed by Capt. G. A. Olsen and the other officers, George Thomas of Denver, Albert Dean of Memphis, H. B. Stoddard of Bryan, Texas, Mrs. Jessie Thornton of Chicago, and eleven other passengers. In substance it declares that at three bells on the evening of June 24, the *Livingstone*, bound from Galveston to Frontera, Mexico, making good weather, and about fifty miles north of Frontera, in the Gulf of Mexico, the serpent was sighted off the port bow.

"The ship got within sixty feet of the creature, and for fifteen minutes stood while all on board viewed the serpent through the glasses. It was apparently sleeping, and not less than 200 feet long, of about the diameter of a flour barrel in the centre of the body, but was not as round. The head was about six feet long by three feet at the widest part.

"The color was dark brown, and near its tail were rings or circles that appeared larger in circumference than the body at that point. As it swam away the tail was erected, and a rattling noise as loud as that made by a gatling gun in action startled the watchers on the *Livingstone*."

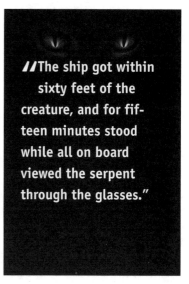

//The ship got within sixty feet of the creature, and for fifteen minutes stood while all on board viewed the serpent through the glasses."

GIANT EEL OF BIRMINGHAM

As is the case with practically every investigator of the unknown, I am sure, occasionally I am on the receiving end of stories, tales, and accounts that sound great, but where the person relating the data insists on either complete or partial anonymity. Of course, such tales can be very interesting indeed; but, equally, they can be extremely frustrating, too. Primarily, this is because at the end of the day, without hard evidence that the person really is who he or she claims to be, very little can be done with the story in terms of investigating it and/or validating it, aside from keeping it on file, and hoping that by making it public—as I'm doing now—it may encourage others to come forward. And the strange story that follows is a classic example.

It comes from a man who claims to be a retired British police constable, who has personal knowledge of a story of truly monstrous proportions, and which focuses on dark goings-on after sunset in the British city of Birmingham in the late 1970s and early 1980s. For what it's worth, here's the tale.

According to the man, who identified himself only by the surname of Sykes, while serving in the British Police Force (service that, he said, began in 1977 and ended in 1988), he heard two tales from colleagues of giant eels seen in the winding canals that run through the city of Birmingham—both of which occurred, he thought, around 1979 or 1980. In both cases, the witnesses had reported seeing very large creatures—the first, amazingly, around twenty feet in length, and both "very dark" in color. Needless to say, if the physical details described in the first encounter were not exaggerations on the part of the witness, then it was, without a shadow of a doubt, a definitive monster.

around the same ••• time that the eels were seen, there had been a spate of mysterious disappearances of pet rabbits in the area.

Notably, Sykes said that although he was not the investigating officer in either case, he recalled that around the same time that the eels were seen, there had been a spate of mysterious disappearances of pet rabbits in the area. And while some of Sykes's colleagues had attributed this to the work of sadists and nutcases, there had been brief talk at the station that "it was the eels' doing."

And there was one other, and very ominous, story that Sykes recalled and related to me as I listened intently. At the height of the rabbit disappearances and the two eel encounters, someone had contacted the Police Station Sykes was working at with a remarkable tale. "It was a local lad, in his twenties; I remember that much," said Sykes. "He hadn't been long married and had just bought a house around here." According to the story-teller, the man had quickly phoned the police after hearing a huge commotion in his small backyard in the early hours of one particular morning.

The wooden fence at the foot of the yard had been partially smashed down; a large area of grass had been flattened and something had broken into his rabbit hutch, utterly destroying it in the process. Needless to say, by the time the man got downstairs and into the yard, there was no sign of the unknown intruder—and, unfortunately, there was no sign of the rabbits, either.

Continuing his tale, Sykes wondered out loud if the eels, hungry for food, had elected to stealthily leave the confines of the canal and had, under the protective cover of overwhelming darkness, slithered around the yards of the nearby homes in search of a tasty rabbit or several. Well, it was as good a theory as any, I thought. And, it was pretty disturbing too, to think that such beasts might secretly be on the loose in a sprawling, industrialized city like Birmingham, and mercilessly prowling the area by night.

As far as Sykes knew, this particularly weird and unsettling incident was never resolved. No more sightings surfaced, and a rigorous search of the canal failed to find anything conclusive at all. And that, in essence, was the tale. Without a doubt, it's one that is fascinating, outrageous, and bizarre in equal measures. And taking into consideration the amount of time that has gone by since the events allegedly occurred, it's unfortunately difficult to prove any-thing with any high degree of certainty. That is, unless anyone reading this knows more.

GLOUCESTER SEA SERPENT

Sightings of so-called sea serpents abound within the domain of monster hunting. More often than not, they are encounters of a fleeting, one-time nature. But not always. One of the most enduring of all such leviathans of the deep is that which haunts the port of Gloucester, Massachusetts, which is situated just north of the city of Boston.

So far as can be determined, the earliest report dates from 1638. The writer was a man named John Josselyn, who said: "They told me of a sea ser-pent, or snake, that lay quoiled [sic] up like a cable upon the rock at Cape Ann; a boat passing by with English on board, and two Indians, they would have shot the serpent, but the Indians dissuaded them, saying that if he were not killed outright, they would all be in danger of their lives."

One year later, Obadiah Turner wrote of the mighty beast, in old-time style and spelling: "Some being on ye great beache gathering of calms and seaweed wch had been cast thereon by ye mightie storm did spy a most wonderful serpent a shorte way off from ye shore. He was big round in ye thickest part as a wine pipe; and they do affirm that he was fifteen fathoms more in length. A most wonderful tale. But ye witnesses be credible, and it would be of no account to them to tell an untrue tale. Wee have likewise heard yt Cape Ann ye people have seene a monster like unto this, whch did there come out of ye land mch to ye terror of them yt did see him."

Moving on to 1817, we have the following notable report from Amos Story: "It was between the hours of twelve and one o'clock when I first saw him, and he continued in sight for an hour and a half. I was setting on the shore, and was about twenty rods from him when he was the nearest to me. His head appeared shaped much like that of the sea turtle, and he carried his head from ten to twelve inches above the surface of the water. His head at that distance appeared larger than the head of any dog I ever saw. From the back of his head to the next part of him that was visible, I should judge to be three or four feet. He moved very rapidly through the water, I should say a mile or two or, at most, in three minutes. I saw no bunches on his back. On this day, I did not see more than ten or twelve feet of his body."

Story's account was swiftly followed by that of Solomon Allen III, a shipmaster. He said of the incredible beast he spied: "His head formed some-

This illustration depicts a sighting of the Gloucester Sea Serpent in 1817.

thing like the head of a rattlesnake, but nearly as large as the head of horse. When he moved on the surface of the water his motion was slow, at times playing in circles, and sometimes moving straight forward."

A particularly detailed account came days later from one Cheever Felch, whose sighting of the Gloucester Sea Serpent was made when he, Felch, was aboard a U.S. schooner, the *Science*. He said of the monstrous thing:

"His color is dark brown with white under his throat. His size we could not accurately ascertain, but his head is about three feet in circumference, flat and much smaller than his body. We did not see his tail; but from the end of the head to the farthest protuberance was not far from one hundred feet. I speak with a degree of certainty, behind much accustomed to measure and estimate distances and length. I counted fourteen bunches on his back, the first one say ten or twelve feet from this head, and the others about seven feet apart. They decreased in size towards the tail. These bunches were sometimes counted with and sometimes without a glass. Mr. Malborne counted thirteen, Mr. Blake thirteen and fourteen, and the boatman the same number.... His motion was partly vertical and partly horizontal, like that of fresh water snakes. I have been much acquainted with snakes in our interior waters. His motion was the same."

And still the reports kept on coming, as seafarer John Brown noted: "I discovered something about three or four miles distant, about two points on the weather bow, which appeared as a mast, as it rose and sunk in a perpendicular manner, once in about eight or ten minutes. I kept the vessel directly for it, and after look at it with my glass, I observed to my mate that it was a wreck, as I could see timbers sticking up, but as we approached nearer, I found what appeared like timbers to be a number of porpoises and black fish playing and jumping around a large Sea-Serpent, which we had supposed to be the mast."

While there have been sporadic sightings of sea serpents in the waters of Gloucester since 1817, none of them—in terms of their frequency, number of witnesses, and credibility—has ever come close to matching those tumultuous, early nineteenth-century days when the people of Gloucester were plagued by a monster.

HENRY LEE'S SEA MONSTERS

Today's instant access to worldwide, online news effectively ensures that whenever a strange creature is seen and reported, we soon know about it. Less easy to determine is the scale of encounters with monstrous beasts in centuries past. Fortunately, there were those who collected and chronicled such incidents. One of those was a man named Henry Lee, who, in the nineteenth century, made it his business to secure just about as many reports as possible. While Lee's dedicated research resulted in the surfacing of numerous accounts of massive and mighty beasts of the oceans, three reports in particular—all from the nineteenth century—stand out in the credibility stakes. In Lee's own words:

"In 1817 a large marine animal, supposed to be a serpent, was seen at Gloucester Harbor, near Cape Ann, Massachusetts, about thirty miles from Boston. The Linnaean Society of New England investigated the matter, and took much trouble to obtain evidence thereon. The depositions of eleven credible witnesses were certified on oath before magistrates, one of whom had himself seen the creature, and who confirmed the statements. All agreed that the animal had the appearance of a serpent, but estimated its length, variously, at from fifty to a hundred feet. Its head was in shape like that of a turtle, or snake, but as large as the head of a horse. There was no appearance of a mane. Its mode of progressing was by vertical undulations; and five of the witnesses described it as having the hunched protuberances mentioned by Captain de Ferry and others. Of this, I can offer no zoological explanation. The testimony given was apparently sincere, but it was received with mistrust; for, as Mr. Gosse says, 'owing to a habit prevalent in the United States of supposing that there is somewhat of wit in gross exaggeration or hoaxing invention, we do naturally look with a lurking suspicion on American statements when they describe unusual or disputed phenomena.'"

Lee also chronicled this amazing encounter of the sea serpent variety:

"On the 15th of May, 1833, a party of British officers, consisting of Captain Sullivan, Lieutenants Maclachlan and Malcolm of the Rifle Brigade, Lieutenant Lister of the Artillery, and Mr. Ince of the Ordnance, whilst crossing Margaret's Bay in a small yacht, on their way from Halifax to Mahone Bay, 'saw, at a distance of a hundred and fifty to two hundred yards, the head and neck of some denizen of the deep, precisely like those of a common snake in the act of swimming, the head so far elevated and thrown forward by the curve of the neck, as to enable them to see the water under and beyond it. The creature rapidly passed, leaving a regular wake, from the commencement of which to the fore part, which was out of water, they judged its length to be about eighty feet.' They 'set down the head at about six feet in length (considerably larger than that of a horse), and that portion of the neck which they saw at the same.' There could be no mistake—no delusion, they say; 'and we were all perfectly satisfied that we had been favored with a view of the true and veritable sea-serpent.'

> //All agreed that the animal had the appearance of a serpent, but estimated its length, variously, at from fifty to a hundred feet."

This account was published in the *Zoologist*, in 1847 (P. 1715), and at that date all the officers above named were still living."

Then we have this one from Lee, which serves even further to demonstrate that our oceans are home to massive, unknown animals:

"The next incident of the kind in point of date that we find recorded carries us back to the locality of which Pontoppidan wrote, and in which was seen the animal vouched for by Captain de Ferry. In 1847 there appeared in a London daily paper a long account translated from the Norse journals of fresh appearances of the sea-serpent. The statement made was that it had recently been frequently seen in the neighborhood of Christians and Molde. In the large bight of the sea at Christians and it had been seen every year, only in the warmest weather, and when the sea was perfectly calm, and the surface of the water unruffled.

"The evidence of three respectable persons was taken, namely, Nils Roe, a workman at Mr. William Knudtzon's, who saw it twice there, John Johnson, merchant, and Lars Johnoen, fisherman at Smolen. The latter said he had frequently seen it, and that one afternoon in the dog-days, as he was sitting in his boat, he saw it twice in the course of two hours, and quite close to him."

Lee continued, "It came, indeed, to within six feet of him [Johnoen], and, becoming alarmed, he commended his soul to God, and lay down in the boat, only holding his head high enough to enable him to observe the monster. It passed him, disappeared, and returned; but, a breeze springing up, it sank, and he saw it no more. He described it as being about six fathoms long, the body (which was as round as a serpent's) two feet across, the head as long as a ten-gallon cask, the eyes large, round, red, sparkling, and about five inches in diameter: close behind the head a mane like a fin commenced along the neck, and spread itself out on both sides, right and left, when swimming.

"The mane, as well as the head, was of the color of mahogany. The body was quite smooth, its movements occasionally fast and slow. It was serpent-like, and moved up and down. The few undulations which those parts of the body and tail that were out of water made, were scarcely a fathom in length. These undulations were not so high that he could see between them and the water. In confirmation of this account Mr. Soren Knudtzon, Dr. Hoffmann, surgeon in Molde, Rector Hammer, Mr. Kraft, curate, and several other persons, testified that they had seen in the neighborhood of Christians and a sea serpent of considerable size."

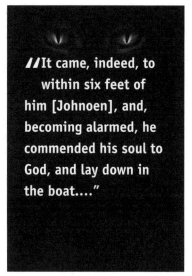

//It came, indeed, to within six feet of him [Johnoen], and, becoming alarmed, he commended his soul to God, and lay down in the boat....''

H.M.S. *Daedalus's* Monster of the Deep

Henry Lee, a dedicated seeker of sea serpents in the nineteenth century, reported on one of the most fascinating and credible encounters with an unknown leviathan of the deep. He said:

"In the *Times* of the 9th of October, 1848, appeared a paragraph stating that a sea-serpent had been met with by the Daedalus frigate, on her homeward voyage from the East Indies. The Admiralty immediately inquired of her commander, Captain M'Quhae, as to the truth of the report; and his official reply, addressed to Admiral Sir W. H. Gage, G. C. H. Devonport, was printed in the *Times* of the 13th of October, 1848.

Captain M'Quhae's account makes for amazing and jaw-dropping reading:

"H.M.S. *Daedalus*, Hamoaze, October 11th, 1848.

"SIR—In reply to your letter of this date, requiring information as to the truth of the statement published in the *Times* newspaper, of a sea-serpent of extraordinary dimensions having been seen from H.M.S. Daedalus, under my command, on her passage from the East Indies, I have the honor to acquaint you, for the information of my Lords Commissioners of the Admiralty, that at 5 o'clock P.m. on the 6th of Aug. last, in lat. 24' 44' S. and long. 9'22 E', the weather dark and cloudy, wind fresh from the N.W. with a long ocean swell from the W., the ship on the port tack, head being N.E. by N., something very unusual was seen by Mr. Sartoris, midshipman, rapidly approaching the ship from before the beam.

"The circumstance was immediately reported by him to the officer of the watch, Lieut. Edgar Drummond, with whom and Mr. Wm. Barrett, the Master, I was at the time walking the quarter-deck. The ship's company were at supper. On our attention being called to the object it was discovered to be an enormous serpent, with head and shoulders kept about four feet constantly above the surface of the sea, and, as nearly as we could approximate by comparing it with the length of what our main topsail yard would show in the water, there was at the very least sixty feet of the animal afleur d'eau, no portion of which was, to our perception, used in propelling it through the water, either by vertical or horizontal undulation.

"It passed rapidly, but so close under our lee quarter that had it been a man of my acquaintance I should easily have recognized his features with the naked eye; and it did not, either in approaching the ship or after it had passed our wake, deviate in the slightest degree from its course to the S.W., which it held on at the pace of from twelve to fifteen miles per hour, apparently on some determined purpose.

"The diameter of the serpent was about fifteen or sixteen inches behind the head, which was without any doubt that of a snake; and it was never, during the twenty minutes it continued in sight of our glasses, once below the surface of the water; its color dark brown, and yellowish white about the throat. It had no fins, but something like the mane of a horse, or rather a bunch of seaweed, washed about its back. It was seen by the quartermaster, the boatswain's mate, and the man at the wheel, in addition to myself and the officers above mentioned.

"I am having a drawing of the serpent made from a sketch taken immediately after it was seen, which I hope to have ready for transmission to my Lords Commissioners of the Admiralty by to-morrow's Post- PETER M'QUHAE, Captain."

Henry Lee also noted:

"Lieutenant Drummond, the officer of the watch mentioned in Captain M'Quhae's report, published his memorandum of the impression made on his

This illustration from the October 28, 1848, issue of the *London News* depicts the *H.M.S. Daedalus*'s encounter with the sea serpent.

mind by the animal at the time of its appearance. It differs somewhat from the captain's description, and is the more cautious of the two.

"I beg to send you the following extract from my journal. *H.M.S. Daedalus*, August 6, 1848, lat. 25' S., long. 9'37'E, St. Helena 1,015 miles. In the 4 to 6 watch, at about 5 o'clock, we observed a most remarkable fish on our lee-quarter, crossing the stern in a S.W. direction.

> **//It had no fins, but something like the mane of a horse, or rather a bunch of sea-weed, washed about its back."**

"The appearance of its head, which with the back fin was the only portion of the animal visible, was long, pointed and flattened at the top, perhaps ten feet in length, the upper jaw projecting considerably; the fin was perhaps 20 feet in the rear of the head, and visible occasionally; the captain also asserted that he saw the tail, or another fin, about the same distance behind it; the upper part of the head and shoulders appeared of a dark brown color, and beneath the under-jaw a brownish white.

"It pursued a steady undeviating course, keeping its head horizontal with the surface of the water, and in rather a raised position, disappearing occasionally beneath a wave for a very brief interval, and not apparently for purposes of respiration. It was going at the rate of perhaps from twelve to fourteen miles an hour, and when nearest was perhaps one hundred yards distant; in fact it gave one quite the idea of a large snake or eel. No one in the ship has ever seen anything similar; so it is at least extraordinary. It was visible to the naked eye for five minutes, and with a glass for perhaps fifteen more. The weather was dark and squally at the time, with some sea running. EDGAR DRUMMOND, Lieut. *H.M.S. Daedalus*; Southampton, Oct. 28, 1845."

HORNED MONSTER OF LAKE BANGWEULU

Richard Freeman, formerly a head keeper at England's Twycross Zoo, says: "An English ex-pat that gathered information on a supposed horned giant animal said to lurk in Lake Bangweulu [which is situated in the upper Congo River basin in Zambia], J. E. Hughes was born in Derbyshire in 1876 and attended Cambridge. The British South Africa Company offered him a job as assistant native commissioner in the newly formed civil service of north-east Rhodesia. After seven years of service Hughes resigned and became a hunter/trader. He lived for the next eighteen years on the Mbawala islands on

Lake Bangweulu. He recorded his life in a book, *Eighteen years on Lake Bang-weulu*, in which he writes of the monster."

Having digested Freeman's words, let's now turn our attention to Hughes himself and his extraordinary story of a rampaging monster.

"For many years now there has been a persistent rumor that a huge pre-historic animal was to be found in the waters of our Lake Bangweulu. Certainly the natives talk about such a beast and 'Chipekwe' or 'Chimpekwe,' is the name by which they call it. I find it is a fact that Herr Hagenbeck sent up an expedition in search of this animal, but none of them ever reached the Luapula, owing to fever, etc.; they had come at the wrong time of year for newcomers.

"Mr. H. Croad, the retired magistrate, is inclined to think there is some-thing to the legend. He told me one night, camped at the edge of a very deep small lake, he heard a tremendous splashing during the night, and in the morning found a spoor on the bank—not that of any animal he knew, and he knows them all.

"Another bit of evidence about it is the story Kanyeshia, son of Mieri-Mieri, the Waushi Paramount Chief, told me. His grandfather had said that he could remember one of these animals being killed in the Luapula in deep water below the Lubwe.

"A good description of the hunt has been handed down by tradition. It took many of their best hunters the whole day spearing it with their 'Viwingo' harpoons—the same as they use for the hippo. It is described as having a smooth dark body, without bristles, and armed with a single smooth white horn fixed like the horn of a rhinoceros, but composed of smooth white ivory, very highly polished. It is a pity they did not keep it, as I would have given them anything they liked for it.

"I noticed in Carl Hagenbeck's book 'Beasts and Men,' abridged edi-tion, 1909, p. 96, that the Chipekwe has been illustrated in bushman paint-ings. This is a very interesting point, which seems to confirm the native legend of the existence of such a beast.

"Lake young is named on the map after its discoverer, Mr. Robert Young, formerly N.C in charge of Chinsali. The native name of the lake is 'Shiwangandu.' When exploring this part in the earliest days of the Adminis-tration, he took a shot at an object in some floating suds that looked like a duck; it dived and went away, leaving a wake like a screw steamer. This lake is drained by the Manshya River, which runs into the Chambezi. The lake itself is just half-way between Mipka and Chinsale Station.

"Mr. Young told me that the natives once pulled their canoes up the Manshya into this lake. There were a party of men, women, and children out on a hippo-harpooning expedition. The natives claimed that the Guardian

> **//The natives claimed that the Guardian Spirit of the lake objected to this and showed his anger by upsetting and destroying all the men and canoes."**

Spirit of the lake objected to this and showed his anger by upsetting and destroying all the men and canoes. The women and children who had remained on the shore all saw this take place. Not a single man returned and the women and children returned alone to the Chambezie. He further said that never since has a canoe been seen on Lake Young. It is true I never saw one there myself. Young thinks the Chipekwe is still surviving there.

"Another bit of hearsay evidence was given me by Mr. Croad. This was told to him by Mr. R. M. Green, who many years ago built his lonely hermitage on our Lulimala in the Ilala country about 1906. Green said that the natives reported a hippo killed by a Chipekwe in the Lukula—the next river. The throat was torn out.

"I have been to the Lukulu many times and explored it from its source via the Lavusi Mountain to where it loses its self in the reeds of the big swamp, without finding the slightest sign of any such survival of prehistoric ages.

"When I first heard about this animal, I circulated the news that I would give a reward of either £5 or a bale of cloth in return for any evidence, such as a bone, a horn, a scrap of hide, of a spoor, that such an animal might possibly exist. For about fifteen years I had native buyers traversing every waterway and picking up other skins for me. No trace of the Chipekwe was ever produced; the reward is still unclaimed."

Hughes concluded: "My own theory is that such an animal did really exist, but is now extinct. Probably disappearing when the Luapula cut its way to a lower level—thus reducing the level of the previously existing big lake, which is shown by the pebbled foothills of the far distant mountains."

It's well worth noting Richard Freeman's comments on this affair, given his extensive knowledge in the fields of both zoology and cryptozoology: "Perhaps, if we are to believe Mr. Young's tale the creature's ferocity kept it from being hunted very often. A picture is emerging of a huge, dangerous, semi-aquatic animal with a single horn and an antipathy towards hippos. Many have come to the conclusion that these are Ceratopsian dinosaurs. These were a sub-order of Ornithischia (bird hipped dinosaurs) and contained such well known horned dinosaurs as *Triceratops* and *Styracosaurus*. They were all herbivores and were typified by bearing horns and a bony frill like an Elizabethan ruff that grew from the rear of the skull to protect the animal's neck. The number of horns varied between the species, some such as *Monoclonius* bore only one horn on the snout.

"There are two main stumbling blocks with the dinosaur theory. First and foremost there is no fossil evidence for any species of non-avian dinosaur surviving beyond the Cretaceous period (which ended 65 million years ago). Secondly there is no indication of any species of being aquatic, let alone Ceratopsians. So we need to look elsewhere for this beast's identity."

Freeman believes that the beast may be some form of gigantic, aquatic rhinoceros. He says: "The idea of a water dwelling rhino may seem strange but the great Indian rhino (*Rhinoceros unicornis*) spends almost as much time in water as a hippopotamus. It feeds mainly on lush water plants such as reeds and water lilies. The Indian rhino also bares only one horn, much like the *Emela-ntouka* and unlike the two savannah dwelling African species who both bare two horns."

Freeman adds, in conclusion: "One group of rhinos, the *Amynodontids*, specialized in an aquatic lifestyle. These flourished in the Oligocene epoch 38 to 25 million years ago, finally dying out around 10 million years ago. Could one species have survived into the present? This is by no means impossible but it is perhaps more likely that our unknown giant is a modern species that has avoided detection, rather than a prehistoric survivor."

The Indian rhinoceros spends much of its life wading through water and eating plants, much like the behavior of the Horned Monster of Lake Bangweulu.

KLAMATH RIVER MONSTER

Beginning in the Cascades of Southern Oregon and extending down to Copco Lake, south of the California-Oregon border, the river is some 250 miles (402 kilometers) in length and takes its name from the Native American term for "swiftness." However, the creature that Jeffrey Shaw and his wife claim to have seen on a summer's day more than forty years ago can hardly be termed swift.

According to Shaw, he and his wife had rented a pleasant wooden cabin on one particular stretch of the river and would most days sit near the water's edge with a couple of bottles of white wine and a well-stocked picnic basket. As someone whose schedule with the military was incredibly hectic, said Shaw, the pair relished some much welcome peace and quiet while simultaneously communing with nature. And commune with nature they most certainly did.

The Shaws had taken a ten-day vacation and all was normal for the first half of the week; however, it was six or seven days into their break from the rigid confines of the Air Force that matters took a very weird and dramatic turn. On the day in question, the Shaws had driven fifteen or twenty miles in search of a particular sandbank they had been told about that was apparently the perfect area for a private water-side feast. Unfortunately, they failed to locate the place in question; and so, as fate would have it, they stopped at a shady, grassy area some two to three hundred yards from the edge of the water. With blankets, wine, and a plentiful supply of food laid out, they enjoyed a romantic lunch under a warm and sunny sky.

It was perhaps a little more than two hours into their day of fun when Jeffrey Shaw's wife saw out of the corner of her eye what she first thought was a large black bear ambling along at the edge of the woods and heading in the direction of the water. Concerned, she whispered to her husband and pointed in the direction where the creature was maneuvering among the trees and the bushes. But a closer look revealed that it was certainly no black bear.

Jeffrey Shaw explained to me that as the trees and bushes became less dense, he and his wife were able to get a much clearer view of the animal that was "shuffling" towards the lake. At first glance, he said, the creature was continually obscured by the woods and therefore initially appeared to be only about six or seven feet in length, which is what had led his wife to assume it had merely been a black bear on all fours. Now, however, they could see that it was closer to thirty feet long, and appeared to resemble either a giant snake or a monstrous eel.

Both of the Shaws confirmed to me that the creature seemed to have great trouble moving on land, hence their "shuffling" description, to which they added that it seemed to "wriggle from side to side" as it moved, while its body appeared to be "continually vibrating" as it did so. They were unable to discern the nature of the beast's head, said Jeffrey Shaw, adding that "the whole thing reminded us of a big black pipe."

The Shaws stated that they did not feel frightened in the presence of the unknown creature, only awestruck. And while they did not actually see it enter the water, they were sure that this was its ultimate destination. At no time did it make any noise as it passed by, said the couple, and it appeared not to notice them in the slightest. On the following two days they returned to the same spot, hoping to see the remarkable animal once again; and Jeffrey Shaw even camped out one night near the water's edge, hoping for a truly close encounter.

it seemed to
• • • "wriggle from side to side" as it moved, while its body appeared to be "continually vibrating" as it did so.

It was unfortunately (or fortunately, depending on your perspective) not to be, however. Whatever the true nature of the beast, it summarily failed to appear again for Jeffrey Shaw and his wife. The Klamath waters continued—and continue to this day—to keep a tight grip on their dark secrets, it would appear.

KRAKEN

A creature that features heavily in Scandinavian folklore and mythology, the Kraken is a terrifying beast, perhaps most reminiscent of H. P. Lovecraft's famous, fictional monster, Cthulhu. A beast of the mysterious deep, the Kraken is a definitive sea monster, albeit, not a sea serpent of the long-necked and hump-backed variety. In many respects, the Kraken sounds like a strange combination of giant octopus and gargantuan squid. Certainly, both animals have the ability to grow to significantly large proportions—with the colossal squid reaching overall lengths, including tentacles, of up to forty-six feet. The Kraken, however, is said to grow much, much bigger—and to the point where, in centuries long gone, it supposedly dragged ships under the waves, drowning their crews in the process.

The story of Örvar-Oddr, a renowned Scandinavian hero of old, whose adventures were chronicled in the 1200s, contains a description of a beast called the hafgufa, but which scholars of Scandinavian folklore and history believe, with hindsight, may well have been a Kraken. It states:

"Now I will tell you that there are two sea-monsters. One is called the *hafgufa* (sea-mist), another *lyngbakr* (heather-back). It (the *lyngbakr*) is the largest whale in the world, but the *hafgufa* is the hugest monster in the sea. It is the nature of this creature to swallow men and ships, and even whales and everything else within reach. It stays submerged for days, then rears its head and nostrils above surface and stays that way at least until the change of tide. Now, that sound we just sailed through was the space between its jaws, and its nostrils and lower jaw were those rocks that appeared in the sea, while the *lyng-bakr* was the island we saw sinking down. However, Ogmund Tussock has sent these creatures to you by means of his magic to cause the death of you (Odd) and all your men. He thought more men would have gone the same way as those that had already drowned (i.e. to the *lyngbakr* which wasn't an island, and sank), and he expected that the *hafgufa* would have swallowed us all.

A circa 1700 illustration of a Kraken form the book *Mystères de l'Ocean.*

Today I sailed through its mouth because I knew that it had recently surfaced."

Then there is the sixteenth century tome *Konungs skuggsjá*, which translates into English as "King's mirror" and also describes what is believed to have been a Kraken:

"There is a fish that is still unmentioned, which it is scarcely advisable to speak about on account of its size, because it will seem to most people incredible. There are only a very few who can speak upon it clearly, because it is seldom near land nor appears where it may be seen by fishermen, and I suppose there are not many of this sort of fish in the sea. Most often in our tongue we call it hafgufa.

"Nor can I conclusively speak about its length in ells, because the times he has shown before men, he has appeared more like land than like a fish. Neither have I heard that one had been caught or found dead; and it seems to me as though there must be no more than two in the oceans, and I deem that each is unable to reproduce itself, for I believe that they are always the same ones. Then too, neither would it do for other fish if the hafgufa were of such a number as other whales, on account of their vastness, and how much subsistence that they need.

"It is said to be the nature of these fish that when one shall desire to eat, then it stretches up its neck with a great belching, and following this belching comes forth much food, so that all kinds of fish that are near to hand will come to present location, then will gather together, both small and large, believing they shall obtain there food and good eating; but this great fish lets its mouth stand open the while, and the gap is no less wide than that of a great sound or fjord. And nor may the fish avoid running together there in their great numbers. But as soon as its stomach and mouth is full, then it locks together its jaws and has the fish all caught and enclosed, that before greedily came there looking for food."

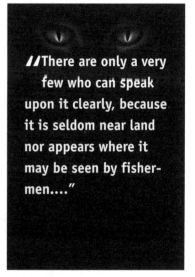

//There are only a very few who can speak upon it clearly, because it is seldom near land nor appears where it may be seen by fishermen...."

In addition, we have the words of a Swedish author, one Jacob Wallenberg. In the pages of his 1781 title *Min son på galejan* (which translates as "My son on the galley"), we're told the following:

"Kraken, also called the Crab-fish, which is not that huge, for heads and tails counted, he is no larger than our Öland is wide [i.e., less than 16 km]. He stays at the sea floor, constantly surrounded by innumerable small fishes, who serve as his food and are fed by him in return: for his meal, (if I remember correctly what E. Pontoppidan writes) lasts no longer than three months, and another three are then needed to digest it. His excrements nurture in the following an army of lesser fish, and for this reason, fishermen plumb after his resting place.

"Gradually, Kraken ascends to the surface, and when he is at ten to twelve fathoms, the boats had better move out of his vicinity, as he will shortly thereafter burst up, like a floating island, spurting water from his dreadful nostrils and making ring waves around him, which can reach many miles. Could one doubt that this is the Leviathan of Job?"

And, finally, we have "The Kraken," an 1830 sonnet from the acclaimed poet laureate Alfred Tennyson. It reads thus:

Below the thunders of the upper deep;
Far far beneath in the abysmal sea,
His ancient, dreamless, uninvaded sleep
The Kraken sleepeth: faintest sunlights flee
About his shadowy sides; above him swell
Huge sponges of millennial growth and height;
And far away into the sickly light,
From many a wondrous grot and secret cell

Unnumber'd and enormous polypi
Winnow with giant arms the slumbering green.
There hath he lain for ages, and will lie
Battening upon huge seaworms in his sleep,
Until the latter fire shall heat the deep;
Then once by man and angels to be seen,
In roaring he shall rise and on the surface die.

Today, sightings and reports of the Kraken are not just rare, they are nonexistent. This suggests one of two possibilities: (a) that the Kraken was purely a mythical beast; or (b) it was hunted to extinction in centuries past. Whatever the truth of the matter, while the Kraken seemingly no longer endures, its legend most assuredly does.

LAKE STORSJÖN CREATURE

Although far less well known than its counterpart in Loch Ness, Scotland, the mysterious beast of Lake Storsjön, Sweden, has been seen on more than a few occasions. While many of the sightings are somewhat vague and open to interpretation, one that occurred in 1878 is not. It came from a man named Martin Olsson, a mechanic at the nearby Ostersund sawmill, who lived in a cabin at the edge of the lake. He described his dramatic encounter with the monster:

"I was fishing near Forson Island when I got a strange feeling someone was watching me. I looked behind me and the lake creature was not more than forty meters behind my boat. I dropped my pole and line in the lake when I saw it. The weather was bright and sunny and I got a good view of the animal. The neck was long, about as round as a man's body at the base where it came up out of the water. It tapered up about six feet to a snake-like head that was larger than what I figured the neck could support. There was a hairy fringe just back of the neck. Hanging down the back. This 'ribbon' was stuck close to the neck, possibly because of the wetness. The color was greyish brown. The thing had two distinct eyes that were reddish in appearance. There were a couple of dark humps visible beyond the neck. Both of these humps, and the part that was out of the water, glistened in the sunlight. I did not see scales. There was a skin on the animal that resembled the skin of a fish.

"I didn't want to alarm the animal, but I did want to get away as quickly as possible. Moving very cautiously, I took my oars and pulled slowly away from the spot. I became even more frightened when I had rowed about ten

Lake Storsjön in Sweden is a little-known sister lake to Loch Ness that is home to its own rather large mystery.

meters distance and the animal began to swim towards me. I stopped rowing, and the thing just lay there in the water staring at me. This must have gone on for about five minutes. I'm uncertain because my mind was on anything but the passage of time. There was no doubt in my mind that this thing could have overturned my little boat. I thanked god when he dropped beneath the water and I saw a blackish hump move out in the opposite direction."

LAKE WINNIPEGOSIS UNKNOWN ANIMAL

In 1903, a man named Oscar Frederickson, of Winnipegosis, Canada, wrote a fascinating and extensive report on his knowledge of huge lake monsters in the early decades of the twentieth century, all of which came from witnesses, both first- and second-hand. He began his account like this:

"In 1903, I lived with my parents on Red Deer Point, Lake Winnipegosis. Our house was situated about two hundred yards from the shore. About a mile south of our place lived a man by the name of Ferdinand Stark. One day Stark was down by the lake shore when he saw what he thought was a huge creature in the lake. It was moving northward along the shore, a short distance out.

"Stark wanted someone else to see the strange animal, and as we were his nearest neighbors, he came running along the lake to our place. All the while, he could see the creature moving in the same direction as he was, only going a little slower than he was running.

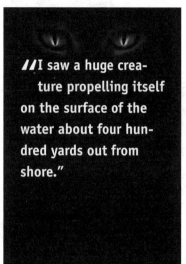

//I saw a huge creature propelling itself on the surface of the water about four hundred yards out from shore."

"Stark arrived at our home very much excited and breathing heavily, and asked my dad and mother to hurry down to the lake to see a strange animal in the water. By the time my parents got down to the lake shore, there was nothing to be seen. Whatever Stark had seen had disappeared. Looking somewhat bewildered, but still visibly excited, Stark began to describe what he had seen.

"All he could see of the creature was its big back sticking out of the water, and it was very dark or black in color. A number of gulls followed it and kept flying down to it as if they were picking at it. My parents did see quite a number of gulls still flying around.

"In 1935, Mr. Cecil Rogers of Mafeking and I made a trip to Grand Rapids on Lake Winnipeg. While there, I called on Mr. Valentine McKay, a resident of Grand Rapids for many years. As we were talking, the conversation drifted to strange animals that had existed at one time. To my surprise, McKay said he had seen some such animal in Lake Winnipegosis."

McKay, very pleased by the fact that Frederickson took his story seriously and did not poke fun at him, prepared a carefully written statement for the monster hunter, which read as follows:

"In September, 1909, I was traveling alone in a canoe from Shoal River on Lake Winnipegosis to Grand Rapids on Lake Winnipeg. At the time I saw this animal I was standing on the lake shore. I had stopped at Graves' Point to make tea. I was at the edge of the bush getting willows for a campfire, when I heard a rumbling sound like distant thunder. As I looked out on the glassy surface of the calm water, I saw a huge creature propelling itself on the surface of the water about four hundred yards out from shore. A large part must have been submerged, judging by the great disturbance of the water around it.

"The creature's dark skin glistened in the autumn sun, and I estimated it was moving at the rate of two to three miles an hour. As I watched it, a member of the body shot up about four feet, vertically, out of the water. This portion seemed to have something to do with the creature's method of locomotion. The course it was taking was toward Sugar Island or Sleep Rock. I watched it till it went out of sight. The number of gulls, hovering around this creature, followed it as far as I could see."

Frederickson had something notable to say on this particular story: "Mr. McKay said he had described this creature to a geologist by the name of Craig who said it was quite possible that it was a remaining specimen of a prehistoric animal that was once plentiful."

On the matter of the two men in question—Ferdinand Stark and Valentine McKay—Frederickson made a number of observations and comments: "A great many people will think these two men just made up a story about seeing some strange animal or creature in Lake Winnipegosis. But, it is hardly probable that both men would think up a yarn about the gulls. Stark and McKay never met, as far as I could find out. Stark moved from Winnipegosis about 1904 or 1905, and where he is now, if still living, I have not been able to find out."

Frederickson had yet another account to relate on this particular matter of unidentified, large beasts on the loose in the early part of the twentieth century: "In 1934, Captain Sandy Vance lived on Graves' Point. One day he was over at Sitting Island, which is on the northeast side of the point. He saw what he thought was a huge animal a short distance off shore. Vance said it was the biggest living creature he had ever seen in water. Mr. Vance had been captain on freight tugs for many years on Lake Winnipeg and Lake Winnipegosis. He said he had often seen moose and deer in water, so there is no reason not to believe that he saw some strange living creature. Captain Vance died some years ago. He was well known here."

And, finally, there is the following short, but intriguing, account from Frederickson: "There are quite a few Natives who have seen some strange thing. They call it 'the big snake.' Those of Shoal River claim that a monstrous animal was seen often off Sugar Island and Steep Rock in Dawson Bay during the latter part of the 19th century."

LOCH NESS MONSTER

The Loch Ness Monster: just about everyone has heard of it. A large number of people claim to have seen the long-necked, humped leviathan of the deep. Some have even photographed and filmed it. Nessie, as the beast is affectionately known, has been a staple part of the world of the unexplained since 1933, when the phenomenon of the monster exploded in spectacular, worldwide fashion. Since then, millions of people have flocked to the shores of the 22.5 miles long and 744 feet deep loch, all in the hopes of seeing the elusive creature. Attempts have been made to seek out Nessie with sonar equipment, aircraft, balloons, and even submarines.

Theories abound as to what Nessie is—or, far more likely and correctly, what the Nessies are. Certainly the most captivating theory, and the one that the Scottish Tourist Board, movie-makers, and the general public find most appealing, is that which suggests the monsters are surviving pockets of plesiosaurs. They were marine reptiles that the domain of zoology assures us became extinct tens of millions of years ago. The possibility that the monsters are actually giant-sized salamanders holds sway in more than a few quarters. As does the idea that perhaps massive eels are the culprits. Then there are scenarios involving sturgeon, oversized turtles, catfish, and even crocodiles, giant frogs, and hippopotami!

To say that Loch Ness has an air and atmosphere of mystery and intrigue about it is an understatement. The gigantic loch is steeped in legend, folklore, mythology, and history. It lies along a huge fault line called the Great Glen Fault, the origins of which date back literally hundreds of millions of years. The fault runs through the similarly named Great Glen, which includes Loch Ness, Loch Lochy, Loch Oich, Loch Linnhe, the River Ness, and the River Lochie. Loch Ness is home to a near-magical-looking thirteenth-century structure called Urquhart Castle.

This photo from 1977 is one of the more famous images of Nessie, although many have considered it to be a fake. It was taken by Anthony "Doc" Shiels, a man many knew was trying to become a noted monster hunter.

The date on which history was really made—as the newspapers and the public saw it, anyway—was April 14, 1933, although the facts didn't surface until May 2. The latter was the date when a man named Alex Campbell splashed the story across the pages of the *Inverness Courier* newspaper. And what a story it was! Campbell told of the encounter of a then-anonymous, well-known businessman and his wife, who lived near Inverness. They had, apparently, been driving along the north side of the loch when they saw to their amazement a "tremendous upheaval" in the water. They watched in complete shock as a massive animal, with a body not unlike that of a whale, broke the water. Campbell upped the intrigue and sensational nature of the story when he added that the water churned like "a simmering cauldron" as the "denizen of the deep" provoked cold fear in the pair.

Then there was the July 22, 1933, encounter of Mr. and Mrs. George Spicer. Incredibly, they saw the monster not in the loch, but lumbering across a road and towards the dark waters. Mr. Spicer said: "It was horrible—an abomination. It did not move in the usual reptilian fashion but with these arches. The body shot across the road in jerks but because of the slope we could not see its lower parts and saw no limbs." He continued that by the time the shocked pair reached the section of the road where the monster appeared, it was already gone. Nevertheless, evidence of its presence was still there. The surrounding bracken had clearly been flattened by something large and heavy; that much was certain. Of two things, however, he was sure: the beast was at least five feet in height and "was quite big enough to have upset our car."

Mr. Spicer added: "I estimated the length to be twenty-five to thirty feet. Its color so far as the body is concerned could only be called a dark elephant grey. We saw no tail, nor did I notice any mouth on what I took to be the head of the creature. We later concluded that the tail must have been curled around alongside it since there was something protruding above its shoulder which

A 1930s-era postcard includes photos of the locations where the Loch Ness monster has been spotted.

gave the impression that it was carrying something on its back. My wife and I looked at each other in amazement. It had been a loathsome sight. To see that arched neck straggle across was something which still haunts us."

And thus was born a mystery that, more than eighty years later, shows no signs of stopping. As one perfect example of the fact that Nessie has not gone away, there is a certain case from the 2000s that remains a classic.

In 2007, one of the most amazing and significant encounters in a very long time occurred at Loch Ness. It was an encounter that had both the Nessie-based research community and monster hunters everywhere practically foaming at the mouth with excitement. This was hardly surprising, since the witness in question, a man named Gordon Holmes, succeeded in filming one of the world-famous, legendary beasts. And this was not a piece of vague or blurry footage of a questionable nature; it was there, clear enough for anyone and everyone to see.

Around 10:00 P.M. on May 26, 2007, Gordon Holmes filmed, well, *something*, in Loch Ness. It was something that turned him into an overnight media sensation—albeit a brief sensation. The day in question was dominated by heavy rain, but which cleared as the evening arrived, allowing Holmes to get clear footage of what looked like some kind of animal moving at a significant rate of knots in the waters of Loch Ness. The specific location from where all the action was captured was a parking area, on the A82 road, just a couple of miles from Drumnadrochit. Holmes said:

"I couldn't believe my eyes when I saw this jet black thing, about 45 feet long, moving fairly fast in the water. My initial thought is it could be a very large eel. They have serpent-like features and they may explain all the sightings in Loch Ness over the years."

Long-time Nessie seeker Adrian Shine was moved to comment in a fairly positive fashion: "I see myself as a skeptical interpreter of what happens in the loch, but I do keep an open mind about these things and there is no doubt this is some of the best footage I have seen." He was careful to add that while Holmes might have filmed "some biological creature," there was always a possibility that "it could just be the waves of the loch," or that it might well have been a "psychological phenomenon, inasmuch we see what we want to see."

LOUGH NAHOOIN MONSTER

In 2015, I was fortunate to acquire a wealth of original notes and files belonging to the late monster hunter F. W. "Ted" Holiday, who spent a great deal of time in the 1960s and 1970s investigating the Loch Ness Monster. Amongst those notes was a summary-report of an interview that Holiday conducted with one Stephen Coyne, in July 1968. Not at Loch Ness, Scotland, however, but at Lough Nahooin, Ireland.

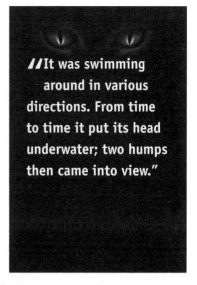

//It was swimming around in various directions. From time to time it put its head underwater; two humps then came into view."

Holiday's notes report the following:

"At about seven on the evening of 22 February 1968, Stephen Coyne went down to the bog by the lough to bring up some dry peat. With him he took his eldest son, a boy of eight, and the family dog. Although the sun had set it was still quite light. On reaching the peat-bed beside Nahooin he suddenly noticed a black object in the water. Thinking it was the dog he whistled to it; however, the dog came bounding along the shore from behind. On seeing the object it stopped and started barking.

"He then saw that the object was an animal with a pole-like head and neck about nine inches to a foot in diameter. It was swimming around in various directions. From time to time it put its head underwater; two humps then came into view. Occasionally, a flat tail appeared. Once this came out near the head which argued length and a high degree of flexibility. The thing was black, slick, and hairless with a texture resembling an eel.

"The dog's barking seemed to irritate the monster and it began to move in-shore, its mouth open. However, when Coyne strode over to support his dog it turned away and resumed swimming around this little lough. At about this point the little boy ran home to bring his mother to see the strange beast. When Mrs. Coyne and the children returned the Peiste [which is Irish terminology for a lake monster] was still busily patrolling the tiny lake.

"Both Mr. and Mrs. Coyne agreed that the creature was about twelve feet long and both agreed they saw no eyes. Mrs. Coyne told us that she noticed two horn-like projections on top of the head. Whereas she thought the thing approached as near as four to five yards, her husband felt that the nearest point was about nine yards. Both agreed that the mouth was under-slung in relation to the snout and neither of them saw any teeth. Coyne described the mouth interior as 'pale.'

"To and fro before the seven members of the Coyne family strutted the Nahooin dragon. As dusk was setting they finally left it and made their way home over the bog."

Whatever the true nature of the Irish beastie of Lough Nahooin, it was never seen again.

MERMAIDS

The word "mermaid" is derived from a combination of "mere," an old English word meaning "sea," and "maid," as in "woman." According to old sea-faring legends, mermaids would often deliberately sing to sailors to try and enchant them with the secret and malevolent intent of distracting them from their work and causing their ships to run disastrously aground. Other ancient tales tell of mermaids inadvertently squeezing the last breaths out of drowning men while attempting to rescue them. They are also said to particularly enjoy taking humans to their underwater lairs. In Hans Christian Andersen's *The Little Mermaid*, for example, it is said that mermaids often forget that humans cannot breathe underwater, while other legends suggest the sinister she-creatures deliberately drown men—out of sheer, venomous spite, no less.

Artist Edvard Eriksen made this statue of the Little Mermaid from the Hans Christian Andersen tale; it sits on a rock by Copenhagen.

The fabled Sirens of Greek mythology are sometimes portrayed in folklore as being mermaid-like in nature and appearance. Other related types of mythical, legendary creatures that fall into this category include water nymphs and selkies, animals that can allegedly transform themselves from seals into human beings—and vice versa, too.

Mermaids were noted in British folklore as being distinctly unlucky omens—occasionally foretelling disaster and sometimes even maliciously provoking it, too. As evidence of this, several variations of the ballad *Sir Patrick Spens* depict a mermaid speaking to the doomed ships. In some, she tells the crews they will never see land again, and in others she claims they are near the shore, which the men are wise and astute enough to know means that deep, malevolent deception is at work. The ballad itself is of Scottish origin and may possibly refer to an actual event—namely, the bringing home of the Scottish Queen Margaret, Maid of Norway, across the North Sea in 1290. There is, however, some speculation that the ballad may actually relate to a voyage by the princess's mother in 1281. But, regardless of the specific truth behind the ballad itself, its words are prime evidence of both the knowledge and the deep fear of mermaids that have existed in the British Isles for an untold number of centuries.

One such account tells of a deadly mermaid inhabiting a small pool in the pleasant little village of Childs Ercall, England. In 1893, the writer Robert Charles Hope described the story as follows:

"[T]here was a mermaid seen there once. It was a good while ago, before my time. I dare say it might be a hundred years ago. There were two men going to work early one morning, and they had got as far as the side of the pond in [a] field, and they saw something on the top of the water which scared them not a little. They thought it was going to take them straight off to the Old Lad himself! I can't say exactly what it was like, I wasn't there, you know, but it was a mermaid, the same as you read of in the papers.

"The fellows had almost run away at first, they were so frightened, but as soon as the mermaid had spoken to them, they thought no more of that. Her voice was so sweet and pleasant, that they fell in love with her there and then, both of them. Well, she told them there was a treasure hidden at the bottom of the pond—lumps of gold, and no one knows what. And she would give them as much as ever they liked if they would come to her in the water and take it out of her hands.

"So they went in, though it was almost up to their chins, and she dived into the water and brought up a lump of gold almost as big as a man's head. And the men were just going to take it, when one of them said: 'Eh!' he said (and swore, you know), 'if this isn't a bit of luck!' And, my word, if the mermaid didn't take it away from them again, and gave a scream, and dived down into the pond, and they saw no more of her, and got none of her gold. And nobody has ever seen her since then. No doubt the story once ran that the oath which scared the uncanny creature involved the mention of the Holy Name."

Moving on, there is the story of Mermaid's Pool (also known as Blakemere Pool), which can be found at the Staffordshire,

One of many English folktales is that of "Clerk Covill and the Mermaid." In it, a young man goes to see a mermaid and is inflicted with head pains that cause him to die (illustration by Arthur Rackham).

England village of Thorncliffe, on the Staffordshire Moorlands, which are dominated by forests, lakes, rolling hills, and crags. It's a story that dates back approximately 1,000 years. Lisa Dowley is someone who has spent a great deal of time and effort pursuing the story and sorting fact from legend. She says:

"The story transpires that this particular mermaid was once a maiden of fair beauty, and it came to pass—for reasons that are unclear—that she was persecuted, and accused of various crimes, by a gentleman named Joshua Linnet. It is not clear whether these accusations included being a witch, or whether he may have had his amorous advances rejected.

"The said Mr. Linnet had this woman bound up, and thrown into the bottomless Blakemere Pool. As she fought for her breath and life, the woman screamed vengeance on her accuser, Joshua Linnet, and that her spirit would haunt the pool from that moment hence, and swore that one day she would drag her accuser and executioner deep down beneath the dark depths of the Blakemere Pool to his own death.

"It is a recorded fact that three days later, Joshua Linnet was found face down, dead in the Blakemere Pool. When his body was dragged out and turned over by the locals, to their horror, what greeted them was that what was once his face, but was now nothing more than tattered shreds of skin, the injuries seemingly caused by sharp claws or talons."

Moving on, situated barely a stone's throw from the Shropshire, England, town of Newport and just over the border from rural Staffordshire, Aqualate Mere—at 1.5 kilometers long and 0.5 kilometers wide—is the largest natural lake in the Midlands; yet it is very shallow, extending down to little more than a uniform three feet. Legend has it that one day many years ago, when the Mere was being cleaned, a mermaid violently rose out of the water—quite naturally scaring the living daylights out of the workmen—while simultaneously making shrieking, disturbing, and damning threats to utterly destroy the town of Newport if any attempt was ever made to empty Aqualate Mere of its precious waters. Very wisely, perhaps, the Mere was not—and, to date, never has been—drained.

MERMEN

George Brisbane Scott Douglas (1856–1935) was the author of such acclaimed books as *Scottish Fairy and Folk Tales* and *New Border Tales*. He was someone who had a fascination for mysteries of the oceans, and particularly so mermaids and the far-less-mentioned matter of mermen. He said of mermen and mermaids that there were many strange tales emanating from

Scotland's Shetland Isles. Beneath the depths of the ocean, according to these stories, Douglas said:

"[A]n atmosphere exists adapted to the respiratory organs of certain beings, resembling in form the human race, possessed of surpassing beauty, of limited supernatural powers, and liable to the incident of death. They dwell in a wide territory of the globe, far below the region of fishes, over which the sea, like the cloudy canopy of our sky, loftily rolls, and they possess habitations constructed of the pearl and coral productions of the ocean. Having lungs not adapted to a watery medium, but to the nature of atmospheric air, it would be impossible for them to pass through the volume of waters that intervenes between the submarine and supramarine world, if it were not for the extraordinary power they inherit of entering the skin of some animal capable of existing in the sea, which they are enabled to occupy by a sort of demoniacal possession."

Douglas noted something that most people—having only a cursory knowledge of the merman/mermaid phenomenon—would likely be completely unware of. He acknowledged that although most people viewed such creatures as "of an animal human above the waist, yet terminating below in the tail and fins of a fish," that was far from always being the case. He explained that the "most favorite form" was actually that of the "larger seal."

He explained that "... possessing an amphibious nature, they are enabled not only to exist in the ocean, but to land on some rock, where they frequently lighten themselves of their sea-dress, resume their proper shape, and with much curiosity examine the nature of the upper world belonging to the human race. Unfortunately, however, each merman or merwoman possesses but one skin, enabling the individual to ascend the seas, and if, on visiting the abode of man, the garb be lost, the hapless being must unavoidably become an inhabitant of the earth."

Douglas was someone who not only was deeply familiar with mermen lore, but someone who collected a number of fascinating accounts of encounters with what appear to have been—rather incredibly—real half-man, half-fish-like entities. As one example of many, we have the following from Douglas:

"A story is told of a boat's crew who landed for the purpose of attacking the seals lying in the hollows of the crags at one of the stacks. The men stunned a number of the animals, and while they were in this state stripped them of their skins, with the fat attached to them. Leaving the carcases on the rock, the crew were about to set off for the shore of Papa Stour, when such a tremendous swell arose that every one flew quickly to the boat. All succeeded in entering it except one man, who had imprudently lingered behind. The crew were unwilling to leave a companion to perish on the skerries, but the surge increased so fast that after many unsuccessful attempts to bring the boat close in to the stack the unfortunate wright was left to his fate."

Most people just think of mermaids when they contemplate the myth of the half human/half fish beings, but the other side of that is, of course, mermen, who also inhabit stories in our folklore.

Douglas continued, detailing how things quickly developed, and in a strange and unforeseen fashion: "A stormy night came on, and the deserted Shetlander saw no prospect before him but that of perishing from cold and hunger, or of being washed into the sea by the breakers which threatened to dash over the rocks. At length he perceived many of the seals, who in their flight had escaped the attack of the boatmen, approach the skerry, disrobe themselves of their amphibious hides, and resume the shape of the sons and daughters of the ocean. Their first object was to assist in the recovery of their friends, who, having been stunned by clubs, had, while in that state, been deprived of their skins.

"When the flayed animals had regained their sensibility," said Douglas, "they assumed their proper form of mermen or merwomen, and began to lament in a mournful way, wildly accompanied by the storm that was raging around, the loss of their sea-dress, which would prevent them from again enjoying their native azure atmosphere and coral mansions that lay below the deep waters of the Atlantic."

The chief lamentation of the mermen, said Douglas, was for one Ollavitinus, the son of Gioga, who, "...having been stripped of his seal's skin, would be forever parted from his mates, and condemned to become an outcast inhabitant of the upper world. Their song was at length broken off by observing one of their enemies viewing, with shivering limbs and looks of comfortless despair, the wild waves that dashed over the stack. Gioga immediately conceived the idea of rendering subservient to the advantage of her son the perilous situation of the man. She addressed him with mildness, proposing to carry him safe on her back across the sea to Papa Stour, on condition of receiving the seal-skin of Ollavitinus."

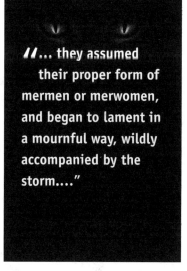

// ... they assumed their proper form of mermen or merwomen, and began to lament in a mournful way, wildly accompanied by the storm...."

A bargain was struck, added Douglas, and "...Gioga clad herself in her amphibious garb; but the Shetlander, alarmed at the sight of the stormy main that he was to ride through, prudently begged leave of the matron, for his better preservation, that he might be allowed to cut a few holes in her shoulders and flanks, in order to procure, between the skin and the flesh, a better, fastening for his hands and feet. The request being complied with, the man grasped the neck of the seal, and committing himself to her care, she landed him safely at Acres Gio in Papa Stour; from which place he immediately repaired to a skeo at Hamna Voe, where the skin was deposited, and honorably fulfilled his part of the contract by affording Gioga the means whereby her son could again revisit the ethereal space over which the sea spread its green mantle."

MOKELE-MBEMBE

For at least two centuries, there has been talk of a deadly and violent monster lurking in the deep and dark waters of Africa, and particularly so in the

Congo. Lakes, rivers, and swampy environments are those most preferred by the monster that has become known as Mokele-Mbembe. In English, it means "the one who stops the flow of rivers." It's a most apt name, since the Mokele-Mbembe is said to be the size of an elephant—and maybe even bigger—and has a long, muscular neck.

Although, at a local level, the existence of the beast was known for generations, it was not until 1980 that the rest of the world, thanks to mainstream media sources, got to hear about this mysterious animal, which sounds not unlike some surviving relic from the Jurassic era. It was in that year that Dr. Roy P. Mackal headed off to Africa to try and determine the true nature of the Mokele-Mbembe. It's important to note that Mackal was not some wide-eyed, amateur sleuth. No, he was a biologist and biochemist who spent much of his time working at the University of Chicago.

Mackal had the very good fortune to interview a large number of native people who had seen Mokele-Mbembe, or who had heard of its exploits. Having listened carefully to what the witnesses said, and studied their descriptions of the appearance of the monster, Mackal came to an astonishing conclusion: the animals were very possibly sauropods. We're talking about huge reptiles that we are told became extinct 65 million years ago, when the dinosaurs' rule of the planet came to a crashing end—possibly as a result of a comet or a massive meteorite slamming into the Earth. Seven years after his trip to Africa, Mackal penned a book on his work, *In Search of Mokele-Mbembe*.

The Mokele-Mbembe is a huge creature resembling a brachiosaurus that lives in the Congo.

Mackal was not the only person to seek out the truth of the monsters of the Congo. The late J. Richard Greenwell also spent much time trying to resolve the riddle of Mokele-Mbembe. His target was the Likouala River—a place where he stumbled on a number of massive tracks, which suggested the presence of a huge, lumbering beast that spent time in both the water and on land.

In 1986, a man named Rory Nugent caught sight of a long-necked animal in the Likouala Swamp, adding further weight to the theory that the Mokele-Mbembes are sauropods. The strangest part of the story is that Nugent managed to secure a couple of clear photographs of the animal. They could, potentially, have resolved the matter once and for all. Except for one thing: the native people of the area viewed the Mokele-Mbembe as a supernatural beast. The result: they demanded Nugent destroy the film, lest the monster would kill them all. Given the hostility shown to Nugent, he, perhaps wisely, did as he was told.

Mokele-Mbembe seeker Bill Gibbons tells a fascinating story from the 1960s:

> the native people of the area viewed the Mokele-Mbembe as a supernatural beast [and they] ... demanded Nugent destroy the film, lest the monster would kill them all.

"Around 1960, the forest dwelling pygmies of the Lake Tele region (the Bangombe tribe) fished daily in the lake near the Molibos, or water channels situated at the north end of the lake. These channels merge with the swamps, and were used by Mokele-mbembes to enter the lake where they would browse on the vegetation. This daily excursion into the lake by the animals disrupted the pygmies fishing activities. Eventually, the pygmies decided to erect a stake barrier across the molibo in order to prevent the animals from entering the lake.

"When two of the animals were observed attempting to break through the barrier, the pygmies speared one of the animals to death and later cut it into pieces. This task apparently took several days due to the size of the animal, which was described as being bigger than a forest elephant with a long neck, a small snake-like or lizard-like head, which was decorated with a comb-like frill."

The search for Mokele-Mbembe continues: Richard Freeman, of the Centre for Fortean Zoology, traveled to the domain of the monster in 2006 and, while he believes the creature exists, he strongly suspects it's an unknown type of huge monitor-lizard. Imagine a thirty-foot-long, ferocious Komodo dragon and you have an idea of what Freeman has in mind.

MONSTER OF THE MERE

It all began on Valentine's Day, 2002, when a Lancashire, England, newspaper announced that "something" had been attacking swans at a picturesque, otherwise tranquil, nature reserve in the north of England. Eyewitnesses reported that a giant, unknown creature had been seen dragging fully grown swans beneath the water—which were never seen again. The location was the Wildfowl and Wetland's Trust Reserve at Martin Mere, Ormskirk, Lancashire.

And, when the media started reporting that the beast was "the size of a small car," things really took off in the publicity stakes.

Pat Wisniewski, the reserve's manager, said that: "Whatever it was out there must have been pretty big to pull a swan back into the water. Swans weigh up to thirteen kilos. This could be an extremely large pike or a Wels catfish." Wisniewski had good reason to take the matter seriously, as four years previously, in 1998, he had spotted something large and dark circling in the mere—much to his consternation and concern. It didn't take long before a team of intrepid investigators from Britain's premier monster hunting group, the Centre for Fortean Zoology, headed from their home base in the south of England to Martin Mere. It was an ambitious project, led by CFZ Director Jon Downes, and with backup provided by Richard Freeman, a former head zoo keeper at Leicestershire's Twycross Zoo.

// Whatever it was out there must have been pretty big to pull a swan back into the water. Swans weigh up to thirteen kilos."

In no time at all, the story went from one of a mystery fish to a tale involving "dragons," "unexplained ancient human mutilation," and even "a resident mermaid." Of course, much of this was due to media hype and sensationalism, but people were clearly seeing something out of the ordinary. The CFZ was determined to know exactly what it was. Freeman and Downes undertook numerous interviews with local folk who had seen the beast. They were pretty much unanimous that it was a powerful, fast-swimming creature with a slick, shiny, muscular back—that moved with astonishing speed.

It was thanks to Freeman's dedication that, in July 2002, he finally caught sight of the monster-fish. Although it was only in view for mere moments, Freeman was pretty sure that what he encountered in the dark waters was a Wels catfish. But, this was no ordinary Wels. It was huge. In all likelihood, said Freeman, it was very old, somewhere in the region of no less than a century in age. The older the Wels, the bigger its size. Freeman opined that it had probably managed to successfully avoid one and all for decades, happily living on the local fish and bird population. And, of course, who would believe it if someone occasionally reported seeing a monster-fish in Martin Mere? Probably no one until—for reasons unknown—the great beast made its presence known more and more in the summer of 2002.

Sightings have subsided in recent years, leading to the possibility that the immense car-sized creature has died, or perhaps more likely, has retreated to the lower, muddy depths of the mere to avoid detection and media attention. Keep that latter possibility in mind should you ever visit Martin Mere and decide to go for a paddle. You may do so at your cost—and possibly at the expense of a few toes or even your very life.

MORAG

Make mention of Scottish lake monsters to most people and they will inevitably conjure up imagery of the world's most famous unknown water beast, the Loch Ness Monster. It's a little known fact, however, that there are more than a few Scottish lakes with legends of diabolical creatures attached to them. While many of the stories are decidedly fragmentary in nature, one of them is not. Welcome to the world of Morag, the resident beasty of Loch Morar.

At just over eleven and a half miles in length, it has the distinction of being the deepest body of fresh water in the British Isles, with a depth of just over 1,000 feet (305 meters). Unlike Loch Ness, the water of which is almost black, Loch Morar can boast of having practically clear water. It takes its name from the village of Morar, which is situated close by and specifically at the western side of the loch, the site of the Battle of Morar—a violent, death-filled confrontation between the Mackenzie and MacDonell clans.

As for the monster, Morag, the tales are many. What makes them so different to the ones coming out of Loch Ness, however, is not the descriptions of the creatures, but that such reports are often hard to uncover. Unlike Loch Ness, Loch Morar is an isolated, seldom visited loch. It is bereft of much in the way of a large population and not particularly easy to access. The result is that tourists to Scotland very rarely visit it. The same goes for native Scots, too! For that reason, just like Las Vegas, what happens at Loch Morar is very often destined to stay there. Nevertheless, there are enough classic cases on record to strongly suggest strange things lurk in Loch Morar.

One of the earliest reports came from a man named James McDonald, who claimed a sighting of a three-humped creature snaking through the waters, late one cold, dark night in January 1887. Rather ominously, superstitious locals perceived this as a distinctly ill omen: the three sections were seen as death, a coffin, and a grave—such was the fear that the villagers had of the monster in their midst. Eight years later, Sir Theodore Brinckman and his wife were fishing at the loch when a long thing, shaped like an upturned boat, surfaced from the depths. "It'll just be the monster," said one of the locals, a man named MacLaren.

An astonishing sighting occurred in 1948, when a man named Alexander MacDonnell saw one of the Morags

> Unlike Loch Ness, Loch Morar is an isolated, seldom visited loch. It is bereft of much in the way of a large population and not particularly easy to access.

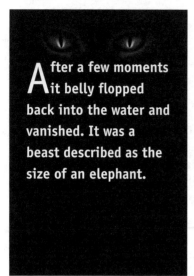

After a few moments it belly flopped back into the water and vanished. It was a beast described as the size of an elephant.

actually on the bank of the shore, at Bracorina Point. After a few moments it belly flopped back into the water and vanished. It was a beast described as the size of an elephant. Needless to say, there is no known, indigenous creature in the British Isles that rivals an elephant in size. In the same year, a number of people, led by a Mr. John Gillies, caught sight of an approximately thirty-foot-long animal, displaying no fewer than four humps. Then, in August 1968, John MacVarish had a close view of an unknown animal in Loch Morar, one that displayed a snake-like head of about six feet in length and had very dark, or black, skin.

Without a doubt the most amazing—and, for the witnesses, nerve-wracking—encounters occurred on the night of August 16, 1969. That was when William Simpson and Duncan McDonnell were traveling on the waters, near the west end of the loch. Suddenly, as if out of nowhere, a large animal—possibly thirty feet in length—loomed into view and actually collided with their motorboat. Or perhaps, *rammed* would be a better term to use. When Simpson tried to blast the creature with his shotgun, it sank beneath the waves—as a result of the ear-splitting sound of the gun, both men concluded, rather than as a result of Simpson having actually shot the monster.

As for what the Morags might really be, monster hunter Richard Freeman says: "As with the Nessie I think the best bet are giant sterile eels. The common eels swim out to the Sargasso Sea to breed then die. The baby eels follow scent trails back to their ancestral fresh water homes and the cycle begins again. Sometimes, however a mutation occurs and the eel is sterile. These stay in fresh water and keep on growing. Known as eunuch eels no one knows how old they get or how big. One theory suggests that these rare, naturally occurring, mutations may now be on the increase due to pollution. PCBs and Beta Blocker chemicals have long been implicated in causing sterility in fish. Could they be causing more eunuch eels in the deep lakes of Scotland? For now, we just don't know."

MORGAWR

In August 2010, an English author, good friend, and seeker of all things weird, Elizabeth Randall, said that according to a sensational article that appeared in the pages of the British *Daily Mail* newspaper that same month, "… a picture has been circulating on the Internet purporting to show a sea monster that, so far seems to have eluded identification. It was seen off Saltern Cove, Devon, U.K., and has been dubbed by many as a 'new Nessie.' The image appears to show a greenish-brown, long-necked 'something,' with a reptilian-like head, that was trailing a shoal of fish just 30 yards offshore. According to reports the fish beached themselves just a few seconds later."

Elizabeth continued: "The photo was sent to the Marine Conservation Society, who have still to decide exactly what it is. Although theories range from a sea serpent to a salt water crocodile. The lady who took the photograph at first thought that it might be a turtle but the Marine Conservation Society (MCS) says that not only do turtles not chase fish, but the description doesn't fit."

Meanwhile, of this very same affair, Jonathan Downes of the Centre for Fortean Zoology, who is an expert on reports of strange and unknown animals, said: "Me? I think it is a basking shark; I think that what appears to be its back is its tail, and the 'head' is the tip of its nose, but golly, wouldn't I love to be proved wrong!"

Others suggested that nothing more than a turtle was possibly the culprit. Photographs that were taken by one of the witnesses, Gill Pearce, however, clearly demonstrated that the neck of the creature was much too long for it to be that of a regular turtle. Pearce took the photos on July 27, and subsequently reported the details of the encounter to the Marine Conservation Society, a spokesperson for whom, Claire Fischer, told the press:

"Gill Pearce spotted the creature about 20 meters from the bay at Saltern Cove, near Goodrington. It was observed at about 15.30 on 27 July but by the time she had got her camera it had moved further out. She spotted it following a shoal of fish which beached themselves in Saltern Cove. The creature remained in the sea, then went out again and followed the shoal—this indicates it's not a turtle as they only eat jellyfish. We would love to know if other people have seen anything like this in the same area and can help clear up the mystery."

It's possible that what was seen was Morgawr, a sea-serpent-style beast that has been reportedly seen for decades in and around Falmouth Bay, Cornwall, England—which, very notably, is situated only one county away from where this latest incident

The very real basking shark has an odd appearance that certainly could mistake it for a sea monster, and that makes it a candidate for one theory behind the Morgawr.

occurred. Variously described as looking like a giant serpent, a monstrous eel, or even a supposedly extinct plesiosaur, Morgawr was first viewed in September 1975 by two witnesses who claimed to have seen a humped animal with "stumpy horns" and with bristles that ran along the length of its long neck, and which apparently had a conger-eel in its huge mouth.

A whole wave of startling encounters with the creature allegedly occurred during the period 1975 to 1976, and such reports continue to surface sporadically from time to time and from this very same location. Did Morgawr possibly decide to take a trip along the coast for a brief vacation and to entertain the nation's media? Maybe so!

NARRABEEN LAGOON MONSTER

Occasionally I get asked: what's the strangest unknown animal lurking in the woods, jungles, or mountain ranges of our world? Well, first and foremost, there are plenty of them! And, second, each and every one of them is undeniably odd. After all, how else would you describe Bigfoot, the Loch Ness Monster, and the Chupacabra than downright weird? But, here's the important thing: some are far, far weirder than others.

Beyond any shadow of doubt, Sydney, Australia, can claim fame to having played host to one of the most mystifying and bizarre of all creatures ever encountered. And I do not use the words "mystifying and bizarre" lightly. After all, how else would you describe a diminutive beast that looks like an elephant but walks on its hind legs and surfaces from the depths of nothing less than a dark lagoon? That was exactly what a woman named Mabel Walsh encountered in Narrabeen—a beachside suburb of Sydney—back in the late 1960s.

> **how else would you describe a diminutive beast that looks like an elephant but walks on its hind legs and surfaces from the depths of nothing less than a dark lagoon?**

While driving home late one April 1968 evening with her nephew, John, Walsh was shocked to fleetingly see the approximately four-foot-tall animal emerge from the watery depths and shuffle its way into the heart of nearby scrubland. It was a creature that Walsh would never forget, even though it was in view for only mere seconds. Gray in color, with what looked like a tough, leathery skin, it had a snout resembling that of an anteater, a slim trunk, long back legs, and a pair of short forelimbs that dangled as it waddled along—sideways, no less—by the edge of the road, before vanishing into the scrub.

The local newspaper, the *Daily Telegraph*, recognizing the publicity the story would surely create, splashed the details across its pages. In an article titled: "And Now It's the Monster of Narrabeen!"—and with the subtitle of: "Loch Ness Was Never Like This"—the details of Mabel Walsh's story tumbled out, which provoked yet more reports of the fantastic creature.

Some of them sounded decidedly sensationalized, since they suggested the monster of the deep had taken to dragging sheep, cows, and even horses to their horrific deaths in the heart of the lagoon, a most unlikely action for a creature barely four feet in height! Others spoke in near-hysterical tones of seeing a bright red-colored, clawed hand come out of a hole in the ground at the lake and try and grab a terrified youngster.

The final word on the matter went to Mabel Walsh, who started the controversy, and who told newspaper staff that people might call her crazy, but she was absolutely sure there was a bizarre creature in Narrabeen Lake. As it transpired, not many did call her crazy. The *Daily Telegraph's* audience excitedly lapped it all up, and, sales-wise, its staff was very happy indeed. Walsh's story is made all the more bizarre by the fact that the creature she saw was not the only resident weirdo in the area.

Still on the matter of Sydney's monsters, we have to now take a trip to the vast and picturesque Blue Mountains. Chiefly composed of a huge plateau that borders Sydney's bustling metropolitan area, the mountains sit in the central region of what is known as the Sydney Basin, and are home to one of the area's most famous attractions: a trio of tall peaks known as the Three Sisters. Many, however, claim that the Blue Mountains are home to something even more spectacular than those three rocky women: the Australian equivalent of Sasquatch. Or, as it's known in the land down under: the Yowie.

Of course, no one would claim that Mabel Walsh saw a Yowie. But, that the creature she encountered was seen not at all far from where huge, hulking apes are also seen only makes her case even more…well…weird!

NORWEGIAN SEA MONSTER

Nineteenth-century sea serpent seeker Henry Lee recorded that "Archdeacon of Molde, gives the following account of an incident that occurred there on the 28th of July, 1845."

In the Archdeacon's (the Reverend Mr. Dein-Boll's) own words:

"J. C. Lund, bookseller and printer; G. S. Krogh, merchant; Christian Flang, Lund's apprentice, and John Elgenses, labourer, were out on Romsdalfjord, fishing. The sea was, after a warm, sunshiny day, quite calm. About seven o'clock in the afternoon, at a little distance from the shore, near the ballast place and Molde Hooe, they saw a long marine animal, which slowly moved itself forward, as it appeared to them, with the help of two fins, on the fore-part of the body nearest the head, which they judged by the boiling of the water on both sides of it.

"The visible part of the body appeared to be between forty and fifty feet in length, and moved in undulations, like a snake. The body was round and of a dark colour, and seemed to be several ells in thickness. As they discerned a waving motion in the water behind the animal, they concluded that part of the body was concealed under water. That it was one continuous animal they saw plainly from its movement.

"When the animal was about one hundred yards from the boat, they noticed tolerably correctly its fore parts, which ended in a sharp snout; its colossal head raised itself above the water in the form of a semi-circle; the lower part was not visible. The colour of the head was dark-brown and the skin smooth; they did not notice the eyes, or any mane or bristles on the throat.

"When the serpent came about a musket-shot near, Lund fired at it, and was certain the shots hit it in the head. After the shot, it dived, but came up immediately. It raised its neck in the air, like a snake preparing to dart on his prey. After he had turned and got his body in a straight line, which he appeared to do with great difficulty, he darted like an arrow against the boat. They reached the shore, and the animal, perceiving it had come into shallow water, dived immediately and disappeared in the deep.

"Such is the declaration of these four men, and no one has cause to question their veracity, or imagine that they were so seized with fear that they could not observe what took place so near them. There are not many here, or on other parts of the Norwegian coast, who longer doubt the existence of the sea-serpent. The writer of this narrative was a long time sceptical, as he had not been so fortunate as to see this monster of the deep; but after the many accounts he has read, and the relations he has received from credible witnesses, he does not dare longer to doubt the existence of the sea-serpent."

OGOPOGO

While Loch Ness, Scotland's Nessie is certainly the world's most famous lake monster, it most assuredly does not stand—or swim—alone. Numerous lakes around the world are said to be the lairs of monstrous serpents of the deep. In all likelihood, some sightings of such alleged creatures are due to mistaken identity—of catfish and sturgeon, both of which can grow to impressive sizes. But there are those reports that simply cannot be dismissed in such a down-to-earth fashion. Take for example, Ogopogo, of Okanagan Lake, British Columbia.

It's interesting to note that Okanagan Lake is, like Loch Ness, a place of considerable size, one in which a colony of predominantly underwater-based creatures could survive and thrive. It is more than eighty miles long, three miles wide, and just short of 250 feet deep.

Like its Scottish cousin Nessie, Ogopogo has a long and rich history of sightings. We may never know for sure how far back into history the creatures of Okanagan Lake extend, but we can say for sure that the Native Americans

A children's playground in British Columbia, Canada, has this charming Ogopogo statue for kids to play on. The real creature, though, would be less fun to meet in person.

who lived in the area as early as the 1700s knew that the waters of the lake were home to something monstrous and terrifying. That much is evident by the name they gave to the beast—or, far more likely of course, beasts. They called it the *n'ha-a-itk*. Very appropriately, it translates into English as "Lake Demon."

Perhaps "Lake Demon" was too horrific for the locals and they settled upon "Ogopogo." The story of the name is an intriguing and winding one, as the late cryptozoologist Mark Chorvinsky noted: "The name Ogopogo might suggest to some that it is an Indian word, but all evidence points to a modern origin. According to Mary Moon, author of *Ogopogo: the Okanagan Mystery* (1977), in 1924 a local named Bill Brimblecomb sang a song parodying a popular British music-hall tune at a Rotary Club luncheon in Vernon, a city in the northern Okanagan Valley. H. F. Beattie adapted the lyrics."

> Literally dozens of people—in no less than thirty vehicles—saw a mysterious creature in the vicinity of Okanagan Mission Beach.

As for those lyrics, they read as follows: "I'm looking for the Ogopogo, his mother was a mutton, his father was a whale, I'm going to put a little bit of salt on his tail."

When it comes to the eyewitness accounts of Ogopogo, the list is impressive. Most witnesses describe a large creature—anywhere from fifteen to twenty-five feet and, on occasion, even as long as fifty feet—serpentine in appearance, and sometimes displaying undulating "humps" and a neck that occasionally rises out of the water, to a height of six to seven feet. If true, then this effectively rules out sturgeon or catfish as being the guilty parties. And with that said, let's now take a look at the evidence in support of the theory that Okanagan Lake is a domain of monsters.

It was on September 16, 1926, that Ogopogo was really thrown into the limelight. Literally dozens of people—in no fewer than thirty vehicles—saw a mysterious creature in the vicinity of Okanagan Mission Beach. Like so many others, all were unanimous in their belief that the beast was an immense serpent-like animal.

On July 2, 1947, a Mr. Kray got a good look at an Ogopogo and said the creature had "a long sinuous body, 30 feet in length, consisting of about five undulations, apparently separated from each other by about a two-foot space, in which that part of the undulations would have been underwater. There appeared to be a forked tail, of which only one-half came above the water. From time to time the whole thing submerged and came up again."

Jumping forward more than forty years, there is the case of Ernie Giroux, a hunting guide, who spotted a fifteen-foot-long creature in the waters of the lake in the summer of 1989. Whatever the beast was, it was like nothing Giroux had ever seen before: it "swam real gracefully," had a head shaped like a football, and a long neck. To date, the number of reports of Ogopogo are in the hundreds. As to what the monsters may be—surviving creatures from the Jurassic era, giant eels, or something entirely unknown to science—the answers still elude both monster hunters and those who have been fortunate enough to encounter the famous monster.

OKLAHOMA OCTOPUS

I t's a deeply strange story that is very much dominated by myth, folklore, and urban legend, but which just might have at its heart a genuine mystery of cryptozoological proportions. And it goes like this. In the waters of Lake Thunderbird, Oklahoma, something monstrous and weird is said to dwell. It's described as being octopus-like—hence the memorable moniker the creature now has—and is somewhat akin to a scaled-down version of horror maestro H. P. Love-craft's most famous creation, Cthulhu.

In Lovecraft's own words, Cthulhu was: "A monster of vaguely anthropoid out-line, but with an octopus-like head whose face was a mass of feelers, a scaly, rubbery-looking body, prodigious claws on hind and fore feet, and long, narrow wings behind."

The wings aside, that's not a bad description of the Oklahoma Octopus, too! Of course, Cthulhu was merely the product of Lovecraft's weird-but-gifted mind, right? Well … *probably*. There is, however, a school of thought that believes Lovecraft based at least some of his works on his own, secret, arcane knowledge of terrible beasts and of fantastic, lost lands and ancient civi-lizations. Lovecraft was somewhat familiar with Oklahoma too: he ghost-wrote *The Mound*, which was focused on dark goings-on in Caddo County, Oklahoma.

And on the subject of Oklahoma.…

As noted above, most of the claimed sightings of the Oklahoma Octopus have

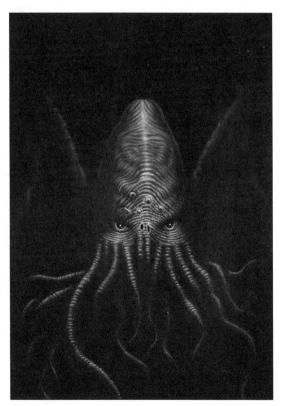

The Oklahoma octopus has been compared to a frightening hell-monster created by horror writer H. P. Lovecraft: Cthulhu.

been reported from within the depths of Lake Thunderbird. This, in itself, is curious, and for three, specific reasons: (A) Lake Thunderbird is a freshwater lake; (B) the lake wasn't built until 1962 (which begs the question: where did the beast, or beasts, come from?); and (C) octopuses live in saltwater environments. Unless, that is, against all the odds an octopus or several have managed to cope with, and adapt to, a freshwater world.

There are other, notable aspects to the story, too: the lake itself is named after another legendary creature of cryptozoological proportions, the Thunderbird, a staple part of Native American lore and history. Plus, the Native Americans who called the area their home centuries ago told stories of monstrous, octopus-like water-beasts in the area way back then—and long before the Oklahoma Octopus was on anyone's radar. The specific locations were the Illinois River (which snakes its way through parts of eastern Oklahoma) and the Verdigris River.

As for the witness reports, they typically revolve around sightings of fairly significantly sized tentacles seen breaking the surface of the lake. Seldom is a complete creature encountered; but there are several such cases that, collectively, still leave the matter wide open.

ONE EYE

Lake Granbury in Texas was constructed in 1969 as a dam for the Brazos River, which is the lake's primary inflow. At more than 1,200 miles (1,930 kilometers) long, the Brazos River is the eleventh-longest river in the United States. And Lake Granbury is hardly small either: it has a surface area of 8,310 acres. The approximately seventy-five-foot-deep lake is home to wide and varied kinds of fish, including catfish, bass, gar, and sunfish. It's a popular spot for a bit of fun, too: water skiing, boating, and fishing are all very popular on weekends and holidays. And then there is the matter of its hideous, terrifying inhabitant. As far as the resident monster is concerned, it goes by the name of One Eye and is described as a classic lake monster: dark gray in color, with a long neck, and a hump-like back. Irish creature-seeker Ronan Coghlan says: "Whether it has attained a one-eyed state by accident or whether it is naturally one-eyed, I cannot say."

Although the lake itself is less than half a century old, the Brazos River has a long history of sightings of huge fish and mysterious creatures. Native Americans and early Spaniards talked of something terrible and savage lurking in the river. In 2010, a huge gar was hauled out of its waters.

Accounts such as these have given rise to the theory that the association between lake, dam, and river has, somehow, allowed the monsters to find their way into Lake Granbury. And, just maybe, there is some truth to the story; maybe a lot of truth. All of which brings us to a close encounter of the beastly variety on a Saturday afternoon in August 1999. According to the witness, Becky, she was standing on a stretch of shoreline—which, I was later able to determine, was not at all far from a row of houses— hanging out with her then-boyfriend, now her husband.

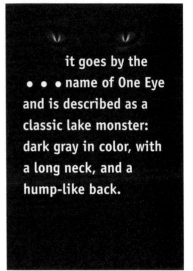

it goes by the
• • • name of One Eye
and is described as a
classic lake monster:
dark gray in color, with
a long neck, and a
hump-like back.

Suddenly, out of nowhere, and at a distance of about forty feet, a large animal lurched out of the water and, for about ten or fifteen seconds, partially beached itself on the land. It thrashed around violently, finally managing to return to the waters and vanishing into the depths. The utterly shocked couple estimated the animal was around seventeen to twenty feet in length, with a body thickness of close to two feet.

Very interestingly, the woman did not describe the creature as resembling a long-extinct plesiosaur, as so many other witnesses have in times past and present. Rather, she had no doubt whatsoever that it was a gigantic eel. As both she and her boyfriend fished regularly, they knew an eel when they saw it. But not usually—or, indeed, ever— of this size!

Certainly, the world of conventional zoology will assure you that eels simply do not—and cannot—reach such immense sizes. But, that doesn't mean they don't exist. Are the legends of One Eye based on sightings of giant eels? If so, how could they get so monstrously huge? The theories and the answers are intriguing.

Richard Freeman, the Zoological Director of Britain's Centre for Fortean Zoology (CFZ), says: "Common eels swim out to the Sargasso Sea to breed then die. The baby eels follow scent trails back to their ancestral fresh waters homes and the cycle begins again. Sometimes, however, a mutation occurs and the eel is sterile. These stay in fresh water and keep on growing. Known as eunuch eels, no one knows how old they get or how big."

The CFZ's head honcho, Jon Downes, offers the following: "In February 2004 two Canadian tourists came upon a 25-foot eel floating in the shallows of Loch Ness. At first they thought it was dead but when it began to move they beat a hasty retreat."

Roland Watson, the author of an excellent book, *The Water Horses of Loch Ness*, says at his *Loch Ness Mystery* blog that "...it is well known that Loch Ness is teeming with eels. No one knows accurately how many eels inhabit the loch because of their behavior. This is because eels are classed as benthic or 'bottom feeders' in that they tend to live on or close to the surface of a sea or lake bottom."

Jon Downes adds: "One theory suggests that these rare, naturally occurring mutations may now be on the increase due to pollution. PCBs [polychlorinated biphenyls] have long been implicated in causing sterility in fish. Could they be causing more eunuch eels in the deep lakes of Scotland?"

Maybe that is exactly what is happening. And, perhaps, not just in Scottish lochs! One Eye might not be just a legend, after all.

PADDLER

Situated in Idaho, Lake Pend Oreille is a huge expanse of water that extends in excess of forty miles (64 kilometers) in length and 1,000 feet (305 meters) in depth. And, it might accurately be said that the lake is the home to a creature not unlike the Loch Ness Monster, Scotland's legendary Nessie. On the other hand, however, Lake Pend Oreille's lake monster—known locally as Paddler—might be something even stranger.

Sightings of the prehistoric-looking thing date back to the 1940s and continue to the present day. A particularly spectacular encounter with Paddler occurred on Memorial Day in 1985. That was when a woman named Julie Green was on the lake with several friends when they all caught sight of something huge and fantastic: a large, gray-colored thing racing across the lake, seemingly partially above and below the surface of the water. That the thing was only around 600 feet away meant Green and her friends were able to determine that whatever it was, it wasn't a wave.

Then, in 1996, the Groves family of Pasadena, California—vacationing with family who lived in the lake area—reported seeing early on a Sunday morning a large, gray-colored object break the waters. It was described as resembling the back of an elephant, in both color and size. Needless to say, Lake Pend Oreille isn't home to a herd of elephants that enjoy taking morning swims.

While monster hunters are content to suggest that Paddler (or *the* Paddlers) is either an unknown animal or one from the Jurassic era that survived extinction, there is another explanation for the presence of the monster. Patrick Huyghe is someone who has undertaken extensive research into the saga of Paddler and he has noted something that could be of deep and relevant significance: "The very first mention of Paddler came straight from the Navy's own Farragut Naval Training Station, established on the southwestern end of Lake Pend Oreille in 1942."

Built in response to the terrible and tragic events at Pearl Harbor in December 1941, the FNTS was created at Lake Pend Oreille and though which around 290,000 servicemen and women passed, as the hostilities with the Axis powers grew. What is particularly interesting, however, is that in the post-war era—that's to say, after 1945—the Navy presence on the lake began to change. The one arm that began to play a more substantial role was the Navy's Acoustic Research Department. The ARD says of its work: "Unique experimental hardware and floating platforms have been developed" at the naval facilities on Lake Pend Oreille, noting too that "future plans include continuation of sonar dome development and submarine silencing and target strength reduction experiments using large-scaled models."

Julie Green was • • • on the lake with several friends when they all caught sight of something huge and fantastic: a large, gray-colored thing racing across the lake....

One has to wonder if some of these "unique experimental hardware," "floating platforms," and "large-scale models" may have been responsible for at least some sightings of what the witnesses believed was Paddler.

Patrick Huyghe notes something that is supportive of this particular theory: "In 1949 and 1950, a few years after this secret Navy test site opened, the next two accounts of the lake monster appeared in local newspapers."

It's not at all unlikely—or unfeasible—that the U.S. Navy might secretly spread tales of lake monsters, such as Paddler, to divert people from learning the truth of what was really afoot deep in Lake Pend Oreille, namely the covert testing of new subsurface military vehicles of a highly classified, experimental nature.

PEPIE OF THE LAKE MONSTER

Just about everyone has heard of Nessie, the famous long-necked monster of Scotland's Loch Ness. As we have seen, however, Nessie is not the only creature inhabiting a lake. Indeed, lake monsters surface here, there, and everywhere. One of them is Pepie of Lake Pepin. Of both the lake and its resident monster, Larry Nielsen—a recognized authority on both—says:

"Lake Pepin is the largest lake on the Mississippi River, over two miles [3.2 kilometers] wide and twenty-two miles [35.4 kilometers] long. It forms the

Lake Pepin, which is located on the border between Wisconsin and Minnesota, is described as one of the most beautiful lakes in the area. Too bad it also harbors a lake monster!

natural border between Minnesota and Wisconsin and is located about sixty miles south of the Twin Cities. Surrounded by scenic bluffs and quaint villages, Lake Pepin is widely described as one of the most scenic spots in North America! The native Dakota people that lived in the area refused to travel on Lake Pepin in bark canoes because of the large 'creatures' that would rise from the depths of the Lake and puncture the thin bark skin of those canoes. They would only travel on Lake Pepin in stouter dugout canoes that were made by hollowing out a large log."

Of the mysterious beast—or, far more likely, beasts—Nielsen notes: "On April 28, 1871 a lake monster is seen swimming in Lake Pepin. Since then, many people have reported sightings of an unidentified creature surfacing from the depths of Lake Pepin. The locals have given this shy and elusive creature a name; Pepie. Over the years the question persists: what is Pepie? Because Lake Pepin is almost identical in size and geography to Scotland's Loch Ness (which is twenty-three miles long and one and a half miles wide), many people feel that Pepie is a relative of the famous Loch Ness creature dubbed Nessie."

The *La Crosse Tribune* notes that Nielsen "claims to have seen the monster twice—The first time, he was out on the lake in a speed boat with his wife.

They were the only craft on the water and the lake was 'smooth as glass,' when suddenly he saw an enormous wake churning in the middle of the lake, about two feet high and 200 feet long, Neilson recalled. 'I have no idea what it was, but whatever it was, it was very, very large,' he said. The second time he was driving along the lake and noticed what looked like a log, 15–20 feet long, floating in the lake. He thought nothing of it, until he realized that the log was floating upstream against the river's current. He pulled to the side of the road and grabbed his camera, but by that time whatever he saw had disappeared."

As for that 1871 encounter, it was chronicled in the April 26, 1871, edition of the *Wabasha County Sentinel.* Under the heading of "Living Curiosity," we're told: "Giles Hyde and C. Page Bonney, report having seen some sort of sea monster, on Monday last, in the lake, between this and Stockholm. It was the size of an elephant and rhinoceros, and moved through the water with great rapidity. It is understood now, since they have told the story, that the same thing, whatever it may be, has been seen on one or two other occasions. The water in the lake is known to be very deep, whales might live in it—but this is not likely to be a whale, the question is, what is it?"

What, indeed? It's a question still being asked to this day. The Pepie is now the subject of a full-length book: *Pepie The Lake Monster of the Mississippi River*, written by Chad Lewis and Noah Voss. Theirs is a refreshingly down-to-earth book, one that addresses a variety of theories for the monsters. Giant eels, long-necked plesiosaurs, mistaken identity, and hoaxes are all given space. While, as their book shows, the number of reports—even in today's world—is nowhere near frequent, clearly something inhabits Lake Pepie. As for its actual identification, just like Nessie, Pepie is definitely an enigma.

RIVER MONSTER

In June 2015, a monster-sized fish was spotted by two astonished and terrified anglers on the River Nene, in the Fens, Cambridgeshire, England. One of the fishermen told BBC Radio Cambridgeshire: "I enjoy going out on my boat. One day we were on our boat going up towards Whittlesey and the boat suddenly juddered as if there was something large in the water. My friend and myself looked at each other and I looked down to see what we had hit. I saw the most extraordinary thing. I saw the biggest fish I have ever seen in my life. I like boating and I like wildlife, but I had never seen a fish like this before. It was absolutely huge—it was over six-foot long. It was swimming alongside us and our boat had struck it and it was as if it was showing us the side of itself where the propeller had hit it and we could see the white flesh. My friend saw it and exclaimed 'Blimey is that a dolphin?' It was so big. We're going to go out again this year and see if we can see it."

The two men speculated that what they had seen was a sturgeon. Not an impossibility, since sturgeon can grow to impressive sizes. But, the catfish was also offered as a potential candidate—echoing the Centre for Fortean Zoology's experiences at Martin Mere in 2002 (see Monster of the Mere). Then there was the theory that the creature was a giant eel, a creature that, on occasion, has been suggested for the Loch Ness Monster.

> **//**It was swimming alongside us and our boat had struck it and it was as if it was showing us the side of itself where the propeller had hit it and we could see the white flesh."

The witness was forty-one-year-old Michelle Cooper, who was prompted to come forward by the June 2015 encounter. Her sighting, however, occurred one year earlier. She spoke out to the *Cambridge News*: "I told people about it last year and they just took the mickey but now that these anglers have seen it too I know what they mean by being terrified. I am 5 ft 4 inches tall and it was bigger than me. The water was crystal clear and I had a good look at it. I didn't see any white like the fishermen.

"I saw dark brown and when I researched what it could [be] I found it looked exactly like the giant eels you get in America. I was really shaken up by it. It was terrifying but I don't think it would hurt anyone. It seems to just stay low down on the river bed. It was so big it did create a wave and knocked my boat. I've seen pike and catfish and it definitely wasn't that. I went for my camera to get a picture of it but it moved too fast and was gone before I could get a shot."

Whatever the true nature of the immense leviathan, its identity remains unknown.

RIVER NESS MONSTER

Just about everyone has heard of Scotland's famous and legendary Loch Ness Monster. But what about the monster of the *River* Ness? Most people, when faced with such a question, would likely say "Huh?" But read on and all will become clear. As incredible as it may sound, there's a distinct possibility that no fewer than *two* breeds of unknown animals call this particularly notable area their home.

It was way back in the sixth century when a certain St. Columba spent time in the vicinity of both Loch Ness and the River Ness. And for those who may not know, the latter is an approximately twelve-mile- (nineteen-kilometer-) long stretch of water located at the northern end of Loch Ness. The life of St. Columba was chronicled by yet another saint: St. Adomnán. In the words of Adomnán himself we have the following, amazing account:

"[W]hen the blessed man was staying for some days in the province of the Picts, he found it necessary to cross the river Ness; and, when he came to the bank thereof, he sees some of the inhabitants burying a poor unfortunate little fellow, whom, as those who were burying him themselves reported, some water monster had a little before snatched at as he was swimming, and bitten with a most savage bite, and whose hapless corpse some men who came in a boat to give assistance, though too late, caught hold of by putting out hooks."

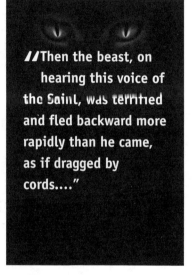

//Then the beast, on hearing this voice of the Saint, was terrified and fled backward more rapidly than he came, as if dragged by cords...."

Adomnán continued: "The blessed man however, on hearing this, directs that some one of his companions shall swim out and bring to him the cable that is on the other bank, sailing it across. On hearing this direction of the holy and famous man, Lugne Mocumin, obeying without delay, throws off all his clothes except his under-garment, and casts himself into the water.

"Now the monster, which before was not so much satiated as made eager for prey, was lying hid in the bottom of the river; but perceiving that the water above was disturbed by him who was crossing, suddenly emerged, and, swimming to the man as he was crossing in the middle of the stream, rushed up with a great roar and open mouth. Then the blessed man looked on, while all who were there, as well the heathen as even the brethren, were stricken with very great terror; and, with his holy hand raised on high, he formed the saving sign of the cross in the empty air, invoked the Name of God, and commanded the fierce monster, saying, 'Think not to go further, nor touch thou the man. Quick! Go back!'"

And, finally, we have this from Adomnán: "Then the beast, on hearing this voice of the Saint, was terrified and fled backward more rapidly than he came, as if dragged by cords, although before it had come so near to Lugne as he swam, that there was not more than the length of one punt-pole between the man and the beast. Then the brethren, seeing that the beast had gone away, and that their comrade Lugne was returned to them safe and sound in the boat, glorified God in the blessed man, greatly marveling. Moreover also the barbarous heathens who were there present, constrained by the greatness of that miracle, which they themselves had seen, magnified the God of the Christians."

The skeptic might say that this story—and the accompanying death by a river monster—is nothing but a piece of folklore. However, it's very intriguing that if the whole thing was merely someone's idea of a hoax—or a means to promote the power of the Christian God—they should have chosen, of all possible places in Scotland, the River Ness as the site of the action and death.

It may well be the case that the creatures of the River Ness and those of Loch Ness are one and the same—or, at the very least, closely related. There is, however, the matter of that violent death recorded by Adomnán. The beast of the river seems to have a particular dislike of people. On the other hand, there is not a single case on record of people losing their lives to the monsters of the loch. In view of that, if, one day, you wish to take a paddle or a swim in those mysterious waters, it's probably very wise to avoid the River Ness and head to Loch Ness. You know; just in case it's feeding time for the monsters.

SOLIMOES RIVER BEAST

In October 1907, a remarkable and terrifying encounter with a water monster occurred on the Solimoes River, Brazil. The story came from a respected German explorer and adventurer, Franz Herrmann Schmidt, who, along with a companion, Captain Rudolph Pfleng, spent weeks exploring the wilder areas of Colombia, and in search of all things wild and wonderful. He certainly found them. Or, at least, one of them.

Twelve days into their trek along the Solimoes River, Schmidt, Pfleng, and their Indian guides reached a remote valley that was filled with thick vegetation and fed by a small, shallow lake. The entire team was excited, but also disturbed, to see a number of huge tracks leading to and from the lake—tracks that were unrecognizable as anything conventional. In addition, there was evidence that whatever left the tracks had been feeding on the leaves of certain trees that extended to heights of around fourteen feet. In other words, this was a formidable, huge creature.

The next day, something astounding occurred. As Schmidt, Pfleng, and their guides negotiated the waters of the lake in canoes, a sudden, loud crashing and splashing was heard coming from the direction of the thick vegetation on the bank to their right side. The guides, seemingly having some pre-existing awareness of the beast that lurked just out of sight, panicked and they furiously paddled their canoes away from the edge and towards the central portion of the lake.

In Schmidt's own words: "There was a sudden outcry among [the monkeys], a large dark something half hidden among the branches shot up among them and there was a great commotion. One of the excited Indians began to paddle the boat away from the shore, and before we could stop him we were one hundred feet from the waterline. Now we could see nothing and the Indians absolutely refused to put in again, while neither Pfleng nor myself cared to lay down our rifles to paddle. There was a great waving of plants and a sound like heavy slaps of a great paddle, mingled with the cries of some of the monkeys moving rapidly away from the lake. One or two that were hurt or held fast were shrieking close at hand, then their cries ceased. For a full ten minutes there was silence, then the green growth began to stir again, and coming back to the lake we beheld the frightful monster that I shall now describe."

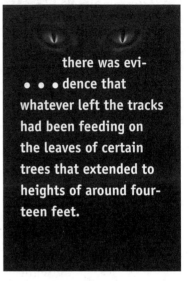

there was evi- ● ● ● dence that whatever left the tracks had been feeding on the leaves of certain trees that extended to heights of around fourteen feet.

"Frightful" was a most apt word for Schmidt to use, as his following words make very clear:

"The head appeared over bushes ten feet tall. It was about the size of a beer keg and was shaped like that of a tapir, as if the snout was used for pulling things or taking hold of them. The eyes were small and dull and set in like those of an alligator. Despite the half dried mud we could see that the neck, which was very snakelike, only thicker in proportion, was rough knotted like an alligator's sides rather than his back.

"Evidently the animal saw nothing odd in us, if he noticed us, and advanced till he was not more than one hundred and fifty feet away. We could see part of the body, which I should judge to have been eight or nine feet thick at the shoulders, if that word may be used, since there were no fore legs, only some great, heavy clawed flippers. The surface was like that of the neck. For a wonder the Indians did not bolt, but they seemed fascinated.

"As far as I was concerned, I would have waited a little longer, but Pfleng threw up his rifle and let drive at the head. I am sure that he struck between the eyes and that the bullet must have struck something bony, horny or very tough, for it cut twigs from a tree higher up and further on after it glanced. I shot as Pfleng shot again and aimed for the base of the neck.

"The animal had remained perfectly still till now. It dropped its nose to the spot at which I had aimed and seemed to bite at it, but there was no blood or any sign of real hurt. As quickly as we could fire we pumped seven shots into it, and I believe all struck. They seemed to annoy the creature but not to work any injury. Suddenly it plunged forward in a silly, clumsy fashion. The Indians nearly upset the dugout getting away, and both Pfleng and I missed the

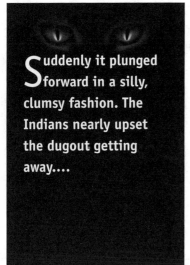

S uddenly it plunged forward in a silly, clumsy fashion. The Indians nearly upset the dugout getting away....

sight as it entered the water. I was very anxious to see its hind legs, if it had any. I looked again only in time to see the last of it leave the land—a heavy blunt tail with rough horny lumps. The head was visible still, though the body was hidden by the splash. From this instant's opportunity I should say that the creature was thirty-five feet long, with at least twelve of this devoted to head and neck.

"In three seconds there was nothing to be seen except the waves of the muddy water, the movements of the waterside growth and a monkey with its hind parts use-less hauling himself up a tree top. As the Indians paddled frantically away I put a bullet through the poor thing to let it out of its misery. We had not gone a hundred yards before Pfleng called to me and pointed to the right.

"Above the water an eighth of a mile away appeared the head and neck of the monster. It must have dived and gone right under us. After a few seconds' gaze it began to swim toward us, and as our bullets seemed to have no effect we took to flight in earnest. Losing sight of it behind an island, we did not pick it up again and were just as well pleased."

Whatever the true identity of the monster, it eludes us today, just as it did Schmidt and Pfleng back in 1907.

St. Helena's Sea Serpents

L ocated just outside of central London, England, is a large and impressive building known as the National Archives. It serves as a repository for declassified and still-classified files from the British Royal Air Force, Royal Navy, Army, and the British equivalents of the FBI, CIA, Department of Defense, and National Security Agency.

As might be expected, the bulk of the records that the British govern-ment has released into the public domain via the passing of its Freedom of Information Act—and that are now available for scrutiny by the public—focus upon such matters as Cold War activities, espionage, the Second World War, and the routine, day-to-day work of governmental bodies.

As well as the strictly down-to-earth material, intriguing files have sur-faced demonstrating that during the nineteenth century, elements of British officialdom took a deep and keen interest in sightings on the high seas of nothing less than fully-fledged sea serpents!

The National Archives in London, England, serves as a repository for documents from the British military, as well as from the FBI, CIA, NSA, and U.S. Department of Defense.

One of the most notable reports of an encounter with such a beast can be found within the archives of the Admiralty. The documentation at issue details the remarkable encounter with a sea serpent that was seen on May 9, 1830, by the crew of the *Rob Roy*, a British Royal Navy ship that was homeward bound after a lengthy sea journey across the Atlantic Ocean. As the ship sailed by the island of St. Helena, something remarkable occurred, as the *Rob Roy*'s captain, James Stockdale, recorded in his official log the following:

"About five P.M. all at once while I was walking on the poop my attention was drawn to the water on the port bow by a scuffling noise. Likewise all the watch on deck were drawn to it. Judge my amazement when what should stare us all in the face as if not knowing whether to come over the deck or to go around the stern—but the great big sea snake! Now I have heard of the fellow before—and I have killed snakes twenty-four feet long in the straits of Malacca, but they would go in his mouth.

"I think he must have been asleep for we were going along very softly two knots an hour, and he seemed as much alarmed as we were—and all taken

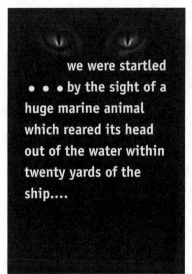

we were startled • • • by the sight of a huge marine animal which reared its head out of the water within twenty yards of the ship....

aback for about fifteen seconds. But he soon was underway and, when fairly off, his head was square with our topsail and his tail was square with the foremast."

Captain Stockdale continued: "My ship is 171 feet long overall—and the foremast is 42 feet from the stern which would make the monster about 129 feet long. If I had not seen it I could not have believed it but there was no mistake or doubt of its length—for the brute was so close I could even smell his nasty fishy smell.

"When underway he carried his head about six feet out of water—with a fin between the shoulders about two feet long. I think he was swimming about five miles an hour—for I watched him from the topsail yard till I lost sight of him in about fifty minutes. I hope never to see him more. It is enough to frighten the strong at heart."

A second report of a sea-monster sighting has been declassified at an official level by the British Government and describes an extraordinary December 13, 1857, encounter that also occurred in the vicinity of the island of St. Helena. A statement prepared by Commander George Henry Harrington revealed the facts:

"While myself and officers were standing on the lee side of the poop—looking toward the island—we were startled by the sight of a huge marine animal which reared its head out of the water within twenty yards of the ship—when it suddenly disappeared for about half a minute and then made a reappearance in the same manner again—showing us its neck and head about ten or twenty feet out of the water.

"Its head was shaped like a long buoy—and I should suppose the diameter to have been seven or eight feet in the largest part with a kind of scroll or ruff encircling it about two feet from the top. The water was discolored for several hundred feet from the head, so much so that on its first appearance my impression was that the ship was in broken waters, produced, as I supposed, by some volcanic agency, since I passed the island before."

And Captain Harrington had far more to impart:

"But the second appearance completely dispelled those fears and assured us that it was a monster of extraordinary length and appeared to be moving slowly towards the land. The ship was going too fast to enable us to reach the masthead in time to form a correct estimate of this extreme length—but from what we saw from the deck we conclude that he must have been over two hundred feet long. The Boatswain and several of the crew, who observed it from the forecastle, state that it was more than double the length of the ship, in which case it must have been five hundred feet."

The captain concluded in his official report: "I am convinced that it belonged to the serpent tribe."

Of that, there seems little doubt!

STORSJÖODJURET

The fifth largest body of water in Sweden, Storsjön Lake, has something in common with Loch Ness, Scotland. No prizes for guessing what it is: a lake monster. Or, perhaps, an entire colony of them. Its name is Storsjöodjuret, and it's a creature with a long history. In 1635, a priest named Morgens Pedersdens wrote the following, which suggests the Swedish Nessie is a beast of supernatural proportions, rather than one of a flesh and blood nature:

"A long, long time ago two trolls, Jata and Kata, stood on the shores of the Great-Lake brewing a concoction in their cauldrons. They brewed and mixed and added to the liquid for days and weeks and years. They knew not what would result from their brew but they wondered about it a great deal. One evening there was heard a strange sound from one of their cauldrons. There was a wailing, a groaning and a crying, then suddenly came a loud bang. A strange animal with a black serpentine body and a cat-like head jumped out of the cauldron and disappeared into the lake. The monster enjoyed living in the lake, grew unbelievably larger and awakened terror among the people whenever it appeared. Finally, it extended all the way round the island of Fröson, and could even bite its own tail. Ketil Runske bound the mighty monster with a strong spell which was carved on a stone and raised on the island of Fröson. The serpent was pictured on the stone. Thus was the spell to be tied till the day someone came who could read and understand the inscription on the stone."

Fifty years later, in 1685, the monster was still attracting the attention of people in the region of Storsjön Lake. Andreas Plantin stated of the serpent of the deep: "It is said that beneath this stone lies a dreadfully large head of a serpent and that the body stretches over Storsjön to Knytta by and Hille Sand where the tail is buried. The serpent was called a rå and therefore shall this stone be risen. Since no one peacefully could cross [Storsjön], the ferryman and his wife states, along with many others, that in the last turbulent time this stone was tore down and bro-

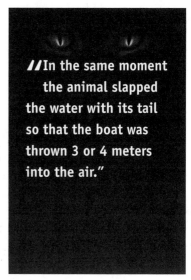

//In the same moment the animal slapped the water with its tail so that the boat was thrown 3 or 4 meters into the air."

A sculpture in Sweden fancifully portrays the Storsjöodjuret lake creature.

ken in two. As long as this stone laid on the ground many strange things occurred in the water, until the stone was risen and assembled anew."

The stone Plantin was referring to was the Frösö runestone. For those who may not know, runestones are ancient, raised stones inscribed with runic symbols. That the Storsjöodjuret has a connection to the Frösö runestone is yet another indication that in times past the beast was perceived as a paranormal one. It's important to note, however, that the Storsjöodjuret is not just a creature of the distant past. The 1970s saw a number of significant encounters with the creature. On August 2, 1973, a man named Ragnar Bjorks had a notable sighting of the monstrous serpent. He said at the time:

"As I am the fisheries officer in this area and I was out checking to see that all the anglers had their valid permits. But instead of anglers I saw something peculiar, a big tail that was about 0.5 meters high just above the surface. At first I thought it was a piece of driftwood. But when I got closer I saw a colossal fish whose tail was out of the water. My rowing boat is 3.8 meters long and I estimate that the fish was 2 meters longer than my boat. When I was by the side of this monster I took my oar and hit it straight over its back."

By Bjorks's own admission, "I shouldn't have done that." He explained why: "In the same moment the animal slapped the water with its tail so that the boat was thrown 3 or 4 meters into the air. Strangely enough, the boat came down again on its keel but I had to balance it. I believe that God was with me then."

As for the specific description of the beast of the waters, Bjorks said: "The creature was grey/brown on top and yellow underneath and was 5 to 6 meters long. I think it was a marl, a voracious, predatory fish that grows over 16 feet long in some countries. Yes, it was a real experience and many people will think that this Storsjöodjuret is a mere fake, but I've seen it with my own eyes and I'm not afraid to talk about it. Some years ago my wife saw it. It had two humps and was slowly moving forward. I didn't believe her but now I'm convinced."

Also convinced were Rolf Larsson and Irene Magnusson, who saw the legendary monster three years after Ragnar Bjorks. It was July 1976 when the pair, fishing on the lake at the time, had an extraordinary encounter. Larsson said:

"We were about 500 meters from land and we were going home when we passed a buoy. Suddenly some waves rocked the boat. Fifty or sixty meters from us between land and the boat we saw something that moved under the surface. Then it came up to the surface, not with a splash but with smooth waves. The part of the body we saw above water was not more than 20-30 cm high and about 1 meter long. But from the amount of water it displaced we could see that it was a large object beneath the surface. I would like to compare it with an upside-down boat; you only see the keel of it. Irene was as pale as a corpse."

Like the Loch Ness Monster, Ogopogo, and Champ, the Storsjöodjuret continues to be seen. And, just like the "big three," it continues to elude capture and identification. The mystery of Sweden's most famous monster lives on.

TEGGIE OF LAKE BALA

Deep in the heart of North Wales there exists a large expanse of water called Lake Bala. You may say, well, there's nothing particularly strange about that. You would be correct. Lake Bala is not out of the ordinary in the slightest. But what is rumored to dwell in its dark depths most assuredly *is* out of the ordinary. It's the domain of a violent lake monster called Teggie. Or, is the story born out of secret, military experiments? It all very much depends on who you ask and who you believe.

Before we get to the matter of Teggie, it's worth noting that within Lake Bala there lurks a creature called the Gwyniad. It can hardly be termed a monster, as it's just a small fish. But there is one issue concerning the Gwyniad that does have a bearing upon the matter of Teggie. The Gwyniad is a fish that dates back to the prehistoric era and is found in Lake Bala and nowhere else—at all. This has, quite naturally, given rise to a thought-provoking question: *what else* of a prehistoric nature might be in Lake Bala? And how big might it grow? The questions are intriguing. The answers are even more so.

Whereas sightings of the Loch Ness Monster date back more than 1,500 years, Lake Bala's resident unknown beast has only been reported for just over a century. Some locals, who claim to have seen the Teggies at close quarters, say the creatures resemble huge, violent northern pike. They are ferocious fish that can easily grow to four feet in length, occasionally five, and rumor has it, even six feet long. If, however, the Teggies *are* northern pike, then they

The Gwyniad is a fish that has survived since prehistoric times and is found only in Lake Bala. Could other ancient species also have survived there?

would have to be true giants, since witnesses claim that the creatures they encountered were in the order of ten to fifteen feet. No one, surely, needs telling that a too close encounter with such a creature would result in a swift and bloody death—but not for a Teggie, though.

Then there are the equally baffling reports of a reptilian monster that vaguely resembles a crocodile. Such a scenario is unlikely, as a colony of crocodiles would stand little chance of adapting to, and surviving, a harsh North Wales' winter—never mind untold numbers of centuries of such winters. There is, however, a third theory for what the Teggies might be. It's just as strange and controversial as the crocodile and northern pike scenarios, but in a very different fashion.

There are longstanding rumors in and around the Bala area that in the buildup to the First World War, the British Royal Navy clandestinely let loose a group of seals into the lake. The reason: to strap them with dynamite and train them to attack specific targets, namely warships. It should be noted that the dynamite was not real and the "warships" were just small rowing boats. In other words, the project was a test run in the event that the Royal Navy might find itself at war with Germany (which it did in 1914, when the First World War broke out), and suicidal seals, strapped with explosives, might be required to fight for their country.

As the story goes, the seals proved impossible to train, and the project was abandoned. And, so today, what people are seeing are brief glimpses of the original seals that bred and bred and so on. Of course, it's very possible this is nothing more than a tall tale, passed on through the generations and without any actual facts to support it. And, it must be said, it would be very difficult to mistake a seal for a crocodile or a huge, violent pike. Thus, the legend of Teggie continues to thrive.

ALMASTY

It should not come as a surprise to learn that the vast wildernesses, thick forests, and massive mountain ranges of Russia are home to Bigfoot-type beasts. They are known to the local folk as Almasty. For some researchers, the creatures are unknown apes. For others, they are nothing less than still-surviving pockets of Neanderthals. Both scenarios are amazing, in terms of their potential implications. But, whatever the true identity of the Almasty, there's very little doubt that it exists. The sheer number of witness reports makes that very clear. The Almasty is a creature that has a long history attached to it, something that also adds to the likelihood of it being a genuine animal of very ancient proportions.

What is very possibly the earliest report on record of the hairy, giant Almasty came from one Hans Schiltenberger. In the 1400s, Schiltenberger was taken prisoner by Turkish forces and was, as David Hatcher Childress notes, placed "in the retinue of a Mongol prince named Egidi."

It transpires that upon his return to Europe in 1427, he began writing a book about his experiences with the Turks. It was a book that surfaced in 1430 and that is made highly notable by its reference to strange and savage creatures that Schiltenberger was told of, which were said to live high in the Tien Shan Mountains of Mongolia, which border upon Russia. Schiltenberger's translated words state:

Some have speculated that the Almasty of Russia are actually the last surviving members of the Neanderthals.

"The inhabitants say that beyond the mountains is the beginning of a wasteland which lies at the edge of the earth. No one can survive there because the desert is populated by so many snakes and tigers. In the mountains themselves live wild people, who have nothing in common with other human beings. A pelt covers the entire body of these creatures. Only the hands and face are free of hair. They run around in the hills like animals and eat foliage and grass and whatever else they can find. The lord of the territory made Egidi a present of a couple of forest people, a man and a woman. They had been caught in the wilderness, together with three untamed horses the size of asses and all sorts of other animals which are not found in German lands and which I cannot put a name to."

Evidently, the creatures still exist: in August 2005, a Ukrainian newspaper, *Situation,* described a then recent encounter with no less than an entire group of Almasty on the Demedzhi Plateau, in the Crimea. The newspaper reported that: "Ivan S., 21, and his group of 12 tourists were spending their second day camped on the plateau. The kids went to sleep early, while the adults stayed up a while. 'The night was very bright with a full moon,' reported Crimean ufologist Anton A. Anfalov."

Anfalov continued: "Ivan's assistant, Sasha and several of the men left the campsite to use the bathroom and when they returned, they looked terrified and trembled with fear. It was then everyone heard a frightful growl near the camp."

Suddenly, the group was confronted by a pack of huge, approximately eight feet tall, "naked, hairy men."

According to Sasha: "There were three creatures. And they were about six meters away from us. The hairy humanoids were 2 to 2.5 meters in height. Their true height was hard to estimate because they were all crouched down and balancing themselves on their fists, like large apes. All three were growling at us. Their faces were very hairy, almost without wrinkles, and their eyes were not shiny at all. Their heads were set or positioned very low, as if they had no necks. On their backs they had something like humps on their spine.

The creatures were very aggressive. Everyone was scared and the beasts' growls awoke the children who became hysterical."

Situation had more to say: "The standoff lasted for about 45 minutes. Finally the creatures turned and bounded away with strange ape-like bouncing leaps. The campers spent a sleepless night around their fire. In the morning Ivan and the others searched the ground around their camp, but due to a dense layer of fallen leaves the creatures didn't leave any distinct prints."

Moving on to 2009, in April of that year the Russian newspaper *Pravda* revealed—in an article titled "Russian scientists use Google maps to find yeti"—that there had been more than twenty sightings of Almasty by hunters in the forests of Kemerovo. Not only that, there were reports of strange, large footprints having been discovered in the depths of nearby caves: "Scientists found two identical yeti footprints. One of them was left on the rock and it dates back 5,000 years ago, and the other footprint which was left not long ago was found at the bottom of the cave."

Pravda spoke with one of the unnamed scientists, who said: "They are absolutely identical. Five thousand years ago yetis settled down in this cave and now their descendants are still living here. The conditions in the cave are suitable for yeti. The cave defends them from rains, snow and wind. There is also a lake in the middle of the cave where yetis can find clean water."

// **On their backs they had something like humps on their spine. The creatures were very aggressive."**

The newspaper added: "Unfortunately, the scientists did not manage to see yetis that time. They say their snowmobiles were too noisy and yetis had to hide somewhere in the forests. However, the scientists say they managed to reach their main goal—they got the proof that yetis are living there. A new expedition to the site will be arranged this summer."

But that was not all, as *Pravda* made very clear: "Members of the Kosmopoisk association have returned from an expedition to Russia's Kirov Region where they searched for a Bigfoot that allegedly lived in that region. Kosmopoisk leader Vadim Chernobrov says the expedition has discovered a den occupied by a mysterious giant and an underground passage dug obviously not by a human."

Ivan Konovalov was a forest warden who, for thirty years, worked in the Kirov Region. He told of his 1985 encounter with an Almasty:

"It was snowing on the day when I was walking along the fir wood and suddenly heard snap of twigs. I turned around and saw an awesome creature covered with dark hair that was much taller than me. It smelt strongly. The beast leant against a pine tree and started bending it down to the ground.

"The tree was rather thick, but it cracked under the creature's burden. Then the creature started breaking the tree against the knee. Its hands were as thick and long as its legs. Quite of a sudden, the creature felt something and turned its 'face' to me. I saw two black eyes and the impression at the bottom of the eyes deeply impressed me. I still remember the look of the eyes. Then the creature flung the tree and quickly left. But I stood thunderstruck and could not move a finger."

BIG GREY MAN OF BEN MACDHUI

A large and mysterious mountain in a Scottish range called the Cairngorms, Ben Macdhui is said to be the lair of a sinister, lumbering, Bigfoot-like creature known as the Big Grey Man (BGM). Legends of its existence date back centuries, and they show no signs of stopping. Although definitively animal-like in both nature and appearance, the Big Grey Man reputedly possesses paranormal powers that allow it to plunge the unwary traveler into states of terror and panic. A form of monster-based mind-control, one might be justified in suggesting.

Without doubt, the foremost expert on the BGM is anomalies expert Andy Roberts. Andy has noted that witnesses to the creepy phenomenon describe how they have heard heavy footsteps on the fog-shrouded mountain, felt a distinct sensation of a threatening presence, and experienced an overwhelming feeling of unbridled terror. The experience is graphic enough to compel witnesses to flee—in fear of their lives—and, in some cases, to run wildly and in crazed, fear-filled fashion for miles. Taking into consideration the fact that encounters almost exclusively take place on rocky, dangerous ground, and often in weather conditions involving mist and snow, Andy stresses that "we should not underestimate the power of the experience."

As far as can be determined, the first encounter of any real note with the BGM occurred in 1791. The witness was a poet and shepherd named James Hogg. He reported seeing a massive figure on Ben Macdhui, which appeared to manifest out of a strange halo. Says Andy: "As he watched the halo which had formed around him due to the combination of sunshine and mist he suddenly noticed a huge, looming figure. It was vaguely human in shape and

the Big Grey • • • Man reputedly possesses paranormal powers that allow it to plunge the unwary traveler into states of terror and panic.

he imagined it to be the devil. Hogg fled in terror, not stopping until he reached fellow shepherds."

Then, from 1831, we have the following from Sir Thomas Dick Lauder. In his own words:

"On descending from the top (of Ben Mac Dhui) at about half-past three P.M., an interesting optical appearance presented itself to our view. We had turned towards the east, and the sun shone on our backs, when we saw a very bright rainbow described on the mist before us. The bow, of beautifully distinct prismatic colors, formed about two-thirds of a circle, the extremities of which appeared to rest on the lower portion of the mountain. In the center of this incomplete circle there was described a luminous disc, surrounded by the prismatic colors displayed in concentric rings. On the disc itself, each of the party (three in number), as they stood about fifty yards apart, saw his own figure most distinctly delineated, although those of the other two were invisible to him. The representation appeared of the natural size, and the outline of the whole person of the spectator was most correctly portrayed. To prove that the shadow seen by each individual was that of himself, we resorted to various gestures, such as waving our hats, flapping our plaids, &c., all which motions were exactly followed by the airy figure."

Moving on to the twentieth century, in 1921, the *Cairngorm Club Journal* reported that a recent letter-writer "called attention to a myth prevalent in Upper Deeside to the effect that a big spectral figure has been seen at various times during the last five years walking about on the tops of the Cairngorms. When approached, so the story goes, the figure disappears."

Andy Roberts reveals a further layer of the puzzle: "In 1924, Dr. Ernest A. Baker's book, *The Highlands with Rope and Rucksack*, appeared. Here, Baker relates the experience of a friend whose job took him into the mountains, a deer stalker or perhaps a shepherd. Alone on Ben Macdhui one day he became aware of a terrifying presence which Affleck Gray [the author of the book *The Big Grey Man of Ben Macdhui*] recounts, 'disturbed him in a manner which was beyond his experience.' Gray makes the point that this was no ordinary fear but something so powerful that Baker's friend fled from Ben Macdhui, the terror only subsiding when he reached low ground. Baker also reports how one mountain climber had

The path to Ben Macdhui goes through desolate, wet, rugged terrain, leading to the home range of the Big Grey Man.

told him that he would under no circumstances spend any time on Ben Macd-hui alone, even in daylight."

One year later, in 1925, Professor Norman Collie revealed the facts concerning his very own encounter with the Big Grey Man, decades earlier. Collie recalled:

"I was returning from the cairn on the summit in a mist when I began to think I heard something else than merely the noise of my own footsteps. For every few steps I took I heard a crunch, and then another crunch as if someone was walking after me but taking steps three or four times the length of my own. I said to myself: This is all nonsense. I listened and heard it again but could see nothing in the mist. As I walked on and the eerie crunch, crunch, sounded behind me I was seized with terror and took to my heels, staggering blindly among the boulders for four or five miles nearly down to Rothiemurchus Forest. Whatever you make of it I do not know, but there is something very queer about the top of Ben Macdhui and I will not go back there by myself, I know."

> **// ... he became aware of a terrifying presence which ... 'disturbed him in a manner which was beyond his experience.'"**

A man named Alexander Tewnion told of his very own encounter with the terrifying thing of Ben Macdhui in the 1940s:

"In October 1943 I spent a ten day leave climbing alone in the Cairngorms. One afternoon, just as I reached the summit cairn of Ben MacDhui, mist swirled across the Lairig Ghru and enveloped the mountain. The atmosphere became dark and oppressive, a fierce, bitter wind whisked among the boulders, and an odd sound echoed through the mist—a loud footstep, it seemed. Then another, and another. A strange shape loomed up, receded, came charging at me! Without hesitation I whipped out the revolver and fired three times at the figure. When it still came on I turned and hared down the path, reaching Glen Derry in a time that I have never bettered. You may ask was it really the Fear Laith Mhor? Frankly, I think it was."

Cryptozoologist Dr. Karl Shuker says: "Even more incredible, however, was the entity reportedly spied one night on Ben MacDhui by a friend of climber-writer Richard Frere. Having pitched a tent beside the Cairn, Frere's friend awoke, to see a brown shape standing between his tent and the moon. So as soon as the shape moved away, his friend peered outside his tent, only to discover (according to Frere's subsequent description, which follows) that just twenty yards away...."

"[A] great brown creature was swaggering down the hill. He uses the word 'swaggering' because the creature had an air of insolent strength about it:

and because it rolled slightly from side to side, taking huge measured steps. It looked as though it was covered with shortish, brown hair … its head was disproportionately large, its neck very thick and powerful. By the extreme width of its shoulders compared to the relative slimness of its hips he concluded its sex to be male. No, it did not resemble an ape: its hairy arms, though long, were not unduly so, its carriage was extremely erect."

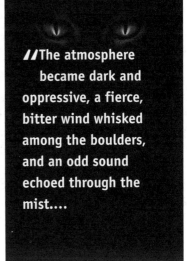

//The atmosphere became dark and oppressive, a fierce, bitter wind whisked among the boulders, and an odd sound echoed through the mist....

A sensational story surfaced in 2004 from Tom Robertson, a noted expert on paranormal phenomena and the author of *Ghosthunter: Adventures in the Afterlife*. While on Ben Macdhui in July 2004, Robertson and a colleague had a nerve-jangling experience, at an altitude of around 4,000 feet, as Robertson made abundantly clear:

"At about 1:00 A.M., after we climbed into our sleeping bags we heard the footsteps of something coming to the tent and heard mumbling noises outside. I looked through the air vent in the roof and saw a large arm crashing down. The figure of what seemed like a yeti was standing over the tent, then all hell broke loose and it was trying to get at us. I remember something landed on my foot. My toes are black, kind of bruised. I have never been so scared in all the sixty years I have been interested in such things. I don't know what it is, but it isn't human. I reckon it could be the Gray [sic] Man or something from outer space."

From September 2006, we have the following from someone using the pseudonym of "Big Max." He or she states: "I was climbing back down Ben MacDhui in May 1988 when I experienced the footsteps phenomenon mentioned by others. It was pretty misty and I was alone. But it was like 'something' was behind me, only 10 metres or so, keeping track of me. I back-tracked to see if anyone was there. I didn't see anything, but it was weird enough to scare me, particularly as the sounds occurred both when I was moving or stationary. It was only after I told this story to a Glasgow cousin years later that I first heard about the Grey Man."

As for what the Big Grey Man may be, Dr. Karl Shuker says:

"During the 1970s, inorganic chemistry specialist Dr. Don Robins proposed that some minerals may be capable of encoding a type of electrical energy, in turn yielding a moving image that could be projected under certain specific conditions, i.e. a veritable geological hologram. Could it be that the BGM is one such hologram, stimulated by certain specific, mountain-related mineralogical attributes, and exhibiting an additional aural component?"

Horrific hologram or Scottish Bigfoot, the mystery of Ben Macdhui's Big Grey Man lives on.

As for the final word, it goes to Peter Densham, who, as the leader of the Royal Air Force Rescue Team from 1939 to 1945, was very familiar with Ben Macdhui and its mysterious, foggy and snowy surroundings. He said of the BGM enigma:

"[T]ell me that the whine was but the result of relaxed eardrums, and the presence was only the creation of a mind that was accustomed to take too great an interest in such things. I shall not be convinced. Come, rather, with me at the mysterious dusk time when day and night struggle upon the mountains. Feel the night wind on your faces, and hear it crying amid rocks. See the desert uplands consumed before the racing storms. Though your nerves be of steel, and your mind says it cannot be, you will be acquainted with that fear without name, that intense dread of the unknown that has pursued mankind from the very dawn of time."

BIGFOOT

If the North American Bigfoot really does exist, then what is it? The most likely candidate is *Gigantopithecus blacki*. It was a massive ape that lived in the distant past and which some Bigfoot researchers are convinced may explain sightings of large, anomalous apes in some of the wilder, desolate, and forested areas of our planet today. There is just one problem with this particular theory: mainstream science, biology, and zoology all assure us that *Gigantopithecus* became extinct thousands of years ago. Just maybe, however, it didn't.

In terms of what is known about *Gigantopithecus*, we have to travel back in time to a relatively recent period: the 1930s. The immense beast has the thorny problem of nothing less than male impotence to thank for its discovery. For years, Chinese herbalists and doctors (some accredited and some not) have utilized fossilized teeth to create cocktails that, so they claim, can cure the embarrassing ailment of being unable to "get it up." Since the Chinese landscape is rich in fossilized bones, people have made significant profits from selling such items to apothecaries all across China.

It turns out that in 1936 a German man named Ralph von Koenigswald came across a huge fossilized tooth—specifically a molar—in a Hong Kong apothecary. It was highly fortuitous that von Koenigswald was the man who made the discovery, since he was a paleontologist and instantly recognized the significance of what had fallen into his lap. Not only was the molar giant-sized, von Koenigswald was able to determine it came from a primate—a very large one. In the immediate years that followed, von Koenigswald found further such examples and coined the term *Gigantopithecus blacki*.

An exhibit at San Diego's Museum of Man displays a model of a *Gigantopithecus blacki*.
Could its descendants be the Bigfoot of today?

Von Koenigswald was temporarily, and disastrously, interrupted at the
height of the Second World War when he became a prisoner of war of the
Japanese. Nevertheless, he was not deterred, and, when the hostilities were

over, he continued his quest to understand the true nature and life of *Gigantopithecus*, as did several other people. One of them was an anatomist named Franz Weidenreich.

In his 1946 book *Apes, Giants, and Man*, Weidenreich made the controversial assertion that *Gigantopithecus* may have been far more human-like than ape-like. Chinese scientists also got hot on the trail of *Gigantopithecus* during this same time. Then, in 1956, a massive jawbone of the huge ape was unearthed at a cave in Liucheng, China. The result was that, in a relatively short time, a great deal was learned about this previously unheard of hairy giant.

Perhaps most amazing and impressive of all were *Gigantopithecus's* statistics: estimates suggested that the height for an adult male would have been around ten feet, while it might have tipped the scales at 1,200 pounds in weight. As for when it lived, the estimates were intriguing.

Gigantopithecus authority (and biological anthropologist at the University of Iowa) Russell L. Ciochon, says: "The next development came in 1965 with the discovery of twelve *Gigantopithecus* teeth at Wuming, a few hours' drive north of Nanning. These teeth were significantly larger than their counterparts from Liucheng, and the other animal fossils found with them suggested that the site was considerably younger (current estimates are that Liucheng is one million years old and that Wuming is between 300,000 and 400,000 years old)."

As for when *Gigantopithecus* is believed to have become extinct, Ciochon suggests around 200,000 years ago, but after having lived for roughly six million years. On the matter of why, exactly, the animal finally reached extinction, Erin Wayman, writing for *The Smithsonian*, said:

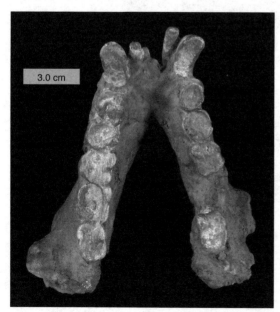

3.0 cm

"...the rise of the Tibetan plateau 1.6 million to 800,000 years ago altered the climate of South Asia, ushering in a colder, drier period when forests shrank. Other factors could have exacerbated this crisis. *Gigantopithecus's* neighbor, *Homo erectus*, may have over-hunted and/or outcompeted their larger ape cousin. And at least one dental study indicates *Gigantopithecus* developed and matured very slowly—a sign they probably had low reproductive rates, which can elevate a species' risk of going extinct."

Of course, one could make an extremely valid argument that since people are still claiming to see giant apes in the very areas where we know *Gigantopithecus*

A mandible (jawbone) of a *Gigantopithecus blacki*.

roamed—such as Tibet, Vietnam, China, and India—this is evidence that the mighty, hairy giant is still amongst us, but now known by its far more famous name of Bigfoot.

There is, however, one problem: due to its massive size, there is a general consensus among primatologists that *Gigantopithecus* walked on its knuckles, in very much the same way that today's baboons move around. Bigfoot, the Yeti, and the rest of the monstrous pack are almost exclusively described as standing and walking in an upright fashion. Plus, many of the cryptid apes of our world are described as tall—we're generally talking about creatures of seven to eight feet in height. Encounters with man-beasts in excess of ten feet in height are far fewer in number. On top of that, there are even suggestions that *Gigantopithecus* may have reached—and possibly even surpassed—a height of thirteen feet. This is far in excess of what is generally reported in Bigfoot. Admittedly, however, there are reports from Tibet of a particular type of Yeti referred to as the Nyalmo which, incredibly, is reputed to reach stratospheric heights of twenty feet.

there are even ● ● ● suggestions that *Gigantopithecus* may have reached—and possibly even surpassed—a height of thirteen feet.

Is it possible that *Gigantopithecus* adapted over millions of years, to the extent that the original, huge, knuckle-walker became a generally smaller, upright beast, one popularly and famously known as Bigfoot? Perhaps, given the sheer number of sightings of anomalous apes in the precise areas where the immense creature lived, we should give some deep consideration to this particular theory.

BLUE BELL HILL BEAST

On the topic of unknown, hairy, humanoid animals seen in the U.K.—and ones seen in the direct vicinity of ancient, historical sites—cryptozoologist Neil Arnold told me the following:

"I've always wondered what type of manifestation these U.K. 'wild men' could be. In the autumn of 2011 a psychic lady who I know as a friend and who I trust—I don't often have any interests in psychics—accompanied me to Blue Bell Hill, which is a very haunted village in Kent, a few miles short of the town of Maidstone. I knew of several obscure 'man-beast' reports in the area which she knew nothing about. I took her to one particular spot, near some ancient stones, hoping she'd pick up a ghostly presence and she said she felt nothing whatsoever, but she did state quite categorically that a

Kits Coty House are megalithic burial stones found in Kent, England.

few years previous, around 2003 she'd had a bizarre encounter in the area one night."

Arnold continued: "She had visited Kit's Coty House—a set of stones—with a group of fellow psychics. Her friends were over on one side of the field which harbours the stones and she was in another area when she noticed someone walking towards her a few hundred yards away. The figure seemed to be striding rather aggressively and was coming from the direction of a thicket which runs alongside the field.

"The woman, whose name is Corriene," said Arnold, "stated that from a distance the figure appeared huge in build and covered in hair and she sensed it was not 'real' but gave off an air of malevolence. The figure marched towards her and she could see it had long hair and a beard, covering most of its face. The hulking figure was taller than six feet and appeared to have a loin cloth around its waist and furred boots. No one else saw this figure, but I was intrigued as I knew that in the past several witnesses had come forward to say they'd seen similar figures in woods within miles of Blue Bell Hill."

Arnold told me this set him on an intriguing and alternative pathway: "I began to wonder if people had seen, from a distance, some type of ghostly primitive man—long hair, bearded, muscular, animal fur around the waist—who, from several hundred yards away, or in ill light, may have looked as if he was covered in hair. Blue Bell Hill and much of Kent is steeped in history—so maybe people were seeing some type of Neolithic hunter. Corriene was intrigued by what I said and then, rather startled, mentioned that on another occasion whilst in the area of the stones she'd seen several of these people who she felt were not aggressive, and although armed with spears were simply guarding the area and stooping low in the bushes, curious as to what they were seeing."

BOLAM BEAST

In the early 2000s, much of England found itself in the grip of a wave of bizarre stories of Sasquatch-type creatures. Jon Downes, the director of the

Centre for Fortean Zoology, was someone who was at the forefront of these investigations. More than a decade later, he still recalls the affair, just as if it occurred yesterday:

"There occurred a huge 'flap' of Big Hairy Men (BHM) sightings throughout the British Isles that we could not afford to ignore and that required our immediate attention. Indeed, such was the scale of this extraordinary wave of encounters that, even as we made firm plans for an expedition in March, a handful of new sightings of large, man-beasts from the Bolam Lake area of Northumberland, England, arrived in our e-mail In-Box in January that prompted us to undertake an immediate study of the evidence."

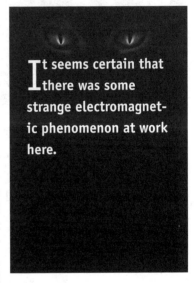

It seems certain that there was some strange electromagnetic phenomenon at work here.

It was a bitterly cold, winter's morning when Jon Downes' Centre for Fortean Zoology hit the road. The trip turned out to be a fortuitous one, however. There was distinct high strangeness afoot, too, as Downes recalls:

"After arriving on-site, a veritable wave of paranormal chaos erupted in the direct vicinity of Bolam Lake. Although we had tested all of our electronic equipment the night before, had charged up batteries where necessary, and had even put new batteries in all of our equipment that needed them, practically without exception all of our new equipment failed. The laptop, for example, has a battery, which usually lasts between 20 and 35 minutes. It lasted just three minutes before failing. Admittedly, we received an enormous number of telephone calls during our stay at the lake, but not anywhere near enough to justify the fact that we had to change handsets four times in as many hours. The batteries in our tape-recorders also failed. It seems certain that there was some strange electromagnetic phenomenon at work here.

"We met with a witness, named Neil, who had been fishing at Bolam Lake one night four or five years previously. Together with two companions he had been making his way back to the car-park when they encountered a huge, dark, man-shaped object about seven to eight feet in height with what he described as sparkling eyes. The three fishermen did not stop to investigate but ran back to the car.

"However, this was by no means the only encounter that Neil had reported to us. Together with one of his companions from the first adventure, he had again been night fishing at Bolam Lake during the summer of 2002. They had been camped out on this occasion, and had heard noises, which they assumed were from an enormous animal moving around in the bushes outside of their camp. Deciding that discretion was most definitely the better part of valor, they decided not to investigate any further; but when they broke camp

Bolam Lake is about twenty miles northwest of Newcastle, England. A bucolic place that is in a park popular with cyclists and others looking for recreation, it is an unexpected spot for a Bigfoot-like beast to roam.

the next morning they found that the fish they had stored in a bait-tin had been taken, and there were distinct signs that something very large had been lumbering around in the immediate vicinity."

As the investigation came to its close, and as the dark skies of winter closed in, something extraordinary and menacing occurred at Bolam Lake, as Downes reveals:

"At about half-past-four, one of the members of Twilight Worlds [a research group that accompanied Downes to the area] reported seeing something large, human-shaped and amorphous in the woods directly in front of the car-park. As the dusk gathered at about 5 o'clock, we again heard the raucous noise of the crows that he had reported just before dawn. Suddenly, once again, they fell silent and one of the Twilight Worlds members shouted that she could hear something large moving around among the undergrowth. All of the car-drivers present were ordered to switch on their headlights and to put them on full-beam. We did not hear any noise in the undergrowth; although other people present did. Eight people were watching the woods and five of us saw an enormous man-shaped object run from right to left, disappear, and then a few moments later run back again."

The most amazing aspect of the encounter, however, was that the hulking, racing thing was one-dimensional; shadow-like, and utterly lacking in any sort of 3-D substance. But, even so, still some form of mystifying entity in its very own right. The bizarre event was over in an instant. And Jon Downes found his life forever changed.

BOULDER BIGFOOT

I'm sometimes asked by those who doubt the existence of such beasts as the Loch Ness Monster, the Chupacabra, the Abominable Snowman and more: do I think that the people I have interviewed about sightings of what appear to be unknown animals of a distinctly monstrous nature are lying or exaggerating to me? Well, I have to say that, in the overwhelming majority of all the cases I've ever studied, my answer is a firm and solid "no." That said, however, there have been a few cases about which I have had my deep suspicions.

Gavin, who I was able to meet personally more than a decade ago, claimed a truly sensational encounter with a Bigfoot-like entity in the county of Staffordshire, England, back in the 1990s. The incident reportedly occurred within the depths of the nation's expansive Cannock Chase woods, and at the site of one of the area's most famous attractions: namely, the Glacial Boulder. Made out of granite, the boulder is both large and impressive. It is also made highly curious by virtue of the illuminating fact that there are no natural granite outcrops anywhere in the area—at all.

the car shot • • • away at high speed, but not before the creature supposedly succeeded in jumping onto the hood of his car.

Indeed, the nearest rock of this specific type can be found within the picturesque confines of the Lake District, which is more than 120 miles (193 kilometers) to the north, and on Dartmoor, Devonshire, no less than 165 miles (266 kilometers) to the southwest. The boulder itself, however, has been matched conclusively to a rocky outcrop at Criffel in Dumfries and Galloway, which is over 170 miles (274 kilometers) from the Chase in the Southern Uplands of Scotland. At some point during the last Ice Age, it is now generally accepted, the great boulder was apparently carried by the massive glaciers down the length of the British Isles and to its present location—and what would prove to be its final resting place—on the Cannock Chase.

Gavin's sensational experience happened on a winter's night in 1997, when he and his girlfriend were parked in his car near the boulder, doing what courting couples have always done since the invention of the automobile, when his girlfriend suddenly let out a loud and hysterical scream. Standing atop the boulder was a large hairy man, waving his arms in a wild, crazed fashion at the starlit sky.

Gavin quickly jumped into the front seat of the car and floored the accelerator. Tires spun, dirt flew into the air, and the car shot away at high speed, but not before the creature supposedly succeeded in jumping onto the hood of his car. For five minutes, it valiantly hung on, before finally being thrown to the ground. Gavin looked in his rear-view mirror and was horrified to see that the creature was already back on its feet and running at high speed into the depths of the surrounding countryside.

In fairness to the more skeptically minded, it must be said at this point that several other people who have also met Gavin are convinced that his tale is simply that: merely a tale (of the very tallest and most outrageous variety) and nothing more. For his part, however, Gavin has been careful—time and time again—to point out in response that he has nothing to gain—and just about absolutely everything to lose—by fabricating such a strange and unbelievable story.

And in that respect he is most certainly not wrong: claiming to all and sundry that you have seen a Bigfoot-type entity roaming around the Cannock Chase at night is, unfortunately, unlikely to result in anything other than the rolling of eyes, a distinct shaking of the head, and overwhelming hoots of both derision and laughter.

It should also be noted that sightings of Bigfoot-type creatures on and around the Cannock Chase absolutely abound, and have done so for centuries. Indeed, I have on file somewhere in the region of thirty or forty such reports, spanning more than 130 years. Typically, the witnesses describe something very similar to that seen by Gavin and his girlfriend: a large, powerful-looking man-beast that typically surfaces at night. Nor is this the only case on record where a Cannock Chase Bigfoot has attacked a car. In 2002, a man named Craig Blackmore found himself caught up in a near-identical, late-night situation, when a Bigfoot-like animal lunged at his vehicle as he drove through the darkened depths of the Cannock Chase. It was a sighting that made the local media and provoked intense interest and debate regarding what may lurk in the thick woods.

We can never prove that the controversial incident did not take place. And, of course, Gavin cannot prove that it did occur. Moreover, the admittedly sensational, and almost over the top, plotline suggests we would be very wise to remain skeptical of this story. Unless, that is, you too have seen the monster of the Glacial Boulder and can add much welcome validation to the account of Gavin.

CASTLE RING MONSTER

Beyond any shadow of a doubt whatsoever, the absolute strangest report I have on record of not just a British wildman of prehistoric proportions, but of an apparent whole *tribe* of them, is one that emanates from Staffordshire's Castle Ring, and which was first related to me many years ago by the witness herself, a woman named Pauline Charlesworth. Pauline knows very well, I need to stress, that while I *do* take her story seriously, I most certainly do *not* take it literally—even in the slightest. Actually, and rather satisfactorily and refreshingly, neither does Pauline. It becomes very clear upon examining her extraordinary testimony that the experience she underwent occurred in some sort of highly altered state, possibly even one of a bizarre, visionary nature.

According to Pauline, it was a bright, summery day in July 1986 that her strange encounter occurred. As she worked on Saturdays, Pauline explained to me when we first met, she had a regular day off work during the week, and had chosen this particular day to prepare a picnic basket, and take a trip up to Castle Ring.

On arriving, she prepared for herself a comfortable place to sit, stretched out a blanket on the ground, and opened up her picnic basket that contained drinks, fruit, and sandwiches. For more than an hour she sat and read a book, but then something very curious happened. It was as if, Pauline explained, she was sitting within the confines of a vacuum and all of the surrounding noises, such as the birds whistling and the branches of the trees gently swaying, stopped—completely. Pauline also said that "what was there wasn't quite right." By that statement, she explained: "The best way I can describe it is to say it was like I wasn't really on the Chase, but it was as if I was

Castle Ring in Staffordshire, England, is the remains of an Iron Age fort. But it is more than just the ancient past that lurks here....

THE MONSTER BOOK: CREATURES, BEASTS, AND FIENDS OF NATURE

in someone's dream of what the Chase should look like; as if it was all a mirage, but a good one."

Then, out of the trees, came a horrific form running directly toward her. It was, said Pauline, a man. The man, however, was quite unlike any that she had ever seen before. He had long, filthy hair, a matted beard, and a 'dumpy' face that was far more prehistoric than modern in appearance. He was relatively short in height, perhaps no more than five feet two inches, and was clad in animal skins that extended from his waist to his knees, and with a long piece of animal skin that was draped over his right shoulder. In his right hand, the man held what were undoubtedly the large antlers of a deer that had been expertly fashioned into a dagger-like weapon that looked like it could inflict some very serious damage indeed, if needed.

> One man, much taller than the rest and who she assumed was the "leader of the group," marched over to her and said something wholly unintelligible....

Pauline said that it was very difficult to ascertain who was more scared—she or the man. While she stared at him in stark terror, he eyed her curiously and in what Pauline described as a disturbing and sinister fashion. On several occasions he uttered what sounded like the words of an unknown language: "It was like he was angry and firing questions at me," she added. But that was not all.

In the distance, Pauline could hear other voices getting ever closer and closer and that, collectively and ultimately, grew into a literal crescendo. And then she found out the source of the noise. Through a break in the trees came perhaps thirty of forty more similarly clad people, mostly men, but also women, and all chanting in an unknown, and presumably ancient, tongue.

It was soon made clear to Pauline that some sort of significant ceremony was about to take place inside Castle Ring—and she, no less, was right in the heart of all the brewing action. The men and women proceeded to sit down at the edges of the Ring. One man, much taller than the rest and who she assumed was the "leader of the group," marched over to her and said something wholly unintelligible; but that she understood by the curt wave of his arm meant that she should get out of the circle. This she quickly did and retreated with shaking legs to the treeline. For more than fifteen minutes she sat, transfixed with overwhelming terror by the sight, as this curious band of people continued to chant and sway in rhythmic, hypnotic fashion.

Then, out of the sky, came the most horrific thing that Pauline had ever seen in her entire life. It was, she recalled, a creature about four feet in height, human in shape, with oily, greasy black skin, thin arms and legs and a pair of large, bat-like leathery wings. And, just for good measure, it had two hideous, red, glowing eyes, too. "It was like the devil," recalled Pauline, perhaps with a high degree of understandable justification.

The creature slowly dropped to the ground and prowled around the Ring for a minute, staring at one and all and emitting hideous, ear-splitting shrieks. Suddenly, seven or eight of the men pounced on the creature, wrestled it to the ground, and bound it firmly with powerful ropes. It writhed and fought to get loose and tore into the flesh of the men with its claws; but it was finally subdued and dragged into the forest by the same tribe members. The remainder of the party followed and Pauline said that the strange atmosphere began to lift and the area eventually returned to its original normality. For several minutes she stood her ground, too afraid to move, but then finally returned on still-unsteady legs to her blanket and quickly scooped up both it and her picnic basket and ran to her car.

I have left until last one factor that, in some fashion, simply has to be connected to the saga related above. The book that Pauline had taken with her to read at Castle Ring was Robert Holdstock's acclaimed fantasy novel, *Mythago Wood*. Ironically, the book is one of my all-time favorites, and one I read at least once a year. The story tells how, after the end of the Second World War, one Steve Huxley returns to England upon getting the news that his father has died. George Huxley had devoted his life to the exploration of the ancient Ryhope Wood that backed up against the family home and kept detailed records of his research into the mysterious area. But Ryhope Wood is unlike any other. It is inhabited by the "mythagos" of the book's title. And what, exactly, might they be? They are creatures and characters from British folklore and mythology, such as Robin Hood and King Arthur, whose curious existence is directly tied to the imaginations and minds of those who believe in them and who, in unconscious, collective fashion, help bring them to some form of quasi-independent life, in the depths of the magical Ryhope Wood.

Of course, in view of the *Mythago Wood* connection, the skeptic would say that Pauline's unearthly experience was merely the result of a bizarre dream—or the absolute worst of all nightmares, perhaps. And, maybe, that really *is* all it was. More than a quarter of a century later, however, Pauline herself is still convinced that something very strange and diabolically evil occurred on that summer day in long-gone July 1986, and that she was provided with a unique glimpse into Staffordshire's very ancient past.

HIBAGON, THE JAPANESE BIGFOOT

In August 1973, a strange and sensational story surfaced in the media that put an entirely new slant on the nature of monsters. Some of them, at least, may be the products of radioactive contamination! The story went as follows:

"A dreadful, real-life 'monster' that looks like an ape and smells like decaying flesh has been observed by several reliable witnesses in the mountains of Japan, near Hiroshima. The creature may be the product of a mutation from the deadly atomic radiation unleashed when the first A-Bomb was dropped on that city more than a quarter-century ago, according to some investigators. Eyewitness reports indicate that the monster lurks amid the low shrubbery clinging to the foothills of Mt. Hiba. The area, one of the few wildernesses that teeming nation has preserved, includes Hibayama National Park."

The article continued: "A typical sighting of the creature is reported by one Mr. Sazawa, the owner of a dry-goods store near the town of Saijo. Mr. Sazawa was scrambling through the foothills digging wild sweet potatoes when he saw the thing."

In Sazawa's very own words: "It is about 5 feet tall, with a face shaped like an inverted triangle, covered with bristles, having a snub nose and large, deep, glaring eyes."

The media coverage continued: "Mr. Sazawa is certain what he saw is not a monkey, for monkeys in Japan grow no taller than 3 feet at the most.

Could the radiation from the nuclear blast at Hiroshima near the end of World War II have created the Hibagon?

The accumulation of these and other bits of data has led to increasingly intense speculation. Is this a gorilla? A wild man? A deserter from the Japanese army, hiding in fear? Or is it the offspring of some unfortunate peasant, grossly deformed by the ravages of atomic radiation?"

It's intriguing to note that during the course of his research, the author of the article noted that there had been a similar encounter to that of Mr. Sazawa, but one year earlier, in 1972. The following was recorded: "Mrs. Reiko Harada 46, a seamstress from the town of Hiwa, was the witness. Walking home with her small son, Mrs. Harada was alerted by the sound of rustling in the underbush. Then she saw something that looked like a gorilla standing at the roadside. It raised its arms, she said, as though begging her to stop. Its face was chocolate brown, she remembers, and its body was covered with dark hair."

She told the press: "When I saw that monster, I suddenly went numb and couldn't walk. I started shaking with fear, but then, somehow, I got the nerve to pick up my little boy and run."

Later that very same evening, the press noted, "four residents armed themselves heavily and went hunting for the beast. They saw nothing but trampled shrubbery. But, one reported, 'the place smelled like a dead body after it starts composing.'"

Whatever the true nature and identity of the Japanese Bigfoot, it failed to be identified by the authorities. And although the Japanese Bigfoot is still occasionally seen, it remains as elusive as its far more well-known American counterpart.

ICEMAN OF MINNESOTA

Over the years, various people within the field of cryptozoology have made controversial claims that they have—or have had—in their possession nothing less than the remains of a dead Bigfoot. Thus far, absolutely none of the claims have proved to be genuine. There is, however, one case in particular that many researchers of the Bigfoot phenomenon suspect may be utterly genuine. It's the strange saga of the Minnesota Iceman.

Frank Hansen was a man who gained deep notoriety when, in the mid-1960s, he maintained that he had acquired the remains of an unusual creature, one that was part-human and part-ape. There were problems from the start, not the least of which was from whom, precisely, Hansen had acquired the body of the beast. The initial story was that the well-preserved corpse was found—floating in a block of ice, no less—in the ocean waters off of Siberia. Reportedly, it was seen, bobbing up and down in the freezing water, by the crew of a boat in the area, who wasted no time hauling it aboard.

That's all well and good, and maybe it's exactly what happened. On the other hand, maybe it's not what happened—in the slightest. A second story links the body of the Iceman to Hong Kong, rather than the waters of Siberia. It's a story that maintains the corpse was found in a Hong Kong deep-freeze and secretly dispatched to the United States. A further theory, that the creature was shot by U.S. troops at the height of the Vietnam War, continues to circulate. Suspicions that the beast was actually slain in Bemidji, Minnesota, by a hunter, Helen Westring, or was the special-effects-based work of one Howard Ball, who was employed by the Walt Disney Corporation, also did the rounds for a while. Even the FBI got in on the act, seeking to determine if the body was actually human—*Homo sapiens* or something else entirely, maybe even a relic Neanderthal.

> he maintained ... that he had acquired the deceased remains of an unusual creature, one that was part-human and part-ape.

Regardless of the origin of the Minnesota Iceman, the word was that the body finally made its winding way to a still-unknown figure in California, one with a sizable amount of money that allowed the person to purchase the potentially priceless remains.

Rumors suggested that the anonymous buyer was none other than the actor James Stewart—of *It's a Wonderful Life* fame—who certainly was deeply fascinated by the controversy of the Yeti. True or not, the unknown individual did a deal with Hansen to have the latter exhibit it at a number of state fairs all across the United States, and Canada too. When Hansen received the body, however, he realized this was no monster. Although covered in hair and savage looking, it had distinct human qualities, too.

Not surprisingly, the cryptozoological community eventually heard of the story and wasted no time in trying to figure out what was going on—and what, exactly, Hansen was displaying for his amazed audiences. Amongst those who had the opportunity to check out the Minnesota Iceman were two highly regarded cryptozoologists, Bernard Heuvelmans and Ivan T. Sanderson. Fortunately, the pair had the opportunity to do so—not in the hectic and crowded atmosphere of a state fair, but at Hansen's very own residence. Both men were sure that what they were looking at had once lived. Even through the ice, the smell of stomach-churning, rotting meat permeated. The body did not appear to be a dummy or some form of special effect. Heuvelmans and Sanderson were, to say the least, excited.

Excitement changed to puzzlement and frustration when the body soon disappeared—back to the unidentified individual who had placed it in the hands of Frank Hansen in the first place. That wasn't the end of the story, however. According to Hansen, after the body was returned to its owner, he was provided with a life-like mannequin of the real Iceman. It was a mannequin that Hansen happily toured with for decades. Today, the fake is on display for the public at the Austin, Texas-based Museum of the Weird. As for the real Minnesota Iceman—presuming it wasn't all just a big con on the part of Hansen, from start to finish—its current resting place remains tantalizingly unknown.

KENTUCKY WILD MAN

On March 27, 1907, the Nevada-based *Reno Evening Gazette* ran a story with the very eye-catching title of "Wild Man Startles People Of Kentucky." The subtitle added even more to the eye-opening and jaw-dropping nature of the story: "Hairy Creature Seen by Farmhand, and Both Are So Scared That They Prepare to Run."

The story began: "Information has been received here that the people in the country around Buena Vista, a village in Garrard County, are much excited over the reports that a wild man has high haunts in the Kentucky River hills near that place. A party is being organized to explore a cave where the creature is believed to have his lair and attempt to capture him."

The saga continued that one Jim Peters, who was a farmhand working for a man named S. D. Scott—the postmaster in Buena Vista—encountered the hair-covered man-thing in Bowman's Woods, in the vicinity of High Bridge. Peters believed that the wild man was attracted by the scent of his dog. Indeed, in the presence of the hair-covered thing, Peters' faithful pet responded by "yelping and showing every evidence of extreme fright." Peters was just as terrified as the dog, and particularly so when it approached to within sixty feet of the pair.

The writer of the newspaper article detailed what happened next: "Peters says he was too frightened to run. The apparition kept its eyes on the dog until asked what it was doing there." Unsurprisingly, the hairy man-beast failed to respond in English—or in any known language. Instead, it turned and vanished into the dense woodland. Fortunately, Peters had been able to get a good look at the monster. He described it as having long, dark, wild hair, a completely hairy body of a dark appearance, wore "a coon skin tied about its loins," and had claw-like talons instead of fingernails.

When petrified Peters finally made it back to Buena Vista, he breathlessly told his boss, S. D. Scott, what had just gone down. Scott, seeing that Peters was serious and not pulling a prank on him, quickly whipped up a posse to track down what may very well have been some type of Bigfoot-like creature. Although the creature was not found, its tracks were seen in the mud of the river bank. Local women and children were said to be too scared to leave their homes, while the most popular theory—albeit an extremely unlikely one, taking into consideration the physical appearance of the thing—was that the man-monster was an escaped lunatic from a nearby asylum. Evidently, the wild man got wind of the fact that he was being hunted down and headed off for new pastures. He was not seen again in Bowman's Woods.

MANDE BURUNG OF INDIA

On October 31, 2010—appropriately Halloween, of course—a team from the British-based Centre for Fortean Zoology (CFZ) embarked upon a truly ambitious expedition to the Garo Hills of Northern India in search of a legendary, hairy, man-like beast known as the Mande Burung. Or, in simpler terminology, the Indian equivalent of the United States' Bigfoot and the Abominable Snowman of Tibet. The five-man team was led by Adam Davies—the author of the monster hunting-themed book *Extreme Expeditions*—and consisted of Dr. Chris Clark, Dave Archer, field naturalist John McGowan, and cryptozoologist Richard Freeman; the latter is a former keeper at England's Twycross Zoo and the author of the book *Dragons: More Than a Myth.*

Jonathan Downes, the founder and director of the CFZ, said of these strange and elusive animals: "The creatures are described as being up to ten feet tall, with predominantly black hair. Most importantly, they are said to walk upright, like a man. Walking apes have been reported in the area for many years. These descriptions sound almost identical to those reported in neighboring Bhutan and Tibet. Witnesses report that the Mande Burung—which translates as forest man—is most often seen in the area in November."

Downes continued: "The Garo Hills are a heavily forested and poorly explored area in Meghalaya state in the cool northern highlands of India. The area is internationally renowned for its wildlife, which includes tigers, bears, elephants and Indian rhino and clouded leopards."

He added: "The Indian team will be led by Dipu Marek, a local expert who has been on the trail of the Indian Yeti for a number of years and has, on previous occasions, found both its nests and 19-inch long 'footprints.' The expedition team has also arranged to interview eyewitnesses who have seen the Mande Burung. Camera traps will be set up in sighting areas in the hope of catching one of the creatures on film."

As for what these creatures may actually represent, Downes had a few thought-provoking ideas: "The Mande Burung may be a surviving form of a giant ape known from its fossilized teeth and jaw bones, called *Gigantopithecus blacki*, which lived in the Pleistocene epoch around three hundred thousand years ago. This creature is, of course, extinct. However, contemporary fauna such as the giant panda, the Asian tapir and the Asian elephant that lived alongside the monster ape, still survive today. It is thought by many that

Noted cryptozoologist Richard Freeman was among those on the expedition to find evidence of a Mande Burung in India.

Gigantopithecus also survives in the impenetrable jungles and mountains of Asia. Its closest known relatives are the Orangutans of Sumatra and Borneo."

And as Downes carefully noted, the CFZ's intrepid explorers were no strangers to heading off into the vast unknown in search of mysterious and elusive creatures: "Last year the team, who investigate mystery animals all over the world, travelled to Sumatra in search of a small, bipedal ape known as the Orang Pendek. Dave Archer and local guide Sahar Didmus saw the creature, and the group brought back hair that was later analyzed by Dr. Lars Thomas at the University of Copenhagen. The DNA proved to be similar to an orangutan's, an animal not found in that part of Sumatra."

While the team was successful in finding a large body of highly credible witnesses to the Indian Bigfoot, they did not uncover a definitive smoking gun. Undeterred, they will one day be embarking on yet another expedition to seek out the legendary beast.

MAN-MONKEY OF THE SHROPSHIRE UNION CANAL

Constructed in the early part of the nineteenth century, England's historic Shropshire Union Canal, or the "Shroppie"—as it has come to be affectionately and popularly known by those who regularly travel its extensive and winding waters—is some sixty-seven miles in length and extends from Ellesmere Port near the city of Liverpool right down to Autherley Junction at Wolverhampton in the Midlands.

The southern end of the old canal, which was originally known as the Birmingham and Liverpool Junction Canal, was the very last of the great British narrow-boat canals to be built and is a true testament to the masterful engineering of Thomas Telford. Deep cuttings and massive embankments are the veritable hallmarks of the canal and they paint a picture that is as eerie as it is picturesque.

The Shropshire Union Canal is quite possibly Britain's most haunted waterway, as the local folk that intimately know and appreciate the history and lore of the canal are only too well aware. At Chester's old Northgate, for example, where the canal was dug into part of the town's old moat, a ghostly Roman centurion can be seen—when circumstances are said to be right, that is—still guarding the ancient entrance to the city. Then there is the "shrieking specter" of Belton Cutting, which is a veritable wailing, Banshee-style monstrosity that strikes cold, stark fear into the hearts of those who have the misfortune and bad luck to cross its terrible path.

One of the spookiest places on Earth is Britain's Shropshire Union Canal.

At the site of the former lock-keeper's cottage at Burgedin, on the nearby Montgomery Canal, come intriguing reports of the ghostly, ethereal figure of an early Welsh princess named Eira. And bringing matters relatively more up to date, there is the spectral American Air Force pilot whose aircraft crashed near the canal at Little Onn, at Church Eaton, Staffordshire, during the Second World War. There is also the "helpful resident ghost" of Tyrley Middle Lock at Market Drayton, which has allegedly been seen opening and closing the lock-gates for those novice, holidaying boaters who, from time to time, negotiate the waters of the long canal. But by far the most famous—or, perhaps, *infamous* would be a much more accurate word to use—ghostly resident of the Shropshire Union Canal is a truly diabolical and devilish entity that has become known as the Man-Monkey. That's right, the very same hairy creature that, back in January 1986, got me into this controversy in the first place!

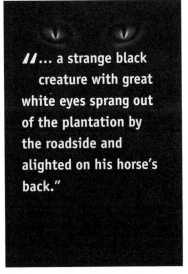

// ... a strange black creature with great white eyes sprang out of the plantation by the roadside and alighted on his horse's back."

It was within the packed pages of Charlotte Sophia Burne's book of 1883, *Shropshire Folklore,* that the unholy antics of what some have since perceived to be the closest thing that Britain may have to the North American Bigfoot and the Yeti of the Himalayas were first unleashed upon an unsuspecting general public. According to Burne:

"A very weird story of an encounter with an animal ghost arose of late years within my knowledge. On the 21st of January 1879, a labouring man was employed to take a cart of luggage from Ranton in Staffordshire to Woodcock, beyond Newport in Shropshire, for the ease of a party of visitors who were going from one house to another. He was late in coming back; his horse was tired, and could only crawl along at a foot's pace, so that it was ten o'clock at night when he arrived at the place where the highroad crosses the Birmingham and Liverpool canal."

It was then, Burne faithfully recorded, that the man received what was undoubtedly the most terrifying shock of his entire life—before or since, it seems pretty safe to assume: "Just before he reached the canal bridge, a strange black creature with great white eyes sprang out of the plantation by the roadside and alighted on his horse's back. He tried to push it off with his whip, but to his horror the whip went through the thing, and he dropped it on the ground in fright."

Needless to say, Burne added: "The poor, tired horse broke into a canter, and rushed onwards at full speed with the ghost still clinging to its back. How the creature at length vanished, the man hardly knew." But the story was far from over, Burne learned: "He told his tale in the village of Woodseaves, a mile further on, and so effectively frightened the hearers that one man actually stayed with friends there all night, rather than cross the terrible bridge which lay between him and his home."

Burne's wild story continued that, by the time he reached the village of Woodseaves, the unnamed man was in a state of "excessive terror" and promptly retired to his bed for several days "so much was he prostrated by his fright." Burne also recorded that, on the following day, another individual travelled back to the sinister bridge and, sure enough, there was the man's whip, still lying at the very place where it had fallen to the ground after the nightmarish and bizarre encounter.

//That was the Man-Monkey, sir, as does come again at that bridge ever since the man was drowned in the cut."

Almost inevitably, dark tales of the crazed beast and its infernal nighttime activities began to spread like absolute wildfire throughout the little villages and hamlets of the area, as Burne quickly learned and recorded thus in her book: "The adventure, as was natural, was much talked of in the neighbourhood, and, of course, with all sorts of variations." Most regrettably, Burne failed to elaborate on the particular nature of these "variations" and gossip.

But, it seems that the local constabulary had heard *all* about the nature and exploits of the hairy demon and knew *exactly* what was afoot, as Burne carefully chronicled: "Some days later the man's master was surprised by a visit from a policeman, who came to request him to give information of his having been stopped and robbed on the Big Bridge on the night of the 21st January."

The "master," who apparently was very much amused by this development in the escalating and seemingly mutating story, carefully explained to the visiting policeman that this was completely untrue, and that, in reality, it was his employee who had reported a strange encounter at the "Big Bridge," but that there was most definitely no robbery involved at all. Interestingly, when the *real* details of what had occurred were related to the policeman, he was seemingly completely nonplussed, came to the realisation that no actual crime had been committed at all, and merely replied in a distinctly matter of fact fashion: "Oh, was that all, sir? Oh, I know what that was. That was the Man-Monkey, sir, as does come again at that bridge ever since the man was drowned in the cut."

Charlotte Burne also revealed that she personally had the opportunity to speak with the man's employer, but, also to our cost today, she did not expand upon the specific nature of the conversation within the pages of *Shropshire Folklore*. Nevertheless, Burne did describe the master as being a "Mr. B_____ of L_____d." And although the man's name remains unknown to us (and probably always will remain so), "L_____d" is very possibly, and probably quite likely, a reference to the ancient, nearby Staffordshire city of Lichfield.

So what, precisely, was the strange, hairy critter that was seen wildly roaming the distinctly darkened corners of the Shropshire Union Canal by moonlight on that winter's night way back in January 1879? Was it truly some form of Bigfoot or Yeti-like entity? Could it potentially have been an exotic escapee of the simian kind, and possibly one that originated with a private zoo somewhere in the area, or even a travelling menagerie of the type that were indeed popular back then? Did it have wholly supernatural and paranormal origins, rather than purely physical ones? Or was it something else entirely? The questions are many. The answers are few. But, still on the matter of the Man-Monkey....

Elliott O'Donnell was a prestigious author, one who penned dozens of titles on the world of the paranormal and who died in 1965, at the age of ninety-three. In his 1912 book, *Werewolves*, O'Donnell said: "It is an old belief that the souls of cataleptic and epileptic people, during the body's unconsciousness, adjourned temporarily to animals, and it is therefore only in keeping with such a view to suggest that on the deaths of such people their spirits take permanently the form of animals."

This, O'Donnell said, accounted for the fact that the places where such people died "are often haunted by semi and wholly animal types of phantasm."

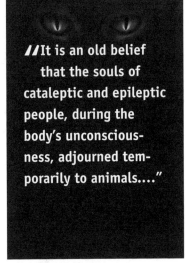

//It is an old belief that the souls of cataleptic and epileptic people, during the body's unconsciousness, adjourned temporarily to animals...."

Dr. David Clarke notes that the story of the Man-Monkey identifies it "as a human revenant who returns to haunt a bridge in animal form. The manner of its appearance, in the form of 'a strange black creature with great white eyes' and the fear it created by its actions leaping on the back of the horse, resonates with contemporary accounts of ghostly activity elsewhere."

The human dead returned in animal form was not the only theory suggested for the presence of the Man-Monkey, however. A rumor quickly circulated in the area that a gorilla had escaped from a traveling menagerie that had recently visited the nearby town of Newport. While it's not entirely impossible that just such a creature could have briefly survived in the cold wilds of Staffordshire, it should be noted that the "circus escapee" theory is one that had been trotted out on numerous occasions—and all across the world—to try and rationalize reports similar to that of the Man-Monkey. In nearly all cases, no evidence of any such escapee is found.

There is, however, clearly something supernatural about the Man-Monkey, since sightings of the always solitary beast have continued to be reported into the twenty-first century. And they are almost identical in nature: the location is usually Bridge 39, the monster leaps out of the trees and terrifies the unwary, and it displays qualities and characteristics that are part flesh and blood and part spectral. Whatever the true nature of Ranton's resident, hairy, monster-man, it shows no signs of leaving its tree-covered haunt anytime soon. Should you, one day, find yourself in the vicinity of Ranton, take great care and heed if you are forced to cross Bridge 39—the Man-Monkey may be waiting in the wooded wings, ready to strike at a moment's notice.

McCOOEY'S MONSTER-APES

While most people have heard of the Bigfoot of the United States and the Abominable Snowman of the Himalayas, somewhat less well known is the Australian equivalent, the Yowie—a tall, hair-covered humanoid that appears to be some form of giant ape. It was in the pages of the December 9, 1882, issue of the *Australian Town and Country Journal* that the story of the Yowie was first told. It was a story that came from an amateur naturalist, Henry James McCooey. He said:

"A few days ago I saw one of these strange animals in an unfrequented locality on the coast between Bateman's Bay and Ulladulla. My attention was attracted to it by the cries of a number of small birds which were pursuing and darting at it. When I first beheld the animal it was standing on its hind legs, partly upright, looking up at the birds above it in the bushes, blinking its eyes and distorting its visage and making a low chattering kind of noise. Being above the animal on a slight elevation and distant from it less than a chain, I had ample opportunity of noting its size and general appearance.

> **//I should think that if it were standing perfectly upright it would be nearly 5ft high. It was tailless and covered with very long black hair...."**

"I should think that if it were standing perfectly upright it would be nearly 5ft high. It was tailless and covered with very long black hair, which was of a dirty red or snuff-color about the throat and breast. Its eyes, which were small and restless, were partly hidden by matted hair that covered its head. The length of the fore legs or arms seemed to be strikingly out of proportion with the rest of its body, but in all other respects its build seemed to be fairly proportional. It would probably weigh about 8 stone [112 pounds].

"On the whole it was a most uncouth and repulsive looking creature, evidently possessed of prodigious strength, and one which I should not care to come to close quarters with. Having sufficiently satisfied my curiosity, I throw a stone at the animal, whereupon it immediately rushed off, followed by the birds, and disappeared in a ravine which was close at hand."

As the debate concerning McCooey's report grew, he submitted more and more communications to the *Australian Town and Country Journal*, all of which are well worth quoting:

"The mere fact of no apes found in the Sydney Museum does not justify us in rushing to the conclusion that there are none in the colony, for it is extremely improbable that any ape will be foolhardy enough to present itself at the museum to undergo the somewhat delicate operation of stuffing; and beyond the fact that there are, none to be found in the Sydney Museum there is not one scintilla of evidence to prove that they are not to be found in the colony, while there is abundance of evidence to show that they are.

> **//The mere fact of no apes found in the Sydney Museum does not justify us in rushing to the conclusion that there are none in the colony...."**

"I do not claim to be the first who has seen this animal, for I can put my finger on half a dozen men at Bateman's Bay who have seen the same, or at any rate an animal of a similar description; but I think I am the first to come forward in the columns of a newspaper and give publicity to the fact of having seen it.

"I may mention that a search party was organized at Bateman's Bay some months ago to surround the locality [and] the supposed ape … and shoot or capture it, but the idea was abandoned in consequence of the likelihood of gun accidents; and I may further state that the skeleton of an ape, 4ft in length, may be seen at any time in a cave 14 miles from Bateman's Bay, in the direction of Ulladulla.

One year later, in 1883, McCooey said that "there are indigenous apes in this colony … they have been frequently seen in Budawong mountains, in Jingera mountains, and in the Abercrombie mountains, at Bateman's Bay, at Mount Macdonald, and on the Guy Fawkes-road between Armidale and Grafton…apes were known to the aborigines of this colony, and were dreaded by them, long before a museum was founded in Australia, or a white man crossed the Murray; and that one was actually captured and killed near Braidwood within the memory of persons still living."

Mono Grande

From various parts of South America, including Colombia, Ecuador, and Venezuela, come stories of a massive, mighty, and extremely violent Bigfoot known as Mono Grande. One of the most fascinating—but also disturbing and tragic—stories came from one Count Pino Turolla, a noted archaeologist who traveled the world, Indiana Jones-style, in pursuit of all things mysterious and fabulous. Turolla (who died in 1984 at the early age of sixty-two) was born in Yugoslavia and later immigrated to Canada. Of note, he developed what became known as the Turolla Control-Descent Parachute that was used by the U.S. military.

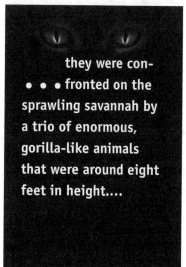

they were con- • • • fronted on the sprawling savannah by a trio of enormous, gorilla-like animals that were around eight feet in height....

It was while traveling across South America in the 1960s that Turolla first heard of the marauding monster. The information came from Turolla's personal guide, Antonio, who told a shocking story. Some years earlier, Antonio and his two sons traveled to a particular range in Venezuela where they were confronted on the sprawling savannah by a trio of enormous, gorilla-like animals that were around eight feet in height, had long and hanging arms, and tiny heads. Not only that, they were armed with large and crudely fashioned wooden clubs. A violent altercation occurred, which resulted in one of Antonio's sons being bludgeoned to death by the merciless monsters.

Turolla didn't have time to investigate the matter of the Mono Grande at the time, but half a year later he was back. And, this time, it wasn't ancient, historical artifacts that he was looking for: it was for the South American Bigfoot itself. He hooked up with Antonio yet again, and they—along with three other native men—headed off to where Antonio's son lost his life in bloody fashion. The story told by Turolla was terrifying:

"When we set out from the camp, we began hiking southeast across the savanna and after a few hours entered the forest, where we followed a narrow track through undergrowth so thick that it reduced our vision to only a few feet on either side. Only now and then did a small clearing enable us to have a field of view of 6 to 10 meters ahead.

"When we entered the canyon where Antonio had seen the big mono, the Indians became very alert and apprehensive, stepping carefully, and sensing every sound and movement in the brush around them. I was carrying a 3.5 Winchester automatic and kept it at the ready. Tension was mounting as we slowly made our way along the trail. The subdued light created lurking shadows and a mood of mystery.

"It was getting toward late afternoon when suddenly we heard a howl, very loud, coming from somewhere in the thick vegetation. The Indians froze. The howl was as loud as the roar of a jaguar, but it was higher and shriller in pitch. It reverberated through the forest, encircling us as if it came from all directions. Something was moving, crashing powerfully through the underbrush.

"The Indians turned abruptly and raced back along the trail, yelling at me to follow. But I was frozen in my tracks; my heart beating so hard that I could hear it. Then, suddenly, the howling stopped. I waited, and when I had regained control of my movements, I advanced slowly along the trail, my finger on the trigger of the gun. Then, as I reached a small clearing, the howling started again, in one crescendo after another. But again, as suddenly as it had started, it stopped.

//Tension was mounting as we slowly made our way along the trail. The subdued light created lurking shadows and a mood of mystery."

"It was then that I saw two furry patches running away from me with a leaping sort of step through the foliage that bordered the clearing. As they bounded across the surface of a group of boulders at the far end of the clearing, I was able to catch a fleeting glimpse of them. They clearly were erect, hairy, apelike creatures, and appeared to be over 5 feet tall. Then they disappeared around the rocks into the jungle, and I heard the cracking sounds of dry twigs and branches as they hastily forged their way through the thick underbrush.

"I waited for what seemed an eternity for something else to happen, trying to impress on my mind what I had just glimpsed. I opened my mouth to yell to my companions, but no sound came out. Finally I turned and retraced my steps, and encountered them advancing cautiously back up the trail. 'They're gone,' I said. No one uttered a word. We continued up the trail. We did not see or hear the creatures again."

MONSTERS OF THE PUBS

Monster hunter Neil Arnold told me, in 2011: "Many years ago when I first began writing for *Animals & Men* magazine [the Centre for Fortean Zoology's in-house magazine] I mentioned to Jon Downes something regarding cryptozoological pub signs. There are many *St. George and the Dragon* signs, and I know a few which also mention unicorns. However, one particular pub sign, which is of great interest to me is that which belongs to the *Wild Man* at 29 Bedford Street in Norwich [England]. Now, most pub signs have a meaning, but the legend which pertains to the *Wild Man* is extremely intriguing.

"So the folklore states, many, many years ago a six year old boy named Peter became lost in a wood in Germany. Around six years later the boy had grown wild, and in naked form would prowl the woods, living alongside the

A painting by William Kent of Peter, who was discovered wild (and apparently mentally ill) in Hanover in 1725 and was adopted by the British royal family.

resident animals. Eventually he was found and picked up by a travelling showman who exhibited throughout Europe."

As Neil also said: "St. Mary's Northchurch adds more to the legend, for within its walls there is an inscription which reads: 'To the memory of Peter, known as the Wild Boy, having been found wild in the forest of Hertswold near Hanover in the year 1725. He then appeared to be about 12 years old. In the following year he was brought to England by the order of the late Queen Caroline, and the ablest masters were provided for him. But proving himself incapable of speaking, or of receiving any instruction, a comfortable provision was made for him at a farm in this parish, where he continued to the end of his inoffensive life. He died on the 22nd of February, 1785, supposed to be aged 72.'" And there the inscription ends.

But why was there an association between wild Peter and the Norwich-based pub itself that led the owner to even name the inn after the slightly tragic soul? Neil provides the answer: "Around 1751 Peter was housed at the public house. In the past the sign would depict the unfortunate chap as a demonic character amid flickering flames. Now the pub sign shows him frequenting the forest alongside bears."

And still on the subject of pubs and primitive people....

As far as the British Isles are concerned, Richard Holland—the author of *Haunted Wales: A Survey of Welsh Ghostlore*—offers his own particular thoughts on the nature of the legendary beast under scrutiny in this chapter: "It has been suggested that the Woodwose is a folk memory of some species of early hominid, a pre-*Homo sapiens* ape man.... Perhaps a few remnants of these 'wild men' still lingered in inaccessible places when prehistoric man first hacked their way through Europe's primeval forest. They might have been glimpsed by Neolithic settlers in the hearts of what remained of their woodland habitat...."

Richard also notes that: "In Sproughton, in Suffolk, according to John Michell and Bob Rickard, the *Wild Man Inn* was so named after a terrifying entity that attacked its builders in the 16th century. They also cite a police report of a 'horrible uncouth creature' which had been living in woods near

Salisbury in Wiltshire and attempted to carry off a farmer's wife: this was recorded as late as 1877. I have also spoken to witnesses who may have encountered a similar man-beast in North-East Wales."

Although some of the stories of the wild man of Sproughton portray him as having been nothing more mysterious than a mad, homeless vagrant who dwelled in the woods and lived a distinctly lawless life, there is a possibility that he may have been something else entirely. On the north side of the River Gipping, which runs from Stowmarket to Ipswich, is a place that just happens to be called—and has been called, for as long as people have inhabited those ancient parts—Devil's Wood, where significant archaeological finds from both Neolithic and Paleolithic times have been made.

the wild man of • • • Sproughton may have been far more than a mere eccentric vagabond or hermit type, after all.

That Sproughton is only twelve miles from Stowmarket, and just three and a half miles from Ipswich, that ancient man dwelled in this very area, and that the place itself became associated with the Devil collectively suggests a distinct possibility that the wild man of Sproughton may have been far more than a mere eccentric vagabond or hermit type, after all. Maybe, incredibly, he was one of the very last of his kind, perhaps even a Neolithic survivor, one who made his lair in old woods that, not surprisingly—given the man's wild appearance and mysterious presence—became so linked with matters so dark and devilish.

MONTAUK SASQUATCH

One of the truly strangest, many have said wholly outrageous, allegations that has been made within conspiracy-themed research circles is that at a relatively innocuous-looking location on Long Island, New York—originally called Camp Hero, and later renamed the Montauk Air Force Station—highly classified research has, for decades, been undertaken into a dizzying array of far-out issues, including time travel, teleportation, invisibility, mind control, and much more—including the creation of Bigfoot-style creatures.

We are not talking about genetic experiments, however. No, the claim is that top secret research is afoot deep below the old base to create Tulpa-style versions of Bigfoot. That's to say, monsters conjured up in the imagination and which can then be projected outwardly and given some degree of quasi-independent life in the real world.

Weird U.S. notes that on one occasion, one of those attached to the secret experiments—a man named Duncan Cameron—envisioned in his mind "a large, angry, powerful Sasquatch-like" entity that "materialized at Montauk and began destroying the base in a rage. It utterly decimated the place, tanking the project and disconnecting it from the past. As soon as the equipment harnessing people's psychic power was destroyed, the beast disappeared."

NYALMO

Bernard Heuvelmans, one of the most important figures within the field of cryptozoology, said that during the course of his research into the Yeti of the Himalayas, he had learned of no fewer than three distinct kinds of creature that roamed the vast mountains.

A Nyalmo is better known as the Yeti or Abominable Snowman.

"This opinion," said Heuvelmans, "was confirmed in 1957 by a Tibetan lama called Punyabayra, high priest of the monastery at Budnath, who spent four months in the high mountains and brought back the surprising but valuable information that the Tibetan mountain people knew three kinds of snowmen."

There was the *rimi*, a man-beast of close to three meters in height that dwelled in the Barun Khola valley, in eastern Nepal, and was specifically omnivorous. Then there was the rackshi bompo, a beast of roughly human proportions, which Heuvelmans said "must be the Sherpas' reddish *yeh-teh* or *mi-teh* which leaves the footprints 20 to 23 cm long that the *Daily Mail* expedition … found in such quantity." Finally, there was the imposing and terrifying Nyalmo.

Heuvelmans came straight to the point: "The *nyalmo* are real giants, between 4 and 5 m high, with enormous conical heads." He continued: "They wander in parties among the eternal snows above 4000m. In such empty country it is hardly surprising that they should be carnivorous and even man-eating."

Heuvelmans asked of the Nyalmo: "Do they really exist, or are they just a myth?" He admitted to having heard of accounts of Yetis with feet around 45 to 60 cm in length but was careful to qualify this by stating that "the evidence is far too slender for us to draw any satisfactory conclusions. Possibly the *nyalmo* are an invented addition based on the belief that *yetis* increase in size the higher you go."

Loren Coleman says: "When [Sir Edmund] Hillary went to the Himalayas to look for the Yeti, he and his collaborator, journalist Desmond Doig, noted that there were several unknown primates said to be there still undiscovered in any formal way. Among the varieties was one called the 'Nyalmo.' Hillary and Doig learned of the Nyalmo in north-central Nepal. It was said to be 'giant-sized (up to twenty feet tall), manlike, hairy, and given to shaking giant pine trees in trials of strength while other Nyalmos sit around and clap their hands.'"

//The creatures were standing as they formed a circle and were chanting, as if they were doing a religious ritual or something of that sort."

The matter of the curious behavior of the Nyalmos—to which Coleman refers—was most graphically told by one Jean Marques-Riviere. It was in 1937 that the details of Marques-Riviere's account first surfaced, one that was eagerly picked up on by Bernard Heuvelmans. According to Marques-Riviere, he had occasion to speak with an Indian pilgrim who personally encountered a group of Nyalmo in the wilds of Nepal. *Crypto Journal* describes the extraordinary encounter in a fashion that suggests the beasts have a high degree of intelligence and may even have some form of spiritual belief-system:

"The creatures were standing as they formed a circle and were chanting, as if they were doing a religious ritual or something of that sort. One of the Yeti-like creatures was enthusiastically beating a hollow trunk of a tree, like a man hitting his drums to create some music. The others continued their 'chants,' but their faces seemed to be filled with a sad expression. With this sight, the adventurers thought that the creatures acted like typical persons and that they should not be feared. But eventually, fears set in due to the creatures' massive build, they decided to walk away stealthily to avoid conflict."

What may very well have been a description of the huge, and reportedly extremely dangerous and violent, Nyalmo came from Charles Stonor, a former assistant curator of the London Zoo, England, who embarked on a quest for the truth of the Yeti in December 1953, an expedition that was organized and funded by the British *Daily Mail* newspaper. While in Darjeeling, Stonor was told of a creature known as the Thloh-Mung that, with hindsight, may very well have been the Nyalmo.

The story told to Stonor went like this:

"Long ago there was a beast in our mountains, known to our forefathers as the Thloh-Mung, meaning in our language Mountain Savage. Its cunning and ferocity were so great as to be a match for anyone who encountered it. It could always outwit our Lepcha hunters, with their bows and arrows. The Thloh-Mung was said to live alone, or with a very few of its kind; and it went sometimes on the ground, and sometimes in the trees."

The account continued: "It was found only in the higher mountains of our country. Although it was made very like a man, it was covered with long, dark hair, and was more intelligent than a monkey, as well as being larger."

It seems that, to a significant degree, the beasts were fighting for their very survival: "The people became more in number, the forest and wild country less; and the Thloh-Mung disappeared. But many people say they are still to be found in the mountains of Nepal, away to the west, where the Sherpa people call them the Yeti."

ORFORD WILD MAN

Consider—as just one example of what actually amounts to far more than a few—the following account of the single-named Ralph, a monk and an abbot of Coggeshall, Essex, England. Recorded way back in the year 1200 in *Chronicon Anglicanum*, the story describes the remarkable capture in the area of nothing less than a definitive wild man of the woods creature:

"In the time of King Henry II, when Bartholomew de Glanville was in charge of the castle at Orford, it happened that some fishermen fishing in the sea there caught in their nets a Wildman. He was naked and was like a man in all his members, covered with hair and with a long shaggy beard. He eagerly ate whatever was brought to him, but if it was raw he pressed it between his hands until all the juice was expelled."

Ralph continued with his monster-themed account:

"He would not talk, even when tortured and hung up by his feet. Brought into church, he showed no sign of reverence or belief. He sought his bed at sunset and always remained there until sunrise. He was allowed to go into the sea, strongly guarded with three lines of nets, but he dived under the nets and came up again and again. Eventually he came back of his own free will. But later on he escaped and was never seen again."

Or, maybe the beast-man—or, far more likely, given the large passage of time, one of its offspring—*was* seen again, albeit hundreds of years further down the line. At some point during the summer of 1968, one Morris Allen—who grew up in the vicinity of Orford—was walking along the coast near, of all places, the town of Orford itself when in the distance he saw someone squatting on the sand and leaning over something.

As he got closer, Morris said, he could see that the man was dressed in what looked like an animal skin and was savagely tearing into the flesh of a dead rabbit. The man was dirt-encrusted, with long, tangled hair and had wild, staring eyes. Morris could only watch with a mixture of fascination and horror. Suddenly the man held his head aloft and quickly looked—or, perhaps, glared would be a far better description—in Morris's direction, as if he had picked up his scent. The wild man quickly scooped up the rabbit, bounded off into the grass and was forever lost from sight. For a highly traumatized Morris Allen, it was an event destined never to be forgotten.

Perhaps, the wild man of Orford, and its surrounding areas, continues to live on, taunting and tantalizing people with the occasional sighting of its bestial form. And, it can now be said with a high degree of accuracy, in the "weird stakes" there is far more to Orford than just its infamous lighthouse.

PUERTO RICAN MAN-APE

On what is now more than a few occasions, I have traveled to Puerto Rico, in hot pursuit of a wide and varied body of mysteries—most of which have had at least some sort of connection to the controversy surrounding the island's resident bloodsucking nightmare, the Chupacabra. Indeed, when it comes to the matter of strange creatures roaming around the many wild and forested areas of Puerto Rico, it's the Chupacabra that automatically springs to mind.

It's a little known fact, however, that the Chupacabra is not the only weird beast rumored to haunt the island of Puerto Rico. Although certainly not on every occasion, but on at least two excursions to the island, I have uncovered fragmentary reports and accounts of encounters with what can only be described as Bigfoot-style creatures, as amazing as it may sound. And, without doubt, the most fascinating body of data on this curious issue surfaced in August of 2013, when I was on the island—again—to chase down the Chupacabra.

That I was on Puerto Rico looking for the infamous Goat-Sucker, but ended up on the receiving end of a varied body of Bigfoot-themed material, was a welcome and refreshing diversion. But, there is something about the Puerto Rican Bigfoot that will not go down well—at all—with those cryptozo-

The Puerto Rican version of Bigfoot reportedly hides in the dense jungles of the El Yunque rain forest.

ologists who believe the Bigfoot of North America, Australia's Yowie, the Yeren of China, and the Himalayan Yeti are nothing more than unknown animals of a flesh and blood nature.

One of the people I interviewed on my latest trek to the island was a ghost hunter and paranormal investigator named Peter—who was originally from Berlin, Germany, but who moved to Puerto Rico to live in 1996. Peter's accounts of Bigfoot activity in Puerto Rico were as fascinating as they were controversial. By that, I mean the reports had far less to do with what one might call unknown animals, and far more to do with what might justifiably be termed downright paranormal anomalies.

It's important, at the very outset, that I stress Peter was not someone whose files on Bigfoot in Puerto Rico were overflowing. In fact, it was quite the opposite. The number of reports in his archives was less than twenty and spanned from the 1970s to 1998, with a spate of reports in 1985. Typically, the beasts closely resembled the North American Bigfoot. That's to say they were large, humanoid, covered in dark hair, and solitary. While most of the reports emanated from—or around—the island's huge El Yunque rainforest, two were—rather incredibly—reported from the fringes of Puerto Rico's capital city, San Juan.

But, as is also the case with so many reports of Bigfoot-type creatures that come out of the British Isles, Peter's Puerto Rican reports were filled with anomalies. As he explained to me, and demonstrated by sharing the case files in question, there were reports of the Puerto Rican Bigfoot seen in conjunction with anomalous lights in the sky—although not structured UFOs, admittedly.

And by "in conjunction" I mean both time-wise and location-wise. There were also reports of the creatures seemingly being impervious to bullets—which is an often-reported aspect of North American cases. Certainly, the most controversial cases of all—of which, granted, Peter only had three examples—were of the creatures seemingly vanishing into nothingness. Again, that "here one minute and gone the next minute" angle of the Bigfoot mystery is not unknown in the United States. I will be the very first to admit that it's incredibly difficult to know what to make of the Puerto Rican Bigfoot. After all, right now we are sorely lacking in a large body of case-files with which to work.

On top of that, even those reports that Peter shared with me were, for the most part, a significant number of years old, and none extended beyond the 1990s. It is, however, my opinion that this lack of hard data is no reason to ignore such cases—nor their attendant anomalies. In fact, I would say quite the opposite.

Regardless of what the Puerto Rican Bigfoot is (or is not), when there is even a small body of material the onus is still on us, the researchers and the investigators, to study the mystery carefully and as thoroughly as possible. I cannot say for sure that Bigfoot (or something like it) really does lurk in the denser and wilder parts of Puerto Rico, but I can say—having sat and chatted with Peter for the best part of a day—that the witnesses most certainly believe that to be the case.

SKUNK APE

When the word "Bigfoot" is mentioned in conversation, for most people it prompts imagery of gigantic, bulky, eight- to nine-feet-tall man-monsters roaming the frozen mountains and massive forests of the Pacific Northwest. Certainly, there's no shortage of such reports. It should be noted, however, that—as incredible as it may sound—Bigfoot might not be the only cryptid ape that calls the United States its home. In Florida, and particularly so in the state's swampy, wooded areas, there lives a beast known as the Skunk Ape. It's a creature whose territory also includes Arkansas and North Carolina. It's in the wilds of Florida, however, where the beast really dominates.

There is a very good reason for suggesting that the Skunk Ape is a distinctly different creature to that reported on the west coast. Predominantly, it's the difference in height and bulk that suggests the Skunk Ape and Bigfoot just might not be one and the same. Admittedly, an argument could be made that the radical differences in the terrain, temperatures, and food supplies in both locations have led to the development of a smaller form of Bigfoot in the Florida region, but that, essentially, both animals are one and the same.

> Predominantly, it's the difference in height and bulk that suggests the Skunk Ape and Bigfoot just might not be one and the same.

Confounding the matter even more, however, there is the fact that some reports of the creature are more befitting a description of the mammoth Bigfoot, as will soon become clear. Although there is no firm consensus on what the Skunk Ape is—Bigfoot or something else of a related nature—there is no denying the rich and diverse body of reports that exists on the creature. It's important to note that sightings of the Skunk Ape can't be blamed on the current craze for Bigfoot that exists today. Reports of the hairy, upright animal are nothing new. They date back decades.

A spate of Skunk Ape encounters occurred in Florida from the late 1970s to 1980. The monstrous matter began in early October. A twenty-two-year-old man was hitchhiking on U.S. 441, around half a mile from the town of Belleview. It was an area noted for its light forestland, something that would have offered perfect cover for a Skunk Ape—and, just maybe it did exactly that. Until, however, it decided to make its presence known to the terrified man. It was the creature's nauseating smell—they don't call it the Skunk Ape for nothing—that first alerted the man to the fact that there was a wild animal in the area. He only realized just how wild when the hairy, dark, and upright thing made a brief appearance, before vanishing into the woods.

Just a couple of days later, a security guard at a nursery in Apopka reported to the local police something that was both amazing and controversial: something resembling Bigfoot—with fur or hair of a grey-red color—attacked him violently and tore off his shirt! Donnie Hall said he let loose with his gun, but to no effect. Then there was the story of a Belleview welder who also saw the man-beast. He said: "I'm six feet tall and it was bigger than me. It smelled horrible, like garbage."

Such was the local attention given to the sightings—by the populace, the press, and even the police—that the Florida Game and Fresh Water Commission got involved. It even sent out one of its personnel to take a look at a line of tracks found at the Apopka nursery. The result was that the tracks appeared to be man-made. Of course, that, essentially, means nothing: if the Skunk Ape is a five-toed, bipedal animal—just like us—then they would look like human prints!

One month later, the Ocala National Forest was the site of a startling encounter with a Skunk Ape. The forest is the perfect terrain for cryptid apes to live and hide in: it runs to more than 600 square miles (1,554 square kilometers) in size, is heavily and densely forested, and is filled with springs and swamps. And, for a large, aggressive, ape, there's no shortage of potential food supplies in the Ocala National Forest. It is home to red foxes, raccoons, boar, deer, squirrels, opossums, and gophers.

The November 1977 case was reported by none other than a sixty-seven-year-old Baptist minister, the Reverend S. L. Whatley, who was the pastor of the Fort

This 2000 photo was taken in Sarasota County, Florida, by an anonymous photographer.

McCoy Baptist Church. It was while he chopped wood on the fringes of the forest that Whatley caught sight of the creature. He said: "It was standing upright, in the middle of some palmetto bushes, and that sapsucker was at least seven and a half, maybe eight feet tall."

The Skunk Ape "had dark, lighter than black hair on its head and chest, not much on its arms, and none on its face. It had kind of a flat face, a flat nose, its eyes were sunk in its sockets."

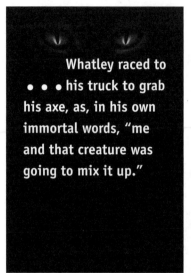

Whatley raced to • • • his truck to grab his axe, as, in his own immortal words, "me and that creature was going to mix it up."

Displaying what some might perceive as behavior not exactly befitting that of a Baptist minister, Whatley raced to his truck to grab his axe, as, in his own immortal words, "me and that creature was going to mix it up." By the time Whatley returned from his truck, however, the monster was gone. His last words on the matter to the press: alcohol hadn't touched his lips since the 1930s.

Three years later, in 1980, Altoona, Florida, became the magnet for Skunk Ape enthusiasts. It so happens that Altoona is also dominated by the Ocala National Forest, where Reverend Whatley almost mixed it up with a monster. It wasn't a sighting of a Skunk Ape that caused so much commotion throughout town, but the discovery of gigantic, size eighteen footprints. Opinion was significantly divided on what the tracks showed.

Doug Sewell was the chief investigator for the Lake County Sheriff's department. He came straight to the point: "I think it's a hoax. There was no indication that something that big enough to make those prints went back through the woods."

Far less sure that fakery could explain away everything was Lake County Sergeant Dee Kirby, who made casts of a number of the massive tracks. Not only did he say that they showed a definitive arching of the step and five toes, he added that there was even some wrinkling in the instep, all of which suggested the tracks were not made by something as down-to-earth as carefully carved "wooden feet."

Kirby also noted: "The prints had a full four feet of distance between each of one." This led Kirby to conclude that the creature had to have weighed somewhere in the region of 1,000 pounds (454 kilograms) and stood somewhere between ten and twelve feet in height! Not only does this suggest something somewhat different than the Skunk Ape, it also describes an animal far bigger than the average Bigfoot.

It is important to note that if the tracks were made by hoaxers, then the perpetrators chose the wrong place to make them. The site of the tracks was a remote area of the forest, and the only reason why they were found, at all, was because contractors working for the U.S. Forestry Service were in the area and stumbled on them. The affair was never resolved.

STALIN'S SUPER-APES

Secret government files generated in Russia in 1926 under the regime of Premier Joseph Stalin reveal the details of an astonishing and shocking story that eerily parallels the scenario presented in H. G. Wells's *The Island of Dr. Moreau*. According to the formerly classified records, Stalin had a crazed idea to try and create an army of creatures that would be a combination of half-ape and half-man, and that would be utterly unbeatable on the battlefield.

As a result Ilya Ivanov, the former Soviet Union's top animal breeding expert at the time, was personally told by Stalin: "I want a new invincible human being, insensitive to pain, resistant and indifferent about the quality of food they eat." Somewhat shrewdly, and perhaps anticipating a scenario similar to the catastrophic ending in *The Island of Dr. Moreau*, Stalin added that the creatures should possess "immense strength but with an underdeveloped brain."

Certainly, in the eyes of Stalin, if anyone could make the crackpot project succeed it was Ivanov. A highly regarded figure, he had established his reputation under the Tsar when, in 1901, he established the world's first center for the artificial insemination of racehorses. But more important to Stalin was the fact that Ivanov had already tried to create a "super-horse" by attempting to crossbreed such animals with zebras.

Despite the fact that the attempts to crossbreed a horse with a zebra failed completely, Moscow's Politburo forwarded Stalin's request to the Academy of Science with the order to build a "living war machine,"

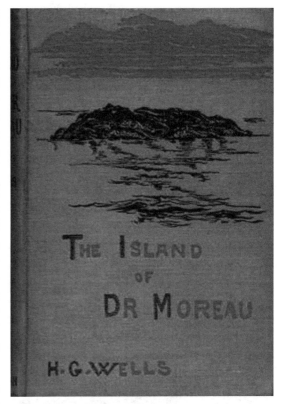

In the classic science fiction novel by H. G. Wells, *The Island of Dr. Moreau,* a scientists finds a way to turn animals into humans. Soviet dictator Joseph Stalin wanted to do something similar, supposedly.

an order that came at a time when the Soviet Union was embarking upon a crusade to turn the world upside down, with social engineering seen as a partner to industrialization.

In addition, Soviet authorities were struggling at the time to rebuild the Red Army after the devastation of the First World War, and there was also intense pressure to find a new labor force, particularly one that would not complain. As a result, in the warped mind of Joseph Stalin, the secret creation of a super race of hybrid creatures that combined the intelligence of human beings with the physical strength of some of the larger primates, such as gorillas and chimpanzees, seemed to be the perfect antidote to every problem.

The Russian scientific community swung into action and Ivanov was quickly dispatched, with $200,000 in his pocket no less, to West Africa where the first such experiment was planned: namely the impregnation of a number of chimpanzees with human sperm. Ivanov's now-archived reports reveal that the Pasteur Institute in Paris, France, secretly granted him permission to use its research station in Guinea, West Africa, for ape-breeding research.

As Ivanov advised the Politburo, however: "The biggest problem is to catch living females." As a result, Ivanov's team learned that the answer to this tricky problem was to burn the trees and chase the apes into cages as they scampered down the trunks. Ivanov also reported, somewhat disturbingly, on the fact that his team had "seized" a number of local African women in the area who were "to be impregnated with ape sperm." No pregnancies resulted. More ambitious plans to impregnate female gorillas with human sperm also ended in complete failure.

At the same time, a center for such experimentation in Russia was stealthily established in Stalin's birthplace of Georgia, where the super-apes were to be raised if impregnation was ever seen to be successful. Unsurprisingly, none of the West African experiments succeeded. Undaunted, however, Stalin pressed on with an even more controversial plan: he arranged for a number of women "volunteers" in Russia to be impregnated with monkey sperm in an

Ilya Ivanov, the brains behind Stalin's twisted experiments with human–animal hybrids.

effort to determine whether or not following this particular route would prove to be more successful. Again, it was not.

That such experimentation did proceed, however, is not in doubt: only recently, workmen engaged in the building of a children's playground in the Georgian Black Sea town of Suchumi found a plethora of ape skeletons and an old abandoned laboratory.

In the eyes of the ruthless Stalin, and a result of the resounding failure to create an army of man-beasts, Ivanov was now in complete disgrace. As a result, Stalin sentenced Ivanov to five years in jail, which was later commuted to five years' exile in the Central Asian republic of Kazakhstan in 1931. He died a year later, after falling sick while standing on a freezing railway platform.

Although Ilya Ivanov's monsters fortunately never lived, their very image alone is enough to provoke the same kind of terrors that real monsters cause.

WENDIGO

The vast majority of reports on record suggest that the Bigfoot creatures are largely solitary and prefer to stay away from humankind as much as possible. Even when Bigfoot and people do cross paths, the beasts generally use intimidation to ward off their unwelcome visitors—and perhaps even stranger methods, too, such as infrasound.

There are, however, rare and not entirely verified accounts of Bigfoot mutilating, killing, and even eating people. Thankfully, such reports are in the minority—unless, that is, one is of the opinion that many of the thousands of people who go missing in the United States every year are helping, in a most unfortunate way, to feed and fuel Bigfoot. All of which brings us to a creature that has, for centuries, been greatly feared by Native Americans: the Wendigo.

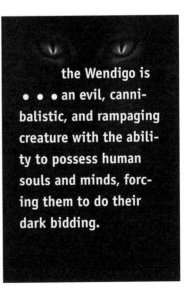

the Wendigo is ● ● ● an evil, cannibalistic, and rampaging creature with the ability to possess human souls and minds, forcing them to do their dark bidding.

A terrifying thing that appears prominently within the lore of the Algonquin people—the most widespread and populated of the Native American groups, with tribes originally numbering in the hundreds—the Wendigo is an evil, cannibalistic, and rampaging creature with the ability to possess human souls and minds, forcing them to do their dark bidding.

Humans have the ability to transform into a Wendigo, especially if they have engaged in cannibalism.

Notably, in centuries past, those who were suspected by the Algonquion of being Wendigos were decapitated after death, to prevent them from rising from the grave and going on slaughtering, people-eating rampages.

Many of the reports of the Wendigo are focused around large forests, freezing cold and winter environments, and dark woods. In light of that, there is a theory that the stories of the Wendigo are the result of (a) a distortion of real events, involving Native Americans who were forced to resort to cannibalism when food was scarce in the winter months; and (b) tales told to try and dissuade people from cannibalism, by making them think that eating human flesh would turn them into Wendigos. That the Wendigo is very often described as a large, marauding, humanoid beast that dwells deep in the forest, however, suggests we should leave the door open to a highly disturbing possibility: that, in the past, and far more than today, Bigfoot viewed us as its prey.

YEREN

Next to the legendary fire-breathing dragon, it's China's most famous monster: the Yeren, a huge, unidentified ape that almost certainly—in terms of its close proximity—has connections to the Abominable Snowman of the Himalayas and the various large and similar animals said to roam the huge mountains, such as the Nyalmo. While Yeren have been seen in a number of areas of China, certainly the one area—more than any other—that is a hotbed for sightings is Hubei, a province located in central China. It's a vast place dominated by numerous mountains—including the Daba Mountains and the Wudang Mountains—and the Jianghan Plain. Hubei is also a province through which flows the massive, nearly 4,000 mile-long Yangtze River.

It's specifically the western portion of Hubei in which the Yeren has been spotted—an area noted for its dense forest and treacherous mountains. As for what the Yerens are, that is the big question: at the top of the list is *Gigantopithecus*, a massive, presumed extinct ape that certainly dwelled in China hundreds of thousands of years ago—and which, perhaps, may not be quite so extinct after all. Coming in at a close second is the theory that the animal represents some form of huge and unacknowledged kind of orangutan.

Interestingly, just like Bigfoot in the United States, the Yeren comes in a variety of colors. Its hair has been described as red, brown, and even—on a few occasions—black. As for its height, while most reports describe creatures of around the average height of an adult human male to about eight feet, there are a number of cases involving colossal mountain monsters in excess of ten feet.

Despite their imposing appearances, however, the Yeren are said to be relatively placid, quiet creatures that shun humankind.

Sightings of the Yeren cannot be blamed upon hype born out of the fascination for Bigfoot. That much is made abundantly clear by the fact that reports of these immense animals have been reported for centuries. A translated, seventeenth-century document from Hubei notes: "In the remote mountains of Fangxian County, there are rock caves, in which live hairy men as tall as three meters. They often come down to hunt dogs and chickens in the villages. They fight with whoever resists."

In Western Hubei Province, China, there is a cave where the locals believe the Yeren resides; nearby, someone painted the warning "Wild Man Cave."

Of course the final comment, about the creatures being prone to violence, suggests that if, one day, you are confronted by a Yeren, do not assume it's as docile as many cryptozoologists claim it to be! Also, the reference to the Yeren hunting dogs adds weight to the notion that dogs and Bigfoot are hardly on friendly terms—as we have seen previously.

The evidence for the existence of the Yeren in more recent years is equally impressive. In 1940, it's said that the body of a dead Yeren turned up in Gansu. Female and over six feet in height, it was examined by a biologist named Wang Zelin. Interestingly, Tselin was unable to figure out if the beast was some form of ape, a primitive human, or something that was an odd combination of both.

In Wang Zelin's own words:

"Around September or October, we were travelling from Baoji to Tianshui via Jiangluo City; our car was between Jiangluo City and Niangniang Plain when we suddenly heard gunshots ahead of us. When the car reached the crowd that surrounded the gunman, all of us got down to satisfy our curiosity. We could see that the 'wildman' was already shot dead and laid on the roadside.

"The body was still supple and the stature very tall, approximately 2 metres. The whole body was covered with a coat of thick greyish-red hair which was very dense.... Since it was lying face-down, the more inquisitive of the passengers turned the body over to have a better look. It turned out to be a mother with a large pair of breasts, the nipples being very red as if it had recently given birth. The hair on the face was shorter. The face was narrow with deep-set eyes, while the cheek bones and lips jutted out. The scalp hair was roughly one chi long and untidy. The appearance was very similar to the plaster model of a female Peking Man. However, its hair seemed to be longer and thicker than that of the ape-man model. It was ugly because of the protruding lips.

"According to the locals, there were two of them, probably one male and the other female. They had been in that area for over a month. The 'wildmen' had great strength, frequently stood erect and were very tall. They were brisk in walking and could move as rapidly uphill as on the plain. As such, ordinary folks could not catch up with them. They did not have a language and could only howl."

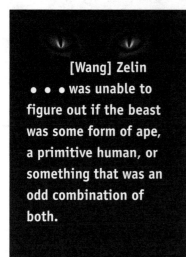

[Wang] Zelin • • • was unable to figure out if the beast was some form of ape, a primitive human, or something that was an odd combination of both.

Moving on to the 1970s, and specifically May 1976, there is a fascinating story of a number of government personnel—all based at Hubei—who, as they drove along a stretch of road dominated by thick woods in the early, predawn hours, came face to face with a Yeren.

In its haste to escape from the approaching jeep, the red-haired creature raced up a slope, but lost its footing and tumbled onto the road, landing right in front of the shocked group. Reportedly, the animal did not rear up onto its legs, but took a crouching stance—perhaps intended to intimidate the group by provoking fear it was about to lunge at them. Fortunately, that did not happen. What did happen is that the beast raced off, yet again—after one of the men hurled a stone in its direction. Although the creature had undeniable physical traits of an ape, its eyes were described as being eerily human-like, displaying intelligence and inquisitiveness.

As sightings of the creatures continued to be reported in the 1970s, and then into the 1980s, the Chinese Academy of Sciences got in on the act and established an ambitious program to try and resolve the mystery of the Yeren, once and for all. It was no easy task, and no hard, undeniable evidence ever surfaced. However, that's not to say there was a shortage of credible witness testimony. The reports poured in.

One such witness said to the Academy of their encounter with a Yeren:

"He was about seven feet tall, with shoulders wider than a man's, a sloping forehead, deep-set eyes and a bulbous nose with slightly upturned nostrils. He had sunken cheeks, ears like a man's but bigger, and round eyes, and also bigger than a man's. His jaw jutted out and he had protruding lips. His front teeth were as broad as a horse's. His eyes were black. His hair was dark brown, more than a foot long and hung loosely over his shoulders. His whole face, except for the nose and ears, was covered with short hairs. His arms hung below his knees. He had big hands with fingers about six inches long and thumbs only slightly separated from the fingers. He didn't have a tail, and the hair on his body was short. He had thick thighs, shorter than the lower part of his leg. He walked upright with his legs apart. His feet were each about 12 inches long and half that broad in front and narrow behind, with splayed toes. He was a male. That much I saw clearly."

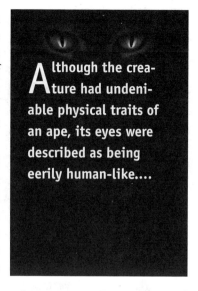

Although the creature had undeniable physical traits of an ape, its eyes were described as being eerily human-like....

Moving onto the 1990s, as monster authority Brad Steiger notes: "In October 1994, the Chinese government established the Committee for the Search for Strange and Rare Creatures, including among its members specialists in vertebrate paleontology and paleoanthropology. A loose consensus among interested members from the Chinese Academy of Sciences maintains that the Yeren are some species of unknown primates."

Today, the search for the Yeren continues in China, in much the same way that Bigfoot is sought in the United States and the Yowie in Australia.

YETI

Bigfoot is certainly the most famous of the world's many and varied hairy man-beasts. Running a close second, however, is the Yeti, also known as the Abominable Snowman. The specific region in which the legendary beast is said to roam is the Himalayas, a vast, mountainous expanse that dominates Tibet.

In the same way that the United States appears to be the home of several distinctly different creatures—such as the huge, lumbering apes of the Pacific Northwest and the smaller skunk apes of Florida—there also appears to be more than one kind of Yeti. Reportedly, they range from man-sized creatures to enormous giants, close to twenty feet in height. Of course, claims of such extreme and extraordinary heights must be treated cautiously. They may well be distorted accounts of encounters with animals of smaller stature, but no less impressive, perhaps around twelve to thirteen feet tall.

There is another Bigfoot parallel, too. Native American tradition tells of ancient awareness of the hairy beasts of the United States. Likewise, tales of hair-covered giants roaming the Himalayas also extend back into the fog of time. Take, for example, the stories of the Lepcha people. They are amongst the oldest of the various tribes that inhabit Sikkim, situated in northeast

An issue of *Radar* magazine promotes a 1960 story of an encounter with a Yeti in the Himalaya Mountains.

India. Their presence, however, extends to Tibet. It's not surprising, then, that they may have encountered Yetis during the course of their travels and expansions. Indeed, Lepcha lore tells of goliath-sized, hairy humanoids that lived high on the Himalayas and that used rocks to kill their prey, such as goats.

In terms of the relatively modern era, it was in the 1800s that matters became particularly intriguing. In the early 1830s an expedition was launched to the Himalayas by a skilled mountain climber, Brian Houghton Hodgson. According to Hodgson: "My shooters were once alarmed in the Kachár by the apparition of a 'wild man,' possibly an ourang, but I doubt their accuracy. They mistook the creature for a càcodemon or rakshas (demons), and fled from it instead of shooting it. It moved, they said, erectly: was covered with long dark hair, and had no tail."

None of the team expected to encounter giant, hair-covered hominids on the Himalayas, but that was exactly what they encountered. Particularly baffling to the team, the creatures they saw—typically at a distance—walked solely on their hind limbs.

Just one year before the turn of the twentieth century, Laurence Waddell's book, *Among the Himalayas*, was published. In the book, Waddell described how a number of Tibetans had told him of huge, hairy, ape-like animals that moved like people and lived in the mountains. Waddell put little faith in the accounts, despite having personally come across some intriguing large footprints in the snow. The reports from Hodgson's team, coupled with that of Waddell, provoked short waves of interest; it wasn't, however, until the 1920s that matters heated up.

The Everest Reconnaissance Expedition was launched in 1921, under the leadership of Lieutenant-Colonel Charles Howard-Bury, of the British military. No one on the expedition anticipated coming across anything unusual, but that was exactly what they found, in the form of huge, human-like footprints, thousands of feet up in the snow-covered mountains. When word of the strange discoveries began to spread, a newspaper reporter, Henry Newman, decided to look into the matter for himself. It didn't take long, at all, before Newman had collected a respectably sized body of material on the legendary mountain roamer, which he famously dubbed the Abominable Snowman—somewhat of a mistaken distortion of the term used by the locals, *metoh,* meaning "filthy."

Without doubt, it was the decade of the 1950s that really caught the imagination of the media and the scientific community. Britain's media was hot on the trail of the creature, as were respected mountaineers, including Sir Edmund Hillary and Eric Shipton. Although interest in, and reports of, the Yeti dipped in subsequent years, the controversy was revived in 2014, when a professor of genetics at Oxford University, England, revealed his findings, which suggested the Yeti was actually nothing stranger than a bear, possibly one that was part polar bear and part brown bear.

A Yeti footprint has a pickax next to it for comparison. Mountaineers Eric Shipton and Michael Ward took the photo in 1951.

Within the field of cryptozoology, the most likely candidate for the Yeti is *Gigantopithecus,* a truly gigantic ape that science tells us has been extinct for tens of thousands of years. That the immense beast dwelled in the very areas where Yetis are seen to this day suggests a distinct, but astounding, possibility that *Gigantopithecus* may still be with us.

YOWIE

Creatures of a Bigfoot-like appearance are not exclusive to the United States, the Himalayas, and the wilds of South America, Russia, and China. Australia is the domain of the huge, apish Yowie. In the same way that Native Americans have a long history of reports of Sasquatch—and particularly so in the Pacific Northwest—Australia's aboriginal people have long told of the existence of the towering Yowie. There is another parallel between the North American Bigfoot and the Yowie of Australia: a careful perusal of old newspapers shows that the Yowie, just like Bigfoot, was known of long before the term "Bigfoot" was created, back in the 1950s.

Many of the sightings of Yowies occur in and around the vast Blue Mountains that dominate the city of Sydney and what is termed the Sydney

A statue of a Yowie stands in a park in Kilcoy, Queensland, Australia.

Basin. A firsthand report, from February 1842, offers a graphic description of the beasts. It was published, as a letter, in the pages of the *Australian and New Zealand Monthly Magazine*:

"This being they describe as resembling a man of nearly the same height, with long white hair hanging down from the head over the features, the arms as extraordinarily long, furnished at the extremities with great talons, and the feet turned backwards, so that, on flying from man, the imprint of the foot appears as if the being had traveled in the opposite direction. Altogether, they describe it as a hideous monster of an unearthly character and ape-like appearance."

Then, on December 9, 1882, a firsthand account surfaced from a Mr. H. J. McCooey, who told the *Australian Town and Country Journal* newspaper the following:

"A few days ago I saw one of these strange creatures. I should think that if it were standing upright it would be nearly five feet high. It was tailless and covered with very long black hair, which was of a dirty red or snuff-color about the throat and breast. Its eyes, which were small and restless, were partly hidden by matted hair that covered its head. I threw a stone at the animal, whereupon it immediately rushed off."

And, make no mistake, sightings of the Australian Yowie are not limited to the past. In early 1993, a man named Neil Frost, who lived in the Blue Mountains area, encountered in the shadows of his backyard an animal that Frost estimated weighed close to 300 pounds, walked on two legs, and had a thick coat of hair and bright red eyes. When the beast realized it had been spotted, it shot away at high speed and into the shadows. Despite attempts on the part of Frost and a friend, Ian Price, to track down the beast on several occasions, the Yowie skillfully eluded them—just like its American cousin, Bigfoot, so very often does, too.

Bringing matters even further up to date, midway through June 2013, Australia's *Northern Star* newspaper reported on a recent encounter. Journalist Jamie Brown wrote: "The latest sighting took place recently just north of Bexhill when a Lismore resident and music videographer spied the classic creature crossing a moonlit Bangalow Road. The witness, who has asked not to be named for fear of reprisal, said he was driving back home from a night of filming at Eltham and had just turned onto the Bangalow Road heading for Lismore when he spied a creature jumping a barbed wire paddock fence before briefly pausing at the edge of the road. Suddenly the beast moved across the two lanes of bitumen, raising his arm to apparently shield its eyes from the bright high beam glare of the approaching car."

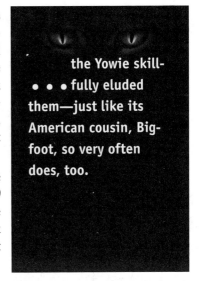

the Yowie skill- • • • fully eluded them—just like its American cousin, Bigfoot, so very often does, too.

As for the witness, who insisted on anonymity, he commented: "I would have seen it for between 20 and 30 seconds. It was really moving at the time. It leapt the fence no problem. All I can remember was seeing this large black object with a solid build, lanky legs and long lanky arms. It wasn't clothed … it wasn't wearing clothes like a human."

The Yowie, it seems, lives on.

ZANA

It was in 1964 that Professor Boris Porshnev uncovered, in Russia's Caucasus Mountains, what was described to him by the villagers of Tkhina as the bones of a female Almasty, Russia's very own Bigfoot. Brad Steiger says that according to Porshnev, a "preliminary investigation of the skeleton determined that its skeletal structure was different to that of a female member of *Homo sapiens*."

It was a discovery that became inextricably linked to a story that dated back to the 1800s, specifically to the mid-1860s. There was a story in the area that a nobleman by the name of Edgi Genaba, who had an estate in Tkhina, returned to the village one day with something remarkable in tow. It was a strange, savage-looking thing of primitive proportions. Clearly, in some respects, at least, it was human. But, as to whether it was actually *Homo sapiens*, that is a very different matter entirely. Reportedly, the creature—a female—was given to Genaba by a vassal of one Prince D. M. Achba, a keen and expert hunter and the ruler of the Zaadan region, who took the wild woman alive while out in the woods.

Genaba wasted no time in building a secure enclosure, one in which the creature, soon named Zana, could be housed. Initially, there were understandable concerns that Zana might prove to be hostile and downright murderous, hence the reason why she was kept confined. For a while, at least, the actions of Genaba were seen as making a great deal of sense: Zana was defini-tively unstable, lived in a hole she dug in the enclosure, and ate like a wild animal. Over the course of a couple of years, however, things began to change.

Eventually, the people of Tkhina came to accept that Zana was no longer the threat they had feared she might originally have been, and as a result, she was given a significant amount of freedom to wander around the village and interact with the people of the area. Zana was, by all accounts, a quick learner and quite intelligent: she helped around the village, hauling sacks of grain and preparing firewood, and seemingly enjoying her daily tasks, too.

> Zana was ... a quick learner and quite intelligent: she helped around the village, hauling sacks of grain and preparing fire-wood....

It's clear from the descriptions that Zana was no nor-mal woman: her immense body was covered in dark hair, she shunned clothing—even in the freezing temperatures of the Caucasus Mountains—and she could not speak a word. Of her physical appearance, Igor Bourtsev said:

"Her face was terrifying; broad, with high cheek-bones, flat nose, turned out nostrils, muzzle like jaws, wide mouth with large teeth, low forehead and eyes of a reddish tinge. But the most frightening feature was her expression which was purely animal, not human. Sometimes, she would give a spontaneous laugh, baring those big white teeth of hers. The latter were so strong that she easily cracked the hardest walnuts."

Despite repeated attempts to try and have Zana learn to speak the local Russian dialect, it came to nothing: mumble and squeal was just about all that Zana could manage, depending on her mood and demeanor. She was, however, a creature obsessed with cleanliness, never missing a day of bathing in the cold waters of a local spring. Zana had another obsession, too: with rocks. She enjoyed chipping away at them and placing them into various designs and piles, as if doing so held some form of significance for her.

The most controversial claim made about Zana is that she gave birth to no fewer than five children. The fathers, however, were reportedly not male Almasty, but the men of Tkhina. Brad Steiger has made a valuable observation on this claim: "If true, the implications of Zana's having bred with men of the village are really quite staggering. If the wild woman truly did conceive with human males, then she was not an ape."

Related to this aspect of the story is the rumor that four of the children died, while the solitary survivor fled for the vast mountains from which its mother reportedly originated. Zana supposedly lived until the 1880s, when she passed away, and her life was celebrated by the people of Tkhina, who had come to embrace her as one of their very own.

Not So Human

ASWANG

For centuries, the people of the Philippines have told of a violent, malevolent monster that has provoked terror and mayhem and which has been responsible for an untold number of savage, violent deaths. It goes by the name of the Aswang—and is also known as the Tik-Tik and the Sok-Sok, due to the strange clicking noises it makes when it is about to launch an attack on its prey, which is almost exclusively humans. Although reports of the Aswang can be found all across the Philippines, the monster is most often seen on Mindanao—the second largest island in the Philippines—and on the Visayas Islands, and particularly so on the islands of Bohol and Negros.

While outsiders might take the view that the Aswang is merely a beast of legend and folklore, the people of the Philippines have a very different opinion: to them, the monster is all too real. And it's a gruesome, marauding thing, to be sure. According to local lore, most Aswangs are female. They are not, however, of the beautiful, seductive type that one might expect to see in a Gothic-style vampire movie. The Aswangs just might be your very worst nightmare. They are scrawny, emaciated things with gray and mottled skin, and milk-white eyes that are as cold-looking as they are emotion-free. Sores and boils cover their bodies. They give off a stench of rotting meat. And they are typically garbed in ragged, torn clothing. Despite their rotted appearance and odor, the Aswangs are highly athletic, having the ability to run at phenomenal speeds and to leap to heights of around fifteen feet or more, as they pursue their terrified soon-to-be victims and dinner combined. Indeed, the Aswangs live exclusively on two things: human blood and human meat. No wonder, then, that zombie-vampire legends surrounding the Aswangs have taken such a firm hold.

Worse still, the Aswangs have a particular taste for the flesh of newborn babies and children. They will do their utmost to seek out the young and the vulnerable, silently and stealthily breaking into homes in the middle of the night, and slaughtering and taking away the corpses of those targeted. Although the Aswangs will devour just about every part of the human body, they are most partial to the liver and the heart, which are seen as definitive delicacies to these infernal things. When an Aswang is unable to seek out a tasty human, he or she will resort to prowling around cemeteries and graveyards, clawing into the dirt and digging up the recently buried.

> **They are scrawny, emaciated things with gray and mottled skin, and milk-white eyes that are as cold-looking as they are emotion-free.**

Also mirroring the lore surrounding zombies and vampires, if a person is attacked and bitten by an Aswang, but manages to escape its clutches, he or she too will soon become an Aswang. Infection takes no time at all to set in, and the process of mutation from human to monster is unstoppable. There is no cure for the deadly infection that the Aswang delivers and which quickly surges through the bloodstream.

As infection spreads, the poor victim develops a craving for blood and for human flesh. Violent mood swings develop. The person is affected by sudden bouts of rage. It's only a matter of time before the infected lose all of their humanity and become fearsome, cannibalistic monsters.

It's not just vampires and zombies that the Aswangs resemble: like the classic werewolf of folklore, history, and Hollywood, the Aswang can shape-shift itself into multiple, animal-based forms, including a huge black dog with glowing eyes, a bipedal wolf, and a huge and violent pig.

BATSQUATCH

Practically everyone has heard of Bigfoot and Mothman. Along with the likes of the Loch Ness Monster and the Abominable Snowman, they are two of the world's most famous monsters. But, what do you get when you combine the aforementioned Bigfoot and Mothman? Well, what you get is Batsquatch: a terrifying, malevolent, hair-covered humanoid that sports a pair of huge, gargoyle-like wings.

It was a diabolical beast encountered by a young man on the night of Saturday, April 16, 1994. The location was southeast of Buckley, Washington, and with Mount Rainier in the background. Interestingly, Mount Rainier has another strange and now-famous aerial mystery attached to it: it was over the mountain, on June 24, 1947, that a pilot named Kenneth Arnold encountered a squadron of strange, flying vehicles that, when the media got hold of the story, became famously known as flying saucers. Meanwhile, however, back to 1994.

The man who became the unfortunate witness to the terrible beast was Brian Canfield, who, at the time in question, was driving his truck to Camp One, a settlement in the area, that is situated near Lake Kapowsin. All was normal until Canfield's headlights began to fade. That was bad enough. But, in mere moments, his engine completely quit and his vehicle silently coasted to a stop at the side of the road. All thoughts of what he should do, on a lonely stretch of Washington road at around 9:30 P.M., went totally out of the window when an infernal monstrosity loomed into view.

It did so in a curious semi-gliding, semi-flying fashion, finally coming to rest right in front of his vehicle.

Canfield could only look on, terror-stricken, as a large, dark-colored humanoid descended from the black skies. It did so in a curious semi-gliding, semi-flying fashion, finally coming to rest right in front of his vehicle. Canfield was unable to move, such was his level of terror. All he could do was grip the steering wheel and stare in stark terror at the beast before him.

It was a shocking sight, to say the least. The winged, hair-covered monster was around nine feet in height and, as Canfield could now see, those wings spanned the entire road. It was at this point, despite his terror, that Canfield finally got a good look at the creature. Its fur was actually a dark blue, rather than the assumed black or brown. Its eyes shone yellow, and its white fangs protruded menacingly from its werewolf-like visage. For at least a couple of minutes, both man and monster confronted each other, neither making any kind of move. That is, until the creature, without warning, flapped its wings powerfully and violently and took to the skies.

Perhaps demonstrating the creature's supernatural powers, when the beast vanished, Canfield's vehicle returned to normal: both its headlights and engine worked perfectly. Canfield raced back to the home he shared with his parents, charged into the house, and spluttered and gasped his way through his astounding story of what happened. Canfield's mother, clearly realizing this was no prank, decided that the best thing they could do would be to get back out there and try and figure things out—as in right now. Perhaps luckily for both of them, Batsquatch—an undeniably memorable name—was nowhere to be seen. And, so far as can be determined, it has never been seen again. Unless, that is, you know better.

DONKEY WOMAN

Her name might sound somewhat comical, but there's nothing to laugh about when it comes to this truly diabolical and infernal entity that haunts various parts of the Texas city of San Antonio. Indeed, she—or, perhaps more correctly, *it*—has, for decades, provoked both fear and mayhem in the city's residents. Which is hardly surprising, as you will now come to appreciate.

The story of the monster-woman dates back to the 1800s, and specifically to the vicinity of an area of the city called Elm Creek. It was on the creek, legend says, that a woman lived with her husband and two children, and eked a living from farming. In fact, it was barely a living, which ensured the family lived in poverty and at near-starvation levels.

As fate would unfortunately have it, on one particular day a man on horseback appeared near the family's property. He was a young man, the son of a rich landowner in the area, and someone with a cruel propensity for torturing animals. And, when he saw the family's solitary mule standing all alone in a particular field, he decided to embark on a bit of what he, in his warped state, termed fun. That's to say, he proceeded to violently beat the poor, defenseless animal. It was only the loud cries of the mule that saved its life: its owners came running to see what was going on and were confronted by the man attacking the mule. Not surprisingly, they tried to beat the man away, which they did by throwing stones at him, some of which were right on target. The man cursed both husband and wife, swearing to get even with them. It was a curse that soon came tragically to life.

Later that night, a posse, led by the man himself, stealthily crept up on the family home and set it ablaze. In moments, the house was engulfed in flames and terror overwhelmed all four. The owner of the house tried to distract the group so his wife and children could escape, but it was to no avail. He was shot and killed and his children were burned alive. His wife was terribly burned. Her fingers were burned down to charred stumps, her entire body was blackened, and her face was dreadfully disfigured—to the extent that her face appeared to have semi-melted and took on elongated, donkey-like proportions; hence her name. Crazed, in agony, and hideously burned, she fled the house and threw herself into the waters below nearby Elm Creek Bridge. She vanished under the water as the farmhouse continued to burn, ominously lighting up the dark, night sky. She was never seen again. Or was she?

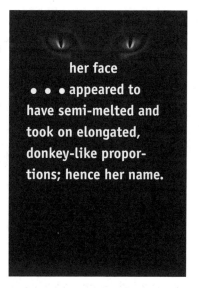

her face • • • appeared to have semi-melted and took on elongated, donkey-like proportions; hence her name.

On more than a few occasions, and right up to modern times, people crossing the bridge—whether walking or in vehicles—have heard terrible shrieks coming from the waters below and from within the surrounding woods. A vile, wailing, she-monster, with long and lank hair, dressed in rags and with her skin peeling off, has reportedly jumped onto the cars of terrified drivers, and on more than a few occasions. Others have seen the beast-woman walking through the waters, insanely seeking revenge on the people who made her life a misery and who killed her family.

"Texas Cryptid Hunter" says of the affair of the Donkey Lady:

"What interests me more than whether or not the stories are true is what people are still seeing on or near the Elm Creek Bridge. Could there be a flesh and blood creature responsible for the legends? If so, what could it be? Many have screwed up their courage and ventured under the bridge to examine the muddy bank for clues. Some have come back with photos of hoof-like tracks. Is this proof that the 'Donkey Lady' exists? I would hesitate to say that. This is Texas, after all, and finding the tracks of a horse or mule anywhere in this state, even under the 'Donkey Lady Bridge,' would not be all that unusual; however, whatever haunts this bridge and the surrounding woods is still seen on occasion and is heard more often than that to this very day."

GOAT MAN OF TEXAS

In the very early hours of one particularly fateful morning in the hot and sticky summer of 1969, six petrified residents of the Texas city of Fort Worth raced for the safety of their local police station and related a controversial and amazing story. John Reichart, his wife, and two other couples were parked at Lake Worth—and, yes, it was indeed at the stroke of midnight—when a truly vile and monstrous-looking creature came storming out of the thick branches of a large, nearby tree.

Reportedly covered in a coat that seemed to be comprised of both scales and fur, it slammed with a crashing bang onto the hood of the Reicharts' car and even tried to grab hold of the not-surprisingly-terrified Mrs. Reichart, before racing off into the pitch-black night and the camouflage of the dense, surrounding trees. The solitary evidence of its dark and foreboding presence was a deep, foot-and-a-half-long scratch along the side of the Reicharts' vehicle.

While this specific event rapidly, and unsurprisingly, generated deep media interest, and was actually taken extremely seriously by the Fort Worth police—as prime evidence of this, no fewer than four police cars quickly headed to the scene of the Reicharts' encounter—it was most certainly not the first occasion upon which Fort Worth officialdom had become the recipient of ominous accounts of diabolical beasts roaming around Lake Worth.

The solitary evidence of its dark and fore-boding presence was a deep, foot-and-a-half-long scratch along the side of the Reicharts' vehicle.

Indeed, until the Reicharts' story hit the newspapers, it was a little-known fact that for approximately two months the police had been clandestinely investigating reports of a distinctly weird beast that was said to be spooking the locals on a disturbingly regular basis. While some of the officers concluded that at least some of the sightings might have been the work of local kids running around in ape costumes, others were not quite so sure that fakery was a dominating factor and took the Reicharts' story to heart.

For example, Patrolman James S. McGee conceded that the report John Reichart filed with the Fort Worth constabulary was treated very seriously, as a result of the fact that "those people were really scared." Of course, the Dallas-Fort Worth media loved the story, and did their utmost to promote it just about as much as was humanly possible. Notably, one particular feature that appeared in the pages of the *Fort Worth Star-Telegram* was written by acclaimed author Jim Marrs—very well-known today for his books on 9/11, the JFK assassination of November 1963, and countless other conspiracies and cover-ups.

The headline that leapt out of the *Star-Telegram* was a news editor's absolute dream: *Fishy Man-Goat Terrifies Couples Parked at Lake Worth*. Beyond any shadow of doubt, it was this particular story that made the Goat Man both infamous and even feared among the residents of Lake Worth. And it would not be long at all before the monster's ugly form surfaced once again. In fact, it was almost twenty-four hours to the minute: midnight was looming around the corner and the creature was reportedly seen racing across a stretch of road close to the Lake Worth Nature Center. Interestingly, the prime witness, one Jack Harris of Fort Worth, stated that when he attempted to take a picture of the monster, the flash on his camera failed to work—a phenomenon that is curiously and eerily prevalent in mystery animal reports and encounters.

The beast, whatever its ultimate nature and origin, was shortly thereafter seen to charge across the landscape to a nearby bluff, with three dozen hyped-up locals in hot pursuit, and all hysterically baying for the blood of the beast. The Goat Man wasn't about to become the victim of some crazed posse, however. He had an unforeseen ace up his sleeve—allegedly, at least. Towering over the crowd at approximately ten yards, the Goat Man hurled a huge tire at the group, which resulted in the throng wildly scattering in all directions. One of those present, a man named Jack Harris, said that "everybody jumped back into their cars" and got out of there quickly. The Goat Man had won the day.

Respected journalist Jim Marrs wrote about the Goat Man in the *Star-Telegram*.

But the story was far from over. Yet more accounts surfaced, with some witnesses stating that the creature had dark fur or hair all over its body, while others maintained that its coat was overwhelmingly white in color. Then there were disturbing tales of horrific mutilations of animals in the area: dogs, cats, and more—most of which surfaced amid theories that the Goat Man had made a home (or, more likely, a lair) for himself in a relatively small piece of land, called Greer Island, that is connected to the mainland by a small walkway.

The story was on the verge of spinning wildly out of control, when one Helmuth Naumer, who was an employee of the Fort Worth Museum of Science and History, offered the theory that the Goat Man was probably nothing stranger than a pet bobcat that someone had clandestinely released into Lake Worth Park, and one that presumably took a great deal of pleasure in jumping onto people's cars at midnight. Precisely how the bobcat was able to change its color from brown to white, or throw a large tire through the air—for what was estimated to be a distance of no less than 500 feet—remained sadly unanswered, however.

Of course, it's not impossible that Naumer's theories might indeed have provided answers to the questions that pertained to at least some of the sightings; however, it most assuredly could not explain the truly surreal photo taken by a man named Allen Plaster, who was a local dress shop owner. Plaster's picture displayed a giant, white-hued beast with a torso that appeared to be constructed out of dozens of cotton-balls, and atop which sat a truly tiny head. And while stories and friend-of-a-friend tales suggested Fort Worth police had found evidence that some of the sightings were the work of costumed hoaxers, this was an issue that to this day remains murky and not fully resolved. Indeed, the legend of the Goat Man still lives on at Lake Worth—and long may it do so!

GOAT MAN OF WHITE ROCK LAKE

The most terrifying resident of White Rock Lake in Dallas, Texas, is the legendary Goat Man. As the story goes, on several occasions in the 1970s and 1980s a distinctly odd creature was seen flitting in and out of the trees after sunset, and was described as being man-like in form, around seven feet in height, with goat-style protrusions sticking out of its head, and hooves instead of feet. The description of the animal was eerily like that of the fabled satyrs of Greek and Roman legend. And it must be noted that numerous other cultures had an awareness that such strange creatures were lurking among them—and for millennia. There was, for example, the demon goat-man Azazel, the goat-beast of the mountains that was feared by the herdsmen of Parnassus. There was also the Greek god Pan.

The deity of woods and fields and of flocks and shepherds, Pan dwelt in grottos, roamed both mountains and valleys, was a lover of music, and was universally feared. In ancient days, any form of overwhelming dread without a discernible cause was very often ascribed to the actions and presence of Pan, and became known as a Panic terror. Pan came to be considered a symbol of the universe and the personification of Nature, and was almost certainly the inspiration for the Latin divinities, Sylvanus and Faunus.

A fascinating account that deserves mention was brought to my attention by Sandy Grace, who saw the Goat Man up close and personal in August 2001—at White Rock Lake. Grace had been jogging around the lake on the nine-mile-long trail when, at around 2:00 P.M., out of the trees, she told me, stepped the strangest looking thing she had ever seen.

The fallen angel Azazel appears goatlike in Christian and Jewish mythology.

Large, covered in thin, coarse brown hair and with two large horn-like protrusions, the half-man half-beast strode purposefully in her direction with a malevolent, sneering grin on its face. Bizarrely, when it got within about fifteen feet of the terror-stricken Grace, the animal crouched on its four limbs and vanished in a flash of light. She was sure that it had not been a hallucination, but was equally sure that such a thing could not live within the confines of White Rock Lake—or, indeed, anywhere on the face of the Earth.

Very interestingly, Grace told me that less than a minute before the Goat Man appeared, she was overcome by an intense feeling of fear—albeit for no particular reason she could fathom, then or now. She had never suffered from panic attacks (before or since) but figured that this was probably the best way to describe how she felt. I thought to myself that it could also have been a classic description of an encounter with Pan, the God of the Woods, centuries ago.

GRINNING MAN

❙❙Christine" grew up in West Texas and was confronted on more than a few occasions by one of the weirdest and creepiest offshoots of the Men in Black mystery—namely, the so-called "Grinning Man." She says:

"I haven't told a lot of people about it. When I first saw the person I was about 1 or 2 years old. I have a very long memory. It was like the typical thing that you hear: it was this man who would stand in the doorway of my bedroom. I remember standing up in my crib and holding onto the bars and he wore a fedora and a tan raincoat and black trousers, shiny shoes and black leather gloves. His face wasn't like someone who had been burned, but he just stood there and would grin. There was nothing friendly about the way he was grinning. It was horrible. Emotionless, didn't blink. And he came off and on for a few years.

"Even as I got older and slept in my own bed I would wake up sometimes, like at 3 o'clock in the morning, and that went on. That still happens: all of a sudden I'll be wide awake at 3 o'clock in the morning, for no apparent reason. But as a kid I'd wake up at 3 o'clock and he'd be there. I didn't have any frame of reference for it. Of course, my mom didn't believe me; she just thought I was dreaming.

"But there were all sorts of strange paranormal things that happened throughout my childhood and I won-

> **❙❙**I remember standing up in my crib and holding onto the bars and he wore a fedora and a tan raincoat and black trousers, shiny shoes and black leather gloves."

der if it was all part of the same thing. I even got weird phone calls as a teenager. The phone would ring and it sounded like a little kid speaking in another language; just rapidly talking into the phone. I thought at the time it was some little kid who got on a payphone and started dialing numbers from another country. But, when I read *The Mothman Prophecies*, I went: Wow! This was the same thing.

"What kind of validated that this person was real was that when I was twelve, a friend and I were out riding our bikes about 9.30 at night in the summer—it was a small town in west Texas. And we stopped and were looking in the doors of the Baptist church, as they had just put in new carpets. A big Saturday night! But, we both turned at the same time to look behind us and this man appeared like right on the edge of the street light and started walking towards us, and he was wearing the exact same outfit: the fedora and the tan overcoat and black pants. But, this time, his whole head and hands were bandaged. We didn't speak; we just took off like a shot, around the corner, to her house. We didn't know what to make of it, but I thought it was probably that same person that I used to see. I never saw him again.

> **//One night, she woke up and he was looking at her, but he was petting her sister's head while she slept."**

"When I got into my early twenties, I was living in Dallas and I met a girl; we got to talking about paranormal stuff and she lived in Lufkin, in east Texas. She said that she and her sister shared a room and that sometimes she would wake up and there would be this man in her room. She said he wore a hat and a long coat. He reminded her of the McDonald's 'Hamburglar' and he would just stand there grinning at her. One night, she woke up and he was looking at her, but he was petting her sister's head while she slept.

"And, then, a few years later, another friend of mine who had grown up in New York, she had seen a similar man and that would stand in her room. I thought, okay that's great; I am absolutely not nuts. I had lights that would turn off and on. My stuff got moved around all the time. I still have my things get moved around. I had a poster of Marilyn Monroe jump off my wall. It was like 6 o'clock, I think I was sixteen, and it just flew off the wall and into middle of the floor. I grew up in a really religious family: southern Baptist; so that was all something of the Devil, although I don't believe that now.

"There was another visible entity that used to show up. It was black, sort of shapeless, but had these enormous eyes, kind of like the quintessential way we depict aliens. The great big eyes, but they were silvery with no pupil. They had a reflective quality. Again, it would be 3 o'clock in the morning and I would feel my bed jolt. And I would look down and see those eyes, right over the edge of my bed, and the black shapelessness around it. I turned on the light once I got my courage up. I thought: if I don't move it's going to kill me, and if I do move it's going to kill me. Again, I was sixteen or seventeen. I screamed for my mom. I just told her I had a nightmare. But then I saw it again; one morning I was getting ready to go to school and I turned toward the shower and I could see the eyes looking between the hooks on the shower curtain.

//I asked her what it looked like and she said the same thing: these big eyes and just black."

"The final time this thing ever appeared I didn't see it. I had a friend sleeping over, a senior in high school. She had never been to my house and I had never told her about any of this kind of stuff. She was very religious; didn't really believe in any of this or would have said it was the Devil. We're up the next morning, and she was helping me make my bed and I said: 'It was a lot of fun; you should come back over.' And she looked at me and said: 'I'm sorry, I'm never gonna come back here.'

"I said: 'What did I do?' She said: 'You didn't do anything. How do you not remember?' I said: 'I really don't know what you're talking about; you'll have to tell me.' She said she woke up suddenly during the night and she thought that she couldn't see. Then, when her eyes adjusted, there was a face so close to hers that she couldn't see anything else. I asked her what it looked like and she said the same thing: these big eyes and just black. She said she screamed so loud she figured she woke the whole neighborhood.

"All I did, according to her, was lift up and sit up on my elbow and look at her and said: 'Are you okay?' And she said she was and went back to sleep. My mom didn't hear it either. And, surely enough, she never came back to my house.

"I did have a person who would actually call me and talk to me while I was in high school. It may have just been some nut, but he seemed to know everywhere that I went. I took dance classes in Abilene and I had friends that lived there as well. And this person would call late at night and ask: 'How was your dance class?' He knew my every move, which was odd. They wouldn't tell me who they were. They knew a week's worth of my activities. I might have decided to see a friend and not had those plans prior. So, no one would know where I was going, but this person knew where I had been.

"The last time I saw him was in a dream when I was thirteen and it was like a lucid dream, and I was in a store, looking at a rack of magazines. And I turned and looked to my left and there he is, and he's got a magazine in his hand and staring right at me and grinning. And in the dream I put my magazine down and I walked right past him and told him: 'Don't ever come here again.' And he never did. That was the last time I saw him, physically or in a dream. I just decided, right there, in my dream I'm not having this anymore.

"I know that when I do think about him it does spur activity in my house; when I look into it again or the paranormal. I wonder how much of that is like energy that I'm putting out. I never had any sightings of UFO phenomena attached to it. There was one thing: I was driving home from Abilene one night—and there is an Air Force base in Abilene—and there was apparently an aircraft, although there were no lights on it. But it left a green, glowing vapor behind it and it was traveling really, really fast. But it could have been some kind of Air Force thing."

HORSE-KILLING CREATURES

Over the last couple of decades, I have spent a lot of time digging into matters relative to Bigfoot, the Men in Black, the Chupacabra, Roswell, and lake monsters. But, back when I was in my early teens, I was exposed to something else. It was as chilling as it was downright bizarre. And it was something that occurred just a short drive from where I lived as a kid, in central England. Namely, the village of Pelsall, the origins of which hark way back in time to the tenth century.

Barely a stone's throw from Pelsall is the village of Great Wyrley. On the surface, there's nothing odd or disturbing about the place. At least, not until you do a bit of digging into its history. That's when you find Great Wyrley has a dark shadow hanging over it. And it has been there for more than a century. In late 1903, a resident of Great Wyrley—a certain young man named George Edalji—was sentenced to serve significant jail time for violently attacking horses in the area. The late-night attacks were so ferocious and deadly that the entire populace of Great Wyrley was shocked to its collective core. Both the local and national media covered the killings and reported extensively on Edalji's sentence. But was Edalji really guilty of the crimes attributed to him?

Someone who suspected there had been a major miscarriage of justice in the Edalji affair was none other than Sir Arthur Conan Doyle, the famous creator of the world's equally famous, fictional "consulting detective." We're talking, of course, about Sherlock Holmes, of 221b Baker Street, London. Such was the extent to which Conan Doyle tackled the Edalji case, the latter's seven-year sentence was cut and he walked out of prison in 1906. Edalji was a free man, albeit, not a pardoned man. The local police remained convinced that Edalji was the guilty party, regardless of what Sir Arthur may have thought, and equally regardless of Sir Arthur's fame and influence.

The apparently peaceful village of Great Wyrley, England, where disturbing acts of violence have occurred in the past.

Now, some might say that the strange saga of George Edalji was nothing more than a case of some deranged individual—whether Edalji, or possibly a local butcher's boy named Royden Sharp, or someone else whose identity has never been ascertained—performing terrible acts that warranted incarceration. No one, surely, would have a problem about placing such a person behind bars—and for a very long time. But was the culprit George Edalji? Well, that's the big question.

There are a number of valid reasons as to why Edalji may not have been the guilty party. Born in 1876 to a mother of Scottish descent and a father who was from Bombay, India, George—along with the rest of his family—suffered from racist taunts, some of which came from the local police. Indeed, the Chief Constable of the Staffordshire Police loudly and outrageously proclaimed "black men [were] less than beasts." Locals viewed the family with suspicion. Anonymous, threatening letters were sent to the Edalji home, and a campaign of intimidation and terror rolled on for years, and which culminated in George Edalji's arrest and conviction for horse maiming. Until, that is, Conan Doyle stepped into the swirling mystery and Edalji became a free man.

Living very close to where George Edalji dwelled decades earlier, I—like most of my family and friends—had heard the tales of the animal mutilations, of the Conan Doyle connection, and of the menace that the entire affair created in and around Great Wyrley, back at the turn of the twentieth century. But with a growing interest in matters relative to the domains of the mysterious, the supernatural, and the occult, I began to realize that there were some aspects to the controversy that pushed things down very strange pathways, possibly even supernatural pathways.

There was talk—often hushed talk—of the unfortunate horses being sacrificed to appease ancient, terrible, supernatural entities. One of the strangest of all accounts suggested that the culprit was a large and monstrous ape. This is intriguing, since Staffordshire has a long and controversial history of "out-of-place apes" and of "British Bigfoot." A similar story in circulation posited that well-trained and aggressive boars were responsible.

Large and violent birds of an unknown kind—possibly of what, today, we might call the Mothman kind—and even a wild and marauding cat were suggested. In terms of the latter, we're talking about an ocelot, which is known as the "dwarf leopard" and which exists in South America, Central America, and Mexico. It just so happens that the creature in question was a very real one. It was owned by a man named Dr. John Kerr Butter. He lived not at all far from where the attacks occurred, and, at the time of Edalji's arrest, Butter was retained by the police to check for any incriminating horse hairs on Edalji's clothing. Whispers suggest that it was Butter's ocelot (he may have owned several over the years …) that was the real cause of the horse attacks, and not Edalji after all. Darker whispers suggest that Butter might well have had a vested interest in placing the blame on Edalji, specifically to direct people away from himself and his wild cat. Whatever the truth, Butter's ocelot vanished under odd circumstances, although a second is rumored to have come into his hands a few years later.

Well, as I'm sure you can guess, all this entertained and intrigued a very young Nick Redfern, to the extent that I still take note of any and all new developments in the strange saga of George Edalji. As for the latest development, it occurred in 2015. The PBS channel aired a three-part, dramatized series on the mystery titled *Arthur & George*, which is based upon a novel of the same name by Julian Barnes. It demonstrates that this macabre and unsettling piece of Great Wyrley history is unlikely to fade away anytime soon.

LIZARD MAN

In the summer of 1988, a terrifying creature began haunting the woods and little towns of Lee County, South Carolina—and specifically the Scape Ore

Swamp area. It quickly became known as Lizard Man, as a result of its alleged green and scaly body. For all intents and purposes, it was a case of *The Creature from the Black Lagoon* come to life. A bipedal lizard roaming the neighborhood? Maybe, yes. On the other hand, research undertaken years later suggested that the Lizard Man was something far more akin to Bigfoot. We'll return to the matter of Bigfoot shortly, but, first, some much needed information and background on the creature.

It all began—publicly if not chronologically—on July 14, 1988, when the Waye family phoned the Lee County Sheriff's office and made a very strange and disturbing claim. Something wild and animalistic had attacked their 1985 Ford. It looked as if something large, powerful, and deeply savage had viciously clawed, and maybe even bitten into, the body of the vehicle—and particularly so the hood. Somewhat baffled, the deputies responded to the call, nevertheless. Sure enough, the Wayes were right on target: their vehicle was battered and bruised in the extreme. In addition, there were footprints across the muddy area. It was clearly time to bring in Sheriff Liston Truesdale. There was a strong probability that the prints were those of a fox. Larger prints, also found, were suspected of being those of a bear—although some observers suggested they had human qualities.

In such a closeknit neighborhood, it didn't take long before news got around and numerous locals turned up to see what all the fuss was about. It's notable that Sheriff Truesdale told Bigfoot investigator Lyle Blackburn, who wrote the definitive book on the affair—titled, of course, *Lizard Man*—that "While we were there looking over this situation, we learned that people in the Browntown community had been seeing a strange creature about seven feet tall with red eyes. Some of them described it as green, but some of them as brown. They thought it might be responsible for what happened."

A mystery—and a monster—was unleashed.

The publicity afforded the Waye incident prompted someone who ultimately became the key player in the matter to come forward. His name was Chris Davis, and at the time he was seventeen years of age. Chris's father, Tommy, had seen the sensationalized coverage given by the media to the attack on the Hayes's vehicle and contacted Sheriff Truesdale. Specifically, Tommy took his son to tell the police what he had told him. It was quite a story.

The creature that became known as the Lizard Man haunted the Scape Ore Swamp in South Carolina.

Back in 1988, Chris was working at a local McDonald's. On the night of June 29—roughly two weeks before the Waye affair exploded—Chris was on the late shift, which meant he didn't finish work until after 2:00 A.M. His journey home ensured that he had to take a road across the swamp—and specifically a heavily forested part of the swamp. It was just minutes later that he had a blowout. Chris pulled up at a cross-roads and, via the bright moonlight, changed the tire. As he finished the job and put the tools back into the trunk, Chris saw something looming out of the trees. Large, humanlike in shape, and possessing two glowing, red eyes and three fingers on each hand, it was something horrif-ic. Chris panicked and jumped in his vehicle and sped off. Based on what Chris had to say next, that was a very wise move:

> We learned that people in the Browntown community had been seeing a strange creature about seven feet tall with red eyes.

"I looked back and saw something running across the field towards me. It was about 25 yards away and I saw red eyes glowing. I ran into the car and as I locked it, the thing grabbed the door handle. I could see him from the neck down—the three big fingers, long black nails and green rough skin. It was strong and angry. I looked in my mirror and saw a blur of green running. I could see his toes and then he jumped on the roof of my car. I thought I heard a grunt and then I could see his fingers through the front windshield, where they curled around on the roof. I sped up and swerved to shake the creature off."

The reports didn't end there: Sheriff Truesdale received more and more reports, to the extent that a near-*X-Files*-style dossier was compiled. It was an official police dossier that contained the fascinating account of Johnny Blythers, who, on July 31, 1990, described for the Sheriff's department the events of the previous night:

"Last night about 10:30 P.M., we were coming home from the Brown-town section of Lee County. It was me, my mother (Bertha Mae Blyther), [and] two sisters.... I started talking about the time we passed the flowing well in Scape Ore Swamp. I said 'they ain't [sic] no such thing as a Lizzard [sic] Man. If there was, somebody would be seeing it or caught it.

"We got up about a mile or mile and one half passed the butter bean shed, about 50 feet from the dirt road by those two signs, my mother was dri-ving the car.

"It was on the right side, it came out of the bushes. It jumped out in the road. My mother swerved to miss it, and mashed the brakes and sped up. It jumped out of the bushes like he was going to jump on the car. When my mother mashed the brakes, it looked like it wanted to get in the car."

Johnny's mother, Bertha Mae, gave her own statement on that terrifying drive through the spooky swamp:

"This past Monday night I went to my mother's house in Browntown to pick up my son. We went to McDonald's on Highway 15 near Bishopville to get something to eat. We left there about 20 minutes after 10:00 P.M., was headed home and came through Browntown and Scape Ore Swamp....

"We passed the bridge and was down the road near a mile. I was looking straight ahead going about 25 M.P.H., and I saw this big brown thing; it jumped up at the window. I quickly sped up and went on the other side of the road to keep him from dragging my 11-year-old girl out of the car. I didn't see with my lights directly on it. It nearly scared me to death."

Then there was the statement of Tamacia Blythers, Bertha's daughter:

"Tall-Taller than the car, brown looking, a big chest had big eyes, had two arms. Don't know how his face looked, first seen his eyes. Never seen nothing like it before. I didn't see a tail. Mother says if she hadn't whiped [sic] over he would have hit her car or jumped on it. Mother said she was so scared her body light and she held her heart all the way home."

//...it jumped up at the window. I quickly sped up and went on the other side of the road to keep him from dragging my 11-year-old girl out of the car."

In addition, Lyle Blackburn has uncovered other reports of the beast—dating from 1986 to well into the 2000s. Two of the key players in this saga are now dead: Johnny Blythers and Chris Davis. The former in a car accident, in 1999, and the latter from a shotgun blast, the result of a drug deal gone bad, almost a decade to the day after Blythers's death.

As for the legendary Lizard Man, what, exactly, was it? Certainly the name provoked imagery of a malevolent scaly, green monster. On the other hand, let's not forget that there were references to the beast having a brown color. All of which leads us to Lyle Blackburn's conclusions. To his credit, Blackburn undertook a personal, on-site investigation with his colleague, Cindy Lee, and studied all of the evidence in unbiased fashion. Blackburn noted that, despite the undeniably memorable name, the various descriptions of the beast as being brown in color simply did not accord with anything of a reptilian nature.

Blackburn suggests that if a Bigfoot dwelled in watery bottomlands, where it might become "covered in algae-rich mud or moss, this could explain its green, wet-like appearance. It doesn't explain the three fingers, but greenish mud which has dried and cracked could certainly give a scaly appearance."

Certainly, it's a good theory, and far more likely than a huge, bipedal lizard roaming around the swamps of South Carolina.

MAPINGUARI

A terrifying man-beast that has a particular penchant for ripping out the tongues of cattle, the Mapinguari is a violent thing that haunts the Mato Grosso, a huge Brazilian state, the name of which translates into English as "thick bushes," and which is dominated by plains, plateaus, and rainforest—the ideal locations in which hairy man-beasts just might hide and thrive.

Randy Merrill, who has studied the history of the Mapinguari, says that, according to local native legends, the Mapinguari is "a prehistoric cryptid that reportedly lived (and is still reported to live) in the Amazon rain forests of South America, particularly in Brazil and Patagonia. It was consistently described as … having red hair, long arms, powerful claws that could tear apart palm trees … a sloping back, a crocodile-like hide that arrows and bullets could not penetrate, a second mouth on its belly and backwards feet (said to make a bottle-shaped footprint)."

Readers will, yet again, note the odd reference to the creatures having feet facing backwards. Merrill continued:

"It was said to stand up to 6 feet tall when it assumed a bear-like stance on its hind legs, which it did when it smelled a nearby human. It also gave off a putrid, disorienting stench, emitted a frightening shriek, and could move slowly and stealthily through the forest, often surprising unsuspecting locals. Although it was believed to be carnivorous, by all accounts it did not eat humans. Finally, it was said to sometimes speak and to enjoy punishing hunters who violated religious holidays. Certain lore even seemed to link it with the South American werewolf. The more werewolf-like version of the creature is called the 'wolf's cape' and is thought to have originally been human."

> It was consistently described as ... having red hair, long arms, powerful claws ... a sloping back, a crocodile-like hide ..., a second mouth on its belly and backwards feet....

We have to thank the late and renowned Dr. Bernard Heuvelmans for bringing much of the story of the Mapinguari to the attention of the media, the public, and the Bigfoot-hunting community. One story that really stood out in the menacing stakes occurred decades ago and involves a man identified as Inocencio, an explorer taking part in an expedition on the Urubu River.

Reportedly, Inocencio and his team were in hot pursuit of what were described as a group of mysterious "black monkeys" that they intended bagging and taking back to civilization. Unfortunately for Inocencio it didn't quite work out as planned. It was one particular night, when the sun was long gone, and the area was bathed in darkness, that something vile and marauding put in an appearance. It was an appearance accompanied by something hair-raising: what sounded like the panic-filled cries of a man, echoing around the dense jungle environment.

Then, something worse still happened: Inocencio's ears were filled with the sound of heavy feet, resonating loudly on the forest floor. There was no doubt in Inocencio's mind what was going on: some, huge, lumbering, bipedal thing was racing towards him. That was not good news, not at all. Suddenly, the loud footsteps were replaced by something else: ear-splitting silence. To Inocencio's horror, he could see something large, dark, and manlike lurking in the shadows—possibly waiting for the right time to launch an all-out attack. Inocencio was frozen to the spot, fearful of what might happen next. What did happen is that the beast let loose with an almighty, ear-splitting roar.

Dr. Bernard Heuvelmans, the "father of cryptozoology," researched the Mapinguari and brought his findings to the world.

Acting on instinct more than anything else, Inocencio fired his rifle in the direction of the creature, which only enraged the crazed monster even more, as it hurtled towards him. Fortunately, another bullet deterred the mapinguari from coming any closer and it vanished into the undergrowth. Showing a high degree of common sense, Inocencio spent the night perched in a high tree, kept awake by the hideous, malevolent roaring of the unknown animal.

When morning finally came, and Inocencio finally plucked up the courage to climb down the tree, the only calling cards of the night's turmoil were splashes of blood on the ground, and a strong, sour odor that filled the air. The violent visitor was never identified.

Interestingly, local folklore suggests that the mapinguari has the ability to make a person disoriented, to induce a nauseous sense of vertigo, and even to instill unconsciousness in a person. This may not be mere myth and legend: it's entirely possible that potentially like its American cousin, Bigfoot, the mapinguari has the ability to disable people via the manipulation of infrasound.

Although many researchers of the worldwide man-beast mystery take the view that the mapinguari may be some form of unknown ape, or even an ape man, there is another popular theory to explain the existence and presence of the creature in the Mato Grosso.

An ornithologist who has extensively traveled the Amazon, David Oren believes that the mapinguaris may not be unknown man-beasts, after all, but surviving pockets of massive creatures that are supposed to have become extinct thousands of years ago: giant sloths, possibly Mylodons, which could reach heights of around nine feet and that weighed in at a hefty 500 pounds.

Cryptid Chronicles notes:

"The first rumors that a giant ground sloth species may still exist reached Europe in the 16th century. Sailors brought home stories of 'water tigers' backed up by fossil bones.

In 1789, Dr. Bartolome de Muñoz found Megatherium bones near what is now Buenos Aires. He gave them to the King of Spain, prompting the King to order a complete specimen of the animal alive or dead. The rumors gained more credence in the late 19th century. The future governor of Santa Cruz province in southern Patagonia, Ramón Lista, was riding in Santa Cruz in the late 1880s when a shaggy red-haired beast resembling what he called a 'giant pangolin' trotted across his path."

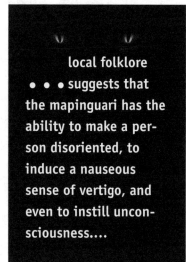

local folklore • • • suggests that the mapinguari has the ability to make a person disoriented, to induce a nauseous sense of vertigo, and even to instill unconsciousness....

Craig Woolheater runs the hugely popular website *Cryptomundo*, which is dedicated to the world of unknown animals. In October 2005, Woolheater said: "Several years back, actually in August of 1999 or so, I ran across a very interesting article in *Discover* magazine. It chronicled an ornithologist named David Oren's treks into the Amazon in search of the Mapinguari, what is thought to be the still living giant ground sloth. The article detailed the derision that Oren suffered from his fellow scientists."

In his article, Woolheater quoted the following from the *Discover* feature: "Oren has gathered a certain amount of derision in the scientific community over the last few years because of his determination to keep tramping through the jungle in search of the giant ground sloth. His detractors suspect he's as likely to find the beast as other adventurers are to find Bigfoot, the mythical creature said to be roaming the wilderness of the Pacific Northwest."

Having read this, Woolheater said: "I felt that this article had many parallels to Bigfoot research. The Mapinguari was known to the locals, much as the anecdotal evidence we are collecting regarding sightings of Bigfoot here in our country."

Woolheater cited another section of the article as being of some particular note:

"One might argue how much faith Oren should put in anecdotal evidence provided to him by 50 or so people who say they've had encounters with the sloth. Still, it seems odd that scientists, of all people, would question the search for anything thought to be elusive or even impossible to find. Think of the naysayers who used to scoff every time Carl Sagan said there had to be other planets orbiting other suns in other solar systems; now other planets are discovered so often it's hard to keep track of how many there are."

As Woolheater rightly noted: "People think that every inch of the earth has been explored. Quite the contrary...."

Some people, such as ornithologist David Oren, thought the Mapinguari might be related to the giant ground sloth shown in this drawing.

MENACING ALBINO

Neville Jacques is a social worker who lives with his wife, Barbara, in Cleveland in the North East of England. He has a casual interest in UFOs and the paranormal, while Barbara is generally skeptical of such things. Neville shares with us a strange, MIB-themed encounter he and Barbara had in Fuerteventura, Costa Caleta, in 2012....

"Hi Nick, I listened to your show on *Coast to Coast*, re men in black recently, the header photo for that gave me some relief! Let me explain, I was on holiday with my wife in Fuerteventura, Costa Caleta, in the Canaries, November–December 2012. We were walking back to our hotel on a very long promenade walk. It was close to 4 P.M. There were other people milling about. It's kind of high up on a volcanic rock face, directly at the sea's edge and a wide open area. We noticed about 100 meters in front of us a tall thin man, at least 6 foot 2 with a big rimmed black hat, round feature hugging black sixties type sunglasses, a long sleeved shirt and a light coloured jumper over his shoulders and long trousers!

> **//When we where about 5 feet from him I noticed his skin was almost translucent, that's the only way I can describe it...."**

"What made it more strange was his face looked white as if it was plastered in sun block, (whiter than white). We both laughed and watched him walk towards us. I got the feeling he was watching me, although I couldn't see his eyes. As he drew closer it became apparent that it wasn't sun block it was his skin! He had big hands and long fingers, also very white, kind of in front of him, not by his sides!

"When we where about 5 feet from him I noticed his skin was almost translucent, that's the only way I can describe it, his sun glasses covered all of his eye area and wrapped around the full socket area, they were round and black. He had a narrow, sunken face, had a very angular jaw and prominent cheek bones, he looked in his sixties or so. I am a social worker for older people so the age would be a good guess.

"When he was passing us he turned his head looking at me and spoke, with a kind of acknowledging manner and said something that I and my wife couldn't understand or describe as human language, it was high and low pitched all at the same time and very short, that's the best way to describe it! Strangely we didn't look back to see where he went or take a photo, both of us don't know why we didn't, I got the feeling he was watching me from me first noticing him.

"We got back to the hotel and I could not stop thinking and talking about the encounter with my wife, I kept telling her he wasn't from here, his clothes weren't right in fact he was totally alien in appearance to anyone I have ever seen in my life. I went to bed that night and didn't sleep much, every time I tried to go to sleep all I could see was him and I thought about the encounter for the rest of the holiday.

"I searched the internet for all types of albinos that I could find for months after but couldn't find a match for him, then I found your interview on *Coast to Coast* and bingo the artist's impression of the man in black was him, only without the hat and glasses.

"It still freaks me out to this day Nick, we can still not explain it!

"Kind Regards, Nev Jacques, I I K "

MONSTER OF GLAMIS

Situated just west of Forfar, Scotland, Glamis Castle is referred to by Shakespeare in *Macbeth*; the castle is where Macbeth killed King Duncan in 1040. And it is also at the castle where assassins murdered King Malcolm II in 1034. In addition, Glamis Castle was the childhood home of Elizabeth (the Queen Mother) and the birthplace of Princess Margaret. Then there is the castle's very own monster.

Jonathan Downes, the director of the British-based Centre for Fortean Zoology—one of the few full-time groups dedicated to the search for unknown creatures—notes that "the castle is the site of a well-known and semi-legendary beast known as the Monster of Glamis. It's said that the creature was supposed to have been the hideously deformed heir to the Bowes-Lyon family and who was, according to popular rumor, born in about 1800, and died as recently as 1921."

Downes digs further into the puzzle: "Legend has it that the monster was supposed to look like an enormous flabby egg, having no neck and only minute arms and legs but possessed incredible strength and had an air of evil about it. Certainly, there is a family secret concerning the monster, which is only told to the male heir of the Bowes-Lyon family when they attain majority."

He continues: "But according to the author Peter Underwood, who has looked into this case, the present Lord Strathmore knows nothing about the

Glamis Castle in Scotland is the site of historic regicides … and a monster.

monster, presumably because the creature has long been dead, but he always felt that there was a corpse or coffin bricked up behind the walls."

According to folklore and oral tradition, the existence of the terrifying creature was allegedly known to only four men at any given time, namely the Earl of Strathmore, his direct heir, the family's lawyer, and the broker of the estate. At the age of twenty-one each succeeding heir was told the truth of the terrible secret and shown the rightful—and horrendously deformed—Earl, and succeeding family lawyers and brokers were also informed of the family's shocking secret.

As no Countess of Strathmore was ever told the story, one Lady Strathmore, having indirectly heard of such tales, quietly approached the then broker, a certain Mr. Ralston, who flatly refused to reveal the secret and who would only say by way of a reply, "It is fortunate you do not know the truth for if you did you would never be happy."

So, was the strange creature of the castle a terribly deformed soul with some bizarre genetic affliction or something else? While the jury, inevitably, remains steadfastly out, it's an intriguing fact that in 1912, in his book, *Scottish Ghost Stories*, Elliott O'Donnell published the contents of a letter that he had received from a Mrs. Bond who had spent time at Glamis Castle and had undergone an undeniably weird encounter while staying there.

In her letter to O'Donnell, rather notably, Mrs. Bond described a somewhat supernatural encounter with a beast that was possessed of nothing less than distinct ape-like qualities, rather than specifically human attributes.

Might it be the case, then, that the beast of Glamis was not simply a man with appalling genetic abnormalities, but some terrifying ape-like beast—a definitive wild-man or ape-man, perhaps? Not surprisingly, the truth—whatever it may one day prove to be—remains hidden behind closed doors. Just like the creature itself.

NIGHTMARE HALL MONSTERS

Longstanding rumors suggest that a vast underground alien base exists within, and below, a massive mesa at Dulce, Rio Arriba County, New Mexico. Interestingly, we can prove there has been a wealth of weird activity in the area. For example, the FBI has officially declassified a large file on cattle mutilations in and around Dulce, spanning the mid- to late 1970s. And, on December 10, 1967, the Atomic Energy Commission (AEC) detonated a twenty-nine-kiloton-yield nuclear device 4,240 feet below ground level, in an attempt to provoke the release and, as a direct consequence, production of natural gas. Thus was born Gasbuggy: a program of an overall project known as Operation Plowshare, which, ostensibly, was designed to explore the peaceful uses of atomic energy. Notably, the location of the Gasbuggy test—that covered an area of 640 acres—was New Mexico's Carson National Forest, which just happens to be situated only twelve miles from the town of Dulce. Today, people are forbidden from digging underground in that very area—which is very interesting in view of the underground base allegations.

Within conspiracy-based research circles, it has been suggested that the nuclear detonation had a very different goal—namely, to destroy the aforementioned alien base and wipe out the deadly, hostile ETs. Certainly, it's a strange and foreboding story. And there are no shortages of accounts suggesting that such a base existed (and may still exist), and in which freakish monsters were being created by the alien entities. As one example of many, we have the following from someone we might justifiably call a ufological whistleblower/Edward Snowden:

"Sir, first off, if you want the full story let me know. But this will explain how Mothman came about. U.S. Energy Secretary John Herrington named the Lawrence Berkeley Laboratory and New Mexico's Los Alamos National Laboratory to house advanced genetic research centers as part of a project to

A crater created by a 1962 nuclear test that was part of Operation Plowshare. The crater is 1,280 feet (390 meters) wide and 320 feet (97.5 meters) deep.

decipher the human genome. The genome holds the genetically coded instructions that guide the transformation of a single cell, a fertilized egg, into a biological organism.

"'The Human Genome Project may well have the greatest direct impact on humanity of any scientific initiative before us today,' said David Shirley, Director of the Berkeley Laboratory. Covertly, this research has been going on for years at the Dulce biogenetics labs. Level 6 is hauntingly known by employees as 'Nightmare Hall.' It holds the genetic labs at Dulce. Reports from workers who have seen bizarre experimentation, are as follows:

"I have seen multi-legged 'humans' that look like half-human/half-octopus. Also reptilian-humans, and furry creatures that have hands like humans and cries like a baby, it mimics human words. Also, huge mixtures of lizard-humans in cages. There are fish, seals, birds and mice that can barely be considered those species. There are several cages (and vats) of winged-humanoids, grotesque bat-like creatures, but 3 1/2 to 7 feet tall. Gargoyle-like beings and Draco-Reptoids.

"Level 7 is worse, row after row of thousands of humans and human mixtures in cold storage. Here too are embryo storage vats of humanoids in various stages of development. I frequently encountered humans in cages, usually dazed or drugged, but sometimes they cried and begged for help. We were told they were hopelessly insane, and involved in high risk drug tests to cure insanity. We were told to never try to speak to them at all. At the beginning we believed that story. Finally in 1978 a small group of workers discovered the truth."

REPTILE MAN

Certainly, one of the strangest of all encounters with what can only be described as a definitive monster, occurred on the night of Saturday, November 8, 1958. The unlucky soul who had the misfortune to fall foul of the unearthly beast was Charles Wetzel, who at the time was driving his green, two-door Buick Super along North Main Street, Riverside, California—near the Santa Ana River. As Wetzel reached one particular stretch of the road that had flooded, the radio of his car began to crackle loudly and in a highly distorted fashion. With the water levels high, and Wetzel trying to figure out what was wrong with the radio, he slowed down, purely and simply to ensure that he didn't find himself driving off the side of the road. He didn't know it at the time—but he soon would—that there were far worse things than a flooded road and a wonky radio.

As Wetzel continued to slowly negotiate the road, he was shocked to the core by the sight of an extraordinary creature that surfaced from the shadows, and, in brazen fashion, stood in the middle of the road, preventing Wetzel from going any further. He could only sit and stare, in a combination of fear and awe, as he tried to take in and comprehend the thing that stood before him.

Humanoid in shape, and in excess of six feet in height, it had a large round head described as being "pumpkin"-like, glowing eyes, a prominent mouth that had beak-like qualities to it, and scaly skin that resembled leaves. Strangest of all, the legs of the beast did not extend from beneath its torso, but from its sides. Actually, that may not have been so strange after all: both reptiles and lizards are built in precisely that fashion. Add to that a pair of long, muscular arms and you have a definitive monster.

What began as a bone-chilling stand-off quickly mutated into something else entirely. The reptile man issued a loud, high-pitched noise that was partit had a large • • • round head described as being "pumpkin"-like, glowing eyes, a prominent mouth that had beak-like qualities to it, and scaly skin that resembled leaves.

scream and part-gurgle, after which it suddenly charged at Wetzel's Buick. He could only sit, paralyzed with fear, as the scaly thing raced towards the hood of the vehicle, then lunged even closer and violently clawed the windshield.

Although it was good fortune that led Wetzel to have a rifle with him, by his own admission he was fearful about using it. Not because it might injure or kill the animal-man. Wetzel's big concern was that if he fired through the windshield and failed to kill it, the shattered glass would allow the monster to reach inside and haul him out of the car, possibly to tear him to pieces. With his body flooded with adrenalin, Wetzel took the only option he felt was available to him: he floored the accelerator, spun the wheels and shot away. In doing so, he ran the beast down, which was evident by the fact that Wetzel felt the car go over its large body.

While some might consider a story like this to be nothing more than a hoax, the likelihood is that it was not. The rationale for this is that Wetzel quickly reported the affair to the local police, who launched an investigation. It's most unlikely that a hoaxer would run the risk of being charged for wasting police time or for filing a bogus report. Such was the seriousness with which the police took Wetzel's story, they sent not just officers out to the scene, but a pack of bloodhounds too. The monster, whatever it was, was never found—dead or alive. There were, however, two pieces of evidence that corroborated Wetzel's amazing experience: vicious-looking claw marks on the windshield and on the underside of the Buick. They were calling cards that Wetzel preferred to forget about—if he ever could.

SLENDERMAN

In 2015 publicity was given to a story coming out of the U.K. of sightings in and around Britain's Cannock Chase woods, of something described as looking like the legendary "Slenderman." It's a fictional character created in June 2009 by Eric Knudsen (using the alias of "Victor Surge," at the forum section of the *Something Awful* website), who took his inspiration from the world of horror-fiction.

The Slenderman (also spelled as Slender Man) is a creepy creature indeed: tall, thin, with long arms, a blank (faceless, even) expression, and wearing a dark suit, sounding almost like a night-marish version of the Men in Black. While there is no doubt that Knudsen was the creator of what quickly became a definitive, viral meme, people have since claimed to have seen the Slenderman in the real world.

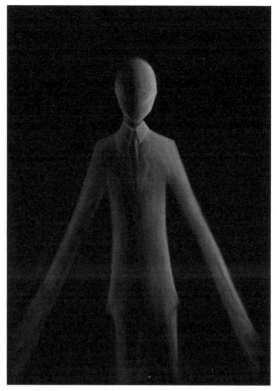

In other words, so the theory goes, it's a case of believing in the existence of the Slenderman and, as a result, causing it to actually exist, which is very much akin to the phenomenon of the Tulpa. An entity is envisaged in the mind, and the imagery becomes so powerful and intense that it causes that same, mind-based imagery to emerge into the real world, with some degree of independent existence and self-awareness. Such a scenario may well explain why people are now seeing something that began as a piece of fiction.

All of which brings us to the matter of the recent story on the Slenderman of the Cannock Chase. As people who have followed my writings will know, I grew up only a very short drive from the Chase, which is an undeniably deeply strange area.

An artist's rendering of Slenderman based on witness descriptions.

It's filled with reports of so-called "Alien Big Cats," Bigfoot-type beasts, flying humanoids, giant snakes, and much more of a monstrous nature.

And now, it seems, the Slenderman has started to call those dark woods his domain, too. In a January 24, 2015, article that appeared in the *Birmingham Mail* newspaper (titled "Spooky Slender Men spotted in Cannock"), Mike Lockley wrote:

"A paranormal probe has been launched in the Midlands following FOUR sightings of Slender Men—long, stick thin specters feared around the world. Each of the chilling close encounters took place in the Cannock area, and now X Files investigator Lee Brickley is trying to fathom why the ghoul has descended on the Staffordshire mining town. Slender Men have been a part of global folklore for centuries. They may be known by different names, but their harrowing, elongated appearance remains the same around the world."

There's little doubt that the controversy concerning this story will run and run. But, there's something else I want to bring to your attention, something that I think is pretty intriguing. Back in 2007 and 2008, I corresponded

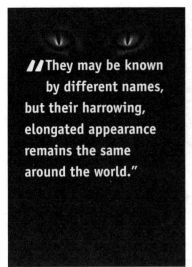

> **❚❚They may be known by different names, but their harrowing, elongated appearance remains the same around the world."**

with an Englishman named Mike Johnson. Back in 2001, Mike had an encounter on the Cannock Chase with a paranormal entity that—with hindsight—sounds very much like … wait for it … the Slenderman.

In Mike's own words: "This character was tall, with very thin arms and legs, dressed in what I presumed were grey trousers and a tight long sleeved shirt of the same color. His hairless head was elongated and neck spindly, and his arms reached practically past his knees; I could not discern a facial feature. I realized he was around three meters tall."

It must be said that just about every aspect of this description conjures up Slenderman-style imagery. Of course, the Slenderman meme was still a year away when my book was published back in 2008, and the encounter took place in 2001—seven years before the publication date of *There's Something in the Woods.*

In view of this, one has to wonder: did the 2009 creation of the Slenderman meme create a Tulpa-like, living equivalent? Or did a real, earlier Slenderman exist before the fictional one was looming on the horizon?

TERRIBLE OLD MAN-THING

The following account, from Terry—in Shingle Springs, California—is without doubt one of the most chilling Man in Black-themed reports ever to have reached me. Read on and you'll see why.

"This encounter occurred during the day time thirty five years ago in 1977 at a Winchell's in Sunnyvale, California, I was just sixteen years of age at the time. My best friend and I had just finished our coffee and were heading for the doorway to leave. As we were passing a man seated at one of the tables, he reached out and firmly grabbed my wrist. In that moment my first reaction was to jerk away from his grip, but looking down at him I realized that he was a very old man and I felt in that moment that he was harmless. He was dressed in black wearing an old fashioned hat and suit, his clothing looked like it was from the 1930's. He was extremely pale, very thin and appeared to be very old, I guessed in his 80's or 90's.

"He told my friend and I that he was a palm reader, a very good one, he claimed and could he please do us a favor by giving us each a reading. My friend and I talked briefly to each other about his offer and agreed to let him. I first sat down across the table from him, then as my friend was starting to sit down along side of me, he stopped her and asked her to please go sit a few tables away out of earshot from us, explaining that the information was going to be direct and personal, we would need some privacy. She complied and moved several tables away.

"Once my friend was seated away from the us, I placed my hands on the table in front of him, palms up and looked into the man's face, it was then that I noticed the old man's eyes were completely glazed over with cataracts, he was surely blind I thought, as his gaze was unfixed and unfocused in my direction. I asked him how long had he been a psychic? He responded by saying that his ability had nothing to do with being psychic and emphasized that it had everything to do with 'science.'

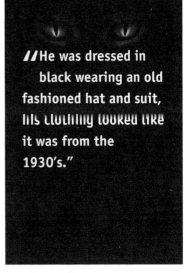

//He was dressed in black wearing an old fashioned hat and suit, his clothing looked like it was from the 1930's."

"He began by talking about my early childhood experiences along with some very painful incidents that had occurred to me in which he had precise and detailed information that I was sure no one could have known about. Quite suddenly I felt very vulnerable and exposed as he recounted these events, his knowledge unnerved me to my very core. Staring straight ahead he moved along into my present situation, lecturing and chastising me like a father would a child, for some poor choices I had made during that time. All the while he broke a doughnut down into tiny pieces. My mind raced as I tried to figure out how on earth could he know this stuff? It was then in that moment that I would forever change my ideas of 'secrets kept' and how I viewed my own identity in the world. Apparently 'nothing' could be hidden from myself or anyone else for that matter. I felt naked in the truth.

"He continued this reading now delving into my future and that of upcoming world events, with stories sometimes so harsh and brutal that I clearly remember wondering if I would ever 'catch a break in life'? Among other things, he warned me of a time when that by speaking about my UFO experiences I would anger 'the governmental powers that be' and he cautioned that I would be dealing with very dangerous people and circumstances. He rambled on often emphasizing again that this all had to do with 'science.'

"I then asked him if he could see any kind of success coming to me, ever? He responded by telling me, 'You will not find success in life, you will die of a broken heart. It will be a better stronger woman who will be successful.' As I listened to his words I began to cry and he sharply asked me, 'Are you going to lay down and die like a frightened whore, or are you going to be willing to stand up and fight like a worthy warrior?' I was stunned into silence and then he said,

'Whether you realize this or not, I have done you a huge favor today and I will be returning to see you in the future, ___ years from now to collect on it.'

"As a side note, I do not recall the exact time he said, but do recall thinking 'You'll be long dead by then, old man.' Our reading ended, he asked me to leave the table and he then waved for my friend to come over to sit with him. He spent all of five minutes with her and when she arose from the table she was badly shaken and would only say that she hoped that what he predicted for her was not true.

// You will not find success in life, you will die of a broken heart. It will be a better stronger woman who will be successful."

"As we exited the doughnut shop I tried to press my friend for more information because she was crying, but she was too upset to speak about what he had said to her. Once out on the street the both of us walking together toward home, my friend asked me to tell her about what the old man said to me in my reading with him, she pointed out that the reading he gave went on for an hour and forty five minutes with me. I was lost for words when she spoke up and said, 'Linda I don't think he was a person, I think that old man was an alien.'

"Right in that moment as she was speaking we watched as an old black 1930's or 40's gangster type car with running boards pull out of the parking lot and pass us on the street, there was no driver at the wheel and the same old man that we had met, was riding in the back seat. Our mouths dropped as we watched the car pass by us and at the same time a whirlwind picked up and swirled around our feet. We watched the car disappear from view making a turn further down the street, I then shook my head and responded to her with 'No, he was just a creepy old man in black.'

"Over the years during the course of our friendship my friend and I would many times ponder and question our meeting with 'the old man in black.' We could not understand who or what he was and neither of us would reveal to the other exactly what his frightening messages to each of us separately were, agreeing only that we felt that he was speaking the truth and that it was frightening for both us. We would part ways and our friendship ended in 1988 when I came out to her about my lifelong UFO experiences and the old man's messages to me. She mocked and ridiculed me in that moment. It was a very painful ending to our relationship for me. I would struggle with it for years.

"In 1988 when I began to seriously study the UFO phenomena I came across stories about these Men in Black, Master Tricksters and the like. It was then that I began to understand who and what they are and how this 'old man in black' specifically related to me as that young teenager all those years ago and yet, I was still haunted by his promise to return to collect on that favor.

"During Christmas of 2009, alone in my mother's apartment while she traveled, I found myself slipping into a deep depression and I was filled with despair. During the course of that year I had lost a job that I loved due to the economy, gone through a terrible break up with a man I could no longer love, I found out that my old friend who was with me in 1977 on that day with the 'old man in black' in Sunnyvale had died in 2008 from cancer and I had still not gotten over losing my beloved horse Meaghan, who had also died the year before, leaving me filled with a sorrow that I was not able to overcome.

"Starting on Christmas day I fasted and prayed for three days hoping that I could find some peace and comfort. It was then I realized that, I was indeed 'heart broken' over my losses and suddenly the encounter with 'the old man in black' came flooding back into my mind and would not leave me alone. In trying to escape his words and his terrible messages to me, I began drinking heavily at night until I could find some peace in sleep. This would go on into the beginning of 2011 when I finally began to slowly recover from the pain. I finally thought I had come to terms with that old man's warnings and I successfully quit drinking, my attitude shifted and I was now looking forward to a great new year.

// ... there was no driver at the wheel and the same old man that we had met, was riding in the back seat."

"In April of last year I discovered a lump in my breast and was at first unconcerned about it, I thought that it was probably a just a fibroid cyst that would go away on its own. I put off having it checked out until July when the lump had grown quite large and when the results came back positive for cancer I was shocked. Last month after trying a lot of alternative therapies in the prior months since July, I had a mastectomy. The pathology indicates that I have advanced stage cancer and once again the 'old man in black' and his words are haunting me. Oddly I find myself both eager and apprehensive as I await his return, but know that above all, I am no longer afraid."

FLYING BEINGS

AFRICA'S SKY-CREATURES

The continent of Africa is the reported home of numerous unknown creatures and wild monsters. They range from goliath-sized ape-men to lake monsters and from dinosaur-like lizards to massive spiders. Africa is also the domain of more than a few large winged flying monsters. A wealth of such stories comes from the Kaonde (or Bakahonde) tribes of Zambia. It's largely thanks to an early twentieth-century explorer, Frank H. Melland, that we know of the accounts of these immense and fearsome fliers. Melland's sources in the tribes told him that the most feared of all the monsters of the skies was the Kongamato. Its name means "over-whelmer of boats." The name is a very apt one, since it had the habit of swooping down on canoes and savagely attacking and killing those within. It was a huge beast that lived and hunted in the Jiundu swamps, and which deeply terrified the people of the area.

As for the appearance of the Kongamato, it looked somewhat like a bird—at first glance. That it utterly lacked feathers and the fact that its red body was leathery-looking, was membranous, and had wings far more befitting those of a bat suggests it was something else entirely. Moreover, its immense mouth was filled with sharp teeth that could slice a man in two in an instant, which is not something typical of the average bird.

Acting purely on instinct, when Melland explored the area in 1924—a trip that he chronicled in his 1923 book, *In Witchbound Africa*—he showed the local tribespeople artistic renditions of various presumed extinct pterosaurs, including one of a pterodactyl. On seeing the pictures, the tribespeople cried one word, and one word only: "Kongamato!"

Very likely connected to the tales told by the Bokaonde and Kaonde tribes are similar accounts coming out of the Kitui Wakamba people, also of Zambia. They told their stories to a man named A. Blayney Percival, who, in 1928, penned *A Game Ranger on Safari*. So the Kitui Wakamba said they could always tell when one of the chiefly nocturnal creatures had landed near their villages, as they always left behind them large, telltale tracks on the ground. As with the data shared with Frank H. Melland a few years earlier, the Kitui Wakamba described their resident monster as large, leathery, and possessed of huge membranous wings. Such stories were also handed to, and faithfully recorded by, Colonel Charles R. S. Pitman, the author of *A Game Warden Takes Stock*. On top of that, a well-respected ichthyologist, Dr. J. L. B. Smith, investigated a number of almost identical cases from Tanzania's Mount Kilimanjaro.

If one takes a trip along Africa's Gold Coast, one is likely to eventually come across stories of the Sasabonsam. To the locals, it very much resembles something that is half-man and half-bat. It's notable that a revered cryptozoologist, Ivan Sanderson, wrote in his book, *Investigating the Unexplained*, that while wading in an African creek at some point in 1932, he was suddenly, and out of the blue, dive-bombed by an immense creature with a wingspan of around twelve feet. As someone well acquainted with just about every animal under the sun, Sanderson knew exactly what the beast was. It was a bat, although one of previously unheard of massive proportions. The precise location was Cameroon's Assumbo Mountains. And Sanderson was not alone; also witness to the obscenely huge bat was a biologist named Gerald Russell, who shot at the animal but failed to kill it.

It was this close call with death that led Sanderson to ponder an intriguing possibility. He began to wonder if the Kongamato, the Sasabonsam, and a variety of other flying monsters reported in Africa were not surviving pterosaurs, after all. He came to believe that each and every one of them may have been examples of giant, ferocious bats. In many respects, this makes a great deal of sense. After all, the idea of giant bats is far more plausible than surviving pockets of animals believed to have become extinct tens of millions of years ago.

ANGLEY WOOD DRAGON

A fascinating story of nothing less than a real-life dragon can be found in the pages of Charles Igglesden's 1906 book, *A Saunter through Kent with Pen &*

Pencil. Of a dragon reportedly seen in Cranbrook, Kent (a county in southern England), centuries earlier, Igglesden wrote: "The magnificently wooded park of a hundred and fifty acres is richly watered by a huge lake made in 1812 and a smaller one within the grounds, while further west is an old mill pond that rejoices in a curious legend. It is an old one and the subject of it is very ancient indeed and as rare as it is horrible."

A real-life dragon is said to have made the woods in Cranbrook, Kent, England, its home.

He continued that nothing less than a flying dragon was said to haunt the pond but that "on certain—or uncertain—nights of the year it wings its flight over the park and pays a visit to the big lake yonder. But he always returns to the Mill Pond and it is said to pay special attention of a vicious kind to young men and women who have jilted their lovers. A legend with a moral is this. But a winged dragon! A dragon of the ordinary kind is bad enough. But a flying dragon! Augh!"

Igglesden had more to add to the story: "It is a Mr. Tomlin's opinion that there is stronger evidence of the existence of this dragon than of most of his kind and of his fires gone out in the closing years of the last century. Nothing short of this monster's malign influence could account for the curious fact that, till the coming of Mr. Tomlin's eldest daughter, no child had been born at Angley Park for upwards of a hundred years."

Over the years, numerous monster-seekers have flocked to the specific area in question—in hopes of encountering the dragon. Its presence is far less today, however, than it was in centuries past. Nevertheless, it's worth noting that in December 1997, a local policeman, on duty during the early hours of a chilly, windy Saturday morning, caught a brief sight of a "bloody great bird, about twenty feet across," in the skies of Cranbrook. The ancient dragon crossing the night sky?

BIRD PEOPLE OF BRAZIL

San Antonio, Texas-based cryptozoologist Ken Gerhard is one of the world's leading seekers of strange creatures. His investigations have taken him, quite literally, across the globe, as he has pursued the likes of the Chupacabra, werewolves, Bigfoot, and lake monsters. Gerhard notes:

"One of the greatest experiences of my life was traveling throughout the continent of South America when I was but a lad. My mother, who had been in remission from cancer at the time, had a newfound zeal for life and wanted to expose me and my sister to faraway lands and new experiences. Among the wonders that we were fortunate enough to see were the lofty and mysterious Inca ruins of Machu Picchu in the Andes Mountains, as well as the diverse natural wonders of the Galapagos Islands."

One of Gerhard's favorite memories from that time is of an adventure along the Amazon River, deep within the dense and mysterious jungle environment. It was while there that Gerhard, his mother, and sister were introduced to the people of the Javaro and Yagua tribes, who remained blissfully unchanged by the technological and high-stress-based world of the final years of the twentieth century.

> As the "birds" got closer, however, the dumbstruck pair could see that the creatures were not birds, after all, but winged humanoids.

Gerhard notes: "Surely, if there is anywhere on the planet where strange, new creatures lurk, the Green Continent just might be the place." He was not wrong.

Gerhard has investigated a curious story that occurred back in the 1950s; the location being southern Brazil, specifically close to Pelotas, a coastal city. It involved two witnesses, Luiz de Rosario Real and his wife, Lucy Gerlach Real. As they casually walked along an enchanting forested path, they saw what appeared to be two large birds, silhouetted in the moon-dominated sky. As the "birds" got closer, however, the dumbstruck pair could see that the creatures were not birds, after all, but winged humanoids. When the beasts realized they had been seen they retreated into the dense, surrounding trees. That was scarcely the end of things, however: both husband and wife, as they exited the area with speed, developed a strong and disturbing feeling that the winged monsters were stalking them. Whether to make a meal of them or not, we will never know. They suddenly soared into the skies above, never to be seen again. It was, perhaps, a lucky escape for Luiz and Lucy.

BLACK-WINGED BEAST

A prime mover in the Texas office of the British-based Centre for Fortean Zoology—one of the few, full-time groups that diligently searches the world for unknown animals, such as the Abominable Snowman, the Chupacabra and the Loch Ness Monster—Naomi West has a startling tale to relate that chronicles a series of events that occurred when she was a teenager, and which focuses upon two specific issues: a hat-wearing Man in Black and a Mothman-type entity. In Naomi's very own words:

"When I was sixteen, I lived in Parker City, Indiana. I always felt Indiana in general, and particularly Parker City, was very dark. I hated it there. Anyway, one night my friend Toby and I were at our friend Ralana's house. Ralana had just seen a mysterious light that she claimed occasionally appeared to her in her house. It had gone away just before we had arrived at Ralana's to visit. We all three thought it was probably an angel and we wanted to get it to come back. We decided that perhaps if we created a 'holy atmosphere' by singing hymns and praying, we might get it to come back.

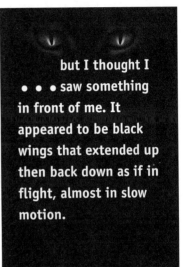

but I thought I ● ● ● saw something in front of me. It appeared to be black wings that extended up then back down as if in flight, almost in slow motion.

"So we shut ourselves in Ralana's parents' bedroom where the light had appeared to Ralana that evening, and we started singing, praying, etc. The room was entirely dark, having not even a window. We made sure that not a crack of light even showed beneath the door so that if the light did appear, we would know for sure it wasn't from a natural source.

"After sitting in this pitch blackness having our impromptu church service, no light appeared, but I thought I saw something in front of me. It appeared to be black wings that extended up then back down as if in flight, almost in slow motion. Then I saw the head of the apparent black winged creature turn to the side. There was a long, snout-like nose on it. Because I didn't even believe what I was seeing—I mean, I truly thought my eyes were playing tricks on me—I dismissed it and said nothing about it. After all, when you are in a pitch black room, your eyes sometimes sort of create things, and this creature being black on black was so vague I just couldn't be sure. Before long, the three of us became bored of waiting for the light and we decided to leave.

"On our way out the front door, it was either Ralana or Toby that said, somewhat tentatively, 'Did anyone see a … black winged thing?'

"The other two of us instantly said yes, we had. Then I remember specifically that Ralana said, 'Did it have a beak-like snout on it?' We all agreed, realizing we had seen the very same creature. I can only assume that none of us had believed in what we were seeing at the time enough to mention it.

"When I told my youth pastor the story later, he told me that we called up the 'wrong' thing by trying to conjure anything at all. Of course, as kids, we hadn't considered our innocent attempts to invoke an angel 'conjuring.'

BRENTFORD GRIFFIN

One might be forgiven for thinking that sightings of large, winged monsters only ever occur in the skies over large forests and jungles, and above remote mountains. Not so. In fact, far from it. In 1984, just such an unearthly beast was seen soaring over the capital city of the United Kingdom: London! The specific location was Brentford, a town situated within west London. The day on which all hell broke loose was hardly of the kind one might expect to associate with a monster. There were no dark and stormy skies, no thunder and lightning, and no howling winds. Instead, there was nothing but a warm, pleasant, sunny day in March.

Griffins have appeared in European mythology going back centuries, as evidenced by this mosaic floor art in St. Mark's Basilica in Venice, Italy.

The man who kicked off the firestorm of controversy was Kevin Chippendale, who, at the time, was walking along Brentford's Braemar Road. As he did so, Chippendale's attention was drawn to something strange in the sky. It was some sort of large, flying animal. Not the kind of thing you see every day, to be sure. And in a decidedly synchronistic fashion, it all went down in the skies directly above a local pub called *The Griffin*. It was the imagery of a legendary griffin of ancient mythology that Chippendale most associated with the thing he briefly encountered. It was winged, fork-tailed, and sported mean-looking talons and a dog-like muzzle. Chippendale could do nothing but stare in awe. And in shock and terror, too.

Stories of so-called griffins date back millennia, to the times of the ancient Greeks, Egyptians, and Persians. In the fourteenth century, Sir John Mandeville wrote of griffins: "Some men say that they have the body upward as an eagle and beneath as a lion; and truly they say sooth that they be of that shape. But one griffin hath the body more great and is more strong than eight lions, of such lions as be on this half, and more great and stronger than an hundred eagles such as we have amongst us. For one griffin there will bear, flying to his nest, a great horse, if he may find him at the point, or two oxen yoked together as they go at the plough. For he hath his talons so long and so large and great upon his feet, as though they were horns of great oxen or of bugles or of kine, so that men make cups of them to drink of. And of their ribs and of the pens of their wings, men make bows, full strong, to shoot with arrows and quarrels."

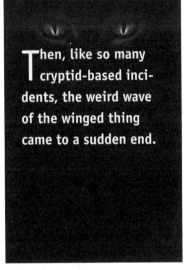

Then, like so many cryptid-based incidents, the weird wave of the winged thing came to a sudden end.

Almost a year later after his extraordinary encounter, specifically in February 1985, Chippendale saw the creature yet again. Others saw the monster, too. They included a psychologist named John Olssen—who encountered the beast while jogging near the River Thames—and a woman named Angela Keyhoe, who saw the griffin squatting in ominous and beady-eyed fashion atop the town's Watermans Arts Centre. Both the local and national media—television and newspapers—were soon onto the story, and major coverage was afforded the mystery. Then, like so many cryptid-based incidents, the weird wave of the winged thing came to a sudden end. It's worth noting, however, that despite the incredible nature of the affair, this is far from being the only occasion upon which a griffin has been encountered in the U.K.

Elliott O'Donnell was an enthusiastic collector and disseminator of data on all manner of wonders, including ghosts, demons, and strange creatures. He was also someone who crossed paths with the English griffin. He said, of a strange story that dated back to the seventeenth century:

"Mr. John Luck, a farmer from Raveley, set out on horseback one morning to the annual fair at Whittlesea. On the way he met a friend, with whom he had a drink at a wayside inn. After drinking somewhat heavily Mr. Luck became very merry, and perceiving that his friend was getting restless and desirous of continuing on his way to the fair, he said, 'Let the devil take him who goeth out of this house today.'

"The more he drank, the merrier he grew. Forgetful of his rash saying, he called for his horse and set out for the fair. The fresh air seemed to have a sobering effect, for he had not travelled very far before he remembered what he had said. He was naturally superstitious and became so perturbed that he lost his bearings. He was endeavoring to find the way home—it was getting dusk and far too late to go to the fair—when he espied 'two grim creatures before him in the likeness of griffins.'

"They handled him roughly, took him up in the air, stripped him, and then dropped him, a sad spectacle, all gory, in a farm yard just outside the town of Doddington. There he was found lying upon some harrows. He was picked up and carried to a house, which belonged to a neighboring gentleman. When he had recovered sufficiently to talk, he related what had happened to him. Before long he 'grew into a frenzy,' so desperate that the inmates of the house were afraid to stay in the room with him.

"Convinced that Luck was under evil influences, they sent for the clergyman of the town. No sooner had the clergyman entered the house than Luck, howling like a demon, rushed at him and would have torn him to pieces, had not the servants of the house come to his rescue. They succeeded with great difficulty in overcoming Luck and tying him to the bed. No one was allowed to enter his room, the door of which was locked."

Neil Arnold, who has carefully studied the affair of the Brentford Griffin, notes: "O'Donnell goes on to describe how Mr. Luck, the next morning, was found dead in his bed. His body a crooked, broken mess, black with bruises, neck snapped, and tongue hanging from his chasm of a mouth. His face an expression of utmost dread. Many believed that the griffin monsters were sent by Satan and had succeeded in their quest."

The griffin: just a myth? Doubtful. Deadly? Undoubtedly.

CHILE MONSTER

In 2003 the South American country of Chile was hit by a spate of reports of traumatic and terrifying encounters with flying monsters. One particularly fantastic incident occurred on the night of July 23. That was when three boys, Jonathan, Diego, and Carlos, were having a sleepover at Diego's grandfather's house, which was situated near San Pedro de Atacama. They were awakened from their sleep by the sound of scratching against the outside of the door to the yard. Tentatively, the brave trio got out of their beds and tiptoed to the door, carefully and quietly opened it, and peered into the darkness.

To their eternal horror, they were confronted by a horrific-looking beast standing at a distance of around fifty feet and staring directly at them. It was humanoid in shape, beaked, and around five feet in height. It had large bat-style wings that extended to a combined length of around eleven feet, and talons instead of toes. And its head was crested. As for its color, it was black and shiny, almost wet-like. It wasn't a local.

It's interesting—and probably not coincidental—to note that a few days earlier a man by the name of Juan Acuqa contacted police to tell them of his trauma-filled, late-night encounter with a pair of strange animals in the Chilean town of Parral. "They were both dog-faced and had wings," Acuqa told the responding officers. And it wasn't just a sighting that Acuqa had: as he walked home, the monsters attacked him out of the sky and out of the blue, something that forced Acuqa to leap into a nearby canal to try and shake them off. Fortunately, it worked, though he was briefly hospitalized for gashes inflicted by the flying, nightmarish things.

Around a month or so later, what were very possibly the same two creatures—along with another pair—were seen by the entire Abbett family, as they drove through Chile's Pampa Acha region. Such was the sheer weirdness of the appearance of the flying things, the family could only describe them as "dog-faced kangaroos" and as "gargoyles." Thankfully, the family was not attacked and the creatures swept by, above the road, with barely a glance in their direction. It was, to be sure, a most lucky escape.

It should also be noted that when the details of the 2003 wave in Chile became publicly known, more than a few investigators of strange creatures and paranormal activity suggested that Puerto Rico's infamous Chupacabra was clearly on the move and had made its way to Chile. It's not an unreasonable thing to muse upon. After all, some of the initial reports of the Chupacabra—and particularly those seen in the

Evidence suggests the Chupacabra of the Caribbean has somehow made its way to Chile.

island's massive El Yunque rainforest—described seeing animals that had monkey-like bodies, that hopped like kangaroos, and that had large, leathery wings. Of course, no one was able to offer a viable explanation for how the Chupacabras had made it from Puerto Rico to Chile. The fact remains, however, that the Chilean monsters and those of Puerto Rico were astonishingly similar in appearance.

DRAGON

For three years Richard Freeman worked as Head of Reptiles at Twycross Zoo, England, and, today, is the Zoological Director of one of the world's premier cryptozoological investigation groups: namely, the Centre for Fortean Zoology. And while Freeman has a passion for all aspects of cryptozoology, it is the dragon that fascinates him most of all.

"I started my career as a zoologist—so I had a grounded training," says Freeman. "But cryptozoology was my passion. Now, I have had a particular passion—an obsession, I suppose—for years with dragons. But there was something that always puzzled me: no one had ever thought, for more than a hundred years, to publish a definitive, non-fiction book on the subject. And as I am a qualified zoologist, I thought: why not me?"

Why not, indeed? In fact, that is precisely what Freeman did in his book, *Dragons: More Than a Myth?* I asked Freeman about his theories and discoveries with regard to dragons. He replied: "Well, that's a bit difficult to answer because there are several things going on. It's important to note that I've traveled the world pursuing these creatures—the Gambia, Mongolia, Thailand, and right here in England with some of the old legends from past centuries. And of one thing I can be certain: there isn't just one answer to the question of what dragons are or what they may be."

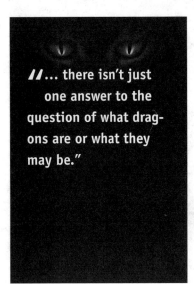

//... there isn't just one answer to the question of what dragons are or what they may be."

Freeman continued: "There are many creatures that have become linked to the lore and legend of what today we perceive and view as dragons, and some of these creatures are distinctly different to each other. But that should not take away from the fact that dragons are a real phenomenon."

On this latter point, Freeman elaborates: "I am absolutely certain, having reviewed many ancient reports of dragon activity, that many sightings—perhaps two or three hundred years ago and probably further back—were genuine encounters, but where the witnesses were seeing what I believe to have been huge snakes, giant crocodiles, and the Australian 'monster lizard' Megalania."

Freeman makes a noteworthy, and thought-provoking, point: "Any mention of dragons always conjures up images of fire-breathing monsters, and there are definitely reports that fall into that group. But, when you look into many of the earliest, ancient legends, you find that the dragon is more often associated with water. So, I have a theory that some of the better lake monster accounts from centuries ago may well have influenced dragon tales."

On this point, he adds: "Personally, I also believe that some classic tales of dragons in England in Medieval times, and tales of beasts such as the Lambton Worm, probably have their origins in lake monster accounts, giant eels, etc., that have then mutated into tales of dragons on the loose. But the important point is that this shouldn't detract from the fact that people did see something."

I asked him: "You mean that the ancients were seeing lake monsters and, having been exposed to dragon legends, believed them to be—or interpreted them as—dragons, too?"

"Exactly," Freeman replied.

Of course, the biggest question of all was: are there creatures still living today that Freeman believes have helped perpetuate the image of the dragon? He is certain there are: "I would pretty much stake my life on the fact that Megalania still exists— or did until very recently—in the large forests of Australia, and that also roamed New Guinea. This was a huge, killer-beast; a massive monitor lizard that exceeded thirty feet in length. In literal terms, this was a classic dragon-type animal."

I questioned Freeman about his research into an animal known as the Naga of Thailand that he believes is responsible for some dragon tales. He told me: "There is no excuse for not getting out into the field and doing firsthand investigations; none at all. In fact, it's vital. I have no time for the

When we think of dragons, most of us have an image of a fire-breathing monster from fantasy novels and films.

armchair theorist. And one of the experiences that I will remember for the rest of my life was traveling to Thailand with the Discovery Channel in 2000, where we chased giant snakes—the Naga—in the caves and tunnels that exist deep below Thailand.

"It's very easy to see why the inhabitants in times past considered them to be dragons. The Naga is apparently a large snake, a very large one—maybe in the order of literally tens of feet in length, oil-drum-sized bodies, and definitely big enough to take a whole man."

And similar accounts abound elsewhere, too: "There have come reports from the Congo of an animal known as Mokele-mbembe. Again, it has crossover qualities with dragon legends, but I'm sure that it will be shown in time to be some sort of giant monitor lizard, too."

But what of the definitive, fire-breathing dragons of legend: does, or did, such a creature exist? Freeman makes a very intriguing observation: "Back in 1979 Peter Dickinson wrote a book that was titled *The Flight of Dragons*. Dickinson had come up with this idea—an excellent theory, in fact—that real-life dragons did exist and that they were the descendants of dinosaurs such as the Tyrannosaurus Rex. Dickinson suggested that these animals developed large, expanded stomachs that would fill with hydrogen gas, which would come from a combination of hydrochloric acid found in the juices of the digestive system that would then mix with calcium found in the bones of their prey.

"Then, from there, the hydrogen—a lighter-than-air gas—allowed these creatures to take to the skies and then control their flight by burning off the excess gas in the form of flame. Anyone seeing this would be seeing the closest thing to the image of the dragon that we all know and love. Dickinson's theory is an excellent one, and may well be a perfect explanation for sightings of real dragons—in times past, and perhaps today, I believe."

I leave the final word to Freeman: "The dragon has its teeth and claws deep into the collective psyche of mankind, and it's not about to let go. Our most ancient fear still stalks the earth today. Beware: this is no fairytale. When your parents told you that there were no such things as dragons, they lied!"

EAST TEXAS AIRBORNE ENIGMA

A startling encounter with a large flying creature—far bigger than anything officially known to exist today—occurred in the piney woods of East Texas in late 1964. The source of the story chose to remain anonymous, which is understandable, as not everyone wants the world to know they have been confronted by a monster. Nevertheless, it's a story that was studied carefully by Texas resident and cryptozoologist Ken Gerhard. He finds it to be highly credible—given that it accords closely with other, similar cases Gerhard has studied, in the Lone Star State and in Mexico and Central America. At the time of the encounter, the source was just fifteen years of age. Most people have traumatic moments during their teenage years. Very few are like this, however. His story goes as follows:

"I was on Thanksgiving break from school, out snake hunting along Pine Island Bayou. I was standing along the bank of the bayou facing north when I looked up and to my right (east) only to see, at a distance of roughly 100 yards away, a positively huge bird flying from south to north. It was approximately flying at a height of 150 feet and I was able to observe its flight for a total of one minute or so before it disappeared into a cloud bank."

M ost people have traumatic moments during their teenage years. Very few are like this, however.

The man continued that the animal was, "a light plum color, normally feathered, wingspan estimated at 10–20 feet (bigger, longer than anything I've ever seen on any living, known bird), greyish clawed feet and greyish beak. In profile it resembled a pterodactyl more so than any bird I am familiar with either in movies, pictures, real life or drawings of same. Its wings moved methodically with an economy of motion which barely seemed fluid enough to support its weight or keep it in motion, let alone airborne. Its wings, when spread, had an almost skeletal semi-transparency about them."

Ken Gerhard has a very intriguing observation to make about this particular report and its location: "Point Island Bayou happens to be in Hardin County, in the heart of the Big Thicket. This remote area in southeast Texas has a rich history of Bigfoot sightings. The first native people in the area, who found parts of it to be literally impenetrable, appropriately named the Thicket. It is a massive network of swampy, dense forests that covers more than 12,000 square miles. On my first Bigfoot expedition there in September of 2002, I discovered an unusual, large three-toed track, which I made a plaster cast of. All those who studied the cast agreed that the track seemed to have a bird-like quality. After one expert proclaimed the track to be from an escaped emu (the tall, flightless relative of the ostrich), I discarded the cast. In retrospect, I wish that I had kept it!"

Just perhaps, whatever it was that left that three-toed print seen and casted by Ken Gerhard in 2002 was a latter-day version of the monster-bird seen by that amazed fifteen-year-old boy back in 1964.

FLYING SERPENTS

In her 1909 book, *Folk Lore and Folk Stories of Wales*, folklorist Marie Trevelyan told a fascinating story of a strange creature said to haunt a particular portion of Wales. She said, of the story provided to her more than a century ago by a then-elderly, local woman:

"The woods around Penllyn Castle, Glamorgan, had the reputation of being frequented by winged serpents, and these were the terror of old and young alike. An aged inhabitant of Penllyn, who died a few years ago, said that in his boyhood the winged serpents were described as very beautiful.

"They were coiled when in repose, and 'looked as if they were covered with jewels of all sorts. Some of them had crests sparkling with all the colors of the rainbow.' When disturbed they glided swiftly, 'sparkling all over,' to their hiding places. When angry, they 'flew over people's heads, with outspread

The Mayan god Quetzacoatl sometimes appeared as a feathered snake rather like the one seen in Wales. This mural in Mexico portrays the god in this form.

wings, bright, and sometimes with eyes too, like the feathers in a peacock's tail.' He said it was 'no old story invented to frighten children,' but a real fact. His father and uncle had killed some of them, for they were as bad as foxes for poultry. The old man attributed the extinction of the winged serpents to the fact that they were 'errors in the farmyards and coverts.'"

A similar story, also provided to Trevelyan, and also from the same area, states:

"An old woman, whose parents in her early childhood took her to visit Penmark Place, Glamorgan, said she often heard the people talking about the ravages of the winged serpents in that neighbourhood. She described them in the same way as the man of Penllyn. There was a 'king and queen' of winged serpents, she said, in the woods round Bewper. The old people in her early days said that wherever winged serpents were to be seen 'there was sure to be buried money or something of value' near at hand. Her grandfather told her of an encounter with a winged serpent in the woods near Porthkerry Park, not far from Penmark. He and his brother 'made up their minds to catch one, and watched a whole day for the serpent to rise. Then they shot at it, and the creature fell wounded, only to rise and attack my uncle, beating him about the head with its wings.' She said a fierce fight ensured between the men and the serpent, which was at last killed. She had seen its skin and feathers, but after the grandfather's death they were thrown away. That serpent was as notorious 'as any fox' in the farmyards and coverts around Penmark."

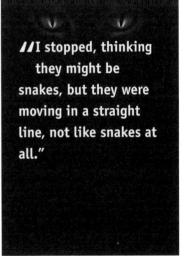

///I stopped, thinking they might be snakes, but they were moving in a straight line, not like snakes at all."

Moving on from Wales, there is the fascinating and eerily similar story of Izzet Goksu, of Bursa, Bulgaria. His story, however, dates from 1947:

"I used to go and fetch fresh water from the spring 200 meters from our house. One lovely summer evening, I picked up two buckets and started to walk towards the spring. After about 40 meters, I noticed what looked like branches on the path, but as I got closer I saw them moving. They were black, grey, and white, thin and one or two meters long. I stopped, thinking they might be snakes, but they were moving in a straight line, not like snakes at all."

Then, there was a sudden and amazing development:

"As I got closer, something alarmed them and they noticed me. They gave the weirdest cry I have ever heard, before taking off and flying two or three meters above the ground straight as arrows. They flew all the way to the spring about 150 meters away and disappeared behind the trees. I don't remember seeing any wings on them. Whenever I remember that cry my hair stands on end."

FLYING WOMAN OF VIETNAM

One of the strangest, and undoubtedly creepiest of all encounters with a weird creature occurred at the height of the Vietnam War, and specifically in Da Nang, Vietnam. It was in August 1969 that a man named Earl Morrison and several comrades had the shock of their lives. It was, very appropriately, in the dead of night when the menacing event occurred—while the men were on guard duty, keeping a careful look out for the Vietcong. Everything was quiet and normal until around 1:30 A.M. That's when the atmosphere changed, and an eerie form made its presence known to the shocked men of the U.S. 1st Division Marine Corps.

Despite being somewhat reluctant to speak out publicly, Morrison eventually changed his mind and, by 1972, was comfortable discussing the incident, even if he wasn't comfortable with what he encountered. His story makes for incredible reading:

"We saw what looked like wings, like a bat's, only it was gigantic compared to what a regular bat would be. After it got close enough so we could see what it was, it looked like a woman. A naked woman. She was black. Her skin was black, her body was black, the wings were black; everything was black. But it glowed. It glowed in the night—kind of a greenish cast to it. She started going over us, and we still didn't hear anything. She was right above us, and when she got over the top of our heads she was maybe 6 or 7 feet up. We watched her go straight over the top of us, and she still didn't make any noise flapping her wings. She blotted out the moon once—that's how close she was to us. And dark—looked like pitch black then, but we could still define her because she just glowed. Real bright like. And she started going past us straight towards our encampment. As we watched her—she had got about ten feet or so away from us—we started hearing her wings flap. And it sounded, you know, like regular wings flapping. And she just started flying off and we watched her for quite a while."

One of those who took a great deal of interest in the story of the flying woman of Da Nang was a UFO researcher named Don Worley. His personal interview with Morrison revealed additional data, such as the fact that the woman's hair was black and straight, that the wings may have had a slight furry quality to them, that she "rippled" as she flew by, that she appeared to lack bones in her body,

> **//She was black. Her skin was black, her body was black, the wings were black; everything was black. But it glowed."**

and that her wings seemed to be directly "molded" to her hands and arms.

The investigators Janet and Colin Bord say of this particularly odd case: "Usually our reports of winged figures describe them as 'men,' but without any indication whether features are seen which tell the witness definitely that it is a man. In view of this we suspect that so-called 'birdmen' should strictly be termed 'bird people' or 'bird persons,' and that no sex attribution can honestly be made. However, the Da Nang sighting does not come into that category. The only other winged figure we have on record is a creature from Welsh folklore, the Gwrach y Rhibyn. She resembled the Irish banshee, moaning and wailing to foretell death in a family."

Like this banshee from Irish folklore, the flying woman of Da Nang was a dark and ominous presence.

Marie Trevelyan—a noted expert on Welsh folklore—made more than a few comments that, with the benefit of hindsight, suggest Earl Morrison and his colleagues were visited by something eerily similar to the Gwrach y Rhibyn. Trevelyan said of the Welsh winged monster that it had "long black hair, black eyes, and a swarthy countenance. Sometimes one of her eyes is grey and the other black. Both are deeply sunken and piercing. Her back was crooked, her figure was very thin and spare, and her pigeon-breasted bust was concealed by a somber scarf. Her trailing robes were black. She was sometimes seen with long flapping wings that fell heavily at her sides, and occasionally she went flying low down along watercourses, or around hoary mansions. Frequently the flapping of her leathern bat-like wings could be heard against the window-panes."

Did the Gwrach y Rhibyn pay a visit to Vietnam in 1969? It's an amazing question to ponder upon. After all, the Welsh monster was noted for her links to looming death. And, no one can deny the tragic and massive numbers of deaths that occurred during the Vietnam War.

HOUSTON BATMAN

Mothman is a bizarre, flying creature that was made famous in the 2002 movie *The Mothman Prophecies* that starred Richard Gere and that, in turn, was based on the book of the same name penned by the late authority on just about everything paranormal and supernatural, John Keel. But long before Mothman dared to surface from his strange and ominous lair in Point Pleasant, West Virginia, in the mid-1960s, there was yet another mysterious winged thing that struck terror into the hearts and minds of those who were unfortunate enough to cross its terrible path.

Certainly, one of the most bizarre of all the many and varied strange beings that haunts the lore and legend of Texas is that which became known, albeit very briefly, as the Houston Batman. The most famous encounter with the beast took place during the early morning hours of June 18, 1953. Given the fact that it was a hot and restless night, twenty-three-year-old housewife Hilda Walker, and her neighbors, fourteen-year-old Judy Meyer and thirty-three-year-old tool plant inspector Howard Phillips, were sitting on the porch of Walker's home, located at 118 East Third Street in the city of Houston.

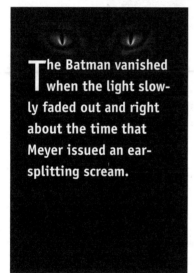

The Batman vanished when the light slowly faded out and right about the time that Meyer issued an ear-splitting scream.

Walker stated what happened next: "…twenty five feet away I saw a huge shadow across the lawn. I thought at first it was the magnified reflection of a big moth caught in the nearby street light. Then the shadow seemed to bounce upward into a pecan tree. We all looked up. That's when we saw it."

She went on to describe the entity as being essentially man-like in shape, sporting a pair of bat-style wings, dressed in a black, tight-fitting outfit, and surrounded by an eerie, glowing haze. The trio all confirmed that the monstrous form stood about six and a half feet tall and also agreed that the strange glow engulfing him was yellow in color. The Batman vanished when the light slowly faded out and right about the time that Meyer issued an ear-splitting scream.

Mrs. Walker also recalled the following: "Immediately afterwards, we heard a loud swoosh over the house tops across the street. It was like the white flash of a torpedo-shaped object…. I've heard so much about flying saucer stories and I thought all those people telling the stories were crazy, but now I don't know what to believe. I may be nuts, but I saw it, whatever it was…. I sat there stupefied. I was amazed."

Meyer added to the newspaper: "I saw it, and nobody can say I didn't."

Phillips, meanwhile, was candid in stating the following: "I can hardly believe it. But I saw it… we looked across the street and saw a flash of light rise from another tree and take off like a jet." For her part, Walker reported the incident to local police the following morning.

As a former resident of Houston, monster hunter Ken Gerhard made valiant attempts to locate the address on East Third Street where the event took place and discovered that it is no longer in existence. It has seemingly been overtaken by the expansion of the nearby Interstate 10. Strangely, and perhaps even appropriately, the location has apparently vanished into the void—much like the Batman did, for a while at least.

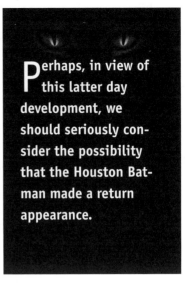

Perhaps, in view of this latter day development, we should seriously consider the possibility that the Houston Batman made a return appearance.

Several years after he first heard about the exploits of the Batman, a close friend of Gerhard told him about the experience of a number of employees at Houston's Bellaire Theater, who claimed to have seen a gigantic, helmeted man, crouched down and attempting to hide on the roof of a downtown city building late one night during the 1990s.

Perhaps, in view of this latter day development, we should seriously consider the possibility that the Houston Batman made a return appearance. Or, maybe, it never went away at all. Instead, possibly, it has been lurking deep within the shadows of Houston, Texas, for more than half a century, carefully biding its time, and only surfacing after the sun has set, and when overwhelming darkness dominates the sprawling metropolis.

HOUSTON SPACE CENTER MOTHMAN

Back in 2004, I interviewed a woman named Desiree, whose father worked at NASA's Houston, Texas-based Johnson Space Center, and who had a story to tell that was bizarre in the extreme. That does not mean, however, that we should dismiss it as being one of no merit, or one that lacks any meaningful value—only that we should view it with minds that are receptive to challenging ideas and bold, new paradigms.

It was late one night in 1986, said Desiree, when her father returned from his daily routine at the Johnson Space Center. There was nothing particularly unusual about that, she elaborated, as her father was occasionally required to work late into the night. On this particular night, however, things were very different: her father was clearly deeply distressed and even seemed to be on the verge of lapsing into a full blown anxiety attack.

After Desiree and her mother were finally able to calm him down, her father told a wild and extraordinary story: while walking to his car that night, he had seen, to his complete and utter horror, perched on a nearby building a large manlike figure that was utterly black in color, and that seemed to have a large cape draped across its shoulders and back—and with two huge, wing-like appendages sticking out of each side of the cape. Looking more bat-like than bird-like, the wings made a cracking noise as they slowly flapped in the strong, howling wind.

The creature, Desiree's father told his amazed family, had clearly realized it had been seen. Not only that, he gained the very distinct impression that the beast was actually relishing that it had been noticed, and was even seemingly deriving some form of deranged, evil pleasure from the fact that it had struck terror into the heart of the man.

The Mothman has been described as human-like, completely black, and with leathery wings that sometimes appear as a cape or cloak.

He could only stand and stare, frozen to the spot in complete and abject fear. The sheer horrific unreality of the situation—namely that of seeing a large, dark, gargoyle-like entity, looming ominously over him from a rooftop at NASA's Johnson Space Center—finally hit home with full force and Desiree's father raced for his car, flung open the door, slammed it shut, and then sped off into the darkness. He did not attempt to look back even once.

Not surprisingly, the family suggested that reporting the encounter to his superiors might not be the wisest move. Desiree's father agreed—for a short while, anyway. After a few weeks, however, the strange event was still gnawing steadily away at his mind and nerves, and he eventually confided in his immediate superior who, to his great surprise and relief, revealed that this was not the first time such a vile entity had been seen late at night roaming around the more shadowy parts of the Johnson Space Center. In other words, he was not going crazy or hallucinating: the beast was real and he was not the only witness, either.

Looking more bat-like than bird-like, the wings made a cracking noise as they slowly flapped in the strong, howling wind.

Indeed, a secret file on the matter had reportedly been opened some months earlier, primarily because on one occasion, and in the very same location where the winged fiend had been seen, the remains of two dead and horrifically-mutilated German Shepherds had been found—their bodies drained of significant amounts of blood. And as a result of this latest encounter Desiree's father was himself grilled intently about his experience by "NASA security people who were flown in from somewhere in Arizona—that much I know," as Desiree succinctly worded it. As for the flying monster, reportedly at least, it was never seen again.

HYTHE MOTHMAN

Midway through November 1963, one of the most chilling and eerie of all monster encounters on record occurred in the dark and shadowy environment of Sandling Park, Hythe, Kent (England). It was an encounter that, in terms of the description of the creature, provokes Mothman-style imagery—even though the latter, famous creature did not hit the headlines in and around Point Pleasant, West Virginia, until the mid-1960s. Although Sandling Park was certainly shrouded in overwhelming darkness at the time of the beastly event, it was hardly the sort of place where one would expect to encounter nothing less than a fully fledged monster. Amazingly, however, and according to a group of terrified witnesses, that is exactly what happened.

John Flaxton, aged seventeen on the night that all hell broke loose, was accompanied by three friends, including eighteen-year-old Mervyn Hutchinson. As they walked along a lane running by the park—after returning from a local Friday night dance—the group of friends became aware of a bright object moving overhead, which they at first took to be nothing stranger than a star. How very wrong they turned out to be.

The teenagers were amazed, and more than a bit scared, by the object's presence, as they watched it hover and then drop out of sight behind a group of trees. The boys decided to leave the area with haste, but the light soon loomed into view again. It hovered around ten feet from the ground, and at an approximate distance of two hundred feet, then once again went out of sight.

"It was a bright and gold oval," one of the boys reported. "And when we moved, it moved. When we stopped, it stopped." That was not necessarily a good sign!

Suddenly, the boys heard the snapping of twigs from a nearby thicket, and out from the wooded area shuffled a creature of horrendous appearance. "It was the size of a human," reported Mervyn Hutchinson. "But it didn't seem to have any head. There were wings on its back, like bat wings." The group fled, perhaps understandably not wanting to hang around and see what developed next.

Matters didn't end there, however. Five nights later, one Keith Croucher saw an unusual object float across a nearby soccer field. Forty-eight hours after that, one John McGoldrick, accompanied by a friend, checked out the location and stumbled upon unusual impressions in the ground, which gave every indication that something solid and significant had landed there.

Neil Arnold, a researcher of paranormal and monstrous phenomena who lives in the county of Kent, has this to say about the matter: "Local UFO experts believed that the case was nothing more than a misinterpretation of natural phenomena, but Flaxton recalled: 'I felt cold all over.'"

And, as Arnold also notes: "Three giant footprints were also found in the vicinity which were said to have measured two feet long and nine inches across. On 11 December, various newspaper reporters accompanied McGoldrick to the area and found that the woods were illuminated by an eerie, glowing light. No one investigated any further and the case faded as mysteriously as it had emerged."

To this date, the saga of the Mothman of Hythe, Kent, remains precisely that: a mystery.

MEXICAN WITCH

It's a story that sounds like the kind of thing one would read in the pages of something penned by horror maestro H. P. Lovecraft. Except for one key issue: it is one hundred percent fact. It was in the early hours of Friday, January 16, 2004, that a Mexican police officer was attacked by a monstrous, flying, hag-like creature in Guadalupe. All was normal until around 3:00 A.M., when all hell broke loose.

Officer Leonardo Samaniego was on his routine patrol in the Colonia Valles de la Silla area when something truly nightmarish occurred. A black figure leapt out of the shadows of a large tree that stood by the side of the road and slowly turned towards the officer's cruiser. This was nothing as down to earth as a large owl, however. Given the time and the darkness, Samaniego put his lights on high beam and directed the car at the thing in the road. The enormity of the situation—and the horrific nature of it—suddenly became all too clear. It was a hideous-looking woman dressed in black. And she was floating just above the ground.

For a few moments, Officer Samaniego could do nothing but stare in absolute terror as the dark-skinned woman's lidless, black eyes stared directly at him. For a moment. Suddenly, the winged fiend pulled her cloak around her eyes, seemingly being affected by the bright light. She then flew at the vehicle, jumped onto the hood and tried to smash her way into the car via the wind-shield with her bony fists. Panicked, Samaniego managed to put his car in reverse and hit the accelerator. As the vehicle shot away at a quick rate, the monster-woman clung onto the windshield, still intent on getting inside the car. Suddenly, the car slammed into a wall and came to a—quite literally—crashing halt.

For a few moments, Samaniego covered his eyes. But it was to no avail: when he moved his hands away the hag was still there, on the hood, and staring malevolently at him. Such was the level of his fear, he actually fainted at the wheel. In minutes paramedics were on the scene. The beast had gone, and Samaniego soon recovered.

The ghastly witch had black, lidless eyes.

Rather incredibly, it turned out that when Samaniego told his story to his superior officers, it prompted others in the department to admit that they, too, had seen the flying witch-woman in the dead of night, but had failed to report their encounters for fear of ridicule.

In May 2009, San Antonio, Texas-based cryptozoologist Ken Gerhard traveled to Mexico and had the very good fortune to interview Officer Samaniego firsthand, along with a television crew from the History Channel's popular show, *MonsterQuest*. Gerhard recalls how traumatic the whole affair was for Samaniego, even five years after it had occurred:

"At several junctures he began to become emotional and tear up as he relived that terrifying evening that had changed his life forever. Leonardo confessed to us that he still had vivid nightmares about the encounter and occasionally woke up in a panic with sweat streaming down his face. I wondered if the fact that I was dressed all in black with my trademark black leather cowboy hat (adorned with a silver skull, no less) made him slightly uncomfortable."

While in Guadalupe, Gerhard had the good fortune to meet with someone else who had had a similar, traumatic experience when he was a young boy. His name is Marco Reynoso, a UFO investigator and the former head of the regional office of the U.S.-based Mutual UFO Network. Back to Gerhard:

"Over breakfast, he told me about a remarkable experience that had set him on a lifelong quest for real answers. Apparently, when he was a young boy growing up in Monterrey, Marco had observed a tiny, winged, humanoid-like creature peeking out from behind his kitchen curtains one evening. The diminutive being reminded him of a gargoyle, with long, black hair covering its body and bat-like wings. To his credit, Marco made an attempt to curtail the goblin, but the entity vanished right before his eyes."

Ken Gerhard has uncovered other reports of flying humanoids in Mexico, some with wings and a few that appear to have the ability to float in the sky and without the need for wings. He has also collected a great deal of reports of what sound astonishingly like presumed extinct pterosaurs from the Jurassic era. Clearly, something strange is afoot in the skies of Mexico. And particularly so after sunset.

MOTHMAN

There can be few people reading this who have not at least heard of the legendary Mothman of Point Pleasant, West Virginia, who so terrorized the town and the surrounding area between November 1966 and December 1967, and whose diabolical exploits were chronicled in the 2002 hit Hollywood movie starring Richard Gere, *The Mothman Prophecies*, so named after the book of the same title written by Mothman authority John Keel.

A devil-like, winged monster with glowing, red eyes, Mothman's appearance came quite literally out of nowhere and, some say, culminated in high tragedy and death. But what was the Mothman of Point Pleasant? And how did the legend begin? To answer those questions we have to go back to the dark night of November 12, 1966, when five grave dig-gers working in a cemetery in the nearby town of Clen-denin were shocked to see what they described as a "brown human shape with wings" rise out of the thick, surrounding trees and soar off into the distance.

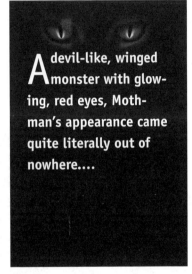

A devil-like, winged monster with glow-ing, red eyes, Moth-man's appearance came quite literally out of nowhere....

Three days later, the unearthly beast surfaced once again. It was at the highly appropriate time of the witch-ing-hour when Roger and Linda Scarberry and Steve and Mary Mallette—two young, married couples from Point Pleasant—were passing the time away by cruising around town in the Scarberrys' car.

As they drove around the old factory, the four were puzzled to see in the shadows what looked like two red lights pointing in their direction. These were no normal lights, however. Rather, all four were shocked and horrified to discover that, in reality, the "lights" were the glowing, self-illuminating red eyes of a huge animal that, as Roger Scarberry would later recall, was "shaped like a Mothman, but bigger, maybe six and a half or seven feet tall, with big wings folded against its back."

Not surprisingly, they fled the area at high speed. Unfortunately for the Scarberrys and the Mallettes, however, the beast seemingly decided to follow them: as they sped off for the safety of Point Pleasant, the winged monster took to the skies and shadowed their vehicle's every movement until it reached the city limits.

The four raced to the sheriff's office and told their astounding story to Deputy Millard Halstead, who later stated that "I've known these kids all their lives. They'd never been in any trouble and they were really scared that night. I took them seriously."

And even though a search of the area by Halstead did not result in an answer to the mystery, the Mothman would soon return.

Early on the morning of November 25, yet another remarkable encounter with the mysterious beast took place, as John Keel noted: "Thomas Ury was driving along Route 62 just north of the TNT area when he noticed a tall, grey manlike figure standing in a field by the road. 'Suddenly it spread a pair of wings,' Ury said, 'and took off straight up, like a helicopter. It veered over my convertible and began going in circles three telephone poles high.'"

Keel reported that Ury quickly hit the accelerator. Nevertheless, Ury added: "It kept flying right over my car even though I was doing about seventy-five." Over the next few days more sightings surfaced, including that of Ruth Foster of nearby Charleston—who saw the winged monster late at night in her garden, and who said: "It was tall with big red eyes that popped out of its face. My husband is six feet one and this bird looked about the same height or a little shorter, maybe."

Needless to say, the local media had a field day with the story. Tales of what were referred to as the "Bird-Monster" hit the headlines while both the skeptics and the police ensured that their views and opinions on the matter were widely known.

Dr. Robert L. Smith, an associate professor of wildlife biology at West Virginia University's Division of Forestry, expressed his firm opinion that Mothman was nothing stranger than a large sandhill crane. This hardly satisfied the witnesses, however. In response to Dr. Smith's assertion, Thomas Ury said: "I've seen big birds, but I've never seen anything like this."

//I've known these kids all their lives. They'd never been in any trouble and they were really scared that night. I took them seriously."

As for the local police, they offered stern warnings to any and all would-be monster hunters contemplating seeking out the mysterious creature, as the *Herald Dispatch* newspaper noted: "Sheriff [George] Johnson said he would arrest anybody caught with a loaded gun in the area after dark [and] warned that the scores of persons searching the abandoned powerhouse in the TNT area after dark risked possible serious injury."

In the weeks and months that followed, further encounters with the bizarre beast were reported; however, they were overshadowed by a tragic event that occurred on December 15, 1967, when the city's Silver Bridge that crossed the Ohio River and connected Point Pleasant to Gallipolis, Ohio, broke away from its moorings and plunged into the river, tragically taking with it nearly fifty lives. Although a down-to-earth explanation was most definitely in evidence—that a problem with a single eye-bar in a suspension chain was to blame—many took the view, and still to this day continue to take the view, that the Mothman was behind it all. Or, perhaps was trying to warn the people of the area of the impending doom that loomed large. But what of today: does the Mothman still fly and terrorize? Maybe so and, perhaps, even outside of the United States, too.

Sometimes the Mothman is fairly small, possibly even mistaken for a bird, and sometime man-sized.

NEEDWOOD FOREST'S FLYING MONSTER

Needwood Forest—of the county of Staffordshire, England—was a chase, or a royal forest, that was given to Henry III's son, Edmund Crouchback, the 1st Earl of Lancaster, in 1266, and was owned by the Duchy of Lancaster until it passed into the possession of Henry IV. In the 1770s, Francis Noel Clarke Mundy published a collection of poetry called *Needwood Forest* that contained his own poem of the same name, one regarded as "one of the most beautiful local poems." And much the same was said about the forest—which was an undeniably enchanting locale, filled with magic, myths, and ancient lore, as forests so curiously often are.

Today, however, things are sadly very different, and most of the ancient woodland is now, tragically, gone: presently, the area is comprised of twenty farms, on which dairy farming is the principal enterprise; and less than 500

Francis Noel Clarke Mundy (1739–1815) was a noted poet and author of the collection *Needwood Forest*.

acres of woodland now remain. Some parts of the forest are still open to the public, including Jackson Bank, a mature, mixed 80-acre area of woodland which can be found at Hoar Cross near Burton upon Trent and which is owned by the Duchy of Lancaster.

And then there is Bagot's Wood near Abbots Bromley, which claims to be the largest remaining part of Needwood Forest, and which takes its name from the Bagot family, seated for centuries at Staffordshire's Blithfield Hall. Situated some nine miles east of Stafford and five miles north of Rugeley, the Hall has been the home of the Bagot family since the late fourteenth century; while the present house is mainly Elizabethan, it has a Gothic façade added in the 1820s.

In 1945 the Hall, then in a neglected and dilapidated state, was sold by Gerald Bagot (the 5th Baron Bagot), together with its 650-acre estate to the South Staffordshire Waterworks Company, whose intention was to build a reservoir, which was completed in 1953. The 5th Baron died in 1946, having sold many of the contents of the house. His successor and cousin, Caryl Bagot, repurchased the property and thirty acres of land from the water company and began an extensive program of both renovation and restoration.

The 6th baron died in 1961 and bequeathed the property to his widow, Nancy, Lady Bagot. In 1986, the Hall was divided into four separate houses, the main part of which incorporates the Great Hall and is owned by the Bagot Jewitt Trust. Lady Bagot and the Bagot Jewitt family remain in residence.

And, it is against this backdrop of ancient woodland and historic and huge old halls that something decidedly strange occurred back in the summer of 1937, when Alfred Tipton was but a ten-year-old boy. And like most adventurous kids, young Alfred enjoyed playing near Blithfield Hall, and in the Bagot's Wood, with his friends on weekends and during the seemingly neverending school holidays. And it was during the summer holidays of 1937 that something strange and monstrous was seen in that small, yet eerie, area of old woodland.

According to Tipton, on one particular morning he and four of his friends had been playing in the woods for several hours and were taking a break, sitting on the warm, dry grass and soaking in the sun. Suddenly, says Tipton, they heard a shrill screeching sound that was coming from the trees directly above them. As they craned their necks to look directly upwards, the five pals were horrified by the sight of a large, black beast sitting on its haunches in one particularly tall and very old tree, and "shaking the branch up and down with its claws tightened around it." But this was no mere large bird.

Tipton says that "it reminded me of a devil: I still don't forget things and that is what I say it looked like." He adds that the creature peered down at the five of them for a few moments and then suddenly opened up its large and shiny wings, which were easily a combined twelve feet across, and took to the skies in a fashion that could be accurately described as part-flying and part-gliding, before being forever lost to sight after perhaps fifteen or twenty seconds or so.

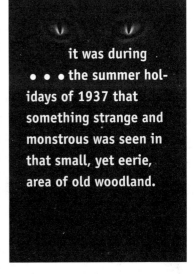

it was during . . . the summer holidays of 1937 that something strange and monstrous was seen in that small, yet eerie, area of old woodland.

Significantly, when shown various pictures, photographs, and drawings of a wide variety of large-winged creatures that either still roam our skies or did so in the past, the one that Tipton said most resembled the creature he and his mates saw was a pterodactyl. Of course, the pterodactyl is long extinct; however, Tipton is adamant that the beast the boys encountered was extremely similar to the legendary winged monster of the distant past.

Were the boys merely spooked and confused by their sighting of a large, exotic bird—albeit one of a conventional nature and origin, and perhaps even a circus- or zoo-escapee? Or, was some hideous winged-thing really haunting Bagot's Wood on that fateful, long-gone morning back in 1937? Sadly, probably neither we nor Alfred Tipton will ever know the answers to those thought-provoking and controversial questions.

NEVADA BIRD-MONSTER

In the latter part of 2006, I had the good fortune to meet with a Las Vegas, Nevada-based bus driver names James, who had a remarkable encounter with a massive, winged beast in the deserts outside of town, in November 2003. James was careful—in fact, *very* careful—about how much he said. This was specifically due to the fact that at the time of his encounter he was high on *Lophophora williamsii*, which is far more famously known as peyote. And, the last thing he wanted was to get into hot water with his employers at the bus company. Nevertheless, he did relate the significant portions of the affair. Those portions alone tell a fantastic story.

Before we get to the encounter itself, first let's acquaint ourselves with a bit of background on peyote, which is also referred to as the Divine Cactus and the Mescal Button. It is a fairly small cactus, one that is chiefly found in the southwestern portions of the United States, as well as in Mexico's Chihuahua desert. And it's most noted for its powerful and profound psychedelic properties. Indeed, one of its primary alkaloids is mescaline. While today it is chiefly used as a recreational drug, peyote has been used for thousands of years in the religious and ceremonial practices of both Native Americans and the people of Mexico. As for its effects, they are typically notable and unforgettable and include graphic imagery and audible hallucinations.

With that in mind, some readers might assume or conclude that James's encounter with the monster-bird was due to nothing more than the effects of peyote. Well, that is exactly what James believes. It's very important to note, however, he is not of the opinion that the peyote made him hallucinate the entire experience. Rather, he is of the opinion that the Divine Cactus opened a portal—or a doorway, perhaps—that gave him a brief glimpse into a magical realm that coexists with ours. One that, in a normal state of mind, we cannot access. In simple terms: what we might justifiably call another dimension. Equally intriguing was the specific location of the sighting: the Valley of Fire, Nevada's oldest state park, which is situated around fifty miles from downtown Las Vegas and has an elevation in excess of 2,000 feet. It's an area with a long and rich history attached to it, too. Certainly, as far back as approximately 300 CE it was home to the Anasazi people, who farmed the nearby Moapa Valley. Now, with the scene firmly set, let's take a look at what, exactly, James had to say.

Peyote is a drug derived from the cactus *Lophophora williamsii*, something the witness had indulged in before seeing the Nevada Monster-Bird.

He explained to me that at the time in question he was chilling out on a rocky ridge when, as the effects of the peyote took firm hold of both his mind and his body, something totally unforeseen occurred. It was something just about as awe-inspiring as it was terrifying. As James stared across the panoramic landscape, his attention was suddenly caught by the sight of something of significant size flying directly towards him. While the object was still at a distance, his first thoughts were that it had to be something along the lines of a hang-glider or a microlight. As it got closer, however, James realized that it was neither. It was something way stranger.

What James encountered—and which glided directly over him at a height of around eighty or ninety feet—was a huge, winged animal, completely black in color, and not unlike a long extinct pterodactyl. As James told me, just about everyone knows what a pterodactyl looks like. Of course, the big problem was: how could such an immense, long dead animal cruise the skies of Nevada in the early years of the twenty-first century? The only answer he had was: the peyote, and the possibility that it allowed him a glimpse of something that few of us ever get to experience, at least not in a normal state of consciousness.

Rather amazingly, this was not James's only encounter with a huge, flying beast in Nevada. A second encounter occurred in the summer of 2005.

Thunderbird imagery is often seen in the art of Native American peoples. The giant bird has been a part of their mythology for thousands of years.

This time, the location was Grapevine Canyon, which is located at Newberry Peak, Nevada. Once again, peyote played a significant role in the experience. The creature that James encountered at Grapevine Canyon, however, was no pterodactyl. Quite the contrary. It sounds far more like the legendary Thunderbird of Native American lore and tradition.

As James lay back on the stones, stared at the stars, and let the peyote do its mind-altering thing, the mighty eagle-like animal loomed into view, its wings beating powerfully and loudly as it circled him at a height of a couple of hundred feet. Oddly, James said that he suddenly felt the Thunderbird was "judging me on what I have done in my life and what I will do in the future." He explained he had no real understanding of why, precisely, he felt that; only that he did. For around ten to fifteen minutes the massive creature—which had a wingspan of, incredibly, around twenty-five feet—continued to circle, yet never made any attempt to come closer to him. Then, suddenly, and without warning, it headed off in a southerly direction, finally vanishing from view as the dusk skies grew rapidly dark. Despite still continuing to use peyote on a regular basis, James's experiences in the 2000s have never been repeated.

James notes, however, that although both experiences were nerve-jangling, he would not turn his nose up at another encounter. For James, opening the door to another world was an enlightening one, even if it involved the manifestation of monsters.

NINETEENTH-CENTURY PTERODACTYL

On April 26, 1890, the *Tombstone Epitaph* newspaper ran a story of extraordinary proportions, one that suggested that nothing less than a gigantic pterosaur had been found. Of course, the sensational nature of the story means that a hoax cannot be ruled out. Nevertheless, it's a saga—and a monster—of incredible proportions and one well worth relating:

"A winged monster, resembling a huge alligator with an extremely elongated tail and an immense pair of wings, was found on the desert between the Whetstone and Huachuca mountains last Sunday by two ranchers who were returning home from the Huachucas. The creature was evidently greatly exhausted by a long flight and when discovered was able to fly but a short distance at a time.

"After the first shock of wild amazement as it passed the two men, who were on horseback and armed with Winchester rifles, they regained sufficient courage to pursue the monster and after an exciting chase of several miles succeeded in getting near enough to open fire with their rifles and wounding it.

Pterodactyls were a species of pterosaur (not dinosaur) that lived during the Jurassic Period.

"The creature then turned on the men but owing to its exhausted condition they were able to keep out of its way and after a few well directed shots the monster partly rolled over and remained motionless.

"The men cautiously approached, their horses snorting in terror and found that the monster was dead. They then proceeded to make an examination and found that it measured about ninety two feet in length and the greatest diameter was about fifty inches.

"The monster had only two feet, these being situated a short distance from where the wings were joined to the body. The head, as near as they could judge was about eight feet long, the jaws being thickly set with strong, sharp teeth.

"Its eyes were as large as a dinner plate and protruded halfway from the head. They had some difficulty in measuring the wings as they were partly folded under the body, but finally got one straightened out sufficiently to obtain a measurement of seventy eight feet, making the total length from tip to tip about 160 feet.

"The wings were composed of a thick and nearly transparent membrane and were devoid of feathers or hair, as was the entire body. The skin of the body was comparatively smooth and easily penetrated by a bullet.

"The men cut off a small portion of the tip of one wing and took it home with them. Late last night one of them arrived in this city for supplies and to make the necessary preparations to skin the creature, when the hide will be sent east for examination by the eminent scientists of the day.

"The finder returned early this morning accompanied by several prominent men who will endeavor to bring the strange creature back to the city before it is mutilated."

O'DONNELL'S HIDEOUS BIRD

Elliott O'Donnell was an acclaimed authority on ghosts and life after death, and penned dozens of books on supernatural phenomena. Born in 1872, he continued writing until his death in 1965, at the age of ninety-three. O'Donnell also had a deep interest in reports of strange creatures, as the following nineteenth-century account demonstrates:

"Henry Spicer, in his *Strange Things amongst Us*, tells the story of a Captain Morgan, an honorable and vivacious gentleman, who, arriving in London in 1841, puts up for the night in a large, old-fashioned hotel. The room in which he slept was full of heavy, antique furniture, reminiscent of the days of King George I, one of the worst periods in modern English history for crime. Despite, however, his grimly suggestive surroundings, Captain Morgan quickly got into bed and was soon asleep. He was abruptly awakened by the sound of flapping, and, on looking up, he saw a huge black bird with outstretched wings and fiery red eyes perched on the rail at the foot of the four-poster bed.

"The creature flew at him and endeavored to peck his eyes. Captain Morgan resisted, and after a desperate struggle succeeded in driving it to a sofa in the corner of the room, where it settled down and regarded him with great fear in its eyes. Determined to destroy it, he flung himself on the top of it, when, to his surprise and terror, it immediately crumbled into nothingness. He left the house early next morning, convinced that what he had seen was a ghost, but Mr. Spicer offers no explanation as to how one should classify the phenomenon.

"It may have been the earth-bound spirit of the criminal or viciously inclined person who had once lived there, or it may have been the phantom of an actual bird. Either alternative is feasible.

I have heard there is an old house near Poole, in Dorset, and another in Essex, which were formerly haunted by spectral birds, and that as late as 1860 the phantasm of a bird, many times the size of a raven, was so frequently seen by the inmates of a house in Dean Street, Soho, that they eventually grew quite accustomed to it.

"But bird hauntings are not confined to houses, and are far more often to be met with out of doors; indeed there are very few woods, and moors, and commons that are not subjected to them. I have constantly seen the spirits of all manner of birds in the parks in Dublin and London. Greenwich Park, in particular, is full of them."

OWLMAN

In 1976, the dense trees surrounding Mawnan Old Church, Cornwall, England, became a veritable magnet for a diabolical beast that was christened the Owlman. The majority of those who crossed paths with the creature asserted that it was human-like in both size and design, and possessed a pair of large wings, fiery red eyes, claws, and exuded an atmosphere of menace. No wonder people make parallels with Mothman.

It all began during the weekend of Easter 1976, when two young girls, June and Vicky Melling, had an encounter of a truly nightmarish kind in Mawnan Woods. The girls were on holiday with their parents when they saw a gigantic, feathery "bird man" hovering over the thirteenth-century church.

It was a story that their father, Don Melling, angrily shared with a man named Tony "Doc" Shiels. I say "angrily" because Shiels was a noted, local magician who Melling came to believe had somehow instigated the whole affair. Or as Shiels, himself, worded it: "…some trick that had badly frightened his daughters." Shiels denied any involvement in the matter whatsoever. But that was only the start of things.

Another one to see the Owlman was Jane Greenwood, also a young girl. She wrote a letter to the local newspaper, the *Falmouth Packet*, during the summer of 1976 that detailed her own startling encounter: "I am on holiday in

Mawnan Church is near Cornwall, England. It was here that the Owlman was spotted in 1976.

Cornwall with my sister and our mother. I, too, have seen a big bird-thing. It was Sunday morning, and the place was in the trees near Mawnan Church, above the rocky beach. It was in the trees standing like a full-grown man, but the legs bent backwards like a bird's. It saw us, and quickly jumped up and rose straight up through the trees. How could it rise up like that?"

Two fourteen-year-old girls, Sally Chapman and Barbara Perry, also had the misfortune to have a run-in with the Owlman in 1976. At around 10:00 P.M., while camping in the woods of Mawnan, and as they sat outside of their tent making a pot of tea, the pair heard a strange hissing noise. On looking around, they saw the infernal Owlman staring in their direction from a distance of about sixty feet.

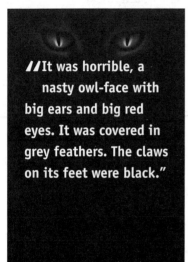

//It was horrible, a nasty owl-face with big ears and big red eyes. It was covered in grey feathers. The claws on its feet were black."

Sally said: "It was like a big owl with pointed ears, as big as a man. The eyes were red and glowing. At first I thought that it was someone dressed-up, playing a joke, trying to scare us. I laughed at it. We both did. Then it went up in the air and we both screamed. When it went up you could see its feet!"

Barbara added: "It's true. It was horrible, a nasty owl-face with big ears and big red eyes. It was covered in grey feathers. The claws on its feet were black. It just flew up and disappeared in the trees."

While there were rumors of additional sightings of the creature in the immediate years that followed, it wasn't until the summer of either 1988 or 1989 that the Owlman put in an appearance that can be documented to a significant degree. In this case, the witness was a young boy, dubbed "Gavin" by a good friend of mine, Jon Downes (who wrote an entire book on the winged monster, titled *The Owlman and Others*), and his then girlfriend, Sally. The beast, Gavin told Jon, was around five feet in height, had large feet, glowing eyes, and significantly sized wings. It was a shocking, awe-inspiring encounter that Gavin and Sally never forgot.

As was the case in the immediate post-1976 era, a few reports from the 1990s and 2000s have surfaced. Chiefly, however, they are from individuals who prefer not to go on the record—which has led to understandable suspicions of fakery and hoaxing. But one could also make a very good argument that going public about having seen a monstrous "birdman" in an English woodland would not be the wisest move to make.

Today, and getting ever-closer to forty years since the original encounters occurred, the matter remains the undeniable controversy that it was back then. For some researchers, Doc Shiels is the man to blame. They perceive him as a trickster, a faker, and someone not to be trusted. Jon Downes, however, suggests something else—something with which I concur.

Namely, that Shiels—dubbed the "Wizard of the Western World"—has profound knowledge of "magic." And by that, I don't mean people pulling rabbits out of hats. We are talking, here, about something far stranger, something ancient, and something filled with swirling mystery.

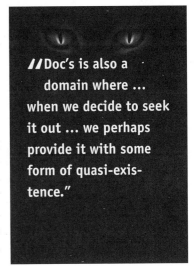

//Doc's is also a domain where ... when we decide to seek it out ... we perhaps provide it with some form of quasi-existence."

In a review of Doc's excellent book *Monstrum*, I noted tbat Doc's "is a world filled with a deep understanding of the real nature of magic (chaos and ritualistic), the secrets of invocation and manifestation, of strange realms just beyond—and that occasionally interact with—our own, and Trickster-like phenomenon. Doc's is also a domain where, when we dare to imagine the fantastic, when we decide to seek it out, and when we finally accept its reality, we perhaps provide it with some form of quasi-existence."

Perhaps Doc, in a decidedly strange way, really did play a role in the formation of the Owlman legend. But, such was the allure of the beast, it quickly stepped out of the world of imagination and storytelling and right into the heart of the real world. And on that last point, be careful what you wish for, lest you unleash into our reality a monster that has no intention of returning to that domain from which it was originally created, imagined, or invoked.

Phantom Bird

The Reverend F. G. Lee was the author of a still-acclaimed book *Glimpses in the Twilight*. Published in 1888, it is filled with all manner of amazing and chilling tales, including one of a terrible monster-bird. Lee, who extensively researched the strange story, said:

"In the middle of the last century, circa 1749, owing to several remarkable circumstances which had then recently occurred, a conviction became almost universal among the inhabitants of the village, that the vaults under the church of West Drayton, near Uxbridge, were haunted."

He continued: "Strange noises were heard in and about the sacred building, and the sexton of that day, a person utterly devoid of superstition, was on inquiry and examination compelled to admit that certain unaccountable occurrences in regard to the vault had taken place. Others maintained that three persons from an adjacent manor-house in company had gone to look through a grating in the side of the foundation of the church—for the ventilation of the vault, and from which screams and noises were heard constantly, and there had seen a very large black raven perched on one of the coffins."

According to the Reverend Lee: "This strange bird was seen more than once by the then parish clerk pecking from within at the grating, and furiously fluttering about within the enclosed vault. On another occasion it was seen by other people in the body of the church itself. The wife of the parish clerk and her daughter often saw it."

Eventually, however, the beastly bird's reign of terror was brought to an end, as the reverend noted:

"The local bell-ringers, who all professed to deny its existence and appearance, one evening, however, came together to ring a peal, when they were told by a youth that the big raven was flying about inside the chancel. Coming together into the church with sticks and stones and a lantern, four men and two boys found it fluttering about amongst the rafters. They gave chase to it, flinging at it, shouting at and endeavoring to catch it. Driven from hither and thither for some time, and twice or thrice beaten with a stick, so that one of its wings seemed to have thus been broken and made to droop, the bird fell down wounded with expanded wings, screaming and fluttering into the eastern part of the chancel, when two of the men on rushing towards it to secure it, and driving it into a corner, vaulted over the communion-rails, and violently proceeded to seize it. As the account stands, it at once sank wounded and exhausted on to the floor, as they believed in their certain grasp, but all of a moment—vanished!"

In relation to this particularly weird saga, the wife of Reverend R. L. Burgh, who served at the church of West Drayton in the 1800s, wrote the following to Reverend Lee: "It was many years ago; and I had quite forgotten it until I got your note. I can remember feeling persuaded that a bird must have got into the family vault, and in going outside to look into it through the iron bars to try if anything could be seen there, the sounds were then always in the chancel in the same place."

Neil Arnold adds a piece of valuable data to this story: "A record of the strange bird also exists from 1869 when two sisters claimed to have seen an enormous bird whilst visiting the church, which they believed would have looked more at home in the zoological gardens."

PTERODACTYL OF ENGLAND

Imagine driving, late at night, across the foggy moors of central England and coming across what looks like nothing less than a living, breathing pterodactyl! Think it couldn't happen? It already has. From 1982 to 1983, a wave of sightings of such a creature—presumed extinct for sixty-five million years—occurred in an area called the Pennines, better known as the "backbone of England" and comprised of rolling hills and mountains.

So far as can be determined, the first encounter occurred at a place with the highly apt name of the Devil's Punchbowl, on September 12, 1982. That was when a man named William Green came forward with an astonishing story of what he encountered at Shipley Glen woods. It was a large, grey-colored creature that flew in "haphazard" style and possessed a pair of large, leathery-looking wings. The latter point is notable, since it effectively rules out a significantly sized feathery bird, and does indeed place matters into a pterodactyl category.

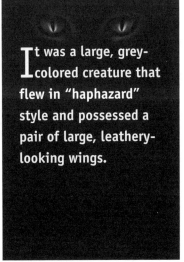

It was a large, grey-colored creature that flew in "haphazard" style and possessed a pair of large, leathery-looking wings.

Seventy-two hours later, a woman named Jean Schofield had the misfortune to see the immense beast at the West Yorkshire town of Yeadon. That the thing was heading for the Leeds/Bradford Airport provoked fears in Schofield's mind of a catastrophic midair collision between a passenger plane and the mighty winged thing.

Perhaps inevitably, the local media soon heard of the sightings and the story was given pride of place in the newspapers of the day. While the theory that a large bird of prey had escaped from a menagerie or zoo satisfied the skeptics, it did not go down well with the witnesses, who were sure that what they had encountered was something straight out of the Jurassic era. Rather notably, the media attention brought forth additional witnesses, including Richard Pollock, who claimed he and his dog had been dive-bombed by the monster, which descended on the pair with alarming speed, "screaming" as it did so. Pollock hit the ground, protecting his dog as he did so. Given the fact that the creature was practically on top of him, Pollock couldn't fail to get a good look at it: he described it as reptilian, and with a face that looked like a cross between a crocodile and a bat, which is actually not a bad description of a pterodactyl.

There was then somewhat of a lull in reports, but they exploded again in May 1983. There was a sighting at Thackley on May 6 by a witness whose attention to the creature was provoked by the sudden sound of heavy wings beating above. Yet again, it was a case that not only caught the media's attention but provoked others to come forward. One of them was a Mr. Harris, who said that in November 1977, at Totley, he saw just such a flying monster that soared overheard, growling as it did so. He was adamant that what he saw was a full-blown pterodactyl.

**he saw just such
• • • a flying monster
that soared overheard,
growling as it did so.
He was adamant that
what he saw was a full-
blown pterodactyl.**

Quite naturally, further attempts were made to try and lay the matter to rest, including the amusing—but utterly unproven—theory that the pterodactyl was actually a radio-controlled model! And claims of escaped, exotic birds were once again trotted out, but without a shred of evidence to support them.

A few more, somewhat vague, reports trickled in. For the most part, however, the curious affair of the Pennines pterosaur was over. If we can rule out models, and mistaken identity, what does that leave us with? It seems downright ridiculous to give credence to the idea that a pterodactyl was flying around the skies of northern England—and possibly from 1977 to 1983. And, yet, that seems to have been precisely what was going on. There is another explanation that might just work. It has been suggested that perhaps what the astonished and terrified witnesses encountered was not a *living* pterodactyl, but the *ghost* of one.

Millions of people believe that the human soul, or life-force, lives on after death. So, why should that not be the case with animals, too? Certainly, there are numerous cases on record of people who claim that beloved, deceased pets have returned to visit them, in spectral form. And, it's important to note that there is some evidence that suggests the ghostly theory is the correct one.

Joshua P. Warren is a highly respected ghost hunter from Asheville, North Carolina. Amongst his many investigations of the spooky kind, one in particular stands out. In the early-to-mid-2000s, Warren investigated and documented a huge amount of supernatural activity at the Jackson Farm, Lancaster, South Carolina. Ghostly apparitions were commonplace on the large property, and particularly so late at night. One of them, amazingly, was described as being a spectral, winged animal that "had a wide wingspan and a long neck with some kind of huge bird head." The terrified witness, Adam Jackson, drew a picture of the ethereal monster he encountered. It would be hard to find a better image of a pterodactyl.

SOUTH AMERICAN MONSTER BIRDS

One of the strangest, yet intriguing, accounts of giant, winged monsters in our very midst came from a man named James Harrison, a resident of Liverpool, England. According to Ken Gerhard's book *Big Bird!* it was in February 1947 that Harrison, who, along with several fellow adventurers and explorers, was boating along the Manaus River—a tributary of the Amazon—encountered something startling. It was a flock of five, huge flying creatures, surfing the sky at an alarmingly low level.

Due to the close proximity, Harrison and his colleagues were easily able to discern that the creatures had leathered skin, were brown in color, and had wingspans that exceeded twelve feet. The wings of the monsters were described as being "ribbed," while their oddly flattened heads were attached to very long necks. In other words, they sounded very much like pterodactyls from a time long gone.

Flying over their heads as they traveled down the river were flying, leathery creatures that looked a lot like pterodactyls.

Cryptozoologist Ken Gerhard has noted that some skeptics suggested what Harrison and his team had really viewed were nothing stranger than storks! It's a most unlikely possibility, and particularly so when one remembers that the entire group was able to see the animals close-up, rather than at a distance. Of pterosaurs in South America, Gerhard says:

"Evidence of relict pterosaurs in South America can be found on the controversial carvings known as the Ica stones of Peru. A local physician named Dr. Javier Cabrera believes that the thousands of intricately carved stones may be ancient, though their true age cannot be scientifically validated. Some of the stones may, in fact, be fakes, generated by local artisans trying to capitalize on the tourists. The original stones were allegedly discovered by a farmer near the mysterious Nazca lines back in the 1960s. Many of the carvings portray humans living alongside dinosaurs. A few stones in particular, display obvious renditions of men riding on the backs of living pterodactyls."

Beyond any shadow of doubt, that would have been an incredible sight to see!

VAN METER MONSTER

One of the strangest of all monsters is Iowa's very own winged thing, the Van Meter Monster. The mystery began in December 1903 when a terrify-

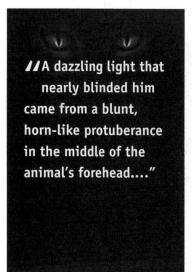

//A dazzling light that nearly blinded him came from a blunt, horn-like protuberance in the middle of the animal's forehead...."

ing beast plunged the town of Van Meter into states of hysteria and fear. The story began with a resident of the town, Dr. A. C. Olcott, whose extraordinary encounter made the pages of the New York-based *Watertown Herald*. According to the press, the doctor "grabbed a shotgun and ran outside the building, where he saw a monster, seemingly half human and half beast, with great bat-like wings. A dazzling light that nearly blinded him came from a blunt, horn-like protuberance in the middle of the animal's forehead and it gave off a stupefying odor that almost overcame him. The doctor discharged his weapon and fled into his office, barring doors and windows, and remained there in abject terror until morning."

For some baffling reason, there were fears in town that the monster would raid the local bank and empty it of cash! This led one Peter Dunn to spend the night in the bank, with a loaded gun. It was a very wise move, as the *Watertown Herald* noted. In the early hours, Dunn was momentarily blinded by a bright light that filled the bank. The beast was back:

"Eventually [Dunn] recovered his senses sufficiently to distinguish the monster and fired through the window. The plate glass and sash were torn out, and the monster disappeared. Next morning imprints of large three-toed feet were discernible in the soft earth. Plaster casts were taken."

The article continues that another sighting was made by one O. V. White, a doctor in town who saw the beast climbing down a telephone pole, "using a beak much in the manner of a parrot." As the creature reached the ground, the *Watertown Herald* told its readers, "…it seemed to travel in leaps like a kangaroo, using its huge featherless wings to assist. It gave off no light. He fired at it and he wounded it. The shot was followed by an overpowering odor. Sydney Gregg, attracted by the shot, saw the monster flying away."

That was not the end of the story, however; far from it:

"The climax came the following night. The whole town was aroused by this time. Professor Martin, principal of the schools, decided that from the description it was an antediluvian animal. Shortly after midnight J. L. Platt, foreman of the brick plant, heard a peculiar sound in an abandoned coal mine, and as the men had reported a similar sound before, a body of volunteers started an investigation. Presently the monster emerged from the shaft, accompanied by a smaller one. A score of shots were fired without effect."

The newspaper rounded things off with the following: "The whole town was aroused, and a vigil was maintained the rest of the night, but without result until just at dawn, when the two monsters returned and disappeared down the shaft."

WINGED MAN

What was without any shadow of a doubt the strangest of all stories of an unidentified flying entity seen in the skies of England surfaced on February 19, 2009. Mike Lockley, then the editor of the now-closed *Chase Post* newspaper—which covered the Staffordshire, England town of Cannock—stated that nothing less than a flying man-thing had been seen soaring over and around the nearby Cannock Chase woods!

Before we get to the heart of the strange saga, it's worth noting that the Cannock Chase, a large area of heathland and forest, has been a veritable hotbed of high strangeness of a monstrous kind for decades. Sightings of large, black cats with glowing eyes, spectral black hounds, Bigfoot-type beasts, werewolf-style entities, and even what are described as giant snakes have been seen deep in the heart of the Cannock Chase. In that sense, the flying monster-man of the Cannock Chase was just the latest in a long line of bizarre creatures to surface in, and above, those dense and mysterious woods. And, now, with that said, back to the story.

"Five locals have contacted the *Post* after witnessing the figure travelling, seemingly unaided, over houses at around 11am on Sunday, February 8. One described it as a 'Superman' moment—a clear case of 'to Chadsmoor and beyond,'" said the newspaper.

Mike Lockley added: "But eagle-eyed Boney Hay villager Clive Wright believes those who reckon they witnessed something supernatural are talking a load of kryptonite. The 68-year-old, who spotted the flying man from the living room window of his Sunnymead Road home, believes the pilot was travelling with the aid of a jet pack—a strap-on engine made famous in the 1965 James Bond movie, *Thunderball.*

"Clive's wife, Janet, 68, and 14-year-old grandson Nicholas also witnessed the

Once again, the woods at Cannock Chase were the source of strange sightings—this time in the form of a manlike figure with wings.

> **✏️I got up to take a closer look and realized it was a flying man. I searched the sky for the plane he had baled-out of, but could see nothing."**

Chase's own rocket man. Clive said: 'To say it was strange would be an understatement. And the bottle didn't come into it because none of us drink. At first I was watching quite a number of seagulls and noticed what I thought was one in the middle moving quite slowly. I got up to take a closer look and realized it was a flying man. I searched the sky for the plane he had baled-out of, but could see nothing.'"

The *Post* additionally quoted Clive Wright as saying: "All I could see was this man travelling in a controlled, straight line, travelling from Ryecroft shops across to Gentleshaw Common. I immediately went upstairs to get my binoculars and went out on the backyard, but he was gone. Some kind of Dan Dare spaceman—that's what it looked like. The only explanation is that he was wearing a jet pack, although I was surprised he was travelling over a densely populated area."

Whether an intrepid flyer equipped with a startlingly high-tech piece of aerial gadgetry, Mothman checking out new areas, or something else entirely, the mystery of Staffordshire's flying whatever-it-was remains.

Winona's Fearsome Fliers

In September 2009, I spent approximately a week in and around the town of Winona, Wisconsin, with a team from the History Channel's popular (but now defunct) cryptozoology-themed series, *MonsterQuest*. We were there to investigate reports of large, winged beasts that in some respects sounded not unlike the infamous Mothman of Point Pleasant, West Virginia. Other reports, however, described more of a giant birdlike nature. And several even seemed like a bizarre combination of both. Being there for a week gave me a very good opportunity to dig deeply into some of the sightings, to gain the confidence and trust of the locals, and to see what I could uncover. I'm pleased to say that what I discovered amounted to a great deal.

One of the stories uncovered for the show revolved around a Winona woman who, back in the 1960s, had seen a large, winged, humanoid creature standing—legs spread wide—on a rooftop on the edge of town. Its wings were bat-like, black in color, and spread wide. Its red eyes stared malevolently at her as she watched it from the yard of her house, which was directly next door to the house atop which the man-beast stood. For a few moments, the terrified

Winona, Wisconsin, is a peaceful, bucolic village nuzzled next to the Mississippi River in the Chippewa Valley. Why were large, winged creatures spotted there, of all places?

woman and beast locked eyes, after which it took to the skies in incredibly fast fashion. Somewhat strangely, it did not take off by flapping its wings, as one might assume or expect. No, it simply spread its wings widely and rose vertically, not unlike a helicopter. The woman was baffled, however, on the matter of how it could do so without utilizing those powerful-looking wings. We had no answer for her. Interestingly, when years later the woman saw the 2001 movie, *Jeepers Creepers*, she declared to her family that the thing she saw all those years earlier was practically identical in appearance. What can be said about that except for jeepers creepers!

Then there was the story that came from the employees of a McDonald's in town. Several of the long-term staff recalled how, only a few years earlier—which would have placed things around 2005 or 2006—a truck driver had come into the McDonald's in what was clearly a shaken state. As they crowded around him, he told them of seeing what he described as a "giant eagle" soaring a certain, large peak that overlooks the town itself. In doing so, it emitted loud, screech-like sounds. Most odd of all, the truck driver said that although there were more than a few other people on the road at the time in question, and the sighting occurred during broad daylight, no one else seemed to see the massive beast. It was as if it manifested for him, and for him alone.

Also on *MonsterQuest's* agenda was a trek to—and up—the nearby huge Trempealeau Mountain. There was a very good reason for this: the mountain, which is contained within the Perrot State Park (named after a French explorer, Nicholas Perrot), has long-standing traditions of sightings of huge birds, not unlike the one reported by the afore-mentioned truck driver in the early 2000s. Many of these stories and legends originated with Native American tribes who believed the creatures to be the legendary Thunderbirds, which are an integral part of their lore and history. We searched the mountain for the best part of a day and night, and—rather intriguingly—did find some large branches that hung over the sometimes near-vertical edges of the mountain. None of us could deny they would have provided large winged things with perfect points of takeoff and to allow them to make use of the thermals to help keep their mighty forms aloft.

> **M**any of these stories and legends originated with Native American tribes who believed the creatures to be the legendary Thunderbirds....

Late at night, we even used full-volume, call-blasting equipment, playing the calls of owls and eagles, as we sought to try and entice our quarry to show itself. It was to no avail; however, the witness testimony, combined with the Native American accounts of centuries past, convinced me that Trempealeau Mountain and its surroundings was, and maybe still is, home to fearsome fliers of the unknown kind.

While in Winona, we also dug deep into a very bizarre case that occurred in La Crosse, Wisconsin, in September 2006. Perhaps not coincidentally, the witness was himself Native American: a member of the Cherokee tribe and someone who had a traumatic and terrifying experience late at night. A good friend of mine, and fellow monster hunter, Linda Godfrey, said of this case:

"Imagine driving down a dark country road, minding your own business, when suddenly a screaming, man-sized creature with bat-like wings flies at your windshield, stares at you, then swoops upwards into the night sky. It happened to a 53-year-old La Crosse man who prefers to be known only by his Cherokee name, Wohali, and the man's 25-year-old son."

Very ominously, after seeing the beast, both father and son felt nauseous and became violently sick, to the point they were forced to make a screeching stop at the side of the road.

Pretty much everyone on the *MonsterQuest* shoot came away from it impressed by the witness testimony, by the centuries-old lore, and by the additional and previously unheard-of stories that came our way. Something monstrous soars the skies of Wisconsin, and particularly so in the vicinity of Winona.

WYVERN

An approximately mile-long body of water in Clwyd, North Wales, Cynwch Lake is renowned for the story of its resident monster, a wyvern—a story that dates back centuries, although the precise date is admittedly unknown. Within ancient legend, the wyvern was very much a dragon-like animal, one to be avoided at all costs. Reptilian, and sporting large and membranous wings of a bat-like appearance, it stands on two powerful legs and has a powerful tail that it uses to sting and kill its prey, not unlike a scorpion. In some cases, and just like the dragon of old, the wyvern was said to occasionally breathe fire. All of which brings us to the monster of Cynwch Lake.

For as long as anyone could remember, the lake and its surrounding landscape made for a peaceful and relaxing environment. But that all changed when the deadly wyvern decided to swoop down on the lake and make it its home. Tranquility, there was no more. The creature was undeniably monstrous. It was described by fear-filled locals as looking like a huge, coiling and writhing monster with a humped back and an undulating neck. On its back were two wings and its feet displayed razor-sharp claws of the kind that could tear a person to pieces. Its breath was reportedly poisonous and green. In no time, the Welsh wyvern began to eat its way through the local populations of sheep, cattle, and pigs. Terrified village folk stayed behind locked doors after the sun set, which was when the beast surfaced from the waters of the lake. The time came, however, when enough was enough.

A local warlock—known as the Wizard of Ganllwyd—believed that he stood a good chance of slaying the deadly beast. As he knew, all previous attempts to kill the animal had failed—as a result of its noxious breath causing instant death to anyone and everyone exposed to it. So, the wizard had a brainwave: he decided to round up a team of archers who could shoot the wyvern from a distance. It was all to no avail. It was as if the beast had a sixth-sense about it, and whenever the bowmen were around the wyvern would stay steadfastly below the waters.

Wyverns resemble dragons, but the difference, traditionally, is that they have wings and two legs versus dragons, which have four legs and wings.

Finally, there was a breakthrough, one that proved to be the turning point in the tumultuous affair. On one particular morning, a bright and sunny one, the wyvern left the waters of the lake and slithered its way onto the shore, where it proceeded to bask under a hot sun. As luck would have it, a young shepherd boy, named Meredydd, happened to be in the area and saw the beast, asleep, as he was directing his sheep to his father's farm.

Realizing that this was, quite possibly, the one time, more than any other, that the wyvern could be killed, Meredydd raced to nearby Cymmer Abbey....

Fortunately, the monster was deep in its slumber—as was evidenced by its hideous, skin-crawling snoring, which was more like the hiss of a gigantic snake. Its body moved rhythmically, its strange form glistening like wet leather. Realizing that this was, quite possibly, the one time, more than any other, that the wyvern could be killed, Meredydd raced to nearby Cymmer Abbey and breathlessly told the monks of what he had just seen. He asked for a much revered axe that hung in the abbey, suggesting that if anything could kill the wyvern it was surely the axe, which allegedly possessed magical powers. The monks agreed and in mere minutes Meredydd was heading back to Cynwch Lake, for a battle to the death. But, of whose death, exactly, Meredydd was not so sure. Nevertheless, he was determined to do his very best to rid the area of the loathsome beast.

Fortunately, as Meredydd got back to the spot where the monster slept, he could see that it had not moved. There was no time to lose. The young shepherd boy used all his might to raise the axe over his head and then brought it down hard and fast on the neck of the sleeping monster. In a spilt second, head and neck were severed. The jaws of the severed head snapped wildly and widely, in a fashion to a headless chicken, while the neck thrashed around for a few moments before falling limp on the grass. The nightmare was over, no thanks to a powerful warlock, but all thanks to a young shepherd.

VAMPIRES AND BLOODSUCKERS

BLADENBORO VAMPIRE

On January 6, 1954, the Lumberton, North Carolina, *Robesonian* newspaper published a sensational article titled "Vampire Strikes at Woman; Police Chief Warns Parents." It began in startling style: "Worried parents kept a close eye on their children today as a strange 'vampire' beast continued to roam the countryside."

Indeed, sightings and killings had been going on since December 29 and plunged the good folk of the small town of Bladenboro, North Carolina, into states of fear and outrage. Although many eyewitnesses described the animal as looking like a black leopard, there were some who said it was more akin to a sleek-looking bear. Adding to the confusion, the tracks of the creature were said to be dog-like, rather than feline in appearance. It was a creepy conundrum, to be sure.

The most terrifying aspect of the story, however, was the claim of both the newspaper and the witnesses that the creature "sucks blood from its victims." And thus was quickly born a vampire legend. *Very* quickly. The victims were, for the most part, dogs. There was, however, one attack on a person; the unfortunate soul being Mrs. C. E. Kinlaw. Fortunately, she was not injured: the animal simply lashed out at her when its attempts to attack and kill her dogs were thwarted.

She stated afterwards: "After we first saw it, and my husband scared it away, it circled back and came running toward the porch where I was standing.

I screamed and it stopped on all fours, turned and ran off. You know, the Bible speaks of sights and wonders before the end of time. This could be one of them. The Bible's coming true, day by day."

One of those whose dogs unfortunately were killed by the creature was Johnny Vause. He said: "My dogs put up a good fight. There was blood all over the porch, big puddles of it. And there was a pool of saliva on the porch. It killed one dog at 10:30 and left it lying there. My dad wrapped the dog up in a blanket. That thing came back and got that dog and nobody's seen the dog since. At 1:30 in the morning, it came back and killed the other dog and took it off. We found it three days later in a hedgerow. The top of one of the dogs heads was torn off and its body was crushed and wet, like it had been in that thing's mouth. The other dog's lower jaw was torn off."

> **After we first saw it, and my husband scared it away, it circled back and came running toward the porch where I was standing."**

As the carnage continued, there were stories of full-grown pigs found with their skulls crushed and their limbs torn off in violent, bloody fashion. Other farm animals were discovered dead, their severed heads completely missing. The entire town was on edge. Children were kept away from school. And practically no one wanted to walk the streets of town after sunset. This was hardly surprising; a deadly, monstrous killer was in their very midst.

An unnamed witness commented: "I got two dogs, Niggy, the little black one, and Peewee, a brown one, that's bigger. Me and my wife were sitting here in the living room. We heard the dogs get awful restless. My front light was on and Larry Moore had his back light on. I glanced out the window and saw this thing. It had me plumb spellbound. It was about 20 inches high. It had a long tail, about 14 inches. The color of it was dark. It had a face exactly like a cat. Only I ain't ever seen a cat that big. It was walking around stealthy, sneaky, moving about trying to get to Niggy and Peewee. I jumped for my shotgun and loaded it and went out to shoot it, but it moved into the darkness right away and I couldn't find him again."

Such was the sheer level of hysteria that gripped Bladenboro that on January 5, 1954, more than five hundred people—all armed to the teeth with rifles and pistols—roamed the area's swamps and woods, something over which the local police took a decidedly dim view. The authorities took an even dimmer view when, on January 6, the figure was estimated to be in the region of eight hundred, and twenty-four hours later, it was in excess of one thousand.

There were sighs of relief when a bobcat was shot and killed in the area and a leopard was reportedly hit by a car. Problematic, however, was the fact that the attacks continued, something that suggested the animal was not a solitary one. Worse, there might even have been an entire pack of the dog/cat/bear drainer of blood.

Whatever the truth of the matter, by mid-January the killings were finally over. Everyone sighed with relief. The saga of the vampire-beast of Bladenboro remains a staple part of the town's history, however, to the extent that, in 2008, the History Channel's popular show *MonsterQuest* dedicated an entire episode to the legend of the bloodsucking, skull-crushing beast that provoked so much terror all those decades earlier.

BLOODSUCKING MONSTER OF THE ARECIBO OBSERVATORY

In September 1959, a groundbreaking paper—"Searching for Interstellar Communications," written by Cornell University physicists Philip Morrison and Giuseppe Cocconi—was published in the pages of *Nature*. The paper was focused upon the idea of searching for extraterrestrial life via the medium of microwaves. Approximately eight months later, one Frank Drake decided to test the theories and ideas of Morrison and Cocconi for himself.

Drake did so at the Green Bank National Radio Astronomy Observatory, located in West Virginia. Despite lasting for 150 hours, the search of the heavens for evidence of messages from alien intelligences was not successful. Drake, however, was not to be dissuaded or defeated quite so easily as that.

In October 1961 the very first conference on what became known as the Search for Extraterrestrial Intelligence (SETI) was convened at Green Bank. It was here that Drake unleashed his now famous and much championed Drake equation upon the world, an admittedly controversial method for attempting to ascertain the scale of intelligent civilizations that may exist in the known universe. Since then, SETI has been at the forefront of research into the search for alien life.

When Frank Drake elected to make it his life's work to search for alien intelligences, he went down a road that eventual-

Wandering around the perimeter of the immense Arecibo Radio Telescope in Puerto Rico, of all places, was a dark-cloaked vampire.

ly led him to the Arecibo Radio Telescope, which is located on the island of Puerto Rico, where Drake eventually rose to the position of director. As Drake noted in his 1994 book, *Is Anyone Out There?*, it was at some point early in his tenure as director—in the mid-1960s—that a guard at the observatory claimed to have seen a sinister-looking man dressed in a black cloak "walking the narrow trail around the perimeter of the bowl."

The guard was of the opinion that the dark figure was nothing less than a blood-draining—and blood-drinking—vampire. Despite his skepticism, Drake politely accepted the guard's report and agreed to at least take a look at it. Forty-eight hours later, said Drake, "I really was forced to look into it … because a cow was found dead on a nearby farm, with all the blood drained from its body. The vampire rumor had already spread through the observatory staff, and now the cow incident whipped the fears of many people into a frenzy."

CHUPACABRA

For years, controversial tales have surfaced from Puerto Rico—or to give it its correct title, the Commonwealth of Puerto Rico, an unincorporated territory of the United States—describing a killer-beast creeping around the landscape, while simultaneously plunging the population into states of deep fear and apprehension. The reason why is as simple as it is distinctly monstrous: the face of the creature is dominated by a pair of glowing red eyes, it has razor-style, claw-like appendages, vicious-looking teeth that could likely inflict some truly serious damage, sharp spikes running down its neck and spine, and even, on occasion, large membranous wings. On top of that, it thrives on blood. Puerto Rico, then, is home to a real-life vampire.

Its moniker is the Chupacabra, meaning Goat-Sucker—which is a reference to the fact that when the tales first surfaced, most of the animals slain by the bloodsucking nightmare were goats. That's right: if you're a goat, it most certainly does not pay to make Puerto Rico your home. It might not be too safe if you're human, either.

Much of the monstrous action is focused upon the Caribbean National Forest—El Yunque as it is known—which is an amazing sight to behold. Around 28,000 acres in size, and located in the rugged Sierra de Luquillo, which is approximately twenty-five miles (forty kilomters) southeast of the city of San Juan, it was named after the Indian spirit, Yuquiye, and is the only rainforest in the U.S. National Forest System.

More than one hundred billion gallons of precipitation fall each year, creating lush foliage, sparkling leaves, spectacular waterfalls, shining wet rocks, and shadowy paths that really have to be seen up close and personal to be appreciated. The Forest contains rare wildlife, too, including the Puerto Rican Parrot, the Puerto Rican boa snake, a multitude of lizards and crabs, and the famous coqui frog, so named after its strange and unique vocalizations.

One artistic interpretation of what the Chupacabra, a blood-sucking goat hunter, looks like.

As for the Chupacabra, its predations and appearance are as legendary as they are feared. And the stories coming from the locals are as notable as they are disturbing. Some years ago, while on one of my many expeditions to Puerto Rico, I had the opportunity to interview a woman named Norka, an elderly lady living in a truly beautiful home high in the El Yunque rainforest that one can only reach by successfully negotiating an infinitely complex series of treacherous roads, built perilously close to the edge of some very steep hills. Although the exact date escapes her, Norka was driving home one night in 1975 or 1976, when she was both startled and horrified by the shocking sight of a bizarre creature shambling across the road.

Norka described the animal as being approximately four feet in height, and having a monkey-like body that was covered in dark brown hair or fur, wings that were a cross between those of a bat and a bird, and glowing eyes that bulged alarmingly from a bat-style visage. Sharp claws flicked ominously in Norka's direction. She could only sit and stare as the beast then turned its back on her and rose slowly into the sky. Since then, eerily similar encounters with such vile entities have haunted the terrified populace of Puerto Rico—and continue to do so.

As evidence of this, in 2004, I traveled to Puerto Rico with fellow monster hunter Jonathan Downes of the British-based Centre for Fortean Zoology. During the course of our week-long expedition in search of the truth behind the beast, we had the opportunity to speak with numerous sources, including a rancher named Noel, who had an amazing account to relate.

Some months previously, he was awakened during the hours of darkness on one particular morning by the sound of his chickens that were practically screaming down the house. Much to his chagrin, however, Noel failed to get out of bed and waited until dawn broke to see what all the fuss had been about. He told us that he was horrified to find all of his prized birds dead. Not only were they dead, they had two small puncture wounds on their necks, and checks by a veterinarian friend determined that their bodies were missing significant amounts of blood.

But what made this particular case so intriguing and memorable was the fact that whatever had killed the chickens had first carefully and quietly opened the complex locks on each of the cages before evacuating them of blood. This suggested to Jon and me that a diabolically sophisticated degree of cunning, intelligence, and dexterity was at work. The Chupacabra, then, may be far more than just your average wild animal. So, with that in mind, precisely what is it?

Certainly, theories wildly abound with respect to the nature of the beast, with some researchers and witnesses suggesting that it is some form of giant bat. Others prefer the controversial theory that it has extraterrestrial origins. And a notably large body of people view the Chupacabra as a wholly supernatural beast, one created—or conjured up—out of devilish rite and ritual. The most bizarre idea postulated, however, is that the Chupacabra is the creation of a top secret, genetic research laboratory hidden somewhere deep within Puerto Rico's El Yunque rainforest. Whichever theory may prove to be correct—and there may be other possibilities, too—of one chilling thing there seems little doubt: Puerto Rico has a monster in its midst.

FLORIDA CHUPACABRA

Although the legendary Chupacabra—that bat-like, vampire-style beast that caused so much mayhem in the 1990s—is most associated with the island of Puerto Rico, there are indications that it, or at least something very much like it, has made its way to Florida. In April 2007, a comment was left at my *There's Something in the Woods* blog by a source using the alias of "Mack the Knife." He told a remarkable and strange story of having encountered not just one monster, but a pair of them. According to Mack:

"I find the possibility of chupacabras particularly interesting, as it is the cryptid I may have gotten a brief glance at. During the Florida drought of 2001 I lived on a farm with my ex-wife. Many of the trees were in great distress because of the heat and dry conditions. One had nearly fallen over on my house. In an effort to help cool and water them I was out spraying down their trunks during the hottest part of the day. I was using a pressure nozzle with some real power."

It was this particular activity that apparently provoked the two creatures to surface from the depths of their hidden lair, as Mack reveals:

"At one point the stream went into an open cavity and out popped two very unhappy looking creatures the like of which I have never seen before.

Rather large, especially given the size of the hole they emerged from, about three feet long, they gave much the appearance of a primate and moved like one. Their shoulder looked strong even bulky. They had flat faces, and I remember they seemed to be squinting against the light. Most curious of all, from their arms to their legs stretched a thick membrane much like a bat. They were startlingly white."

Mack continued: "It could be said that these were just a large albino bat, in and of itself that would be quite a sighting. However, the largest bat in North America is called The Western Mastiff bat which in the United States is only found in southern California, and the body of which is only a foot and a half long. Honestly, as someone who has studied wildlife science, the size of

Sometimes Chupacabras are described as being more monkey- than dog-like. A computer graphics illustrator came up with this interpretation.

the wings doesn't seem large enough to carry a creature of that size. Is that a chupacabra? I don't know. But it was something. It was not an opossum, as there was no gray in the fur, no naked tail, and it moved completely differently. The sighting didn't last long. I remember feeling bad for them actually, as though I had disturbed their privacy. I got the impression they were either siblings or a mated pair. They gave off no sense of menace or evil. Strangely, I did feel as though they were sentient somehow, different than just an animal, and their heads were quite large, with the rounded, side mounted ears of a primate. It's just strange. I looked for them after that, but never saw them again."

There the story ends. To this day, the mystery of Mack's creepy critters remains exactly that—a mystery. Also downright mysterious is this: if the Chupacabra has indeed managed to leave the island of Puerto Rico behind it and make its way to the mainland United States, how on Earth did it achieve such a thing? And how many other countries might it now inhabit as well? They are, without a doubt, sobering and worrying questions.

MOCA VAMPIRE

Since 1995, Puerto Rico has been the domain of a deadly, bloodsucking creature that has infamously become known as the Chupacabra. Long before the now-legendary beast was on anyone's radar, however, there was another vampire-like monster roaming around on the island. It was known as the Moca Vampire—its name taken from the municipality of Moca, which can be found in the northwest of the island, and which is home to around 40,000 people. Unlike the Chupacabra—sightings of which continue to this very day—the "Vampiro de Moca," as it was referred to in Puerto Rico—was a monster of a definitively "here one minute and gone the next" kind.

The controversy all began in late February 1975. That was when the population of Moca was plunged into a collective state of fear, and it was hardly surprising. Numerous ranchers reported how their farm animals were being violently slaughtered under cover of darkness and systematically drained of massive amounts of blood. The first area targeted was the Barrio Rocha region, where several goats, at least four pigs, numerous chickens, and more than a dozen cows were all found dead, with puncture marks on their bodies, deep claw-like wounds on their skin, and all missing one vital ingredient: blood. Villagers and farmers were as outraged as they were terrified. Local authorities, and chiefly the police, tried to diffuse the controversy by attributing the attacks to nothing stranger than the work of packs of wild dogs—a theory that, almost inevitably, was received with nothing but scorn, skepticism, and disdain.

> **N**umerous ranchers reported how their farm animals were being violently slaughtered under cover of darkness and systematically drained of massive amounts of blood.

By the end of the first week in March 1975, the death count was close to three dozen. It was in this same week that an important development was made: the bloodsucking culprit was finally seen, up close and personal, so to speak. The witness was a woman named Maria Acevedo, who caught sight of a monstrously sized, screaming, and screeching winged beast that landed atop her home and clambered about her zinc roof, making an almighty racket in the process. And it was clearly no normal bird: around four to five feet in height, it was described as being similar in appearance to a pterodactyl, a presumed-extinct, flying reptile of the Jurassic era. Whatever the true nature of the monster, it quickly took to the skies and vanished into the starry darkness.

Less than forty-eight hours later, a farmer named Cecilio Hernandez contacted the police after more than thirty of his chickens were killed in a fashion that was quickly becoming attributed to the predations of the Moca Vampire. It was at the same time that Hernandez's story was widely being reported in Puerto Rico that a potential answer to the puzzle was uncovered: two huge snakes were killed in Moca, just before they were about to attack a cow belonging to a rancher named Luis Torres. Of course, this didn't explain the winged monster that Maria Acevedo reported only days earlier. And, it didn't resolve the many and varied additional killings that continued to plague the people of Moca. In addition, while snakes will typically take down and devour—whole, no less—significantly-sized animals, they will not, and cannot, suck blood in either small or large proportions. In other words, while the snake theory might have been a small component of the saga, it most certainly didn't explain everything.

On March 18, 1975, the monster struck again. On this occasion, the victims were a pair of goats owned by Hector Vega, of Moca's Barrio Pueblo. Once again, the culprit had struck in its typical fashion of draining the goats of their blood—and, in this case, of *all* the blood. The creature was not done with Vega, however. On the following night no fewer than seventeen animals were attacked, of which ten were killed, due to deep, penetrating wounds, trauma, and massive blood loss. Five days later, a pig was found dead by farmer Felix Badillo. Blood was removed in significant amounts, and there was a hole in the head of the animal, which gave every appearance of something powerful being violently thrust into the skull. On top of that, one of the pig's ears was missing—in a fashion that, rather intriguingly, was attributed to a surgical procedure. No wonder the people of Moca were as puzzled as they were alarmed.

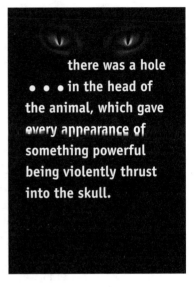

there was a hole • • • in the head of the animal, which gave every appearance of something powerful being violently thrust into the skull.

Forty-eight hours later came the most astonishing development: Juan Muniz was attacked by a huge, bird-like animal that swooped down upon him from above, as he walked through Barrio Pulido. He struggled and fought as the winged nightmare did its very best to force Muniz to the ground. In his panicked, adrenalized state, Muniz managed to escape and alert the authorities.

Then, as April began, the Moca Vampire began to expand its hunting ground: attacks began to be reported all across the island, with farm animals again drained of blood, of rumors of attacks on people, and even of a police coverup of the facts to prevent a public panic exploding. The attacks continued into May—and then into June, too. By this time, hundreds of animals were said to have fallen victim to the blood-drinking monster, and with barely an answer to the problem in sight. As it transpired, however, matters came to a sudden, inexplicable halt. Shortly before the end of June, the sightings, encounters, and attacks were no more.

Whatever the true nature of the Moca Vampire, it vanished as quickly as it originally surfaced. Such was the terror it provoked, however, that the creature is still discussed, in hushed tones, in Moca to this very day.

RHAYADER BLOODSUCKER

Rhayader is the oldest town in mid-Wales. Its origins date back more than five thousand years, and specifically to Neolithic times. Rhayader's long legacy is also evidenced by the fact that, in 1899, a large collection of gold jewelry was found buried on the town's Gwastedyn Hill. Archaeologists were able to date the priceless artifacts to the fifth century and link them to a princess named Rowena. She was the daughter of a local, powerful warlord, Hengest, and the wife of a much-feared character known as High King Vortigen. Neither Hengest nor Vortigen were able to instill as much fear in the people of Rhayader as did a deadly and mysterious beast that surfaced in 1988.

It was between September and December 1988 that the town was hit by a spate of mysterious deaths. Not, thankfully, of people, but of sheep. Although several farms were targeted by the stealthy predator—and always under cover of darkness—it was the Bodalog Farm, owned by the Pugh family that suffered most of all. Over the course of several weeks, they lost close to forty sheep to the deadly intruder. Oddest of all: the sheep were not eaten, whether in whole or in part. The only evidence of the attacks were deep, penetrating bites to the sternum.

That was when the conspiracy theories began to take hold. There were claims of a local police coverup. The stories grew and grew, amid claims that Men in Black-style characters from "the government" were roaming around town, doing their utmost to silence those with knowledge of the attacks. Supposedly, there was good reason why the MIB wanted to stifle all the talk of the deaths: the sheep had been drained of blood, vampire-style. Inevitably, and despite the best efforts of the MIB, the British media soon latched onto the story and it made the headlines across some of the nation's major daily newspapers.

As the death rate increased, so did the wild rumors: there was talk of a large, black cat in the area—such as a black leopard. Of course, such animals are not native to the United Kingdom, something that only added to the mystery. Plus, no one actually saw the big cat, if that is really what it

The tranquil Welsh village of Rhayader by the River Wye was plagued by a bloody terror.

was. It was simply a theory—but, undeniably, one that provoked a great deal of food for thought in the town's pubs on weekend nights. With concern growing, a decision was made to use foxhounds to try and chase the monster in the early hours. And this is when things became decidedly intriguing—and sinister, too.

The dogs soon picked up on the scent—their wild behavior made that very clear. They picked up on something else, too—something that had previously been overlooked. In certain parts of the fields where the sheep had been killed, corridors of flattened ground were uncovered. They gave every indication of something not walking along the fields, but *slithering* along them. In mere moments, all the talk of big cats was gone. In their place were giant snakes. On top of that, and as the dogs continued to chase down the scent, they were led to the banks of the 134-mile-long (216-kilometer) River Wye, the fifth longest river in the U.K. The conclusion was all but inevitable: some form of large, unknown water beast was—under cover of the night—surfacing out of the depths of the river, stealthily crossing the fields, and feeding on the blood of the unfortunate sheep.

> some form of • • • large, unknown water beast was ... surfacing out of the depths of the river, stealthily crossing the fields, and feeding on the blood of the unfortunate sheep.

But what could the creature have been? Certainly, there are no large snakes roaming around the U.K. Yet, the flattened areas of field suggested a beast somewhere around twelve to fifteen feet long had indeed been slithering around. Richard Freeman, of the England-based Centre for Fortean Zoology, took a lot of interest in the case when it surfaced. He said of the snake theory:

"Britain's only venomous snake, the adder, *Vipera berus*, is far too small to have killed the sheep. This case begs many odd questions: why would an animal go to all the trouble of wasting venom and energy killing so many sheep, then not eat any? If it was a large, exotic, venomous snake that had escaped from captivity, how did it cope with October in Wales?"

Freeman's question was—and still is—an important one, as snakes require warm climates in which to survive and thrive. There is nothing warm about mid-Wales in October! Perhaps aware that it was being hunted down, the creature ceased its violent killing spree in early December 1988, and Rhayader finally returned to normality and there were collective sighs of relief all around town. Decades later, the mystery of what that water-borne monstrosity was remains precisely that: a mystery.

There is, however, one last thing to muse upon: in 1912, Ella Leather penned a book titled *The Folk-Lore of Herefordshire*. It told of how, centuries ago, people local to the River Wye believed that the river was home to something terrifying that required a human sacrifice once a year, as a form of appeasement and to ensure that the beast did not launch an all-out, murderous rampage around the area. Based on what happened in Rhayader in 1988, perhaps the old legends had a basis in terrifying, savage fact.

RUSSIAN CHUPACABRA

While it is certainly the case that the vast majority of all Chupacabra reports originate within Puerto Rico, Mexico, the United States, and parts of South America, less well known is the fact that the beast has also surfaced in Russia. Russia's *Pravda* was hot on the trail of the chupacabra in April 2006. In an eye-opening article the Russian people were told:

"The worries began at the end of March 2005 not far from the regional center of Saraktash. On the Sapreka farm two farming families suddenly lost 32 turkeys. The bodies of the birds, found in the morning, had been completely drained of blood. None of the farmers either saw or heard the beast that killed them. Then in the village of Gavrilovka sheep fell victim to the nighttime vampire. The unknown animal was also in the hamlets of Vozdvizhenka and Shishma. In the course of the night 3–4 sheep or goats perished. All together the losses in the region amounted to 30 small horned cattle."

One eyewitness, a rancher by the name of Erbulat Isbasov, caught sight of the monster: "I heard the sheep start to bleat loudly. I run up to them and see a black shadow. It looked like an enormous dog that had stood up on its hind legs. And jumped like a kangaroo. The beast sensed my presence and ran away. It squeezed through an opening in the panels of the fence."

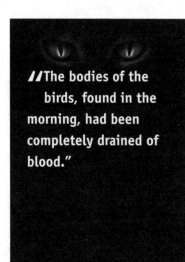

// The bodies of the birds, found in the morning, had been completely drained of blood."

Moving on, in the summer of 2011, the *Moscow News* told its readers the following: "A bloodsucking creature is preying upon goats near Novosibirsk. As rational explanations run thin on the ground, the specter of the so-called chupacabra raises its demon head. Horrified farmers and smallholders are confronted by the drained corpses of their livestock in the morning, bloodless and bearing puncture marks to the neck but otherwise largely intact. But local cops are reluctant to record apparent vampire attacks, as they await official recertification, leaving the locals up in arms."

One year later, the Ukraine was hit by the Goat-Sucker. Or, at least, that's what some thought the hair-free canine was. "The animal doesn't look like a fox or a wolf, or a raccoon," said a representative of the district veterinary service in Mikhailovskoe. He told the media: "It cannot even be a marten. I have never seen such animal before. But, judging by the fangs, I can definitely say that it is a predator."

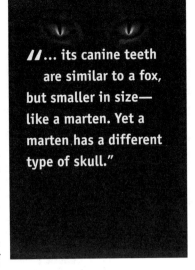

//... its canine teeth are similar to a fox, but smaller in size— like a marten. Yet a marten has a different type of skull."

The British *Daily Mail* newspaper highlighted the affair and said: "It could be a 'mutant' fox poisoned by radiation, while another theory was that it may be a hybrid originating from a Soviet plant conducting tests on animals relating to chemical or biological weapons development. 'A creature we were not supposed to see has escaped from a secret defense lab,' said one comment."

"I cannot identify what kind of animal it is," admitted Alexander Korotya, of the Zoological Museum of Zaporozhye National University, adding: "For example, its canine teeth are similar to a fox, but smaller in size—like a marten. Yet a marten has a different type of skull. If to compare with an otter's head, then the ears are too small. It has a wide nose and a stretched muzzle. My opinion is that it's most likely a hybrid animal or a mutant."

In 2014, Beloomut, Russia, had a deadly visitor. Yep, you know the one. Farm animals were killed. Blood was—*allegedly*, at least—drained from their corpses. People were living in fear. Meanwhile, the world of officialdom was having none of it: "There are no fairytale creatures in the Lukhovitsky district of the Moscow Region," said the Agriculture Ministry. End of story. But the end of the chupacabra in Russia? Time will tell.

SLAUGHTERER AT THE ZOO

For many people, the worlds of cryptozoology and high-level conspiracy make for strange and rarely connected bedfellows. But there are exceptions. And sometimes those exceptions are of a distinctly profound nature, as will now be demonstrated. On the afternoon of a spring day in 1992, Jon Downes, the director of the British-based Centre for Fortean Zoology and a renowned seeker of unknown animals, was deep in conversation with a police officer from Middlemoor Police Station in the English city of Exeter. The subject of the conversation was the so-called "big cat" sightings that have been reported throughout the British counties of Devon and Cornwall for decades.

//... very strange deaths had occurred at the zoo, and wallabies, swans, and geese had been beheaded."

Was Downes aware, the officer inquired, that there had occurred at nearby Newquay Zoo in the late 1970s a series of grisly mutilations of animals under extremely strange circumstances? Downes replied that, no, he was not. Fortunately, however, the officer was able to put Downes in touch with the one man in a position to discuss the facts: the head keeper at the zoo at the time in question. And here's where things began to get distinctly odd. Downes wasted no time in tracking the man down. Elderly and in failing health, he confirmed to Downes the basics of the story: very strange deaths had occurred at the zoo, and wallabies, swans, and geese had been beheaded. But more significantly, their corpses had been totally drained of blood....

"There was no blood left in the animals at all," Downes was informed by the keeper, who added, "I had the area UFO compositor—or whatever he called himself—come down, and the suggestion was that it was beings from outer space who came down and needed the blood—or whatever else it was that they drew out of those animals—to survive. It never developed any further than that. I believe that he got a radiation count in the wallaby paddock at that time."

Was the culprit ever located? "No," was the reply from Downes's source, who added: "But the same thing was happening all over the world. I can tell you that." Downes advised me that the zookeeper was not an adherent of the extraterrestrial hypothesis; rather, he suspected black magic and a witch coven. As he conceded, however, there was also talk of "big cats" in the area—a theory later bolstered by the discovery of large, tell-tale paw-prints.

At that stage the conversation was terminated. Downes, however, felt that the man was keeping something back and resolved to address the matter further at a later date. Regrettably, he did not get the chance. Forty-eight hours later, the man was dead. Although the death seems to have only been as a result of the man's failing health, to this day Downes finds this whole saga particularly strange. But more was to follow.

Two years later, in 1994, Downes received—under somewhat conspiratorial circumstances—a package of documents that consisted of, amongst other things, a police file on the animal killings at Newquay Zoo in 1978. The first such police report of October 2, 1978, stated: "Over the past months a number of incidents have occurred at the Newquay Zoological Gardens at Trenance Gardens, Newquay. These incidents were thought at first to be unconnected and possibly due to the incursion of a marauding animal, but this has now been discounted."

Perhaps most bizarre of all, however, was a further report concerning "something" that had under cover of darkness "attempted to gain entrance to the lion's cage!" It hardly needs to be stressed that only someone very fool-hardy or near-indestructible would dare venture into the cage of a lion! And yet, incredibly, something did. Checks outside of the cage, the report states, revealed prints that were thought to possibly be those of a large cat of some type; however, that the modus operandi behind the killings suggested a degree of sophisticated intelligence is something that leaves this particular aspect of the affair somewhat murky.

> **//The method of killing would indicate that the culprit is an extremely strong 'person' or that some form of drug was used to pacify the animals."**

And most significant of all, the files state: "The method of killing would indicate that the culprit is an extremely strong 'person' or that some form of drug was used to pacify the animals. If tissue samples were available, then the drug, if used, could be detected."

More than twenty years on, the mysterious animal deaths at Newquay Zoo remain just that—a mystery. However, Jon Downes has also been given access to additional papers that ask a number of interesting and perhaps highly relevant questions to the whole affair, including: "Any mysterious disappearances over the relevant period? Have the local population reported any loss of livestock?" Notably, the person posing the question also raised the issue of an abandoned, old mine near the zoo and speculated as to whether it was serving as a "possible refuge" for … well, what?

Perhaps, one day, we'll know what lurked—and may still lurk—in that old mine.

Monsters of Magic and Mind

DANCING DEVIL

My good friend and fellow monster hunter Ken Gerhard shares with us a story he uncovered from the 1970s that is fascinating and creepy, and demonstrates that monsters can turn up in the strangest and most unforeseen of places. Ken says:

"One of my favorite San Antonio [Texas]-based sagas involves a very dubious character, referred to locally as the Dancing Devil. According to many eyewitnesses, as well as newspaper articles from the time, a dashing, handsome, young man dressed in white entered the El Camaroncito Night Club on Old Highway 90 one night, around Halloween 1975. According to all those who were present, the man was a fabulous dancer and wooed many of the ladies who were in attendance that evening.

"As the night progressed, however, things took a very horrific turn when one of the man's dancing partners happened to glance down at his feet. The woman screamed out in terror, broke free of the man's grip and immediately began pointing downward. It was then, amidst a flurry of gasps and shrieks that the patrons noticed the man's shoes had transformed into clawed chicken's feet!

"In some versions of the story, his feet had become goat's hooves. Either way, it was certainly a bad sign, to be sure, as the attendees were now quite sure they were in the presence of none other than the Devil himself. After an

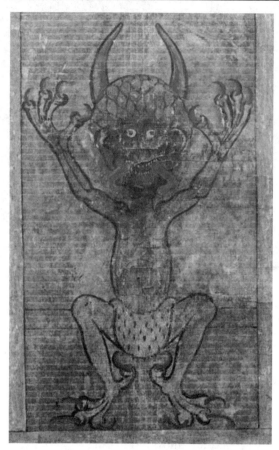

One often thinks of a devil having hooves, but many depictions of Lucifer going back centuries show him with chicken-like claws.

uncomfortable silence, the man dashed, or perhaps waddled or galloped, towards the men's room, where he vanished out of an open window. In his wake remained a cloud of smoke, which was accompanied by a strong, sulfuric smell—surely a classic calling card of the horned and fork-tailed dweller of the underworld."

DOVER DEMON

Some monsters, like Bigfoot, the Chupacabra, the Yeti, and Ogopogo, are seen time and again and across decades—sometimes even centuries. There are, however, a few bizarre beasts that put in very brief appearances for startled eyewitnesses, and soon vanish, never to be seen again. Perhaps there is no better example of the latter than what has become known as the Dover Demon.

It was around 10:30 P.M. on the night of April 21, 1977, when all hell broke loose. William Bartlett, then seventeen, was driving along Farm Street, in Dover, Massachusetts, when he spotted something both amazing and terrifying sitting on a wall. It was nothing less than a small, almost goblin-like beast of about three and a half feet in height that had huge, glowing eyes and "tendrils" for fingers. Very curiously, it lacked ears, a nose, and a mouth. As for its head, it was described as being "melon"-like and extremely pale.

Given that Bartlett later said, "It scared me to death," it's hardly surprising that he didn't hang around to get a good look at it. Fortunately for Bartlett, however, his testimony didn't stand alone. What was almost certainly the same creature was also seen on the same night by a local boy, John Baxter. It was after midnight when Baxter left his girlfriend's house and made his way home, on foot. As he did so, Baxter caught sight in the darkness of a small, humanoid figure heading in his direction. Evidently, the creature hadn't notice Baxter—at least, until the last moment, when it suddenly bounded off into the nearby woods. Baxter decided to give chase, across a field, through the dark woods, and finally to a gully, where he took a break. It was then that Baxter saw the animal, leaning against a tree. He said:

"As I was looking really close there I could see the eyes; it was looking at me. I just stared at it for another few minutes and then I just got all these thoughts that maybe it was something really strange. 'Cause, you know, nothing ever happened to me like this before, so I didn't know what to think. So I finally got the thought that maybe it wasn't as safe as it looked, 'cause the way it was staring at me it just seemed like it was—I don't know. I got all these feelings that it was thinking to itself, or waiting to spring, or whatever, you know? And so I backed up the bank kind of fast, and my heart started beating really fast!"

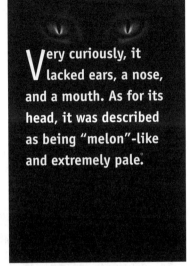

Very curiously, it lacked ears, a nose, and a mouth. As for its head, it was described as being "melon"-like and extremely pale.

The next evening, the Dover Demon scared the life out of Abby Brabham and Will Taintor, who saw it near a bridge on Springdale Avenue. Brabham recalled: "As I looked at it, it kind of looked for a minute like an ape. And then I looked at the head and the head was very big and it was a very weird head. It had bright green eyes and the eyes just glowed like, they were just looking exactly at me."

And, then, it was gone. The town of Dover, only about fifteen miles from the city of Boston, had been visited by a monster—but one that didn't hang around and never returned. Given that all three witnesses were teenagers, skeptical folk suggested the whole thing was nothing stranger than a prank perpetrated by, or on, the trio. To his credit, however, Police Chief Carl Sheridan came to the defense of Bartlett, calling him an "outstanding artist and a reliable witness." So, what was the now-legendary Dover Demon? If not the result of a prank, what could it have been?

Loren Coleman, one of the world's leading cryptozoologists, gave his opinion on the mystery of the Dover Demon:

"The short story (no pun intended) is that over a two day period in April 1977, four people saw a small, 4 foot tall orange sharkskin creature (somewhat like Golem in *Lord of the Rings*) in three separate sightings, in Dover, Massachusetts, a rural location near Boston. The case goes down as unexplainable. I don't know the answer to 'what really happened' as all the eyewitnesses checked out, and were found to be credible by law enforcement and other people in Dover."

There are, however, down-to-earth explanations, even if they sound unlikely. The "Iron Skeptic" says: "Some theorized that the creature was, in fact, a fox that had contracted a disease of some sort that caused severe swelling and bloating. Others have theorized that the creature was in fact a baby moose. Martin Kottmeyer went to great lengths explaining why he thought this, and Loren Coleman went to equally great lengths explaining why this wasn't true. My main problem with this theory was that it was reported to be standing on two legs by Baxter; however, it's not unreasonable to theorize that if it were indeed a moose, it was feeding from the upper parts of the tree, and that it was just leaning on it with its two front legs."

In all likelihood, we will never know the true nature of the Dover Demon. All we can say for sure is that whatever it was, it left a deep impression on the people of that little town—and decades later, still does.

EL CUCUY

Within the Lone Star State, there is a long tradition of a diabolical, goblin-like monster known as El Cucuy. It is most recognizable by its penetrating and evil-looking eyes, which glow a devilish, malevolent red. Typically, they lurk in closets and beneath the beds of children. But, does that mean they are nothing more than bogey-man type tales designed to excite and frighten kids? Maybe not. Very often, there is some degree of truth behind a legend, a very strange truth. And that's certainly the case when it comes to El Cucuy.

The 1799 painting *Que viene el coco* ("Here Comes the Bogey-Man") by Francisco Goya portrays a version of the goblin El Cucuy.

Just a few years ago, a resident of San Benito told researcher Guadalupe Cantu of his encounter with a small, hair-covered humanoid creature that he spotted crawling out of a dumpster in town, late one night. Perhaps wisely, the man chose not to hang around and confront the mini-monster.

Then, in 2006, what sounds very much like a winged version of El Cucuy popped up in the Texas town of Dickens, which is situated east of the city of Lubbock. The location was Highway 70, at a place known as Turkey Crossing. The witness in question was too traumatized to share the details outside of her family. However, the young woman's mother prepared a statement on her behalf, which, in part, read as follows:

"She noticed that there was something sitting on a wide gate post. She did not know what it was so she slowed down to look. As she got closer, she saw a flesh-colored animal, about three feet tall, crouched on top of the post. It had a round head like an owl and a round, sloped face with a tiny round nose, like a short snout and a slit for a mouth. It had eyes that looked like they were slanted down.

"The creature was sitting with its feet together and its knees out, in a bow-legged squat. It had feet like a bird with a set of toes or talons in the back and another set in the front. It had short arms with a flap of triangular skin on the backsides. There was something pointed at the tips of the skin flaps that looked like a bat thumb or claw. It looked like it had paws with four digits on each one and the arms were partly hidden underneath a flap of skin on each side. The skin or short fur was a tan or peach color and it was wrinkled in places like a baby bat."

Monster hunter Ken Gerhard, who has studied this particularly weird case, relates what happened next: "As the eyewitness attempted to pass, the hideous goblin lurched off its perch and landed on the road, causing her to swerve. The little monstrosity crouched for a moment and then started to run on two legs while the terrified girl sped off, apparently in tears as she drove home."

FLYING DEMON

Sometimes a monster is described as being so incredibly strange that one can do very little other than relate the facts—chiefly because the available facts are so strange and near-unfathomable, in terms of what they might represent. A perfect example of just such a uniquely weird case dates back to the 1950s. In terms of the location, all we know for sure is that it was somewhere in the vicinity of Falls City, Richardson County, Nebraska. As for the witness, we know him only as "John Hanks," an admitted pseudonym that the man in question chose to use to protect his real identity. When you read the details of his experience, you will undoubtedly realize why the man was determined to protect his real name from prying, inquiring eyes. It's a case that was carefully investigated by one of the world's foremost experts on bizarre, flying beasts, Ken Gerhard. Even Gerhard, for all the cases of flying anomalies he has investigated, finds the entire affair baffling—which is saying something!

Falls City, Nebraska, site of a creepy flying anomaly.

It was late one night, at some point in the latter part of 1956, said Hanks, when he came face to face with a true giant, a creature in excess of nine feet in height, humanoid in shape, and most certainly not a member of the human race. That much, at least, we can ascertain from Hanks's description. Ken Gerhard says, with a great deal of justification, that Hanks's description of the creature sounds reminiscent of something out of an H. P. Lovecraft story."

Gerhard is not wrong in suggesting that Hanks's monster would have found itself right at home in the pages of one of the legendary horror maestro's novels. In fact, Gerhard is right on target. Hanks's nightmarish thing had a pair of fifteen-foot-wide wings that, rather oddly, appeared to be made of bright, shining aluminum! Not only that, the wings appeared to be strapped to the creatures; almost grafted onto its body in definitive cyborg-style. If that was not nearly strange enough, the robot-birdman displayed numerous, multi-colored lights that spanned the entire undersides of both wings. Whether for illumination, display, or something else, Hanks didn't know. Even stranger still, if such a thing is possible, the winged man-thing had a "panel" attached to its chest that, Hanks assumed, was some kind of control mechanism that allowed the creature to land, take off, and soar the heavens above.

Some, having read the above, might consider and conclude this case to have been nothing stranger than one involving a brilliant, eccentric inventor who had managed to create a portable contraption to allow people to take to the skies in amazing, novel, and previously unheard of fashion. Of course, the height of the figure—around nine feet—effectively rules out such a possibility from the outset, but it would be a scenario at least worth considering. Except for one critical component: the creature's terrifying, unforgettable face.

Described by the witness as being nothing less than "demonic" in appearance, it had skin that was akin to weathered, battered, brown leather. Its eyes were large, staring, evil-looking, and "watery." The only noise it ever made was a malevolent hissing sound that, hardly surprisingly, sent chills throughout Hanks's entire body. Whatever the true nature of the monster that stood before Hanks, it didn't hang around. In mere moments it was airborne, and within a few more seconds it was lost from view, never again to return and plague the people of Falls City in general and the pseudonymous John Hanks in particular. Much to his eternal relief, one strongly suspects.

> Described by the witness as being nothing less than "demonic" in appearance, it had skin that was akin to weathered, battered, brown leather.

GLASTONBURY GARGOYLE

Colin Perks—an Englishman who died prematurely from a heart attack while walking around the fence line of Stonehenge in 2009—was, for years, possessed by a definitive obsession. As a child, Perks became fascinated by the legends pertaining to one of the most well-known and cherished figures of British folklore: King Arthur. For Perks, however, Arthur was far more than mere myth. Perks, like so many other students of Arthurian lore, came to believe that the stories of King Arthur were based upon the exploits and battles of a very real ruler of that name. This Arthur held sway over significant portions of ancient Britain from the latter part of the fifth century to the early part of the sixth. He, and his fearless soldiers, bravely fought off invading hordes of Germanic Saxons and, as a result, left major marks upon British history and mythology.

By the time Perks reached his thirties, he was the proud possessor of a huge library on all things of a King Arthur-themed nature. His research, by now, was not just focused on the past, however. Rather, Perks, following clues that he believed were hidden in a series of complex codes and ciphers that had been provided to him by a fellow Arthur-enthusiast in 1978, was a man on a mission to find the final resting place of King Arthur. The location, Perks concluded, was somewhere in the vicinity of the old English town of Glastonbury.

Late one evening in September 2000, after a day and evening spent digging in the woods, Perks received a very weird, and somewhat disturbing, phone call. It was from a woman who made it very clear that she wanted to discuss with Perks his studies of an Arthurian nature. She also made it clear she would not take "no" for an answer.

Several nights later, and at the arranged time of 7:00 P.M., there was a knock at the door. Perks took a deep breath and opened it. He was confronted by what can only be described as a Woman in Black. Before him stood a beautiful woman, thirty-five to forty years of age. She was dressed in a smart and expensive-looking outfit, had a long and full-bodied head of black hair, and

The pale, beautiful woman warned Perks to stop searching for King Arthur's tomb, for it guarded a door that kept monsters from entering our world.

the palest and smoothest skin. For a moment there was silence. Perks simply stared, feeling various parts captivated, intimidated, and downright frightened. Although the woman's face appeared utterly emotionless, Perks detected a hard-to-define air of hostility, and perhaps even hatred, of him. This was hardly a good start to the evening. And it proceeded to get even worse.

Wasting no time, Sarah Key got straight to the point and informed Perks that she, and what she described as her "colleagues," had been carefully watching him for years. She added, in no uncertain terms, that the purpose of her visit was to request that Perks cease his research. A suddenly defensive Perks loudly responded that there was no way he would ever stop his work to find King Arthur's burial site. On top of that he scoffed at the very idea that shadowy figures were watching his every move, both in Glastonbury and in the heart of the old woods. Or, it's more correct to say he scoffed until Sarah Key reeled off fact upon fact about where Perks was on specific days and nights, even down to which local pubs he visited for dinner and a pint of Guinness after his nightly work in the woods was over. That's when the scoffing came to a shuddering halt.

As Colin Perks sat silently, Sarah Key continued that Arthur's grave—or his "chamber," as she specifically described it—was no ordinary resting place. Rather, it was built atop a paranormal gateway, a portal, to other dimensions where there dwelled hideous and terrible beasts of the kind that H. P. Lovecraft would have been forever proud. The chamber had been constructed as a means to prevent the foul things of this strange realm from entering our world. Perks's dabbling and digging, Key told him, might have been innocent and earnest, but he was playing with definitive fire that could result in catastrophe and carnage if the magical "gateway" was opened.

Sarah Key's tone then became downright menacing and her face became grim in the extreme. She explained that if Perks did not give up his quest, he would receive yet another visit. From whom, or what, was not made entirely clear, but Perks knew it was destined to be nothing positive or friendly.

It was roughly two months later, and late at night, when Perks had a truly terrifying encounter. He was driving back to Glastonbury from the city of Bath—which, like Glastonbury, is also located in the English county of Somerset. On one piece of road that lacked illumination and which was curiously free of any other traffic, a bizarre figure suddenly materialized in the road ahead. Luckily, as the road was a small and winding one, Perks's speed was barely twenty-five miles per hour, which gave him time to quickly apply the brakes. In front of him was what can only be described as the closest thing one could imagine to a gargoyle. That's to say, a tall, man-like figure sporting nothing less than a large pair of bat-style wings. A pair of blazing red eyes penetrated Perks's very soul. Hysterical with fear, Perks hit the accelerator pedal and the creature vanished before his eyes before impact could occur. Matters weren't quite over, however.

One week later, and not long after the witching hour, Perks was awakened from his sleep by the horrific sight of the gargoyle looming menacingly over his bed. Paralyzed with fear, and with the creature gripping his wrists tightly, Perks could only stare in utter shock as the beast delivered a telepathic-style message to stay away from the woods, and to cease looking for the chamber of King Arthur. An instant later, the monstrous form was gone. Perks wondered for a few seconds if it had all been a horrific nightmare. In his heart of hearts, however, he knew it wasn't. In fact, Perks ultimately came to believe that Sarah Key—Perks's very own Woman in Black—and the gargoyle were not just interconnected. Rather, he concluded that Key was a hideous and

> **A** pair of blazing red eyes penetrated Perks's very soul. Hysterical with fear, Perks hit the accelerator pedal and the creature vanished before his eyes....

supernatural shape-shifter, one that could take on any form it desired, including that of something akin to a gargoyle.

Colin Perks did not—despite the traumatic nature of the encounters with the gargoyle—give up his research. Nevertheless, he remained a shell of his former self for the rest of his days, living on his nerves and fearing that the gargoyle lurked around every darkened corner.

GWRACH Y RHIBYN

Of the many and varied monstrous supernatural beasts of Wales, certainly one of the most fear-inducing, was the Gwrach y Rhibyn. The exploits and nature of this nightmarish thing were expertly chronicled back in the nineteenth century by a man named Wirt Sykes who, at the time, was the American consul for Wales. While the story of the Gwrach y Rhibyn is told in Sykes's 1880 book *British Goblins*, it is to Sykes's original notes we turn our attention. They tell a story that is creepy, horrific, and unforgettable:

"A frightful figure among Welsh apparitions is the Gwrach y Rhibyn, whose crowning distinction is its prodigious ugliness. The feminine pronoun is generally used in speaking of this goblin, which unlike the majority of its kind, is supposed to be a female. A Welsh saying, regarding one of her sex who is the reverse of lovely, is, 'Y mae mor salw a Gwrach y Rhibyn.' (She is as ugly as the Gwrach y Rhibyn.)

//A Welsh saying ... is, 'Y mae mor salw a Gwrach y Rhibyn. (She is as ugly as the Gwrach y Rhibyn.)"

"The specter is a hideous being with disheveled hair, long black teeth, long, lank, withered arms, leathern wings, and a cadaverous appearance. In the stillness of night it comes and flaps its wings against the window, uttering at the same time a blood-curdling howl, and calling by name on the person who is to die, in a lengthened dying tone, as thus: 'Da-a-a-vy!' 'De-i-i-o-o-o ba-a-a-ch!' The effect of its shriek or howl is indescribably terrific, and its sight blasting to the eyes of the beholder. It is always an omen of death, though its warning cry is heard under varying circumstances; sometimes it appears in the mist on the mountain side, or at cross-roads, or by a piece of water which it splashes with its hands.

"The gender of apparitions is no doubt as a rule the neuter, but the Gwrach y Rhibyn defies all rules by being a female which at times sees fit to be a male. In its female character it has a trick of crying at intervals, in a most doleful tone, 'Oh! oh! fy ngwr, fy ngwr!' (my husband! my husband!). But when it chooses to be a male, this cry is changed to 'Fy ngwraig! fy ngwraig!' (my wife! my wife!) or 'Fy mlentyn, fy mlentyn bach!' (my child, my little child!). There is a frightful story of a dissipated peasant who met this goblin on the road one night, and thought it was a living woman; he therefore made wicked and improper overtures to it, with the result of having his soul nearly frightened out of his body in the horror of discovering his mistake. As he emphatically exclaimed, 'Och, Dduw! it was the Gwrach y Rhibyn, and not a woman at all.'

"The Gwrach y Rhibyn recently appeared, according to an account given me by a person who claimed to have seen it, at Llandaff. Surely, no more probable site for the appearance of a specter so ancient of lineage could be found, than that ancient cathedral city where some say was the earliest Christian fane in Great Britain, and which was certainly the seat of the earliest Christian bishopric.

"My narrator was a respectable-looking man of the peasant-farmer class, whom I met in one of my walks near Cardiff, in the summer of 1878. 'It was at Llandaff,' he said to me, 'on the fourteenth of last November, when I was on a visit to an old friend, that I saw and heard the Gwrach y Rhibyn. I was sleeping in my bed, and was woke at midnight by a frightful screeching and a shaking of my window. It was a loud and clear screech, and the shaking of the window was very plain, but it seemed to go by like the wind. I was not so much frightened, sir, as you may think; excited I was—that's the word—excited; and I jumped out of bed and rushed to the window and flung it open.

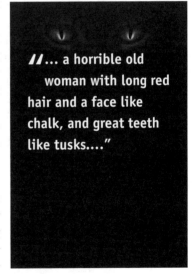

//... a horrible old woman with long red hair and a face like chalk, and great teeth like tusks...."

"Then I saw the Gwrach y Rhibyn, saw her plainly, sir, a horrible old woman with long red hair and a face like chalk, and great teeth like tusks, looking back over her shoulder at me as she went through the air with a long black gown trailing along the ground below her arms, for body I could make out none. She gave another unearthly screech while I looked at her; then I heard her flapping her wings against the window of a house just below the one I was in, and she vanished from my sight. But I kept on staring into the darkness, and as I am a living man, sir, I saw her go in at the door of the Cow and Snuffers Inn, and return no more. I watched the door of the inn a long time, but she did not come out.

"The next day, it's the honest truth I'm telling you, they told me the man who kept the Cow and Snuffers Inn was dead—had died in the night. His name was Llewellyn, sir—you can ask any one about him, at Llandaff—he had kept the inn there for seventy years, and his family before him for three hundred years, just at that very spot. It's not these new families that the Gwrach y Rhibyn ever troubles, sir, it's the old stock.

"The close resemblance of this goblin to the Irish banshee (or benshi) will be at once perceived. The same superstition is found among other peoples of Celtic origin. Sir Walter Scott mentions it among the highlands of Scotland. It is not traced among other than Celtic peoples distinctly, but its association with the primeval mythology is doubtless to be found in the same direction with many other death-omens, to wit, the path of the wind-god Hermes.

"The frightful ugliness of the Gwrach y Rhibyn is a consistent feature of the superstition, in both its forms; it recalls the Black Maiden who came to Caerleon and liberated Peredur: 'Blacker were her face and her two hands than the blackest iron covered with pitch; and her hue was not more frightful than her form. High cheeks had she, and a face lengthened downwards, and a short nose with distended nostrils. And one eye was of a piercing mottled gray, and the other was as black as jet, deep-sunk in her head. And her teeth were long and yellow, more yellow were they than the flower of the broom. And her stomach rose from the breast-bone, higher than her chin. And her back was in the shape of a crook, and her legs were large and bony. And her figure was very thin and spare, except her feet and legs, which were of huge size.' The Welsh word 'gwrach' means a hag or witch, and it has been fancied that there is a connection between this word and the mythical Avagddu, whose wife the gwrach was.

"The Gwrach y Rhibyn appears also as a river-specter, in Glamorganshire."

JERSEY DEVIL

The story of the so-called Jersey Devil is almost as legendary as the tales that surround such famous monsters as Bigfoot, the Loch Ness Monster, and the Chupacabra. It's a very strange saga that dates back to 1735 and to the heart of New Jersey's Pine Barrens, which run to no fewer than 2,000 square miles (5,180 square kilometers) and are dominated by masses of conifer trees. Monster hunter Ken Gerhard says: "Like most remote and uninhabited ranges, the Barrens are also steeped in mystery, with many colorful stories about its history and lore." All of which brings us back to the Jersey Devil.

As the tale goes, a certain Mother Leeds, a sinister figure who lived in the Pine Barrens, was the cause of all the mayhem. When pregnant with her thirteenth child, she placed a curse on the unborn child, which ensured that it took on a hideous form. It was highly appropriate that on the night Mother

Leeds went into labor, a wild storm bruised and battered the area, shaking the trees and filling the skies with crashing thunder and huge lightning bolts. The storm proceeded to get worse and worse, and reached its peak as the demon baby was born, although "baby" is hardly an apt term to use. The hideous child was described as having leathery wings, a horse-like head, and hooves instead of feet. The Jersey Devil wasted no time in making good its escape: it opened its wings, took to the air, and shot out of the chimney of Mother Leeds's home, quickly making a new home for itself in the dense and mysterious Pine Barrens.

While the story sounds like the stuff of legend and nothing else, there can be no denying the fact that people local to the area have reported astonishing encounters with something malevolent and hideous that they believe was the Jersey Devil. For example, on December 14, 1925, the *Bridgeton Evening News* ran an article titled

This drawing of the Jersey Devil was published in a 1909 issue of the *Philadelphia Post*.

"Dog-Like Beast Ate Seven Chickens Before Shot Killed It—Hundreds Fail to Identify Species." The article read as follows:

"What resembled a 'Jersey Devil' as much as anything else was shot and killed near Bacon's Neck last week and was viewed and even photographed by hundreds over the weekend. No one could name the animal with certainty.

"William Hyman, who manages the old Glaspell farm for Barton F. Sharp, was awakened before daybreak by a racket in his chicken coop. He dressed and went out carrying his gun. An animal ran from the coop with a chicken in its mouth. Hyman fired and fur flew but the animal went on.

"As long as he was up at 4 A.M., Hyman decided to start work. Soon the chickens called again and he ran to the coop in time to see the same animal leaving with another fowl. He fired again in the semi-darkness but failed to kill. This time he followed the animal into the meadows.

"A half mile from the house he caught up with it again and the animal turned and attacked him. He blazed away and it fell. He went to it and it was dead.

"About the size of an Airedale dog it has black crinkly hair. On its hind feet it had four webbed toes. It didn't run like a dog but hopped more like a kangaroo. Its front quarters are higher than its hind, which crouched as it ran, Hyman declared. Its rear teeth are prong like, the upper ones fitting into the center of four prong lower ones. Its eyes are still a bright yellow and its jaw is unlike a dog, wolf or coyote.

"There you have the description as given by visitors on the farm yesterday who add that despite the weather, the dead animal is still limber instead of being stiff. It took and apparently ate seven chickens the night it was seen and eventually killed.

"Guesses include one which suggests that it might be a dog, long starved and half wild. Others suggest that it is a cross between a dog and a wolf, but most of those who have seen it haven't any guess to offer. Any one certain of the way a Jersey Devil looks is requested to view the beast and report."

Twelve years later, on July 28, 1937, the *Jersey Evening Bulletin* entertained, and possibly terrified, its readers with a feature headlined "The Devil Went Down to Jersey." The unnamed journalist wrote:

"DOWNINGTOWN, JULY 28.—Chester County's green and verdant countryside was trying to shake itself back into a state of normalcy today after an all-night hunt for the 1937 version of the old Jersey Devil.

"Armed with guns and clubs, and led by a pack of dogs whose barking in the moonlight almost reached blood-curdling heights at times, a hastily-

An artist's concept of what the Jersey Devil looks like.

formed posse of two dozen farmers skipped their sleep last night to scour the hills and fields for a bounding critter with huge eyes.

"The strange monster was reported shortly after 9PM by Cydney Ladley, a paper mill employee, who lives near Milford Mills, just north of here. Rushing into town with bated breath, Ladley, his wife and Mrs. Chester Smith, a neighbor, told of seeing the creature on a back road near their home just as dusk was settling over the hills.

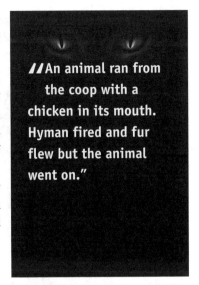

// An animal ran from the coop with a chicken in its mouth. Hyman fired and fur flew but the animal went on."

"'It leaped across the road in front of my car,' Ladley said. 'It was about the size of a kangaroo, was covered with hair four inches long and it hopped like a kangaroo. And eyes! What eyes!'

"'And how it jumped,' chimed in Mrs. Ladley.

"'Right in front of us, too,' added Mrs. Smith.

"The descriptions were enough. Within a half hour more than 20 neighboring farmers had taken their shotguns, unleashed their hounds and were abroad in the moonlight, resolved to track the prowler to its lair."

Today, sightings of the Jersey Devil are far less prevalent and terrifying than they were in decades past. That does not mean, however, that you should let your guard down if, one day, you find yourself deep in the heart of the New Jersey Pine Barrens. The deadly beast just might be circling silently overhead, getting ready to launch a terrifying attack.

LINCOLN IMP

A particularly creepy critter is that which has become known as the "Lincoln Imp." It's actually a carved figure that sits prominently on Lincoln Cathedral, England. The story of the devilish imp is a memorable one, and well known to the cathedral staff, who say:

"Tales of how he came to be perched there have emerged over time. There are several versions of the story however all of them share the same basic plot: Satan sent the imp to Lincoln Cathedral to cause trouble. The imp carried out his orders, and began destroying the Angel Choir. When an angel appeared to prevent him causing further mayhem, the imp jumped up onto the pillar and threw rocks at the angel. In order to put a stop to his mischievousness, the angel turned the little imp to stone.

The carved image of the devilish imp is permanently ensconced in the Lincoln Cathedral in England.

"Some versions of the imp story date to the 14th century and are contemporary with the construction of the Angel Choir. The presence of the imp in the Cathedral acts as a moral symbol and is a constant reminder that ultimately good will triumph over evil.

"Lincoln's imp is a well-known emblem of the Cathedral and the city, to the extent it has been adopted as the symbol of Lincoln and by the 1930s was established as the nickname of the local football club. The imp began a commercial life in the late 19th century, when local jewelers James Usher and Son began advertising a range of 'charming and very appropriate souvenirs of Lincoln' featuring the imp. Lincoln imp merchandise is still available today in the Cathedral's shop.

"Recently Lincoln Cathedral received a surprise when a carved wooden replica of the famous imp was received through the post—all the way from Western Australia! To add to the mystery, the letter accompanying the imp was tantalizingly brief, stating that it was being returned as its custodian had died and that it was removed on behalf of the cathedral during one of the wars. Experts in the Cathedral's Works Department believe the imp is a Victorian copy and is at least 100 years old."

MIND-MONSTER OF THE OLD ABBEY

Psychic questing is a subject that was deeply popular in the United Kingdom from the late 1970s to the early 1990s. It is the process by which ancient, buried artifacts can be located via psychic phenomena. Andrew Collins's books *The Black Alchemist* and *The Second Coming* have long fascinated me and are perfect examples of how psychic questing plays a major role in the discovery of priceless old relics. But, it's Martin Keatman and Graham Phillips's sequel to their book *The Green Stone*—namely, *The Eye of Fire*—that we need to focus on here, and which contains a strange and intriguing reference to Ranton Abbey, which is situated only the very briefest of trips away from the infamous, haunted bridge where the Man-Monkey has for so long made its dark and diabolical dwelling.

Ranton Abbey—known more correctly as the Augustinian Priory—was founded by Robert FitzNoel during the reign of Henry Plantagenet, with the construction having been completed by 1150. In the early nineteenth century, the property became part of the estate of the Anson's of Shugborough, latterly the Earls of Lichfield. Today, the abbey is, unfortunately, in ruins, having been accidentally ravaged and destroyed by fire during the Second World War, while occupied by Dutch soldiers. And, with that said, on to the story.

While much of *The Eye of Fire* is *far* beyond the scope of this book, the relevant data relates to a July 1982 trip to the abbey that the team of investigators in the book embarked upon, as part of their quest to locate the Eye of Fire of the book's title. Basically, the relevant parts of Phillips and

The abandoned building that was once the chapel for the Augustinian Priory (Ranton Abbey).

Keatman's saga reveal how one of the characters in the book, named Mary Heath, created—back in the nineteenth century—a monstrous "Guardian" at the abbey, whose role was to protect an ancient artifact, one that plays a vital role in the story.

Interestingly, the "Guardian" is described in the book's pages in highly ominous tones, and, variously, as "a complete blackness, seething within itself, shapeless but at the same time having substance" as "an abomination" and as a heavy-breathing "great beast."

The "Guardian," we quickly come to learn, is a horrendous, protector-style thought-form, brought into being, and roaming around an ancient abode in the heart of Ranton. But there's more. The vile creature was reportedly created by Mary Heath in 1875. How intriguing that an ominous thought-form was created in Ranton in 1875, and then—only four years later—the Man-Monkey was seen rampaging around the nearby (in fact, the *very* nearby) Bridge 39 on the Shropshire Union Canal.

Could it be that Mary Heath's monstrous offspring and the Man-Monkey were (and still are) one and the very same? Admittedly, this is a highly speculative and controversial question, but it is a question I simply cannot bring myself to dismiss out of hand. Rather, I suspect, it may offer us a most convincing explanation for at least some of the strange beasts that have passed, and that continue to pass, for the enigmatic phenomenon that has become known as the British Bigfoot.

NIGHT HAG

Albert Bender is inextricably linked to the enigma of the Men in Black; it was his 1951 and 1952 encounters with the MIB that led UFO researcher Gray Barker to write the very first book on the darkly clad things: 1956's *They Knew Too Much about Flying Saucers*. For that reason alone, it's unusual that practically every researcher and author who has ever commented on his encounters with the dark-suited ones has overlooked something massively important: his family's links to a *Woman* in Black. She was a spectral crone with an obsession for nothing less than coins.

In 1933, while just a child, Bender's mother told him the spine-tingling story of a family ghost, a Woman in Black. The story revolved around a second cousin of Bender's who, while only six years of age, moved into a creepy old house with his family. It was a house that sat adjacent to an old, abandoned mine shaft. The mine was a downright eerie place: it was filled with angular shadows; old wooden supports creaked and groaned endlessly, and a multitude of bats and rats called it their home.

It was also a mine in which, years earlier, a despondent young woman slit her throat and, as the blood cascaded forth, threw herself into the depths of one of the darkened, old shafts. Her battered and torn body was finally recovered and was taken into the house in which Bender's cousin lived, before being buried in the local graveyard. The woman, noted Bender, was said to have been a definitive witch, one who "lived alone with a great many cats and she was said to prowl about only at night."

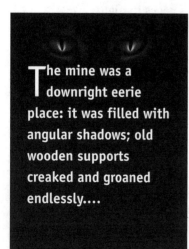

The mine was a downright eerie place: it was filled with angular shadows; old wooden supports creaked and groaned endlessly....

Bender added: "My cousin wore a coin on an unbroken chain around his neck constantly, even to bed. After having lived in the house a few months, his parents noticed his health was failing. He would not eat, and claimed he saw a lady in black in his bedroom at night. Of course they thought it all nonsense and that he was only dreaming, but soon they began to have sleepless nights when the boy would scream out in his sleep and they would find it necessary to go and comfort him."

In the early hours of one particularly fraught morning, Bender's cousin awoke the family, wailing like a veritable banshee. His parents noticed that the coin had been unhooked from the chain and was positioned on the pillow. According to Bender, the boy told his mother and father that "the lady in black was trying to choke him and take his coin away from him." The local doctor said the whole thing was related to nightmares and nothing else. Very soon thereafter, the doctor would be proven catastrophically wrong.

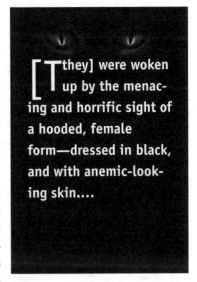

[T]hey] were woken up by the menacing and horrific sight of a hooded, female form—dressed in black, and with anemic-looking skin....

With no end in sight to the night terrors, both parents elected to sleep in the boy's room until things calmed down. On the fourth night, they were woken up by the menacing and horrific sight of a hooded, female form—dressed in black, and with anemic-looking skin—who slowly glided across the room, right in the direction of the boy. A bony hand moved slowly down to grasp the coin, at which point the boy's father lit a candle and firmly thrust it in the face of the WIB. Bender said: "They could see a pale, chalky-white face staring at them." In an instant the terrifying hag was gone—and so was the coin. Not surprisingly, the family vacated the house within a week; the boy, to the relief of everyone, quickly recovered.

Thus, we see that, in reality, Albert Bender's exposure to the blackest mystery of all *did not* begin in the early 1950s, when he received a visit from three menacing MIB that rivaled anything ever written by his hero, Edgar Allan Poe. It all began two decades earlier, in the 1930s, with a monstrous Woman in Black who had a thing for coins, and for making them disappear, too.

TAIGHEIRM TERRORS

Many people with an interest in the issue of powerful, secret societies will be familiar with the likes of the Bilderbergers, the Illuminati, the Freemasons, the Cathars, and Skull and Bones. Very few, however, will be conversant with an equally powerful body of people called the Taigheirm. Like so many other secret societies, the Taigheirm is populated by people who crave absolute power, massive wealth, and elite standing in society. It is, however, the way that the members of the Taigheirm achieve their goals that places them in their own, nearly unique category.

This centuries-old cult, which exists and operates in stealth in the highlands of Scotland, and has done so since at least the seventeenth century, uses ancient sacrificial rituals to get just about anything and everything it desires. It is rumored that numerous Scottish politicians, police officers, bankers, actors, doctors, judges, and landowners are just some of the Taigheirm's many and varied members.

Merrily Harpur is a British researcher who has carefully and deeply studied the history of the Taigheirm. She says that key to the success of the members is "an infernal magical sacrifice of cats in rites dedicated to the subterranean gods of pagan times, from whom particular gifts and benefits were solicited. They were called in the Highlands and the Western Isles of Scotland, the black-cat spirits."

It is rumored that numerous Scottish politicians, police officers, bankers, actors, doctors, judges, and landowners are just some of the Taigheirm's many and varied members.

The process of sacrifice was, and still is, gruesome in the extreme. Isolated and lonely places high in the mountains of Scotland are chosen, chiefly to ensure privacy. Secrecy is paramount. Members arrive, in black cloaks and pointed hats, at the chosen spot in the dead of night, determined at all times to protect their identities and presence from outsiders. Then comes the main event. Huge spits are built, upon which cats are slowly roasted—and while they are still alive—for up to four days and nights, during which the operator of the spit is denied sleep or nourishment, aside from an occasional sip of water. Supposedly, when the ritual is at its height, from the paranormal ether terrifying, huge black cats, with glowing red eyes, appear before the conjurer, demanding to know what it is that he or she wishes to have bestowed on them: money, influence, or something else. In return, and in a fashion befitting the likes of Faust, on his or her death the conjurer agrees to turn over his or her soul to those ancient, mighty gods worshipped by the Taigheirm.

Without doubt, the one person, more than any other, who was conversant with the terrible rituals of the Taigheirm was J. Y. W. Lloyd, who penned an acclaimed 1881 book, *The History of the Prince, the Lord's Marcher, and the Ancient Nobility of Powys Fadog and the Ancient Lords of Arwystli, Cedewen, and Meirionydd*. Lloyd became fascinated by the Taigheirm after reading Horst's *Deuteroscopy*, which was the first published work to expose the actions of this heartless group. Lloyd recorded: "The midnight hour, between Friday and Saturday, was the authentic time for these horrible practices and invocations."

Horst, himself, presented a terrible image: "After the cats were dedicated to all the devils, and put into a magico-sympathetic condition, by the shameful things done to them, and the agony occasioned to them, one of them was at once put alive upon the spit, and amid terrific howlings, roasted before a slow fire. The moment that the howls of one tortured cat ceased in death, another was put upon the spit, for a minute of interval must not take place if they would control hell; and this continued for the four entire days and nights. If the exorcist could hold it out still longer, and even till his physical powers were absolutely exhausted, he must do so."

It was after that four-day period, said Horst, that, "infernal spirits appeared in the shape of black cats. There came continually more and more of these cats; and their howlings, mingled with those roasting on the spit, were terrific. Finally, appeared a cat of a monstrous size, with dreadful menaces. When the Taigheirm was complete, the sacrificer demanded of the spirits the reward of his offering, which consisted of various things; as riches, children, food, and clothing. The gift of second sight, which they had not had before, was, however, the usual recompense; and they retained it to the day of their death."

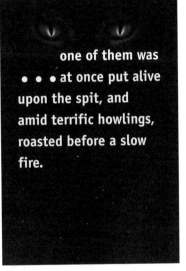

one of them was • • • at once put alive upon the spit, and amid terrific howlings, roasted before a slow fire.

As the nineteenth century reached its end, Lloyd came to believe that while the legend and cruel and cold reputation of the Taigheirm still existed, the group, as a fully functioning entity, no longer did. He recorded that one of the very last Taigheirm rituals was held on the Scottish island of Mull, in the early 1800s. Lloyd added that the folk of Mull "still show the place where Allan Maclean, at that time the incantor, and sacrificial priest, stood with his assistant, Lachlain Maclean, both men of a determined and unbending character."

Theirs was reportedly a frightening, midnight ritual held on a cold, winter's night and under a full moon. Lloyd noted: "Allan Maclean continued his sacrifice to the fourth day, when he was exhausted both in body and mind, and sunk in a swoon; but, from this day he received the second-sight to the time of his death, as also did his assistant. In the people, the belief was unshaken, that the second-sight was the natural consequence of celebrating the Taigheirm."

There is, however, intriguing data strongly suggesting that the Taigheirm are still with us, lurking in the shadows and still extending their power and influence. In 1922, Carl Van Vechten commented on post-nineteenth century Taigheirm activity in a footnote contained in his book, *The Tiger in the House*. It reads: "The night of the day I first learned of the Taigheirm I dined with some friends who were also entertaining Seumas, Chief of Clann Fhearghuis of Strachur. He informed me that to the best of his knowledge the Taigheirm is still celebrated in the Highlands of Scotland."

Then there is the account of one Donald Johnson, a man born and bred in Scotland, but who, just like his late father, worked as a butler for a powerful

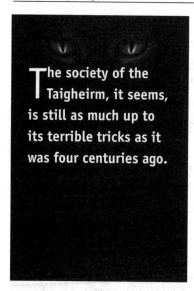

The society of the Taigheirm, it seems, is still as much up to its terrible tricks as it was four centuries ago.

and rich family that had its roots in the ancient English county of Staffordshire. According to Johnson, his father was invited, by his employers, to join an English offshoot of the Taigheirm in the winter of 1982—providing that he was willing to leave his old life and friends behind him, and fully embrace the Taigheirm and its teachings. Johnson Sr. was ready to do so, until, that is, he witnessed one of those monstrous sacrifices deep in the heart of England's Cannock Chase woods, and on the proverbial dark and stormy night, no less.

Johnson Sr.'s decision to walk away—quickly—was not at all appreciated by the Taigheirm, who reportedly made explicit threats about what might happen to him if he ever dared to go public with what he knew and had seen. Such was his fear, he stayed completely and utterly silent on the matter until he told his son, Donald, in 2010—the latter going public with the story in December of that year, out of fear for his own safety. The society of the Taigheirm, it seems, is still as much up to its terrible tricks as it was four centuries ago. Indeed, power, influence, and wealth are hard to give up or deny—even if one has to enter into Faustian pacts with ancient earth gods and supernatural black cats to achieve them.

TROLLS

It was in the early hours of a winter's morning in 1975 when Barry and Elaine, a married couple then in their late twenties and with two small children, were driving towards their then-Slitting Mill, Staffordshire, England, home after attending a Christmas party in the nearby town of Penkridge. As the pair headed towards the small village (its population today, four centuries after its initial foundations were laid, is still less than three hundred), their car's engine began to splutter and, to their consternation and concern, completely died. Having managed to carefully coast the car to the side of the road, Barry proceeded to quickly open the hood and took a look at the engine—"even though I'm mainly useless at mechanical stuff," he states.

There did not appear to be any loose wires, the radiator was certainly not overheated, and a check of the car's fuses did not provide any indication of what might be the problem. But, as the family was less than half a mile or so from home at that point, Barry made a decision, as he explained: "We had a picnic blanket in the boot [a British term for trunk] of the car and I got it out. I got back into the car and I said to Elaine something like: 'Let's cover you up and the kids with the blanket.' They were in the back sleeping and [were] only four and six at the time. So I said to [Elaine]: 'You stay with them, and I'll run back home and get your car, pick the three of you up, and then we'll leave my car here, and we can get someone out from a garage to look at it tomorrow.'"

At that point, however, their plans were thrown into complete and utter disarray. According to Barry, Elaine let out a loud scream, terrified by the sight of a small figure that ran across the road in front of them at a high rate of speed. She explains: "I just about saw it at the last second, and then another one followed it, and then a third one. The best way I can describe them to you is like a hairy troll or something like that. We had some moonlight and they were like little men, but with hunchbacks and big, hooked noses and not a

In children's books such as Walter Stenström's *The Boy and the Trolls* (1915) trolls are friendly, magical creatures. Barry and Elaine had a very different kind of troll experience.

stitch on them at all. Not a stitch, at all; just hair all over them. I'd say they were all four-feet-tallish, and when the third one crossed by us, you could see them at the edge of the trees—wary, or something, anyway."

Things became very hazy indeed, says Barry: "We both know from memory that they came forwards, towards us, very slowly to us, and I've thought since that they were interested in us or wanted to know who we were. They came very slowly, and it was a bit like we were being hunted, to me. Elaine was hysterical; and with the kids with us, I wasn't far-off, either.

"But that's all we remember. The next, it's all gone; nothing. Neither of us remembers seeing them go, and the next thing it was about two o'clock and the car started fine, then. It felt like something had happened to us, but I couldn't quite put my finger on, you know what I mean? But the memory thing is the biggest problem, even now. What was it? I *did* have a dream later about them surrounding the car, but that's it, really. But they were there and we did see them, right up by the Stone House [Author's Note: A reference to a large, old abode that sits on the edge of the village of Slitting Mill and that dates back to 1584, two centuries prior to the emergence of the village in the 1700s]."

Barry states that, to this day, and now both in their mid-sixties, both he and Elaine still feel very uneasy about the loss of memory that they both experienced back in 1975, but he is keen to affirm that "I know, and we know, that we both saw them. The kids don't remember a thing, thankfully. They were horrible little things. All that hair: Trolls, goblins, something. But they were there and they were real." Neither Barry nor Elaine have ever experienced any further such incidents or encounters with the unknown, but they have never forgotten those disturbing events deep in the heart of Slitting Mill on a chilly, winter night all those years ago with a strange band of hairy trolls.

TULPA

Visualize in your mind the fully formed image of a Bigfoot, a werewolf, a huge black dog with glowing red eyes, a Yeti—the list goes on and on. Then, imagine being able to project that same, monstrous imagery externally, and to the point where your "monster of the mind" strides out of your imagination and into the real world. In doing so, it takes on its own quasi-independent form of life, albeit a very strange form of life. You have just given birth to what, in Tibetan lore, is known as a Tulpa.

Creating a mind-monster is not without its hazards, however. In fact, it's an action that is almost always filled with danger. Certainly, no one knew that more than Dame Alexandra David-Néel. Born in 1868, David-Néel—who lived to the impressive and ripe old age of one hundred—extensively explored Tibet and immersed herself in its culture and people. She also learned of the Tibetan lore surrounding the Tulpa—to the extent that she decided to try and create one. It was an action that proved costly—and almost disastrously so for David-Néel. She said:

"Once the Tulpa is endowed with enough vitality to be capable of playing the part of a real being, it tends to free itself from its maker's control. This, say Tibetan occultists, happens nearly mechanically, just as a child, when his body is completed and able to live apart, leaves its mother's womb. Sometimes the phantom becomes a rebellious son and one hears of uncanny struggles that have taken place between magicians and their creatures, the former being severely hurt or even killed by the latter.

"I chose for my experiment a most insignificant character: a Monk, short and fat, of an innocent and jolly type. I proceeded to perform the prescribed concentration of thought and other rites. After a few months, the phantom Monk was formed. His form grew gradually fixed and lifelike looking. He became a kind of guest, living in my apartment. I then broke my seclusion and started for a tour, with my servants and tents.

"The Monk included himself in the party. Though I lived in the open, riding on horseback for miles each day, the illusion persisted. I saw the fat Tulpa; now and then it was not necessary for me to think of him to make him appear. The phantom performed various actions of the kind that are natural to travelers and that I had not commanded. For instance, he walked, stopped, looked around him. The illusion was mostly visual, but sometimes I felt as if a robe was lightly rubbing against me, and once a hand seemed to touch my shoulder.

"The features which I had imagined, when building my phantom, gradually underwent a change. The fat, chubby-cheeked fellow grew leaner, his face assumed a vaguely mocking, sly, malignant look. He became more troublesome and bold. In brief, he escaped my control. Once, a herdsmen who brought me a pre-

Dame Alexandra David-Néel was a Belgian-French explorer, spiritualist, and anarchist best known for visiting Lhasa, Tibet, in 1924, when it was closed to foreigners.

//The fat, chubby-cheeked fellow grew leaner, his face assumed a vaguely mocking, sly, malignant look.″

sent of butter, saw the Tulpa in my tent and took it for a living lama.

"I ought to have let the phenomenon follow its course, but the presence of that unwanted companion began to prove trying to my nerves; it turned into a 'day-nightmare.' Moreover, I was beginning to plan my journey to Lhasa and needed a quiet brain devoid of other preoccupations, so I decided to dissolve the phantom. I succeeded, but only after six months of hard struggle. My mind-creature was tenacious of life. There is nothing strange in the fact that I may have created my own hallucination. The interesting point is that in these cases of materialization, others see the thought-forms that have been created."

Take careful note of Alexandra David-Néel's words and remember this: when we create a Tulpa, we do so at our utmost peril. It's all too easy to unleash the genie from the bottle. It's a very different thing, however, to return it that bottle. Or, to *try* to return it to the bottle.

UFO CREATURES

CRITTERS OF THE SKY

Make mention of Unidentified Flying Objects (UFOs) and it will likely conjure up imagery of flying saucers, diminutive, black-eyed, large-headed extraterrestrials (ETs), and alien abductions. At least some UFOs, however, may have absolutely nothing whatsoever to do with visitors from far-away solar systems and galaxies. Welcome to the world of a man named Trevor James Constable. Having investigated the UFO phenomenon extensively, Constable penned two books on the subject. *They Live in the Sky* was published in 1958 and *Sky Creatures* followed two decades later. In deeply studying the UFO phenomenon, Constable came to a fascinating conclusion concerning what he believed to be the truth of the mystery surrounding flying saucers.

Constable's conclusion was that UFOs are not nuts-and-bolts craft from distant worlds, but rather living creatures that inhabit the highest levels of the Earth's atmosphere. While many UFO investigators scoffed at Constable's undeniably unique ideas, none could deny that his theory was well thought out. Describing them as "critters," Constable believed the creatures to be unicellular and amoeba-like, but having metallic-like outer shells, which gave them their flying saucer-style appearances. He also believed they varied in size from extremely small to lengths approaching half a mile—which admittedly accords with what UFO witnesses tell us: the assumed alien craft that people have reported do indeed vary from a few inches to massive, so-called "motherships."

If the skies of our planet *are* constantly populated by an untold number of airborne critters, then why don't we see them for what they really are—and on a regular basis? Constable had a notable and engaging theory for this, too: he believed the aerial things reflect infrared light, which is not visible to the naked, human eye. However, Constable also believed the critters can change color, something that explains why they are occasionally seen, and sometimes quite out of the blue. It's not a case that they are here one minute and gone the next. For Constable, that was only how it appears. They're always here, in massive numbers; we're just not physically able to see them in their natural state. Constable also concluded that this theory explained why some UFO witnesses had photographed UFOs, but had not seen anything out of the ordinary when they took the picture. In other words, when it comes to Constable's Sky Critters, the camera can see what the human eye cannot.

Constable believed that even though the sky beasts possessed formidable powers that allowed them to remain out of sight—for the most part—they could be seen and photographed if one specifically used an infrared film and a suitable filter. Constable even put his theories into practice—in the heart of the Mojave Desert. He claimed to have had considerable success in California's Lucerne Valley. Constable did not shy away from publishing his photos,

Might UFOs actually be biological beings that inhabit the upper reaches of our planet's atmosphere?

which continue to provoke a great deal of debate—and, at times, unbridled fury—amongst the UFO faithful. It's important to note, however, that Constable's claims did not stand alone.

In May 1977, a UFO investigator named Richard Toronto—who had developed a fascination for Constable's theories—decided to try and replicate Constable's photos, also in the Mojave Desert. He claimed considerable success. As with Constable's pictures—which some researchers felt showed nothing stranger than aircraft landing lights, stars, and planets—down-to-earth claims for the anomalies abounded. At least, they did amongst those UFO enthusiasts who didn't want to see their cherished extraterrestrial theories questioned.

> **I**t was his opinion ... that both men had unknowingly created the sky monsters from the depths of their imaginations and sub-conscious.

There is another theory for what both Trevor James Constable and Richard Toronto photographed. It's a truly fascinating one, which was postulated by the late UFO and paranormal investigator, D. Scott Rogo. It was his opinion—or, perhaps, his "strong suspicion" would be better terminology—that both men had unknowingly created the sky monsters from the depths of their imaginations and subconscious. And their psychic abilities allowed them to project their mind monsters externally, to the point where they had quasi-independent lives and could even be caught on camera.

Whatever the truth of the matter, today, decades after he first began formulating his undeniably alternative theory for what UFOs might be, Trevor James Constable still retains a faithful following who believe our skies are not filled with extraterrestrials, but with large, flying, amoeba-like monsters.

Crop Circle Creatures

Without a doubt, one of the strangest aspects of cryptozoology is its tie-in with the crop circle mystery. Although it's a little-known aspect of both phenomena, more than a few accounts exist of strange creatures seen in and around crop circles. From Matthew Williams—the only British man ever arrested, charged, and convicted for making a crop circle—come several such accounts. Unsurprisingly for someone who has spent years deeply immersed within the crop circle controversy, Matthew is a veritable fountain of knowledge with respect to tales of weird creatures either having been seen in, or at least in the direct vicinity of, complex crop circle formations. One such case is truly strange.

Matthew advised me that the story in question concerned a man who had felt curiously compelled to drive late at night to a certain field in Wiltshire many years ago. On doing so, he parked his car and duly, and carefully, began his walk into the depths of the crop. Suddenly, out of nowhere, a large, black, human-like figure appeared in the air over the field.

"It reminded me a little bit of the Mothman sightings when I heard this story," said Matthew, not without a high degree of justification. Matthew continued that the source of the story could only stand and stare in awe, while suddenly gaining the distinct impression that the hovering entity was the source of at least some of the crop circle formations that were appearing in Wiltshire.

At that precise moment, a simple crop circle suddenly appeared on the ground immediately below the black figure—after which it vanished from the skies and the man was left utterly alone in the field and with no real option other than to make his shocked way back to his vehicle and drive home, baffled and bewildered by both the weird, aerial entity and what it was that had directed him to the field.

Matthew expands: "There was one time, I'd rather not say when or where exactly, as I could get into trouble for admitting I trespassed on the farmer's land and made the crop circle formation. Plus, I had a friend named Paul helping me with this one. We were making this circle when we noticed

A crop cricle in Germany. Some are more elaborate, even graceful, than others.

these three bright lights—small balls of lights coming towards the field. We watched them; we were fascinated. But they split up and each of them went to a corner of the field—and which only left one corner for us to leave by without getting too close to these things.

"That was a bit unsettling. We didn't know what these balls were; so we raced out of the open corner of the field. We looked back as we ran and could see the balls heading towards us: gliding very gracefully just above the top of the crop. It was like they were on a railway track, just moving very smoothly, but it left us sort of disturbed too: like they were almost ghostly and alive."

The story was far from finished, as Matthew notes: "Well, I went to get the car, and told Paul to wait in the bushes at the edge of the road so he wouldn't be seen. The last thing I wanted was for him to get arrested if the police happened to drive past. But by the time I had got the car and got back to Paul, he was walking up the middle of the road with all his crop circle equipment in full view. I pulled up, wound the window down and shouted at him: 'What the hell are you doing? If people see you carrying your [crop circle-making] equipment, we'll get arrested.'

//We looked back as we ran and could see the balls heading towards us: gliding very gracefully just above the top of the crop."

"Paul looked scared stiff and said: 'If they had arrested me, I'd have gone with them, just to get me out of there.' I asked him what he meant, and Paul said that while I was getting the car he had heard these strange, animal-like screaming noises coming from inside the field and he had just charged out of there and onto the road. We never found out what it was though."

Matthew Williams is not alone in commenting on such matters. In the summer of 2007, I spoke with Marcus Matthews, a researcher of mysterious big cats in Britain, who told me that he was then currently investigating a case involving a person who had seen a "huge black cat" sitting inside the confines of a Wiltshire crop circle.

So, how do we define and explain such rogue reports as these? The answer, admittedly, and right now, is that we can't. All I can say is this: if you ever find yourself deep in the heart of a huge crop circle, then keep a careful watch. There may be something monstrous keeping its eyes on you, getting ready to pounce.

FLATWOODS MONSTER

On the night of September 12, 1952, something terrifying descended upon the small, West Virginia town of Flatwoods. Precisely what it was remains a mystery to this very day. All that can be said for sure is that it was hideous, fear-inducing, and downright monstrous. It has, appropriately, become known as the Flatwoods Monster. Situated in Braxton County and dominated by a mountainous, forested landscape, Flatwoods is a distinctly small town—that much is apparent from the fact that, today, its population is less than four hundred. Back in 1952, it was even less. On the night in question, however, the town found its population briefly added to by one visitor from ... well ... no one really knows where.

It all began as the sun was setting on what was a warm, still, September evening. A group of boys from Flatwoods were playing football in the town's schoolyard when they were frozen to the spot by the sight of a brightly lit, fiery object that shot overhead, provoking amazement and wonder in the process. All that the boys could be sure of was that the object appeared to be either egg-shaped or circular. Its color fluctuated from orange to fiery red.

As the stunned children watched in awe, they saw the object begin to descend—at a high rate of speed, no less—and then appear to come down on one of Flatwood's largest hilltops. Not surprisingly, being kids, they saw this as a big adventure looming large. The result: they, with a woman named Kathleen May and a recent U.S. Army recruit, Eugene Lemon, headed off for the scene of all the action. It wasn't long before the group reached the hill in question—and with nightfall rapidly closing in.

they were frozen • • • to the spot by the sight of a brightly lit, fiery object that shot overhead, provoking amazement and wonder in the process.

The first thing the group noticed, as they reached the darkened peak, was something brightly lit within the trees. What it was, no one had a clue. But, it clearly wasn't the lights of a farmhouse, truck, or car. Suddenly, the air was filled with a sickening odor—not unlike that of devilish brimstone. That was not a good sign. To their credit, however, they pushed on, determined to figure out the true nature of the source behind the lights. They soon found out: as the air became filled with a strange, sizzling sound, nothing less than a pair of self-illuminated red eyes could be seen getting ever closer. Kathleen May had the presence of mind to bring a flashlight with her and she quickly focused it on the eyes. In doing so, she also lit up the abominable creature that possessed those fiery eyes.

Looming before the now-hysterical band of intrepid souls was an approximately ten-foot-tall floating monster, which appeared to be humanoid in shape and had a large black cowling behind its head—that gave the entire head a kind of "Ace of Spades" appearance—and that was possibly even cloaked. Oddly, its lower half was ice cream cone-shaped and had wires and cables running from it. This issue of the cone-shaped lower portion led flying saucer sleuths to later suggest the monster may actually have been encased within some kind of remotely piloted vehicle.

As the creature then turned its attention to the group and wildly fired laser-like beams from its eyes, the brave band lost their nerve. They didn't wait to see what might happen next. One and all fled, screaming—possibly for their lives. Mrs. May breathlessly shouted to the boys to follow her to her home, which they all did. On arrival, and possibly as a result of exposure to the noxious odor that hung around the hill, several of the boys became violently ill, feeling nauseated and even vomiting.

Kathleen May quickly and shakily called the local police, who, rather intriguingly, were busy responding to reports of what was described as an "airplane crash" in the area. It turns out that no such crashed aircraft was ever found—something that suggests the "airplane" and the brightly lit UFO that descended upon the high hill that night were one and the very same. As a result of the fact that Flatwoods was, and still is, a very small town, word soon got out about what had happened. Local media were quickly on the scene, and even the U.S. Air Force sat up and took notice. Despite intense investigations by the press and the military, the mystery of the Flatwoods Monster was never solved—the creature was long gone by the time anyone else was on the scene. It is, however, decidedly interesting to note that Flatwoods is only around 125 miles from the town of Point Pleasant, West Virginia, where, from 1966 to 1967, yet another red-eyed monster, Mothman, was seen.

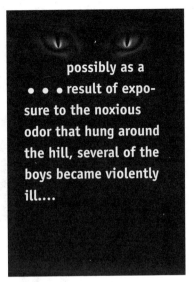

possibly as a • • • result of exposure to the noxious odor that hung around the hill, several of the boys became violently ill....

KELLY-HOPKINSVILLE GOBLINS

Kelly was, and still is, a small, rural town that is situated just short of ten miles from Hopkinsville. They are the kinds of places where people keep to themselves, and nothing of a particularly sensational matter ever happens—apart, that is, from the fateful night of August 21, 1955, when absolute chaos broke out. It all went down at the farmhouse of the Sutton family, who had visitors in from Pennsylvania: Billy Ray Taylor and his wife. It was roughly 7:00 P.M. when Billy Ray left the farmhouse to fetch water from the family's well. And what a big mistake that was.

In mere minutes, Billy Ray was back, minus the water. Terrified, Billy Ray told the Suttons and his wife that as he headed towards the well he saw a significantly sized, illuminated, circular-shaped object come to rest in a nearby gully. As the group tried to figure out what on Earth (or off it) was going on, they mused upon the possibilities of shooting stars, meteorites, and good old leg-pulling. By all accounts, it was none of those. In just a few minutes, the Suttons' dog began to bark, growl, and snarl in aggressive, uncontrollable fashion—after which it raced for cover underneath the porch. Clearly, something strange was going down. Exactly how strange, soon became very apparent.

Intent on making sure they were in control of the situation, Elmer "Lucky" Sutton and Billy Ray Taylor armed themselves with shotguns and

Respected ufologist Dr. J. Allen Hynek determined the sighting did not involve a monkey of some kind, though he could not reach a definitive answer.

headed out into the darkness. In no time, they were confronted by something terrifying: a small, silvery, creature—in the region of three feet tall—that was scurrying towards them with its long, ape-like, arms held high in the air. Sutton did what most folk might do when confronted by a strange, goblin-like thing after sunset: he blasted the beast with his shotgun. To the consternation of both men, the gun had no effect, aside from causing the creature to do a quick and impressive backflip, after which it disappeared into the darkness—for a while.

Rather wisely, Elmer and Billy Ray raced for the safety of the farmhouse and locked the doors behind them. In mere moments, the same creature—or, at least, a very similar one—was seen peering and leering through one of the windows. Elmer's son, J. C., took a shot at it. The only damage was to the window. The small beast scurried away at lightning speed. The curiously named Lucky Sutton, along with Billy Ray, took a tentative walk outside to see if they could see the creature—or creatures. That was a very bad move: as they prowled around the property, a clawed hand came down from the roof and seized Billy Ray's hair and head.

Terrified, Billy Ray pulled away, screaming, to see the goblin charge across the roof. To their horror, a second creature was seen staring at them from the branch of a nearby tree. A second shoot-out achieved nothing, aside from the remarkably weird sight of the creatures floating—rather than leaping or falling—to the ground and then racing into the darkness. The tumultuous events continued throughout the night, with guns firing, and the wizened little beasts seemingly doing their very best to create as much havoc and mayhem as was conceivably possible.

Realizing that the situation might very well go on all night, the group decided there was only one option available to them: they had to flee the farmhouse, which they did in two cars, making their speedy way to the sheriff's office in nearby Hopkinsville. The sheer, collective state of fear into which the Suttons and the Taylors had been plunged pretty much immediately convinced the sheriff that whatever had happened it was no drunken prank.

Unfortunately (or fortunately, depending on one's perspective), by the time the sheriff and the family arrived back at the farmhouse, the creatures were gone—they did, however, put in a reappearance in the early hours, and conveniently after the police had left. In no time at all, the media got onto the story, as did the U.S. Air Force—the latter coming up with a very bizarre explanation as its staff sought to lay matters to rest.

Before we get to the matter of the explanation, it's important to have a full understanding of the physical appearance of the creatures, drawn from the memories and recollections of the players: the Suttons and the Taylors. All of the strange entities were near-identical: long arms, skinny legs, large ears, and yellow eyes. As for their gait, they moved in a strange, pivoting fashion. And, there was the fact that they were all silver in color. Cue the Air Force's best estimate of what really happened.

With absolutely nothing solid—at all—to back up its claims, the Air Force suggested the goblins were actually monkeys, painted silver, that had escaped from a traveling circus! As cryptozoologist Ken Gerhard notes, it's "a theory more ridiculous than the notion of invading aliens." Nevertheless, the Air Force stuck to its guns, with Major John E. Albert being the major proponent of the circus escapee/painted monkeys theory.

Ufologists did not just accept this theory without question. One of the most respected of all UFO researchers was Dr. J. Allen Hynek. He said of his investigation of the Air Force's claim:

"I did make an attempt to find out whether there had been any traveling circuses in the area from which some monkeys could have escaped. The monkey hypothesis fails, however, if the basic testimony of the witnesses can be accepted. Under a barrage of gunfire from Kentuckians, over a somewhat extended period, it is unthinkable that at least one cadaver would not have been found. Furthermore, monkeys do not float down from trees: they either jump or fall. And, anyway, I was unable to find any trace of a traveling circus!"

The 1955 Kelly-Hopkinsville saga remains unresolved to this day. The fact that the incident began with the sighting of what may well have been a UFO has led flying saucer sleuths to conclude a mini alien invasion briefly broke out in rural Kentucky. On the other hand, is it possible that the Air Force was, at least partly, on the right track? Could the creatures have been monkeys, after all? They are questions that, decades later, we are unlikely to ever have answers for.

LOCH NESS'S OTHER MONSTERS

In 1968, Alistair Baxter—who had a lifelong interest in stories and folklore relative to Irish and Scottish lake monsters—travelled to Loch Ness and spent nine weeks armed with a camera and binoculars quietly and carefully monitoring the loch for any unusual activity of the long-necked and humped variety. Baxter never did see the elusive beast of Loch Ness, but he was able to speak with numerous people who *had* seen it. After being at the loch-side almost constantly for five weeks, however, an unusual event occurred. Baxter was awoken in the middle of the night by a curious humming sound that was emanating from a bright, small ball of light about the size of a football that—at a height of around fifteen feet from the ground—was slowly and carefully making its way through the surrounding trees that enveloped Baxter's modestly sized tent.

Suddenly, and without warning, the ball of light shot into the sky to a height of several hundred feet and hovered in deathly silence over the still waters of Loch Ness. For reasons that Baxter was at a loss to explain, he felt an overwhelming urge to go back to sleep and the next thing he knew it was daybreak. But the strangeness had barely begun.

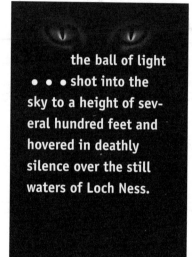

the ball of light • • • shot into the sky to a height of several hundred feet and hovered in deathly silence over the still waters of Loch Ness.

Shortly after breakfast three men in black suits appeared outside of Baxter's tent seemingly out of nowhere and proceeded to ask him if he had seen anything unusual during the night. He replied that he hadn't, at which point one of the three men turned to his two colleagues and made what Baxter said was "a strange smile." He turned to face Baxter. "We might return," said one of the mysterious men in black and all three departed by simply walking off into the woods. They never did return.

Most interesting of all, and of deep relevance to the overall story this book tells, for the following three nights, Baxter had a recurring and frightening dream of a large and lumbering ape-man that would pace outside of his tent and head down to the shores of the loch, whereupon, under a star-lit sky, it would tilt its head back, wail loudly, and stand staring at the ink-black water. The dream would always end the same way: with an image of a huge and ominous atomic mushroom cloud exploding in the distance, and the beginning of the Third World War and the end of civilization.

Baxter's story is made more thought-provoking for the following reason: I have numerous accounts in my own files from people who believe that they have undergone some form of "alien abduction" and who, they maintain, have been shown images by "the aliens" of a desolate and irradiated Earth of the near-future that had been ravaged by a worldwide nuclear war. "This is a warning of what will happen if we don't change our ways," one of the abductees—Ann-Marie—said to me.

Interestingly, she told of a frightening and futuristic scene that she believed showed a ruined and permanently cloud-covered city of London where the starving survivors were forced to do battle for food with strange, hairy ape men that would surface at night out of the rubble and remains of the flattened London Underground rail tunnels.

How do we explain such undeniably rogue events like those of Alistair Baxter and Ann-Marie? Well, right now, we don't, simply because we can't. All we *can* really say is that they offer yet further food for thought that the British Bigfoot is not all that it initially appears to be. Perhaps, until we *do* know more, it's apposite and wise to place such hard-to-define cases in our definitive grey-basket and leave them there to languish.

MINI-FROGMEN

Beyond any shadow of doubt, at all, one of the most bizarre of all encounters with strange and unknown animals occurred at Juminda, Estonia, at some point in the late 1930s; the exact date being unclear. According to an investigation undertaken by acclaimed and renowned UFO expert Dr. Jacques Vallée, two witnesses encountered a small—approximately three-foot tall—humanoid creature with brown-green skin and distinct froglike characteristics. Its eyes were slit-like, as was its mouth. And it appeared to be not at all accustomed to walking on land; its awkward gait made that abundantly clear, and particularly so when it caught sight of the pair and made good its escape. While it outran its pursuers, it did so in a very odd, near-drunken-like state.

A similar state of affairs occurred in the heart of woodland in Orland Park, Illinois, on September 24, 1951. The man who witnessed something both remarkable and disturbing was a steelworker named Harrison Bailey. As he walked through the park, Bailey was suddenly plagued by a burning sensation to his neck, which was accompanied by a sense of cramp in his neck, too. Sensing he was being watched, Bailey quickly swung around. He found himself confronted by a grey-colored object of a large size that was described as being "whirlwind"-like in shape.

two witnesses • • • encountered a small—approximately three foot tall—humanoid creature with brown-green skin and distinct froglike characteristics.

Things then became decidedly weird: Bailey felt groggy, confused, and almost in a dream-like state. And then nothing. His next memory was vague, but revolved around being surrounded by a large group of eighteen-inch-high humanoids that resembled frogs. They asked bizarre questions, such as where he was from and where he was going. All that Bailey could focus on was the fact that he felt somewhat paralyzed and unable to move properly. The unsettling feeling soon wore off, however, and Bailey was left to make his stumbling, slightly out of it, way back home.

He was able to build a much clearer image: the frog-men had slits for mouths, large, staring eyes, stripy brown skin, and just three toes.

Despite having come out of the odd encounter unscathed, Bailey had a nagging feeling that there was more to the experience than he could consciously recall. Finally, he elected to do something about it and underwent regressive hypnosis. It proved to be beneficial, although whether Bailey was pleased and relieved by what he learned after being placed in an altered state of mind is quite another matter entirely.

In his hypnotic state Bailey found himself back in the park, surrounded by those odd, diminutive things. He was able to build a much clearer image: the frog-men had slits for mouths, large, staring eyes, stripy brown skin, and just three toes. And all around the creatures were dozens of smaller bug-like things that wildly raced around the woodland floor. There then followed an amazing situation in which Bailey found himself in telepathic conversation with the frog-men, who informed him that humankind's warlike ways would be its downfall—and that they wanted Bailey to spread their warnings. Bailey then found himself back in the woods and on a path back home.

In many respects Harrison Bailey's encounter sounds like a classic example of what has infamously become known as "alien abduction." Except for one thing: the creatures that Bailey met with sound far more cryptozoological in nature than they do ufological.

THING IN DISGUISE

Karen Totten is an artist and sculptor who has had a wealth of anomalous experiences throughout her life, one of which was with an entity that falls definitively into a Woman in Black category. Yes, never mind the Men in Black; they have their female counterparts, too. Totten says:

"[W]hen I was seventeen I was working in a small convenience store, when a 'woman' came in to buy cigarettes. At first I didn't pay any attention to her until I saw her hand (when she handed me the money)—it was not like a normal human hand. This startled me so I looked up and saw a very pale entity, wearing a thin black coat (like a rain coat) with collar turned up to cover her neck, a heavy long haired wig, and very large black glasses. This did not entirely hide her strange face: a very pointed chin, scant lip and nose. She did not speak. Took her cigarettes and left! I was kinda stunned. Oddly I cannot remember the details of her hand (though it was the first thing I noticed). Nor do I think she left in a car which was odd since most patrons drove up the store (it was somewhat isolated)."

She continues: "[W]hether this entity is a 'gray' or a 'hybrid', I can only guess. I have never seen what is described as a classic gray alien. Perhaps 'hybrid' is most fitting simply because there seems to be some variety of attributes associated with this general category; i.e., that do not fit perfectly with the classic gray alien type (size of head being foremost). Some details that I do recall with some clarity: First, her skin: it was very pale, white with an almost bluish-gray tint to it, and of an unusually smooth texture. I have never seen anything like it before or since. I had previously seen an albino person; it was nothing like that; i.e., her skin was not UN-pigmented though there was an almost translucent quality to it."

And there were other anomalies, too.

"Second, her facial features: Though I could not see her eyes due to the large Jackie-O style sunglasses she wore, other aspects were evident: an unusually long pointy chin. Exaggerated cheekbones out of proportion to the rest of the face. Practically no lips, only enough to discern that there was any mouth. A nose that was almost not there: there was very little structure to it, a small bridge area, and some structure around the nostrils, but not much.

"Finally, her neck: though her coat collar was turned up, I could see some of the neck which was oddly thin. The wig (obviously such: a long thick dishwater blonde mane made of cheap imitation hair easily obtainable at a K-mart in those days) seemed placed to hide other features of the head, so I cannot comment on these (ears, shape of head).

"It puzzles me why I cannot recall her hand. Perhaps because it was what most startled me at first. The only thing I can relate to this lack of recall to is a nasty car accident I had years later: afterwards I completely blanked out the memory of the worst part of the accident (the part when it was occurring). I asked my doctor about this and was told that it was not uncommon for the human brain to "forget" traumatic or difficult events. I can only surmise the initial part of the encounter with the cigarette lady falls into this category.

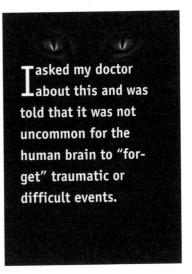

I asked my doctor about this and was told that it was not uncommon for the human brain to "forget" traumatic or difficult events.

"There were no other people in the store. I was alone. It was afternoon. The year of this encounter was 1974, possibly 1975 (I worked both summers between high school and college, and between my 1st and 2nd years of college); but most likely 1974. The location was an area south of St. Louis, Missouri.

"I felt no lingering psychological effect from this encounter that I am aware of, other than extreme puzzlement (and the blocked memory of her hand). As to whether this changed me, I don't know."

FURTHER READING

"1953 Sighting of the Houston Batman Remains Unsolved." http://doubtfulnews.com/2012/11/1953-sighting-of-the-houston-batman-remains-unsolved/. November 1, 2012.

"Alexandra David Neel—Tulpa." http://www.tulpa.com/explain/alexandra.html. 2015.

Amanda. "The Gwrach y Rhibyn." http://www.vampires.com/the-gwrach-y-rhibyn/. July 11, 2010.

Andy. "The Sea Serpent." http://maritimetexas.net/wordpress/?p=3510. December 26, 2011.

Arment, Chad. *Boss Snakes: Stories and Sightings of Great Snakes in North America.* Greenville, OH: Coachwhip Publications, 2015.

Ashliman, D. L. "Werewolf Legends from Germany." http://www.pitt.edu/~dash/werewolf.html. 2010.

"Aswang." http://www.read-legends-and-myths.com/aswang.html. 2015.

"Australian Apes." *Australian Town and County Journal.* December 9, 1882.

"Australia Giant Reptilian Monsters." http://www.mysteriousaustralia.com/australian_giant_reptilian_monsters-qld.html. 2015.

Baring-Gould, Sabine. *The Book of Werewolves.* New York: Causeway Books, 1973.

"Basilisk." http://bestiary.ca/beasts/beast265.htm. January 15, 2011.

"Batsquatch." http://pararational.com/batsquatch/. 2015.

Bayanov, Dmitri. *In the Footsteps of the Russian Snowman.* Surrey, British Columbia: Hancock House Publishers Limited, 2004.

"Beast of Dartmoor 'Is My Pet Dog.'" http://news.bbc.co.uk/2/hi/uk_news/england/devon/6929397.stm. August 3, 2007.

"Beast of Glamis Castle." http://anilbalan.com/2011/10/12/the-beast-of-glamis-castle/. October 12, 2011.

Bill. "The Legendary Kraken." http://www.ancient-origins.net/myths-legends-europe/legendary-kraken-00267. March 26, 2013.

Blackburn, Lyle. *Lizard Man: The True Story of the Bishopville Monster.* San Antonio, TX: Anomalist Books, 2013.

Bord, Janet, and Colin Bord. *Alien Animals.* London, UK: Panther Books, 1985.

————. *Bigfoot Casebook*. Enumclaw, WA: Pine Winds Press, 2006.

Bourtsev, Igor. "A Skeleton Still Buried and a Skull Unearthed: The Story of Zana." http://www.bigfootencounters.com/creatures/zana2.htm. 2014.

Bravo, Damian. "The Mande Burung (Jungle Man) of India." http://bigfootevidence.blogspot.com/2012/07/the-mande-burung-jungle-man-of-india.html. July 18, 2012.

Brown, Jamie. "Yowie Sighted at Bexhill—Witness Asks to Stay Anonymous." http://web.archive.org/web/20130819074211/http://www.northernstar.com.au/news/call-it-what-you-will-a-yeren-a-yeti-or-a-yowie-bu/1908497/. June 15, 2013.

Brown, Raymond. "Mystery Monster Fish in Cambridgeshire River Terrifies Anglers." http://www.cambridge-news.co.uk/Mystery-monster-fish-Cambridgeshire-river/story-26729586-detail/story.html. June 19, 2015.

————. "'Terrifying' Mystery Monster Lurking in Canbridgeshire River Now Sighted Twice Could Be Giant Eel." http://www.cambridge-news.co.uk/Mystery-monster-lurking-Cambridgeshire-river/story-26766152-detail/story.html. June 25, 2015.

"Caddy Captured on Video!" http://www.americanmonsters.com/site/2011/07/monster-captured-on-video/. July 22, 2011.

Campbell, Elizabeth. *The Search for Morag*. Letchworth, UK: Garden City Press, 1972.

Capps, Chris. "The Elephant Men of Narrabeen Lake." http://www.unexplainable.net/simply-unexplainable/the-elephant-men-of-nar.php. November 30, 2011.

"Champ, the Lake Champlain 'Monster.'" http://www.paranormal-encyclopedia.com/c/champ/. 2015.

"Chinese Wildman." http://www.bigfootencounters.com/creatures/wildman.htm. 2015.

Chorvinsky, Mark. "'Champ of Lake Champlain." http://www.strangemag.com/champ.html. 2015.

————. "The Lake Storjson Monster." http://www.strangemag.com/lakestorsjonmonster.html. 2015.

"Chupacabra on Rampage in Russia." https://www.rt.com/news/sheep-killing-vampire-chupacabra-773/. October 1, 2011.

Coleman, Loren. "Lake Winnipegosis Monster Sighting." http://cryptomundo.com/cryptozoo-news/winnipegogo/. August 19, 2006.

————. *Tom Slick and the Search for the Yeti*. London, UK: Faber & Faber, 1989.

————. "The Myakka 'Skunk Ape' Photographs." http://www.lorencoleman.com/myakka.html. 2002.

————, and & Patrick Huyghe. *The Field Guide to Lake Monsters, Sea Serpents, and Other Mystery Denizens of the Deep*. New York: Penguin, 2003.

Collins, Andrew. *The Brentford Griffin*. Wickford, UK: Earthquest Books, 1985.

Constable, Trevor James. *Sky Creatures: Living UFOs*. New York: Pocket Books, 1978.

Cope, Tabitca. "Paddler—Lake Creature, Submarine or Fish?" http://cryptozoo-oscity.blogspot.com/2009/11/paddler-lake-creature-submarine-or-fish.html. November 24, 2009.

————. "The Woodwose, the Origin of Bigfoot?" http://cryptozoo-oscity.blogspot.com/2012/02/wodewose-origin-of-bigfoot.html. February 27, 2012.

————. "Wally the Wallow Lake Creature." http://cryptozoo-oscity.blogspot.com/2009/10/wally-wallowa-lake-creature.html. October 6, 2009.

Costello, Peter. *In Search of Lake Monsters*. San Antonio, TX: Anomalist Books, 2015.

Courage, Katherine Harmon. "Could an Octopus Really Be Terrorizing Oklahoma's Lakes?" http://blogs.scientificamerican.com/octopus-chronicles/could-an-octopus-really-be-terrorizing-oklahomae28099s-lakes/. December 19, 2013.

Couzins, Daniel. "Morgawr—Sea Serpent of Cornwall." http://www.ufodigest.com/news/1007/morgawr.html. October 25, 2007.

Dash, Mike. "On the Trail of the Warsaw Basilisk." http://www.smithsonianmag.com/history/on-the-trail-of-the-warsaw-basilisk-5691840/?no-ist. July 23, 2012.

Douglas, George Brisbane. *Scottish Fairy and Folk Tales*. New York: A.L. Burt Company, 1892.

"Dover Demon." http://www.americanmonsters.com/site/2010/03/dover-demon-massachusetts-usa/. March 20, 2010.

Downes, Jonathan. *Monster of the Mere*. Woolsery, UK: CFZ Press, 2002.

———. "The Hunt for the Bolam 'Beast.'" http://www.cfz.org.uk/expeditions/03bolam/. January 23, 2003.

———. *The Owlman and Others*. Woolsery, UK: CFZ Press, 2006.

———, and Nigel Wright. *The Rising of the Moon*. Bangor, Northern Ireland: Xiphos Books, 2005.

Dr. Beachcombing. "Marco Polo Meets a Dragon?" http://www.strangehistory.net/2011/05/30/marco-polo-meets-a-dragon/. May 30, 2011.

Drake, Frank, and Dava Sobel. *Is Anyone Out There?* New York: Delacorte Press, 1992.

Drinnon, Dale A. "Storsjoodjuret in Lake Storsjon." http://frontiersofzoology.blogspot.com/2013/05/storsjoodjuret-in-lake-storsjon.html. May 12, 2013.

Emery, David. "Alligators in the Sewers." http://urbanlegends.about.com/od/alligators/a/sewer_gators.htm. July 5, 2015.

Erika. "The monster of Rhayader." http://freakyphenomena.com/strange-happenings/article/monster-rhayader. September 11, 2013.

"Expeditions: Loch Morar." http://www.cfz.org.uk/expeditions/morag/morag.htm. 2015.

Feschino, Frank. *The Braxton County Monster: The Cover-Up of the "Flatwoods Monster" Revealed*. Lulu, 2012.

Freeman, Richard. *Dragons: More Than a Myth?* Woolsery, UK: CFZ Press, 2005.

Friedman, Megan. "The Hunt Is on for China's Bigfoot." http://newsfeed.time.com/2010/10/12/the-hunt-is-on-for-chinas-bigfoot/. October 12, 2010.

Gaal, Arlene. *In Search of Ogopogo*. British Columbia, Canada: Hancock House Publishers, 2001.

Gerhard, Ken. "El Cucuy … South Texas' Official Boogeyman." http://www.sacurrent.com/Blogs/archives/2012/10/17/el-cucuy-south-texas-official-boogeyman. October 17, 2012.

———. *Encounters with Flying Humanoids*. Woodbury, MN: Llewellyn Worldwide, 2013.

———, and Nick Redfern. *Monsters of Texas*. Woolsery, UK: CFZ Press, 2010.

"The Ghosts of the Tower of London—Ghost Bear." https://www.youtube.com/watch?v=g1HYaPrttzw. October 31, 2013.

Gibbons, William J. Mokele-Mbembe: *Mystery Beast of the Congo Basin*. Greenville, OH: Coachwhip Publications, 2010.

"Glacial Boulder, Cannock Chase." https://foursquare.com/v/glacial-boulder-cannock-chase/4bf027b1c8d920a1bc7c9430. 2015.

Godfrey, Linda. *The Beast of Bray Road*. Black Earth, WI: Prairie Oak Press, 2003.

———. *The Michigan Dogman*. Eau Claire, WI: Unexplained Research Publishing Company, 2010.

Hall, Mark A., and Loren Coleman. *True Giants: Is Gigantopithecus Still Alive?* San Antonio, TX: Anomalist Books, 2010.

Hanks, Micah. "Vietnam and (High) Humanoid Strangeness in Wartime." http://mysterious universe.org/2012/11/vietnam-and-high-humanoid-strangeness-in-wartime/. November 28, 2012.

Harpur, Merrily. *Alien Big Cats.* Loughborough, UK: Heart of Albion Press, 2006.

Haslam, Garth. "1975, February-July: The Vampire of Moca." http://anomalyinfo.com/Stories/1975-vampire-moca. 2015.

"A History of the Lincoln Imp." http://lincolncathedral.com/2011/12/a-history-of-the-lincoln-imp/. December 16, 2011.

Hotz, Amy. "The Beast of Bladenboro." http://www.starnewsonline.com/article/20061029/NEWS/61027007. October 29, 2006.

Hynek, J. Allen. *The Hynek UFO Report.* New York: Sphere Books, 1978.

Johnson, Ben. "The Mermaids of the Peak District." http://www.historic-uk.com/CultureUK/The-Mermaids-of-the-Peak-District/. 2015.

Justice, Aaron. "Megalania Prisca: Dragon of the Australian Outback." http://thecryptozoolo gist.webs.com/apps/blog/show/15615981-megalania-prisca-dragon-of-the-australian-out back. May 31, 2012.

Kaldera, Rave. "Who Is Fenrir?" http://www.northernpaganism.org/shrines/fenrir/about.html. 2013.

Keating, Kevin. "Did Navy Use Fish Story as Cloak? Pend Oreille Paddler Said to Be Subs." http://m.spokesman.com/stories/1996/nov/15/did-navy-use-fish-story-as-cloak-pend-oreille/. November 15, 1996.

Keel, John A. *The Mothman Prophecies.* New York: Tor Books, 1991.

Krystek, Lee. "The Monstrous Sea Serpent of Gloucester." http://www.unmuseum.org/glserpent.htm. 2000.

"Lake Monster in Granbury, TX the Terror of One-Eye Strange Creature in Lake Granbury Texas Bigfoot?" https://www.youtube.com/watch?v=Te0HaqxaMSU. April 12, 2015.

"The Lambton Worm and Penshaw Hill." http://www.mysteriousbritain.co.uk/england/durham/legends/the-lambton-worm-and-penshaw-hill.html. 2015.

Lewis, Chad, Noah Voss, and Kevin Lee Nelson. *The Van Meter Visitor.* Eau Claire, WI: On the Road Publications, 2013.

"The Lindorm." http://www.santharia.com/bestiary/lindorm.htm. 2015.

"The Linton Worm." http://www.scotclans.com/scotland/scottish-myths/scottish-monsters/lin ton-worm/. 2015.

"Loch Morar Monster Morag Sightings Uncovered." http://www.bbc.com/news/uk-scotland-highlands-islands-21574832. February 25, 2013.

Lockley, Mike. "Spooky Slender Man Spotted in Cannock." http://www.birminghammail.co.uk/news/midlands-news/spooky-slender-men-spotted-cannock-8505191. January 24, 2015.

"Loveland Frog-Men: (Ohio, USA)." http://www.americanmonsters.com/site/2009/12/loveland-frog-men-ohio-usa/. December 16, 2009.

Lyman, Robert R. *Forbidden Land: Strange Events in the Black Forest*, Vol. 1: *1614–1895.*

Point Pleasant, WV: New Saucerian Books, 2014.

Mackal, Roy P. *The Monsters of Loch Ness.* Chicago, IL: Swallow Press, 1980.

Matthews, Marcus. *Big Cats Loose in Britain.* Woolsery, UK: CFZ Press, 2007.

"Mermaid Mythology." http://www.gods-and-monsters.com/mermaid-mythology.html. 2015.

"Military Mayhem in Montauk, Long Island." http://www.weirdus.com/states/new_york/unex plained_phenomena/montauk_project/index.php. 2015.

"The Mongolian Death Worm." http://www.mongolia-travel-guide.com/mongolian-death-worm .html. 2011.

"MonsterQuest." https://en.wikipedia.org/wiki/MonsterQuest. 2015.

"Montauk-Monster: The Truth, the Legend, the Mystery." http://www.montauk-monster.com/. 2015.

Moon, Jim. "The Wyvern of Wonderland." http://hypnogoria.blogspot.com/2015/02/folklore-on-friday-wyvern-of-wonderland.html. February 27, 2015.

"Mysteries at the National Parks: Chupacabra Island." Travel Channel, 2015.

"Mysterious 'Chupacabra'-like Predator Wipes Out Poultry Stock in Russian Village." http://www.rt.com/news/311331-voronezh-chupacabra-chickens-dog/. August 1, 2015.

Nicholson, Andrew. "Australian Big Cats. No So Alien?" http://mysteriousuniverse.org/2013/04/australian-big-cats-not-so-alien/. April 30, 2013.

Nielson, Larry. "The Legend of Pepie." http://pepie.net/. 2015.

"The Other Side: The Wildman of Orford." http://www.visitsuffolk.com/suffolk-stories/the-other-side-wildman-of-orford/. October 24, 2014.

Pain, Stephanie. "Blasts from the Past: The Soviet Ape-Man Scandal." http://www.newscientist .com/article/mg19926701.000-blasts-from-the-past-the-soviet-apeman-scandal.html#.VEVB 5RaEeSo. August 23, 2008.

"Paul Devereux Speaking at the Rollright Stones." http://www.megalithic.co.uk/mm/book/ devereux1trans.htm. 2015.

"The Pennine Pterodactyl." http://www.unexplained-mysteries.com/forum/index.php?show topic=30634. January 2, 2005.

Perticaro, Anthony. "The Jersey Devil of the Pine Barrens." http://www.strangemag.com/ jersey-devil1.html. 2015.

Plambeck, Steve. "The Loch Ness Monster Giant Salamander." http://thelochnessgiantsala mander.blogspot.com/. 2015.

"Probing Deeper into the Dulce 'Enigma.'" http://www.bibliotecapleyades.net/branton/esp_ dulcebook21.htm. 2015.

Radford, Benjamin. "Mokele-Mbembe: The Search for a Living Dinosaur." http://www.lives cience.com/38871-mokele-mbembe.html. August 13, 2013.

Randall, Elizabeth. *From Lyonesse to Alien Big Cats and Back Again.* CreateSpace, 2014.

Ranelagh, John. *The Agency: The Rise and Decline of the CIA.* New York: Simon & Schuster, 1986.

Redfern, Nick. *The Bigfoot Book: The Encyclopedia of Sasquatch, Yeti, and Cryptid Primates.* Detroit: Visible Ink Press, 2015.

———. *Chupacabra Road Trip.* Woodbury, MN: Llewellyn Publications, 2015.

———. "Do Werewolves Roam the Woods of England?" http://monsterusa.blogspot.com/2007/05/do-werewolves-roam-woods-of-england.html. May 17, 2007.

———. "The Great Eel of Birmingham." http://monsterusa.blogspot.com/2008/04/great-eel-of-birmingham.html. April 18, 2008.

———. *Man-Monkey: In Search of the British Bigfoot.* Woolsery, UK: CFZ Press, 2007.

———. *Wildman! The Monstrous and Mysterious Saga of the "British Bigfoot."* Woolsery, UK: CFZ Press, 2012.

————, and & Glen Vaudrey. *Mystery Animals of the British Isles: Staffordshire.* Woolsery, UK: CFZ Press, 2013.

Roberts, Andy. "The Big Grey Man of Ben Macdhui and Other Mountain Panics." In *Strangely Strange but Oddly Normal.* Woolsery, UK: CFZ Press, 2010.

Roberts, Paul Dale. "Batsquatch Sighted at Mt. Shasta." http://www.unexplained-mysteries .com/column.php?id=150840. April 4, 2009.

Ronanus, Ego. "One Eyed Monster." http://cfz-usa.blogspot.com/2014/06/one-eyed-monster .html. June 9, 2014.

Sanderson, Ivan T. "The Minnesota Iceman: The Missing Link?" Argosy, May 1969.

Sanidopoulos, John. "Saint Columba and the Loch Ness Monster." http://www.johnsanidopou los.com/2010/11/saint-columba-and-loch-ness-monster.html. November 12, 2010.

Screeton, Paul. *Quest for the Hexham Heads.* Woolsery, UK: CFZ Press, 2012.

Sergent, Jr., Donnie, and Jeff Wamsley. *Mothman: The Facts behind the Legend.* Point Pleasant, WV: Mothman Lives Publishing, 2002.

Shuker, Karl P.N. *Dragons: In Zoology, Cryptozoology, and Culture.* Greenville, OH: Coachwhip Publications, 2013.

————. "Giant Spiders—Monstrous Myth, or Terrifying Truth?" http://karlshuker.blogspot .com/2014/07/giant-spiders-monstrous-myth-or.html. July 30, 2014.

————. *Mirabilis: A Carnival of Cryptozoology and Unnatural History.* San Antonio, TX: Anomalist Books, 2013.

————. "Wulvers and Wolfen and Werewolves, Oh My!—Tales of the Uninvited." http:// karl-shuker.blogspot.com/2012/07/wulvers-and-wolfen-and-werewolves-oh-my.html. July 28, 2012.

Simpson, Jacqueline. *British Dragons.* London, UK: B.T. Batsford, 1980.

Speed, Barbara. "Yes, They Really Have Found Alligators in the New York Sewer System." http:// www.citymetric.com/yes-they-really-have-found-alligators-new-york-sewer-system-102. August 12, 2014.

Steadman, Ian. "The Bloop Mystery Has Been Solved: It Was Never a Giant Sea Monster." http:// www.wired.co.uk/news/archive/2012-11/29/bloop-mystery-not-solved-sort-of. November 29, 2012.

Stewart, Will. "Fabled 'Chupacabra' or Mutant Fox Poisoned by Radiation? Hunters Baffled by Dog-like Animal in Former Soviet Republic." http://www.dailymail.co.uk/news/article-2192561/Fabled-Chupacabra-mutant-fox-poisoned-radiation-Russian-hunters-baffled-dog-like-animal.html. August 23, 2012.

"Strange and Unexplained—Mothman." http://www.skygaze.com/content/strange/Mothman .shtml. 2015.

"Strange Encounters with the Nyalmo." *The Crypto Journal.* http://bfsearcher.blogspot.com/ 2012/08/strange-encounters-with-nyalmo.html. August 13, 2012.

Strickler, Lon. "The Thetis Lake Monster Legend." http://www.phantomsandmonsters.com/ 2010/02/thetis-lake-monster-legend.html. February 6, 2010.

Sullivan, Mark. "Decades Later, the Dover Demon Still Haunts." http://www.boston.com/ news/local/articles/2006/10/29/decades_later_the_dover_demon_still_haunts/. October 29, 2006.

Swancer, Brent. "Carnivorous Cryptid Plants of the World." http://mysteriousuniverse.org/ 2014/05/carnivorous-cryptid-plants-of-the-world/. May 13, 2014.

"Taigheirm." http://www.encyclopedia.com/doc/1G2-3403804433.html. 2015.

Tarr, Daniel. "The Sky Critters by Trevor James Constable." http://www.tarrdaniel.com/documents/Ufology/skycritters.html. 2007.

Taylor, Troy. "The Jersey Devil: Legend or Truth?" http://www.prairieghosts.com/jerseydevil.html. 2002.

Texas Cryptid Hunter. "The Legend of the 'Donkey Lady' of San Antonio." http://texascryptidhunter.blogspot.com/2014/02/the-legend-of-donkey-lady-of-san-antonio.html. February 18, 2014.

"The Vampire Beast of Bladenboro." http://www.northcarolinaghosts.com/piedmont/beast-of-bladenboro.php. 2015.

Thomson, David. *The People of the Sea*. Edinburgh, UK: Canongate Classic, 1996.

Treat, Wesley, Heather Shade, and Rob Riggs. *Weird Texas*. New York: Sterling Publishing, 2005.

Trubshaw, Bob. *Explore Phantom Black Dogs*. Loughborough, UK: Heart of Albion Press, 2005.

U.S. Geological Survey. "Malformed Frogs in Minnesota: An Update." http://pubs.usgs.gov/fs/fs-043-01/. May 2001.

Vocelle, L.A. "Witchcraft and the Cat's Persecution: Taigheirm." http://www.thegreatcat.org/history-of-the-cat-in-the-middle-ages-part-14-taigheirm/. May 3, 2013.

"Wales Lake Bala Monster—Teggie." *CryPtoReporter*. http://cryptoreports.com/wales-lake-bala-monster-teggie. April 3, 2012.

Warms, John. *Strange Creatures Seldom Seen*. Greenville, OH: Coachwhip Publications, 2015.

Wayman, Erin. "Did Bigfoot Really Exist? How Gigantopithecus Became Exitinct." http://www.smithsonianmag.com/science-nature/did-bigfoot-really-exist-how-gigantopithecus-became-extinct-16649201/. January 9, 2012.

Weaver, Gordon. *Conan Doyle and the Parson's Son: The George Edalji Case*. Cambridge, UK: Vanguard Press, 2006.

Weeks, Linton. "The Elegant Secrets of Flying Snakes." http://www.npr.org/sections/theprotojournalist/2014/03/07/286833436/the-elegant-secrets-of-flying-snakes. March 7, 2014.

"Wendigo Legend, The." http://www.gods-and-monsters.com/wendigo-legend.html. 2014.

"Werecats." http://www.therianthropes.com/werecats.htm. 2015.

"Werecats." http://unnaturalworld.wikia.com/wiki/Werecats. 2015.

"What Does a Bunyip Look Like?" http://www.cfzaustralia.com/2012/04/what-does-bunyip-look-like.html. April 2, 2012.

Whitcomb, Jonathan. "'Batman' of Houston, Texas, 1953." http://www.livepterosaur.com/LP_Blog/archives/2767. February 16, 2012.

———. "Ropens: Live Pterosaurs in Papua New Guinea." http://www.ropens.com/. 2015.

———. "Tunnel Pterodactyl of 1856." http://livepterosaurs.blogspot.com/2010/04/tunnel-pterodactyl-of-1856.html. April 8, 2010.

"Wisht Hounds Part 1—Wistman's Wood." *Faery Folklorist*. http://faeryfolklorist.blogspot.com/2011/10/wisht-hounds-part-1-wistmans-wood.html. October 4, 2011.

Witchell, Nicholas. *The Loch Ness Story*. London, UK: Corgi Books, 1982.

Woolheater, Craig. "Beasts in the Midst—The Mapinguari." http://cryptomundo.com/bigfoot-report/beasts-in-the-mist-the-mapinguari/. October 24, 2005.

———. "Bio of Craig Woolheater." http://cryptomundo.com/craigwoolheater/. 2014.

"Wyvern." http://www.mythical-creatures-and-beasts.com/wyvern.html. 2015.

"The Yeren." http://cryptozoo.monstrous.com/the_yeren.htm. 2015.

"Yorkshire Pterodactyl." http://forum.forteantimes.com/index.php?threads/yorkshire-pterodactyl.5254/. 2015.

Yturria, Santiago. "Mexican Policeman Attacked by a Flying Humanoid Entity." http://www.rense.com/general48/entity.htm. January 23, 2004.

INDEX

Note: (ill.) indicates photos and illustrations.